D1458968

SCHOOL LAW
FOR THE
PRACTITIONER

SCHOOL LAW
FOR THE
PRACTITIONER

ROBERT C. O'REILLY
AND EDWARD T. GREEN

CONTRIBUTIONS TO THE STUDY OF EDUCATION,
NUMBER 6

GREENWOOD PRESS
WESTPORT, CONNECTICUT • LONDON, ENGLAND

Library of Congress Cataloging in Publication Data

O'Reilly, Robert C., 1928-
  School law for the practitioner.

  (Contributions to the study of education, ISSN 0196-707X ; no. 6)
  Bibliography: p.
  Includes index.
  1. Educational law and legislation—United States.
I. Green, Edward T., 1921-   II. Title. III. Series.
KF4119.O73 1983   344.73'071   82-11982
ISBN 0-313-23639-9 (lib. bdg.) 347.30471

Library of Congress Catalog Card Number: 82-11982
ISBN: 0-313-23639-9
ISSN: 0196-707X

First published in 1983

Greenwood Press
A division of Congressional Information Service, Inc.
88 Post Road West
Westport, Connecticut 06881

Printed in the United States of America

10 9 8 7 6 5 4 3 2 1

For Marge and Meg

CONTENTS

PREFACE

The notion that people should all be governed by and responsive to a common set of laws is accepted by twentieth-century Americans—to a degree. Rules that are admired are most easily accepted and enforced; however, since ours is a pluralistic society with many viewpoints and backgrounds, not every rule is admired by all, and many Americans view some rules, some laws, as downright oppressive.

Considered as an occupational group, the teachers and administrators of American elementary and secondary schools comprise what is perhaps the largest single group of rule enforcers in society. Operating under legislative statutes, court cases, board policies, program regulations, and so on, there is no end to the part of the teacher's professional task that calls for the teacher to be an on-the-spot rule enforcer.

Viewed historically, it might be said that the first American schools that originated in response to mandates from Massachusetts legislators were simple, straightforward, no-frills institutions. Yet it is conceivable, too, that many of the affected citizens who had to develop and maintain in those schools a basic curriculum grumbled some about that mandating legislating body. A retrospective view from the twentieth century may not have been the reality view of the times. There is in the American nature an aversion to governance, to imposed rules of behavior. There is a gravitation toward the concept of independence, of freedom for decision making. Groups of people, that is, society, necessitate some rules and some common agreements on both acceptable and unacceptable behaviors.

In a sense, schools are miniature societies. Schools are also part of a larger society. Institutionalized education has a money cost; that money must be raised from the citizens. Calls for curriculum extension and development have costs. Mandated programs coming from the federal or state government or locally requested grass-roots curriculums can only be carried out under some kind of recognized and accepted set of rules. If not mutually acceptable, the rules must at least be tolerated by all who are affected by them. Rules and costs combine, sometimes.

The rate of social change in America has been increasingly rapid. Although the conventional public school district that evolved in the nineteenth century continues to be the basic governance unit through which the obligations of public education are carried out, some of those general social changes are reflected in school districts themselves. Some districts have grown so large that just by virtue of size any realistic expectation of local governance must be set aside. In a school district enrolling hundreds of thousands of pupils it can hardly be seriously contended that such a political subdivision has the operational characteristics generally associated with localism. Should those districts be subdivided? Should they be dismantled? Should localism be forsaken? What stipulations should the laws impose?

Although there are, on the opposite end, many exceedingly small school districts, the total number is decreasing steadily, and there are now about sixteen thousand of those political subdivisions created to offer public education. California has about one thousand districts for 230 million people; Nebraska has about one thousand districts for 1.6 million people. Can both states be correct; or are both in need of new statutes to restructure school districts? If new structures for their education delivery systems are developed, what should they look like? From where should the new laws originate, the state or federal level? Some changes in district organization and governance are occurring. Evolutionary change will be by law—case law, statutes, referendums—or by some other way.

The laws affecting schools exist within a much broader legal framework. Nonetheless, for teachers and administrators, the discrete part of the law that pertains especially to schools, is an area of law that can be separated out, studied, and understood and, through study and understanding, can make for greater ease and efficiency in school operation. Some laws are categorically specific to schools. This volume takes both the broader and the narrower aspects of the law and combines them to provide an extended understanding of the realities in which professionals must perform as employees in elementary and secondary schools. Law applications to university settings are minimal.

The content is a reflection of experiences that the authors have had in a long-term engagement with public schools. Among others, the experiences include those of teacher, building principal, superintendent, and board of education member. Additional experiences stand behind the authors, since each now teaches classes in school law for school administrators in his respective institution. Each maintains extended contacts with practicing school administrators, and each has honed in on problems that relate to school law. Those experiences have been matched with knowledge of school law to assist students toward understanding basic legal principles. Those legal principles are topically treated, by chapter. Not all of law pertinent to schools has been included. Author experience and contact were the deciding force on what topics to include and what to exclude. Fine legal distinctions that might be essential to a law student are not emphasized. Legal principles for professionals in elementary and secondary schools are emphasized. The result is a volume that is usable for teachers interested in school law as well as those preparing for school administration.

From those professional and academic experiences and with those goals, organization of the text evolved, and pertinent material was selected. The flow of authority in the American polity is depicted, from the Constitutional power grant of the Tenth Amendment to the development of policy by a local school board. Statutes and cases have been selected to provide some sense of the national picture, yet to make clear each state is the critical force in decision making about its schools. The hierarchy of law is described so that students can recognize that in the event of conflicts between a Constitutionally protected right and particular state statutes, and if that conflict is litigated, the federal judiciary will set aside the state statutes. The hierarchy does prevail.

The cases should not only be a source of information but should have practical value when professionals are confronted with similar problems in a job setting. They should stimulate reflective thought and discussion, leading readers to consider what courts might decide if similar issues from their own school were to be litigated. For students who are serious about knowing school law comprehensively, selected major cases should be identified and prepared in brief form for a long-term reference. A brief should contain seven parts that answer to the criteria, scholarliness, and practicality:

1. Identification should include the names of the litigants, the primary source of the report, the court that pronounced the decision, and the date.

2. Action should be a statement of what the plaintiff desires.

3. Facts should be a recitation of the pertinent, predominant evidence as it was developed for and recounted by the last court to hear the case.

4. Question(s) should be the specific, limited inquiry that was allowed in the last court hearing.

5. Answers should be the response of the court, yes or no or whatever else might be an accurate and suitable answer to the question.

(Note: Actually, inasmuch as lower and higher courts may address the same case by way of different questions, it might enhance accuracy and understanding to identify every question and answer by every court involved in hearing a case, up to and including the United States Supreme Court, if the case is appealed that far.)

6. Reasons revealed by the court for the answers given, and that substantiate the court's decision, should be listed. Frequently, five or six reasons might be given.

7. Application should reveal the general—or specific—applications of the findings to current organization and operation of schools.

A well-written, precise, seven-part brief can be done for most major cases in four hundred to five hundred words maximum. Techniques for finding cases in the reporting systems are given in Chapter 1.

The authors acknowledge the stimulating conversations with many colleagues in the National Conference of Professors of Educational Administration (NCPEA) and the National Organization for Law in Public Education (NOLPE). Graduate students in classes of school law at both institutions have presented many challenges as the actions of legislatures and courts have been questioned in the best scholarly fashion. Many of those same students have provided substantial research assistance. Finally, a special thanks is due to Inga Ronke, University of Nebraska at Omaha (UNO), the patient typist for much of this manuscript.

SCHOOL LAW
FOR THE
PRACTITIONER

chapter 1

THE LEGAL SYSTEM AND LOCATION OF CASES

The Legal System

Laws came into existence as people became aware of a need for them. When thought of as external guides to acceptable behavior, it can be seen that from an early time laws provided an alternative to brutality and violence as ways to settle disputes. Laws can be operational in a wide variety of political systems, ranging from open-participation democracies to closed, absolute dictatorships. Every system has its own unique group of law-enforcing government officials.

In the United States of America, law has been conceptualized as the minimum restraint that must be imposed on individuals to achieve an acceptable level of social orderliness. Whether it is the revolutionary spirit, the frontier spirit, or something else, it is clear that since American citizens came into their own in 1776, there has been a steady resistance to power increases by central-government authorities. Americans want to make most of their decisions for themselves with minimum guidance from governing officials. Not incidentally, that prevailing spirit of those early Americans provides the basis for much of the litigation involving schools.

At the same time, those Americans of the latter eighteenth century candidly recognized that some laws were necessary if property rights were to exist. Likewise, the same concept called for laws to protect certain rights of citizens in regard to individual freedoms. To incorporate such concerns and give them political reality, a Constitution was adopted that called into being a three-part government, one in which checks and balances were provided. The Constitution called for a United States Congress (Article I); an executive, the President of the nation (Article II); and a judiciary consisting of one Supreme Court and necessary inferior courts (Article III).

Over the decades, certain parts of the Constitution selected from the whole document have proved to be most pertinent to education and schools:

1. Article I, Section 8: The Congress shall have Power to lay and collect Taxes, Duties, Imposts and Excises, to pay the Debts and provide for the common Defence and general Welfare of the United States; but all Duties, Imposts and Excises shall be uniform throughout the United States.

2. Amendment I: Congress shall make no law respecting an establishment of religion, or prohibiting the free exercise thereof; or abridging the freedom of speech, or of the press; or the right of the people peaceably to assemble, and to petition the Government for a redress of grievances.

3. Amendment IV: The right of the people to be secure in their persons, houses, papers and effects, against unreasonable searches and seizures, shall not be violated, and no Warrants shall issue, but upon probable cause, supported by Oath or affirmation, and particularly describing the place to be searched, and the persons or things to be seized.

4. Amendment IX: The enumeration in the Constitution, of certain rights, shall not be construed to deny or disparage others retained by the people.

5. Amendment X: The powers not delegated to the United States by the Constitution, nor prohibited by it to the States, are reserved to the States respectively, or to the people.

6. Amendment XIV, Section 1: All persons born or naturalized in the United States, and subject to the jurisdiction thereof, are citizens of the United States and of the State wherein they reside. No State shall make or enforce any law which shall abridge the privileges or immunities of citizens of the United States; nor shall any State deprive any person of life, liberty, or property, without due process of law; nor deny to any person within its jurisdiction the equal protection of the laws.

Much of the essence of what can or must be done or not done in the nation's elementary and secondary schools is determined by consulting the pertinent portions of the Constitution.

With the Constitution as the benchmark or primary reference point, a substantial experience has developed in regard to the relationship of the federal government and education. The executive branch is involved but little; the legislative branch is involved more than that but still less than the judiciary. The judiciary is deeply involved in many decisions that are mandatory or influential upon local school districts, and that level of influence has increased markedly since the end of World War II.

Any survey of government structures—the legal system—is definitionally brief, and fine points must be omitted. Nonetheless, a general picture, resting upon specifics and basic principles, is a necessary base from which a student of school law can make some important connections. For example, out of a case concerning agricultural subsidies, *United States v. Butler,* 297 U.S. 1 (USSC, 1936), the right of the U.S. Congress to act broadly within Article I, Section 8, was recognized. Presumably, that Congressional power can transfer to other areas of general welfare, for example, education, and that Court interpretation legitimized earlier but unquestioned action by Congress and paved the way for later statutes such as the National Defense Education Act of 1958 and the Elementary and Secondary Education Act of 1965.

Education is not a government function mentioned in the Constitution. The Tenth Amendment is a plenary power grant, stating that all functions not given to the federal government are to become state functions, or functions of the people. Federal powers are restrictive and proscriptive. State powers are much broader; theoretically, states have all power not reserved to the people or the federal government.

In the American political system, a representative democracy, two streams of governmental action exist. Not only does the federal government consist of three parts—legislative, executive, and judicial—but the same is true for every state. Every state has its own constitution, and it is harmonious with the U.S. Constitution. That is, before admission to statehood, conflicts between territorial constitutions and the U.S. Constitution were removed. State constitutions may be "stricter" than the U.S. Constitution, and on some issues, such as separation of church and state, many are more strict.

Every state legislature is active, passing, amending, and repealing laws. Those laws can be different from laws on a similar subject in another state but cannot be in contradiction to federal statutes or the Constitution. Legislation is often tested by citizens who feel adverse effects from it, through the American procedure of judicial review. In its political system, Britain accepts the principle of Parliamentary supremacy. There, laws enacted by the federal legislature—Parliament—become the laws, without question. Although a common political heritage is shared by the English-speaking peoples, in the American political system, another principle prevails. It is called judicial review. In the American system, the laws passed by any legislature— state or federal—may, with cause, be called into question to determine whether they conflict with either the state constitution or the U.S. Constitution. Courts resolve that conflict, if it exists, and those decisions become part of case law, that is, law derived from court decisions in cases brought before them.

Suppose, for example, that a state legislature mandated some additional part of the secondary curriculum for all schools, and that a teacher(s) found it ethically offensive to be so directed, without relief, to teach that new part. That teacher might seek relief in a state court, challenging the power of the legislature to be so prescriptive. The state court would examine the state constitution and decide, yes or no, upon the amount of power conveyed to the legislature by the state constitution. Or perhaps that teacher might seek relief in the federal judiciary, asserting that the mandate to teach the new curriculum was contradictory to personal religious beliefs, beliefs protected in the First Amendment of the Constitution. The example is grossly oversimplified at several points. Yet it portrays accurately three aspects of the legal system: a role of state legislatures; the separate-question roles of state and federal courts; and the rights of citizens to question government actions. In the example, the judiciary served as a kind of political safety valve, assuring individual citizens who, when they want to do so and are willing to face some costs, may challenge the actions of legislatures. Such challenge may not be done on a citizen's whimsy; that is, there must be some probable cause. It is clear, however, that the action of one citizen may be enough to overcome the action of a legislature—if the court so decides.

For schools and questions that have some base in education, the disputes frequently seek court orders or damages. Damages are generally for a money amount—restitution for some wrong and injurious thing done by the school or its employees. Court orders are negative or positive. *Injunctions* are orders to cease and desist; a *mandamus* is an order to start and to do something. In abbreviated form, the judicial system is depicted in Figure 1.

To assist in understanding the system and the linkages, a concise explanation of a real school argument, *Wisconsin v. Yoder,* 406 U.S. 205 (WI, 1972), should be helpful. Wisconsin's compulsory education law forced Amish children to attend secondary schools. The legislature had passed that compulsory education law. The secondary curriculum, also under the general control of the legislature had parts that violated the religious beliefs of the Amish, forcing children to inquire into some deeper meanings of life that the Amish considered closed areas. Argued before the Wisconsin Supreme Court, that decision declared that compulsory-education laws of the state violated the free(religious)-exercise clause of the First Amendment that had been made applicable to the states by the Fourteenth Amendment. Wisconsin, through its attorney general, appealed to the Supreme Court, and Chief Justice Burger delivered the Court's opinion, affirming the Wisconsin decision. So compulsory education laws of the states, as they applied to Amish children who had completed the eighth grade, were set aside.

There is certainly no intention in this book to diminish the role of legislators in making laws that affect schools. They are a primary agency, for every state constitution has conveyed to its legislature the responsibility to provide for public education. Some of those constitutional clauses are

Figure 1
The Judiciary

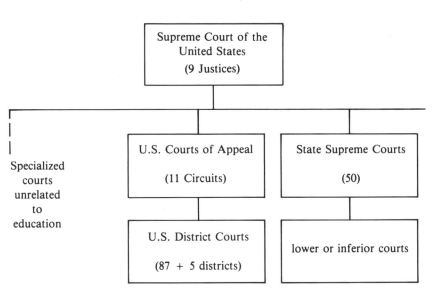

general and some are specific. Some even specify the role to be played by a state department of education. So the legislatures create, in any rational way they desire, the school districts that are charged as the local agencies for the educational effort of the state. It is the whole effort of the legislative branch, combined with the judiciary branch that has chiefly impinged upon education, forming it into what it is and reforming it as new ideas and contentions are expressed within the nation's political system.

Locating Court Cases

Cases are carried before courts and argued there. The decisions of lower, or inferior, courts go unrecorded, in the main. From Figure 1 four courts may be seen that are courts of record: United States district courts, United States courts of appeal, State supreme courts, and the United States Supreme Court. There are, then, 154 courts of record, any of which may handle questions related to schools, and all of which report their findings in the reporter systems. The reports are not transcripts but are summary recapitulations, with conclusions. Authoring judges are usually identified.

Legal citations, as the device for locating any given case, are different from other scholarly citing systems but are really quite simple. Cases have names. Generally, they are the names of the plaintiff and defendant; for example, *Smith v. Jones.* Although those positional labels, *plaintiff* and *defendant* in that hypothetical case, may change upon appeal, and although new labels may be used—*appellant* and *appellee*—the basic statement still is the critical truth. Cases have names.

Civil cases predominate in school litigation. Very little of it involves criminal law. In civil cases damages or court orders are sought. So in *Smith v. Jones,* Smith may have wanted a court to order Jones to do—or not to do—something; or Smith may have sought some kind of damage award from Jones for an alleged injury.

Real citations have names and numbers as well. The numbers reveal the volume and page number of a book in which the case can be found, as reported by the deciding court. For example, in a real case in which the defendant was the state, because a state law was being challenged, the citation was *Meyer v. State of Nebraska,* 262 U.S. 390, 43 S. Ct. 625, 67 *L.Ed.* 1042. This case originated from a complaint filed in 1920 and decided by the Supreme Court in 1923. It can be found in volume 262 of the *U.S. Reports* (the reports of the U.S. Supreme Court decisions) commencing on page 390. It also occurs in other primary reporting systems, the *Supreme Court Reporter* and the *United States Supreme Court Reports, Lawyer's Edition.* Also recounted in the *American Law Review* (ALR), it is enough for school law students to know about and be able to find cases in the primary reporting source. In the example of *Meyer,* and with three citations, the first one listed is the primary, or the official source. In this book a single citing system to the primary source has been used. The identification of each case is the same as was suggested in the preface for the writing of a case brief. If *Meyer* had not been appealed to the U.S. Supreme Court, the decision of the Nebraska Supreme Court would have been final. That court's decisions can be found in the *Nebraska Reports* and also in the *Northwest Reports.* There is a reporter system for each state supreme court. In addition, every such decision is carried in the regional reporter system, such as the *Northwest Reports.*

After locating a case, it should be read to understand clearly the primary aspects of the case. What was the argument? What was the judgment? Who won, the plaintiff or the defendant? Remembering that courts of record report their actions upon the appeals of decisions from lower courts, the reader must come to know what happened in the lower court, separating that part of the report from the final reporting court's action. The seven parts of the brief described in the preface as suitable for students in school administration are the identification of the case, action sought, facts, question(s) raised, answer(s) given, reasons for the answer, applicability to schools, generally. It is a mechanical approach to reading the report of a case, but it is also an assurance that if the reader can grasp how those seven parts fit, the case will be understood.

In addition to locating and reading, a few additional technical concepts are necessary to accurate understanding. The Bill of Rights reserved to the people certain individual liberties. Each amendment in the Bill of Rights places prohibitions and limits upon the powers of governments. Originally, those power restrictions were applicable to the federal government only; however, interpretations by the Supreme Court of the Fourteenth Amendment made them applicable to state government as well.

Interpretations of the Fourteenth Amendment have led the Supreme Court to consider questions such as the meaning of "privilege," "liberty," and "due process of law," as those terms occur in the Fourteenth Amendment, Section 1: "No state shall make or enforce any law which shall abridge the privileges or immunities of citizens of the United States; nor shall any state deprive any person of life, liberty, or property, without due process of law; nor deny to any person within its jurisdiction the equal protection of the laws." Consideration over the past century has revealed several philosophical-legal positions that can stand scrutiny as logical systems in which applications and relationships between the Bill of Rights and the Fourteenth Amendment can be used to settle disputes. The currently prevailing view of the Supreme Court is one of the least rigorous in terms of its ability to meet the tests of a system of logic and one of the most flexible in terms of its ability to allow discretion of interpretation to the Court. Readers should anticipate that viewpoint as a necessary aspect to understanding why court opinions are finally rendered as they are. It provides a vantage point of general understanding and an ability to anticipate or predict decisions. It also serves to explain why many decisions are made by sharply split panels of judges.

chapter 2

THE ORIGIN OF PUBLIC SCHOOL DISTRICTS

Public school districts are political subdivisions of the states, the local education agencies having their base in that single community of interest. Featuring free public education as a partial response to the compulsory education laws of the states, these local education agencies (LEA) are a kind of nonsystem. That is, each LEA has considerable power to determine what will be done for the schoolchildren in its own geographical area. In any international comparison of the ways that nations have designed to provide for the education of the children, American schools are unique. That uniqueness stems from both tradition and laws.

The traditions that developed in Western Europe, before the establishment of the United States of America, had a far-reaching effect upon schooling in America. Experiments in group education, developing philosophies addressed to social and economic problems, and individualistic approaches to religion each played a part. Immigrants to the American colonies from England, Scotland, France, Holland, and other nearby areas sought to transplant ideas and services that held appeal for them. Ideas that were sourced in political elitism, when transferred to the American colonies, came to include many more egalitarian views. That influence for change did not have an exclusive origin in the colonies—many of those notions originated and were developed in a European heritage and were transferred. Eventually, by the turn of the eighteenth century, many of those American colonials saw a need for widely available education, and that need was sourced in diverse social interests such as commerce, transportation, manufacturing, religion, and politics. The time and the place—rich in resources that could help pay for educational costs—proved to be a very hospitable environment for ideas about the extension of educational opportunities. Ordinances and statutes mandated by legislatures upon colonial settlements proved to be handy devices for implementing those ideas.

Early American Schools

By the middle of the seventeenth century, more than one American colony had, by statute, provided for freedom of worship. It was indicative of the New World attitude that included a strong tendency toward expanded individualistic religious viewpoints. This called for literacy as a necessary preliminary to Bible reading and scripture understanding. Initially, those seventeenth-century New World colonials carried out a kind of home instruction that had as its goal preparation for better participation in all aspects of worship.

Then, in the 1630s and 1640s, several colonial towns passed ordinances calling for the establishment of schools. Elementary schools were established to provide a rudimentary education. Popularly called Latin grammar schools, those elementary schools continued to exist for about one hundred years. Several of them were in Massachusetts. That colony became the leader in higher education, too, when under action of its legislature, the General Court, a college was founded that in 1639 was named Harvard College. A few years later, the legislature granted a charter to the college, addressing operational characteristics such as admissions, curriculum, religious obligations, and degree requirements.

In statutes of 1642 and 1646, the Massachusetts legislature spelled out the requirements for public elementary schools and ordered that children should be taught to read. That is, a legislative body, speaking for the state (colony) and to the state ordered a system to provide for widespread literacy. The legislature addressed questions of curriculum, organization, finance, staffing, and admissions. The state asserted its power to levy an obligation upon local communities for a welfare service—education—and even stipulated fines for any community found not in compliance with the statutes. It was an early recognition of the values of education, and it included expectations that good things would happen for the Massachusetts Bay Colony following education of the children. Not only would their children be more capable in the practice of religion but they would also become better tradesmen and craftsmen, returning the costs of their education by way of maturing into better workers than those in other colonies. It was a powerful and persuasive argument, and other colonies, such as Maine, Vermont, New Hampshire, and Connecticut, followed suit in the 1650s.

In other colonies church-sponsored schools were begun. Only in the New England colonies did state initiative and control over education prevail. However, through the decades that followed, and into the founding of the American nation, the model of state control over education was encouraged, and it flourished.

As time passed and the Revolutionary War was concluded, the states—formerly, the colonies—engaged in the development of constitutions as the baseline document for governance within each state. Excerpts from a few such documents reveal that the ideas and ideals of extended education as a part of the "normal" preparation for adulthood and citizenship had taken root. Taken as a whole, they called for systematic learning in schools established by the states, and that sentiment can be seen in the two selections that follow.

Vermont, 1787

Laws for the encouragement of virtue, and prevention of vice and immorality, ought to be constantly kept in force, and duly executed; and a competent number of schools ought to be maintained in each town for the convenient instruction of youth; and one or more grammar schools be incorporated, and properly supported in each county in this State. And all religious societies, or bodies of men, that may be hereafter united or incorporated, for the advancement of religion and learning, or for other pious and charitable purposes, shall be encouraged and protected in the enjoyment of the privileges, immunities, and estates which they in justice ought to enjoy under such regulations as the General Assembly of this State shall direct. Chapter II, Sec. 38.

Delaware, 1792

The Legislature shall, as soon as conveniently may be, provided by law for . . . establishing schools, and promoting the arts and sciences. Article VIII, Sec. 12.

In both states subsequent constitutions were adopted, and in both states these portions were included in the later documents.

Legislatures and Education

Operating under constitutional mandates that called for programs in education, legislatures commenced to specify what should be done. Even before curriculum was addressed, the matter of finance came up for attention. From the present perspective, it is possible to look back and see several ideas for support, proposed at different times. Once school communities passed beyond the idea that central to finance should be some kind of fee system paid largely by parents of schoolchildren, a number of alternatives began to get legislative treatment. Lotteries, special-target taxation, locally levied taxes, state-appropriation support, and land grants were but a few of the school-finance sources introduced into those early American legislatures.

Lotteries designed to funnel revenues into public schools were introduced at the turn of the nineteenth century in two of the larger cities, New York and Washington. In various other communities, taxes were levied on certain commercial endeavors, with the revenue going to schools. Included in such special-target taxation were theaters, liquor stores, and banks. The licenses and charters that were necessary to operate those businesses were granted with a stipulation that a percentage of earnings should be paid annually for the support of public schools. Such a money flow is an *indirect tax.* That is, the money, when paid by a consumer or customer, is not labeled as a tax; it is only one of the many costs of doing business and is buried in the charge for the commodity or service. Such indirect taxes do provide a reasonable money source for the support of public services such as education, but they create an unreality, too, an expectation that free public education is really free. Indirect taxes obscure the fact of real cost for free public education, with someone, somewhere, paying real dollars for the operation of the schools. Moreover, such taxes have never been in favor with the commercial ventures targeted to pay them; those businesses exert effort to secure the repeal of such taxes in order to reduce the price of their product, increase their profit, or both.

Free public education was an idea that was growing with the fledgling nation. It was harmonious with the basic political statements that made up the foundation of the United States. Popular as was the idea of free public education, it was balanced with the unpopularity of the realization that additional taxation would be necessary to fund it. With very uneven accomplishments that included some regressive movements for public education, the idea of direct taxes—levied in local settings, counties, and states to support free elementary education—was firmly in place in the laws of the nation by 1850.

The great land mass of the United States as it was finally acquired gave rise to particular economic ideas and expectations that directly affected ideas about schools. That land was viewed as a national commodity with no individual owners. To prepare the land for ownership and settlement, it was surveyed and platted. Uniformly, townships were measured and marked. They consisted of 36 sections of land, and each section contained 640 acres—a vast national wealth. Knowing that free public education could be used as an inducement to settlement, the National Land Act was passed by the United States Congress, and it called for the 16th section to be set aside for the support of public schools. With that federal statute as a base, each state that joined the union after 1802 had a public school-support base, created from the value of the land—at least 1 section from every 36, in every township in the state. For nearly two centuries, that base has formed part of the revenue for public schools. In a way, it was a relatively unrestricted federal endowment for public education.

The nation's growth was paralleled by the popular desire for extended public education. There was widespread dispute about the idea that an LEA, which was created through each state's constitution and by its legislature, had any power to provide education beyond a basic primary or elementary education. That is, could the governing board of a local school district use tax funds to offer at public expense a postelementary, or secondary, education? That question was settled in the *Kalamazoo* case with a sweeping pronouncement stated by Judge Cooley.

Charles E. Stuart v. School District of Kalamazoo, 30 Mich 69
(MI SC, 1874)

GENERALIZATION

With this decision, it became an accepted idea that local public school authorities had the power to levy a tax for that public school including a program for study beyond the elementary levels, that is, for the purpose of maintaining a high school.

DESCRIPTION

To provide for the secondary school, the Kalamazoo board of education hired a superintendent to oversee the organization, allowed the introduction of new curriculum, and then was forced to levy additional money to support the program. Some taxpayers, against whom the levy had been assessed, brought suit, finally asking relief before the Michigan Supreme Court, and a few excerpts from Judge Cooley's decision reveal its importance for present education systems.

The bill in this case is filed to restrain the collection of such portion of the school taxes assessed against complainants for the year 1872, as have been voted for the support of the high school in that village, and for the payment of the salary of the superintendent. While, nominally, this is the end sought to be attained by the bill, the real purpose of the suit is wider and vastly more comprehensive than this brief statement would indicate, inasmuch as it seeks a judicial determination of the right of school authorities in what are called union school districts of the state, to levy taxes upon the general public for the support of what in this state are known as high schools, and to make free by such taxation the instruction of children in other languages than the English. The bill is, consequently, of no small interest to all the people of the state; and to a large number of very flourishing schools, it is of the very highest interest, as their prosperity and usefulness, in a large degree, depend upon the method in which they are supported, so that a blow at this method seems a blow at the schools themselves. The suit, however, is not to be regarded as a blow purposely aimed at the schools. It can never be unimportant to know that taxation, even for the most useful or indispensable purposes, is warranted by the strict letter of the law; and whoever doubts its being so in any particular case, may well be justified by his doubts in asking a legal investigation that, if errors or defects in the law are found to exist, there may be a review of the subject in legislation, and the whole matter be settled on legal grounds, in such manner and on such principles as the public will may indicate, and as the legislature may prescribe.

The instrument submitted by the (Constitutional) convention to the people and adopted by them provided for the establishment of free schools in every school district for at least three months each year, and for the university. By the aid of these we have every reason to believe the people expected a complete collegiate education might be obtained. . . . The inference seems irresistible that the people expected the tendency towards the establishment of high schools in the primary school districts would continue until every locality capable of supporting one was supplied. And this inference is strengthened by the fact that a considerable number of our union schools date their establishment from the year 1850 and the two or three years following.

The more general question . . . is that there is no authority in this state to make the high schools free by taxation levied on the people at large. The argument is that while there may be no constitutional provision expressly prohibiting such taxation, the general course of legislation in the state, and the general understanding of the people have been such as to require us to regard the instruction in the classics and in living modern languages in these schools as in the nature not of practical and therefore necessary instruction for the benefit of the people at large, but rather as accomplishments for the few, to be sought after in the main by those best able to pay for them, and to be paid for by those who seek them, and not by general tax. And not only has this been the general state policy, but this higher learning of itself, when supplied by the state, is so far a matter of private concern to those who receive it that the courts ought to declare it incompetent to supply it wholly at the public expense. . . .

We content ourselves with the statement that neither in our state policy, in our constitution, or in our laws, do we find the primary school districts restricted in the branches of knowledge which their officers may cause to be taught, or the grade of instruction that may be given, if their voters consent in regular form to bear the expense and raise the taxes for the purpose.

Having reached this conclusion, we shall spend no time upon the objection that the district in question had no authority to appoint a superintendent of schools, and that the duties of superintendency should be performed by the district board. We think the power to make the appointment was incident to the full control which by law the board had over the schools of the district, and that the board and the people of the district have been wisely left by the legislature to follow their own judgment in the premises.

It follows that the decree dismissing the bill was right, and should be affirmed.

In that same year, a California court spoke to the right of citizens to an education. In *Ward v. Flood*, 48 Cal 36, the California Supreme Court declared that access to public school was a right under the "sanction of positive law." Elaborating, the court further stated that such access was a right in the same sense that citizens had the legal right to own property and was a condition entitled to legal protection for those years that the legislature might specify for compulsory attendance.

School Districts

School districts are political subdivisions of the states, created to provide educational opportunities, and they are common to every state. Hawaii is unique, having only one school district. That is, the state, with its own political boundaries is also the school district. In 1980 four states—Illinois, California, Nebraska, and Texas—had more than one thousand school districts each. The 1980 median number of school districts was two hundred and ten per state. There are nearly sixteen thousand public school districts in the nation, geographically defined areas that have been created through state laws and that are charged with the responsibility to provide education to the children who are residents of that area. Boundaries of school districts may change, and they do. Since 1950 the most constant change has been in the consolidation of geographical areas—bigger school districts but fewer in number—creating a very substantial decrease in the total number of public school districts. In *Scoun v. Czarnecki,* 106 N.E. 276, an Illinois court defined school districts as involuntary political divisions of the state and identified some pertinent characteristics of each such unit:

1. Embraced a geographical territory
2. Created for the public advantage
3. Not created for the interest of individuals
4. Provided with sufficient statutory power to serve the citizens of that area with the educational opportunities that are due them

School districts are local agents for the state, carrying out the state function of public education; they have an identity separate from cities or counties, even when boundaries and names may be similar or the same.

The source of state power in regard to education is found in the absence of the treatment of this function in the United States Constitution. Although the Constitution addresses general welfare of each citizen, and what government may or should do for each, education is not mentioned. Then, too, there is the Tenth Amendment:

The powers not delegated to the United States by the Constitution, nor prohibited by it to the States, are reserved to the States respectively, or to the people.

That amendment, called the "plenary power grant," has been accepted as the foundation upon which it has been declared that states are responsible for education. As each state was admitted to the union and by comparable developments in the older states, each accepted constitutional and legislative responsibility for public education.

It was pointed out in a Colorado case, *Hazlett v. Gaunt,* 250 P. 2d 188, that the broad power that is vested in legislatures for the creation or alteration of school districts may be delegated by statutes, enabling selected administrative bodies to carry out such action within given sets of conditions. This balance of power and governmental articulation between state and local government was further amplified in *Farrell v. Sibley County,* 161 N.W. 152 (Minnesota Supreme Court, 1917). That court stated that after the legislature had delegated such powers for alteration of public school district boundaries, in this case to the county board of commissioners, that local board was free to act without judicial review, except for fraud or arbitrary and unreasonable disregard for the educational welfare of the concerned areas. The court finding none, the board's realignment of some school district boundaries within that county were allowed to stand.

Every square mile of each state is located within the boundaries of its counties. The same is true of school districts. The states include no territory outside of public school districts, except for federal land reserves and other similar land parcels. For practical purposes, it can be said that every legislature has attended the complete saturation of its own state by public school districts. Those districts provide for governance, attendance, taxation, and operation in their own area. In some states school districts are fiscally dependent upon other political subdivisions, such as townships or municipalities. Generally, public school districts are independent; that is, they can make their own budget and set the tax rates necessary to raise money to operate. Likewise, in some states, the district's governing board is composed of appointed officials; much more commonly, members of governing boards for school districts are elected from within that district under laws specific to each state. Board members serve for stipulated terms of office.

When sitting as a board, those members operate under statutory powers and can conduct business as a quasi corporation, buying and selling property, hiring and firing personnel, and so on. In *Dappen v. Weber,* 184 N.W. 952 (Nebraska Supreme Court, 1921), the court ruled on a question of school district formation and stipulated that such districts were quasi corporations of a public character. "This rule is applicable to school districts, as like municipal corporations, they obtain their franchise from the state and are created for public purposes to carry out strictly public policies." In *Iverson v. School Districts of Springfield and Curran,* 202 N.W. 788 (Wisconsin Supreme Court, 1925) a further refinement was made when the court stated that a school district "is not a municipal corporation but merely a quasi municipal corporation, constituting the states system of public education." School districts have corporation-style powers but are somewhat restricted. Some of those restrictions have been established to protect the public funds that comprise the school district's treasury.

So public school districts are geographical areas that must maintain schools or at least provide for the education of eligible schoolchildren living within their boundaries. They are political subdivisions of the state. Where the boundary of one district ends, another starts. Governing boards can make a variety of decisions, but no state law allows local boards to ignore the educational needs of their children who fall within the compulsory-attendance age range. That age range varies among the states, but characteristically, children between the ages of six and sixteen must attend a free public school or its equivalent or be labeled as a truant under the laws of the state.

The New England states set the pattern for the nation, enacting laws that in their intent are now nearly two hundred years old. They established the provisions for the management of state systems of (elementary) schools.

Their influence on all that has happened to public education since then is obvious. Those laws attended fundamental legal characteristics of educational organization and management such as:

1. Public school districts as geographical entities

2. Taxation on people and property within a school district

3. Aid to local school districts from state appropriations

4. Courses of study for the pupils

5. Examination and certification of persons to become teachers

6. Erection of public school buildings

7. Inspection of local schools by the state

Although legislatures enacted statutes mandating public schools, those statutes were not always well received or promptly put into place. Records of those early LEA committees and inspectors appointed by the state reveal some typical problems. Districts sometimes lacked classroom space. A lack of desks and books was a common complaint. Some schools employed schoolmasters who did not meet minimum legal requirements for the appointment. School terms were sometimes so short—less than three months out of the entire year—that before all eligible students could be enrolled and supplied with books, the term ended.

For example, the Pennsylvania Free-School Act of 1834 called for all land of the state to be within 987 public school districts. Resistance formed from four sentiments.

1. Citizens resented an imposed state education upon their own locality.

2. Citizens resented the taxation that would be assessed against them to support the schools.

3. Recently arrived immigrants objected to the demand that instruction should be in English.

4. Some citizens saw the law as a threat to parochial (that is, church-supported) schools.

The particulars may have varied somewhat, but in each state there was always some strong resistance to the concept of tax-supported, free public education under the supervision of some local governing board but also under mandates from state legislatures.

As an excellent conceptual design, Thomas Jefferson addressed the need for organized schooling in his plan of 1799. It never became law in Virginia; however, when viewed in retrospect, it is clear that the plan had an effect upon the forming United States, influencing early American schools. Many of the plan's specifics became part of educational organizations, right up to the present. He recommended

1. Small districts within every county
2. Each small district with one teacher
3. A curriculum of reading, writing, and arithmetic
4. Children attending three years at no charge
5. Selection of the best scholars for the next step, that is, grammar school
6. Establishment of twenty grammar schools in the state
7. Continuation in education by competitive examination
8. Graduation after six years
9. Time for choice: college or an occupation

As those early American schools developed and as conceptual designs were set forward by political leaders, the schools were closely harmonized with the public interest. It was quickly recognized that all shared in the advantages of a knowledgeable citizenry, and that recognition formed a base for stable and reasonable regulation as well as for the exclusion or restriction of interference by the general citizenry into the operation of the schools. From the outset, schools were organized for the benefit of students, and of society, and not for the benefit of teachers. That view has prevailed. In *Thompson v. Wallin,* 342 U.S. 801 (1951), the Supreme Court dismissed and let stand a decision from the Court of Appeals of New York that had decided that the state of New York could act in the promotion of a more efficient school system. The state had exercised disciplinary authority over employees with the intention of enhancing the integrity and quality of the public schools, of maintaining the usefulness of the school system.

The authority for a state to provide for the educational needs within the state is in the state's constitution, implicitly or explicitly. Inasmuch as education is a state responsibility, many state constitutions speak to that obligation, explicitly setting forward certain directives and minimum requirements for the state legislature and calling for the establishment of a state department of education. Implicitly, the legislatures are free to act in areas of constitutional omission; so state legislative power is not limited to the constitutionally admonished "things to do." Legislative power is limited in the other direction. That is, legislatures may not do anything that is forbidden by the constitution. Constitutions are limiting documents, but are not denying documents. Under such a broad construction of constitutional meanings, then, the educational power of the state is comprehensive, limited only by the stipulating and circumscribing provisions of the state constitution. (Of course, neither state constitutions nor statutes may be at variance from the United States Constitution, which is the supreme law of the land.) Excerpts from the Nebraska constitution provide a picture that is characteristic of most states, although there may be state-by-state disagreements on highly specific aspects of the education-oriented portions of those documents.

The Legislature shall provide for the free instruction in the common schools of this state of all persons between the ages of five and twenty-one years. The Legislature may provide for the education of other persons in educational institutions owned and controlled by the state or a political subdivision thereof. Article VII, Sec. 1, Amended.

The State Department of Education shall be comprised of a State Board of Education and a Commissioner of Education. The State Department of Education shall have general supervision and administration of the school system of the state and of such other activities as the Legislature may direct. Article VII, Sec. 2, Amended.

The State Board of Education shall appoint and fix the compensation of the Commissioner of Education, who shall be the executive officer of the State Board of Education and the administrative head of the State Department of Education, and who shall have such powers and duties as the Legislature may direct. The board shall appoint all employees of the State Department of Education on the recommendation of the Commissioner of Education. Article VII, Sec. 4, Amended.

No lands now owned or hereafter acquired by the state for educational purposes shall be sold except at public auction under such conditions as the Legislature shall provide. The general management of all lands set apart for educational purposes shall be vested, under the direction of the Legislature, in a board of five members to be known as the Board of Educational Lands and Funds. The members shall be appointed by the Governer, subject to the approval of the Legislature, with such qualifications and for such terms and compensation as the Legislature may provide. Article VII, Sec. 4, Amended.

* * *

An evolutionary development of free elementary-secondary public education is clearly traceable in the nation's records. The sentiments that provided the political mainspring to energize that institution have changed but little since those early colonial "legislators" took matters into their own hands and called for local taxes to support local public schools. That is, the strong belief that individual and social improvement would be a consequence of an educated citizenry is a belief that has stood the test of time—over three hundred years—in America. The fact that American schools of the present are criticized frequently and severely for not educating the children up to some high level of expectation may be more a comment upon things such as too restricted funding, too broad a responsibility, and unrealistically high performance expectations than upon a failing institution. Schools are influenced by many factors beyond the control of the governing boards of the LEAs. There is a limit to the quality of performance in any organization or institution that operates in such a contradictory environment.

Early, the federal government used the prospect of education as an enticement to encourage settlement of the western lands. It was effective, for it did influence that westward movement. Those land endowments for public elementary-secondary education still constitute an important part of the financial base in many states. In some states most of that land was sold to provide the capital to erect school buildings. In whatever way it has been used, those federal grants of land—or equivalency—to support public education did accomplish just that.

Public schools have developed amidst a controversy over finance that is not likely to be much abated in future years. In many instances, courts have been called upon to settle those disputes. Controversy has been a constant, and has its source in the disagreements surrounding decisions about who will be taxed—and in what ways and for how much—to support the public schools. With the given that it is the duty and obligation of each state to provide for the education of schoolchildren, the question concerns where those resources will come from to support those schools. In survey after survey, the property tax has emerged as the most hated tax by Americans, but it is the tax most available as a revenue source for local school districts. History, coupled with obligation, indicates that the contentions about desirable support and desirable taxation cannot lead to a steady solution, because all citizens will not be satisfied at any one point in time. It appears to be a political question, one that exists in and helps create a state of tension, and that will sometimes elicit from the American political system more—and sometimes less—support for free public education, carried on in the LEAs under the general direction of the state legislatures and the state departments of education.

chapter 3

THE BOARD OF EDUCATION

Boards of education are unique American institutions. These boards are charged with the management of school districts and are created as state entities having authority to manage local school systems. The powers and organizational patterns of boards of education vary from state to state and within many states, according to the sizes and types of school districts.

Local boards of education derive their powers from the state constitutions, state statutes, and court decisions. Such powers may be *expressed*—those that are statutory (mandatory) requirements; or *implied*—those that evolve from delegated powers. The courts have provided fairly broad interpretations of the implied powers and have, thus, encouraged freedom and experimentation somewhat beyond that which the legal structure might suggest. Unless a practice not expressly permitted by statute is challenged judicially, it may continue to grow and spread until it becomes generally accepted. If it is challenged and sustained, it acquires a status that is as if permission for the practice had been given through statute. One of the early examples of this process can be found in the decision of *Stuart v. Kalamazoo,* 30 Mich. 69 (MI, 1874). In this instance the Kalamazoo school board extended the common school system to include a high school, hired a superintendent of schools, and levied a tax to pay for these extensions, thereby establishing a process that spread across the nation and was not judicially challenged to the extent that it was judicially impermissible.

Boards of education have been charged with managing the affairs of a local school district and with administering the laws of the state that apply to the public schools within the school district. The board is the governing unit for those political subdivisions charged with the responsibility for education in that state.

Local boards of education are comprised of members who have been selected by a process defined in the statutes or the state constitution. These members serve in their official capacity only when sitting in a duly constituted board of education meeting during which they are to transact the business of the school district in accordance with the authority granted to them by the state constitution, statutes, or court decisions.

Boards of education are considered to be bodies corporate in certain states (for example, Michigan and New York) whereas the school district is considered to be a body corporate in other states (for example, Georgia).

The purpose of this chapter is to explore the board of education's relationships to the state, intermediate and local school districts, and municipal bodies; the basis for board powers; the board's authority to carry out its functions; the board's operational procedures; and the board's relationship to the courts.

The Board of Education and the State

The Tenth Amendment of the United States Constitution states, "The powers not delegated to the United States by the Constitution, nor prohibited by it to the States, are reserved to the States respectively, or to the people." The state constitutions of the fifty states make provisions for education within the particular state. As examples, the state of Georgia places the responsibility for public schools on the state that in turn, delegates this responsibility to the state board of education; Section 1, Article XI, of the New York State constitution instructs the legislature to provide for a system of free common schools wherein all the children of the state may be educated; Section 1, Article 8, of the Michigan constitution states that "Religion, morality and knowledge being necessary to good government and the happiness of mankind, schools and the means of education shall forever be encouraged," and Section 2 provides that "The legislature shall maintain and support a system of free public elementary and secondary schools as defined by law. Every school district shall provide for the education of its pupils without discrimination as to religion, creed, race, color or national origin."

The determination of those policies and statutes that govern the operation of the schools stems from the legislature that, in turn, has delegated those matters of day-to-day management of the schools to local school districts. These same legislatures have made provisions for local governing boards. Since local school districts are creatures of the legislature and have been created, altered, or dissolved by legislative acts, local boards of education depend for their existence on state constitutional or legislative processes. Thus local boards of education have no power or authority except that which is provided through constitutional or legislative enactments for them.

In each state a governing body at the state level is responsible for carrying out the constitutional and legislative mandate for providing public schools. One state—Hawaii—has one school system; thus the state board of education is, at the same time, the board of education for the school system. The other forty-nine states have governing bodies at the state level that are responsible for carrying out the constitutional and legislative mandate for providing public education. They vary in name and structure and provide for a state department of education to carry out the administrative and organizational functions of the state board of education. Citing the same three states, previously mentioned, we find that Georgia and Michigan's governing bodies are state boards of education whereas the New York board of regents has the responsibility for the governance of the public schools.

Technically, then, it must be recognized that although local boards of education provide for the day-to-day operation of the schools, local board of education members—regardless of the manner in which they are appointed or elected—are state, not local, officers. This applies even if local board of education members are appointed by the mayor; they are state and are not considered to be municipal officers.

The Georgia State Department of Education is the administrative unit and organization through which the policies, directives, and powers of the state board of education and the duties of the state superintendent of schools are administered. Section 3, Article 8, of the Michigan State constitution provides that

Leadership and general supervision over all public education, including adult education and instructional programs in state institutions, except as to institutions of higher education granting baccalaureate degrees, is vested in a state board of education. It shall serve as the general planning and coordinating body for all public education, including higher education, and shall advise the legislature as to the financial requirements in connection therewith.

The New York State education department is the administrative arm of the board of regents. These three state systems that have been cited are representative of the remaining systems in the United States.

The Board of Education and the Intermediate School District

The nature and responsibilities of the intermediate school districts vary from state to state. In general, they are formed by a group of local school districts to provide services to the component districts that otherwise could not be economically or efficiently provided for. This "shared service" concept is found in the formation of cooperative educational service areas (CESA) in Georgia, intermediate school districts in Michigan, and boards of cooperative educational services (BOCES) in New York. Most states have some such intermediate education units.

In New York the boards of cooperative education services are voluntary, cooperative associations of school districts in a geographic area that have joined forces to provide educational or auxiliary services more economically than each could provide by itself. Such services may include—but not be limited to—education for handicapped students, vocational education, drug and health education and services, continuing (adult) education, staff development, data processing, consultative services, psychological and psychiatric services, cooperative purchasing, and repair and maintenance of equipment. The services that are supplied are those that each component school district may request—subject to approval, in some instances (that is, New York State) by the appropriate division in the state education department.

Governance of the intermediate school district is through intermediate boards of education or boards of control. Members of these boards are selected, usually, by electors designated by the local school district board of education or by the local board of education itself, as is the case in Georgia. Section 615 of the Michigan School Code provides an alternate method of selection—election at popular elections in the intermediate district.

Financing of intermediate districts varies and may be through the payment of service and administrative costs by the component districts, as in New York; through direct allocations from the state board of education and service fees from component districts, as in Georgia; or by combinations thereof. Wide variances in financial support systems exist from state to state, each provided for in statute.

The intermediate school district is a service unit that serves more than one local school system and is, thus, an intermediary between the state and the local school. These units are governed by specific statutory enactments. (Georgia—Adequate Program for Education in Georgia Act, State Code Sections 32-628a through 32-636a; Michigan—The School Code of 1976, Article 1, Part 7—Intermediate School Districts; New York—Educational Law, Section 1950, Boards of Cooperative Educational Services, are examples of such statutes). It should be noted that the intermediate districts to which we have referred are shared service units in contrast to the type of intermediate districts that are found in major metropolitan areas such as New York City. These latter districts were created for the purpose of decentralizing inordinately large school systems.

The Board of Education and the Local School District

Legally, the local board of education is considered to be the governing body of the school district. Where the duties and powers of the school district have been delineated, they, then, are considered to be the duties and powers of the board of education. The very existence of the board of education is dependent upon the existence of the school district.

Legislative enactments that provide for the organization and establishment of school districts provide, also, for the selection of boards of education. Such enactments include the qualifications, method of nomination and selection, terms of office, duties and responsibilities, procedures for removal from office, composition of the board of education, renumeration of board members, reimbursement for expenditures in the line of duty, and other specifications that may be pertinent to that particular state and the operation of the local boards.

Since boards of education depend upon statutory authority for their acts, duties, and responsibilities, a search of each state's education code can provide the specific information that is applicable to that particular state. As an example, the three states that are cited in this chapter have the following citations pertaining to school districts and boards of education:

Georgia—Chapter 32-9 County Boards of Education
       Chapter 32-11 Local Tax for Public Schools

Michigan—School Code of 1976, Article 2, Part 15—School Districts Powers and Duties Generally
       School Code of 1976, Article 2, Part 16—Boards of Education, Powers and Duties Generally

New York—Education Law, Section 1709—Powers and Duties of a Board of Education of Union Free School Districts (Applicable, also, to Central School Districts)
       Education Law, Section 2503—Powers and Duties of City Boards of Education of Cities under 125,000 Population

Only the board of education can act for the school district and exercise the powers that have been granted by the statutes and the state constitution. Furthermore, a board of education has authority only over the school district that it serves. It is the governing body for one local education agency (LEA).

In some states the qualified electors of a school district meet in an annual meeting of the district. Those voters who attend these meetings have been granted specific statutory authority by the legislature. They are empowered to act upon a variety of items, including adoption of the district's annual budget, election of board of education members, and the transaction of other business that may be properly brought before the meeting. Frequently, questions arise about which body holds the ultimate authority over controversies that might arise in the conduct of the school district's business. In *State v. Anderson,* 22 N.W. 2d 516 (WI, 1946), it was held that a school board is not inherently superior to the annual school district meeting that elects the board. Only when the statutes specifically place a matter within the control of the board of education may the board overrule an action of the school district annual meeting.

Another area in which questions arise is that dealing with the transfer of power when district reorganization takes place. Generally, the powers that the previous board of education possessed are transferred to the successor board. One major concern in district reorganization is the effect of such reorganization on contracts. In *McClure v. Princeton Reorganized School District R-5,* 307 S.W. 2d 726 (MO, 1957), it was held that contracts entered into by a previous board of education must be honored by the successor boards. Unless there is a statutory prohibition, generally, the successor board has the same powers as its predecessor.

The Board of Education and Municipal Bodies

It should be remembered that the local board of education derives its duties and powers from legislative enactments. These statutes prescribe the authority granted to the board of education to manage and control the operations of the school district it serves. It follows, then, that the municipal authorities may not contravene the legislative intent by limiting or controlling the authority granted to the local board of education. Given the fact that some school districts have coterminous boundaries with a municipality of the same name, the separateness is not always clear.

Fiscally independent boards of education are free to adopt budgets—subject in certain jurisdictions to a referendum by the qualified voters of the district; they can levy—or cause to be levied—taxes within the constitutional or statutory limits prescribed by the state and expend the funds received in accordance with the prescribed fiscal procedures. Fiscally dependent boards of education, although having the authority to determine the budget, must depend upon another body, for example, the board of estimate, the city council, or the county board of commissioners, to provide the funds to underwrite the budgetary needs of the school district. In this latter instance, that other local governmental body becomes the fiscal agent and, thereby, assumes some indirect control over the school district's educational program. If the funds requested by the board of education are not granted, the two bodies—the board of education and its fiscal agency—shall confer in an attempt to reach a satisfactory agreement on funds. When an agreement has been reached, the budget must be amended, accordingly. It is in this manner that the "outside" fiscal agency can exercise some control over the school district's affairs.

Bases for Board Powers

SOURCE AND NATURE

In a decision in the case *Board of Education of Oklahoma City v. Cloudman,* 92 P. 2d 837 (OK, 1939), the court defined, judicially, the powers of a board of education as follows: "The school board has and can exercise those powers that are granted in express words, those fairly implied in or necessarily incidental to the powers expressly granted, and those essential to the declared objects and purposes of the corporation.''

Powers and authority residing in a board of education come from three sources—the state constitution, legislative enactments, and judicial decisions. Those powers granted by the state constitution can be changed only through amendment of that document; powers granted by legislative enactment can be modified as the legislature sees fit; powers decreed by judicial decision may be changed only as the decision is reversed by a higher court or superseded by a new opinion.

Unless the statutory authority granted to a board of education proves to be unconstitutional, the courts will not interfere with it. Where express legislative approval has not been given, the courts must determine whether the statutes clearly imply authority to pursue the activity or whether the activity is necessary to accomplish the school district's purpose. We often find challenges to a board of education's authority when that board has embarked upon educational innovations. Typically, such challenges maintain that these innovations are beyond the powers of the board of education.

The decision about how the statutes are to be construed rests with the court. Courts in certain jurisdictions have held that the statutes that confer power or impose duties upon the boards of education must be given strict construction. They hold that the statutes must be viewed not only as grants of powers but also as limitations of that power. Courts in other jurisdictions see the matter differently and give the statutes a more liberal construction. However, as a general rule, wherever doubt exists about whether a board possesses a given power, the courts will deny the power's existence.

There is a rule known as *ejusdem generis* that states that a general grant of power following an enumeration of specific powers is to be interpreted as applying to the same general kind of powers as those that are specifically mentioned. Thus if specific powers regarding the provisions of educational programs have been conferred upon the board of education, a general provision granting powers to the board of education to do those things that are necessary for maintaining the educational program does not expand the specific powers.

Boards of education, as state bodies, have been created to perform a state function. They have been granted the necessary authority to act when the occasion demands action. Thus the board of education possesses powers that have been conferred upon it by statute. Not only may the board of education exercise these powers, but the board must act when the situation requires the board to exercise its granted powers.

POWERS AND DUTIES

No state constitution or statutes are sufficiently all-inclusive to provide for every act that may be performed by a local board of education. It can be noted that many of the practices being followed in American schools were first implemented by one or more local boards of education before those practices were specifically authorized by the statutes. Included in this list might be educational data processing, programmed instruction, nongraded groupings, and the use of paraprofessionals.

Examination of developments in educational programs reveals other areas that were introduced by boards of education before authorization by the legislature and are now provided for by legislative enactment. Among them are pupil health services, school food services, guidance and counseling services, and machine accounting practices and procedures.

Boards of education assumed that those powers were implied to permit them to carry out the *expressed* duties with the expressed powers defined in the statutes. The powers of local boards of education may be changed at any time by the same authority that granted them—the legislature. The courts have agreed that because it is not possible to foresee and legislate particularly for every problem that may arise in the administration of the schools, boards of education may exercise *implied* powers so that they may carry out the express powers granted by the statute. The *doctrine of necessity* is the assumption of implied powers that are necessary to carry out the educational functions of the school district. However, in the eyes of the law, boards of education have implied powers related to education only. Boards of education are not vested with inherent powers. Even though the courts, when in doubt, under common law, are inclined to find against an implied power, most courts tend to construe implied powers broadly.

One of the fears under this tendency is that boards of education will be permitted to expend funds for any purpose they deem to be for the educational cause of children. "Not so," said the Georgia Supreme Court in ruling on the question of whether the school lunch program may be tax supported as an "educational expense." The Court ruled that "educational purposes" could not be construed to include the feeding of children in *Wright v. Absalom,* 159 S.E. 2d 413 (GA, 1968).

Unless the courts find decisions to be arbitrary, capricious, or unreasonable, they have used a rule of expediency as a basis for sustaining board actions that to the court appear to use implied powers to provide educationally sound programs and practices. That the court's determination will be based upon the particulars presented and the outcome of such a proceeding cannot be predicted perfectly. If the court wants to apply a strict construction, limitations may be placed upon the board of education's powers. A remedy for this would be to seek a change in the empowering statute to provide express powers to cover the board of education's action. Should the court interpretation of the board of education's implied powers be extended, this could result in "judge-made law," wherein judicial approval is given to educational programs that were not considered when the legislature enacted the statutes that conferred express powers on boards of education.

One area of board of education powers that should be examined is that of delegated powers. A common law principle is that a delegated power may not be further delegated by the body or the person to whom it was originally delegated. Boards of education, to whom the legislature has delegated specific powers, must exercise the powers that have been delegated. Before exercising these powers, the board may seek counsel and advice from parties who may be affected by their decision; but the final decision must be made by the board of education.

With the development of collective bargaining in the public sector, we find contracts being written sometimes to include powers that are nondelegable. Such contract provisions are null and void. A Georgia case wherein the board of education granted a teachers' association the right to allocate at least $339,600 as increased economic benefits among the board's professional employees was denied by the Court in *Chatham Association of Educators, Teacher Unit v. Board of Public Education,* 204 S.E. 2d 138 (GA, 1974). This case was further complicated by the fact that the state of Georgia had not enacted a public employee bargaining law.

In summary, then, boards of education have no powers or duties other than those expressed by or implied from delegating statutes. Although courts may be fairly liberal in construing implied powers broadly, each case is determined on its merit under the particular circumstances that are presented to the court.

CONTINUING NATURE OF THE BOARD

Where a school district exists, by the nature of the statute that provided for its existence, there, too, is the provision that a governing body shall be formed to manage the day-to-day operations of the school district. The answer to a question about whether one board of education can bind a future board to take a specific action on a proposition that may come before the successor board in the future turns on the statutory authority given to the board of education.

If statutory authority is granted to a board of education to undertake an action that will cover a period that extends into the future, and the board does so in good faith without intent to defraud another, succeeding boards will be bound by the action.

There has been much litigation over this question of binding future boards of education. Even though the courts are not in complete agreement on the question, the weight of the evidence leads to the conclusion that a board of education may enter into a contract extending beyond the terms of office of its individual members (that is, three, four, five, or whatever years the term of office may occupy) even without the benefit of legislative enactment. Georgia is one state that has provided for continuity of a board of education and settled this issue. Where the board of education has been declared a continuing body through the statutes, it can be argued that it

would be contrary to public policy to limit the board's contractual powers
to the official life of its individual members.

An area where the matter of a continuing board of education is of much
concern is that which involves incurred debt. States make provision to
protect against an abuse of the power and authority to incur debt by
providing for public bond referendums before the issuance of such debt
instruments. In addition, many states have constitutional limitations on
debt as well as on the ability to tax that serve as protections against the
misuse of the debt-incurring powers of boards of education.

Because there are such wide variations in state statutes with regard to
entering into contracts that extend beyond the term of office of individual
board of education members and because there are conflicting court
decisions, boards of education should seek legal advice regarding their state
statutes relative to their power to enter into obligations that extend beyond
their term of office and, thereby, bind successor boards.

BOARD STATUS, ROLES, AND FUNCTIONS

The status of a board of education varies from state to state. The board
of education's primary functions are goal setting and policymaking. In
addition, major responsibilities that are assigned to boards of education
include the selection and appointment of the superintendent of schools and
the approval of the annual budget. The board should develop and adhere to
strong, workable policies so that the district might be operated in an
efficient manner. Boards of education do not have plenary powers in many
situations. Their authority to make policies is proscribed by the
Constitution of the United States (through the Fourteenth Amendment),
the state constitution, state and federal statutes, federal and state court
rulings, attorney general opinions, and state board of education policies.
Written policies establish a legal base for the board of each LEA and carry
the force of law.

In *Mullin v. Board of Education of E. Ramapo Cent. School District,* 421
N.Y. 2d 523 (NY, 1979), the court held for the defendant when it weighed
the balance between the teacher's interest "as a citizen in commenting upon
matters of public concern and the intent of the State as an employer, in
promoting the efficiency of the public services it performs through its
employees." In part, the court relied upon *Pickering v. Board of Education
No. 205,* 319 U.S. 568 (IL, 1968), in arriving at its decision.

In *Mullin,* the teachers' union had developed a "success card" and was
mailing this to the parents of the pupils in the school system. The board of
education sought and obtained an injunction against this practice. The
union appealed. The court, in its decision, supported the board of
education's contention that the teachers' union had violated board policy
concerning communication with parents through the use of the "success
card." The board of education's contention was that establishment of

educational policy was within the sole province of the board and the school administration. The court agreed.

Policies must be consistent with and may not contravene the statutes. Thus under the provisions of its policies, a board of education must act only in the manner prescribed or authorized by statute. Where boards of education choose to ignore the duties imposed by the statutes, their failure to comply with the statutes may—and frequently does—result in legal action that contests the board of education's act. Even if the board of education should successfully defend the action, there are those who consider the board to be suspect.

An important point to remember is the general rule that a board of education can act only as a body at a meeting that has been legally called and held. No individual member of the board of education has power to act legally for or bind the board of education. If a board of education's actions are to be considered valid, the board must act at the time, in the place, and in the manner prescribed by law.

There are two types of actions that govern or describe the board of education's behavior. The first type is *discretionary acts,* which require the full consideration, counsel, and deliberation of the entire board of education. The board cannot delegate to an individual or to a committee any act that requires the exercise of discretion. The second type is *ministerial acts* (for example, a board may direct its presiding officer to execute a contract in the name of the board), which are somewhat mechanical and do not require the board's discretion. Moreover, ministerial acts are typically those acts mandated by the state; the local board merely acts for the state.

Many boards of education have adopted a committee system to assist in the conduct of the board's business. It should be pointed out that these committees have no power to act; they may investigate a situation, report their findings, and make their recommendations to the entire board of education for consideration and action. Committees are designed to influence action.

The Board's Authority to Make and Enforce Rules and Regulations

Boards of education have implied power to make and enforce *reasonable* rules and regulations for the efficient conduct of the schools. The key word here is *reasonable.* Because the scope of rules and regulations is so wide, the courts have been asked to consider a vast range of cases. The general presumption by courts is that boards of education have acted reasonably in reaching their determination. Except where a fundamental constitutional right of the plaintiff is involved, the burden of proof is placed upon the plaintiff. In the matter of rules and regulations, we are dealing with discretionary powers of the board of education. Where such powers have been exercised, it remains for the court to examine such actions to determine if they were arbitrary, capricious, unreasonable, or unlawful. It has been established that a court will not substitute its judgment for that of the board of education where the board's judgment has been reasonable. The finding in *Parrish v. Moss,* 106 N.Y.S. 2d 577 (NY, 1951), supports this thesis.

We must realize, however, that a board of education's power to make and enforce rules and regulations is not unlimited. If such rules and regulations conflict with existing statutes and/or constitutional provisions, they are invalid. Should a subsequent statutory enactment conflict with a board of education's rule or regulation, such enactment automatically repeals the board's rule or regulation.

It is virtually impossible to foresee every emergency situation that might arise. Thus it is impossible, also, to promulgate rules and regulations to meet every contingency. Consequently, the court held in *Tanton v. McKenney*, 197 N.W. 510 (MI, 1924), that a reasonable rule that may be adopted by a teacher or a school administrator that is not inconsistent with rules or statutes adopted by a higher authority shall be binding upon pupils.

With the adoption of rules and regulations by a board of education comes the obligation to provide due process to those to whom the rules and regulations will apply. Such due process requires notice. Notice may be provided by the publication of the rules and regulations and the placement of them in the hands of the persons who are to be subject to these rules and regulations. As an example, in the realm of secondary students, the publication of the rules and regulations in a student handbook and the provision of the handbook to each pupil will suffice.

An area where boards of education have been called upon to use discretionary powers is in determining an entrance to school "cut-off" date. If the statute or the state constitution provides a "free" public education for all children, beginning with age six, does that mean that entry could/should/must occur on the sixth birthday?

One such case was brought before the Supreme Court of Montana. In *State ex. rel. Ronish* v. *School District No. 1 of Fergus County*, 348 P. 2d 797 (MT, 1960), the board of education had adopted a rule that a child must be five years of age on or before October 31 to be enrolled in kindergarten during that school year. The board provided, furthermore, that parents could request a test to determine if their child, whose birthday fell between November 1 and November 15, could be enrolled in the kindergarten at the commencement of the fall term. The parents of a child whose birthdate was November 18 sought to enroll their child—claiming that the statute provided for schools to be open to all persons between the ages of six and twenty-one and that the cut-off date was arbitrary. Their request was denied and they sought judicial relief. The question before the court was, "Does a school board have power under our Constitution and statutes to set an arbitrary date, after the beginning of a school term, after which a child who reaches his sixth birthday may not be admitted for that particular term?'' The court answered the question in the affirmative and held, furthermore, that the board of education had made a reasonable rule that was not in conflict with the intent and purpose of the state statute.

Once adopted by a board of education, rules must be administered equitably and in like manner to all persons similarly situated. An example of this requirement is found in *Wood v. School District No. 65,* 309 N.E. 2d 408 (IL, 1974), wherein an Illinois appellate court held that if the board of education used a mailing list to communicate with parents relative to a referendum, that list must be made available to others wishing to express their opinions in the same matter.

If the test to determine the validity of a rule or regulation is its reasonableness, it follows that there should be a "paper trail" that provides a record of facts upon which the rule or regulation is based. Such evidence should show the procedures—for example, study of facts, consultations with experts in the matter, review of similar situations in other districts, public hearings on the matter, and a determination that the rule or regulation is educationally sound—that the board of education has followed.

The Board's Authority to Establish and Regulate Curriculum, Courses of Study, and Activities

Each state legislature has enacted statutes related to the curriculum of the public schools. It has been well established that the legislatures have plenary power over the curriculum, except where there are constitutional restraints. Furthermore, compulsory attendance laws have been held to be valid. The issue of whether all children who are governed by these compulsory attendance laws must attend public schools was decided in *Pierce v. Society of Sisters,* 268 U.S. 510 (OR, 1925), where the Supreme Court of the United States held that "The state (Oregon) may reasonably regulate all schools and may require that all children attend some school, but the state may not deny children the right to attend *adequate* private schools and force them to attend only public schools."

With the requirement of compulsory attendance, it might be expected that there would be challenges to the curricular determinations of legislatures, state boards of education, and local boards of education. That expectation is the reality of much of the litigation involving schools.

One such challenge is found in *Epperson v. State of Arkansas,* 303 U.S. 97 (AR, 1968). The challenge in this instance was to individual freedom. In 1928 the state of Arkansas enacted a statute that prohibited teachers in any state-supported school from teaching the Darwinian theory of the evolution of man. The Supreme Court of the United States found that the statute was unconstitutional on the ground that the establishment of religion clause of the Constitution was breached. Because the statute proscribed a discussion of the subject that was considered by a religious group to be in conflict with the Bible, the statute was held to be in violation of the First Amendment's prohibition of state establishment of religion as incorporated through the Fourteenth Amendment.

The state of Nebraska enacted a statute that prohibited the in-school teaching of any subject in a foreign language or of any modern foreign language to children who had not yet completed the eighth grade. A private schoolteacher who had been convicted for teaching German to a child who had not yet completed the eighth grade appealed the conviction. In *Meyer v. Nebraska,* 262 U.S. 390 (NE, 1923), the court held that a state law that prohibits the teaching of modern foreign language to children in kindergarten through eighth grade is unconstitutional. The state legislature, in enacting the statute, reasoned that children who knew English through grade eight would be better citizens. The court held that this reason was unconstitutionally unreasonable and arbitrary. It, therefore, was insufficient to support the limitation to teach. The court affirmed that the power of the state over curriculum in general in the tax-supported public schools was not in question. The main thrust of this decision was the constitutional right of an individual to pursue an occupation that was not contrary to the public interest, the right of parental choice, and the educational rights of children.

Religious exercises in the schools, for example, the recitation of the Lord's Prayer and Bible reading, were barred in *School District of Abington Twp. Pa. v. Schempp,* 374 U.S. 203 (PA, 1963). This put to rest marked disagreement within the various states about the Constitutionality of Bible reading as a religious exercise. It did not deny the study of the Bible or the study of religion from a literature or historical position.

Implied delegated powers of boards of education have given rise to the inclusion of courses of study and organizational patterns that are not mandated by the state but that have been offered locally over a period of time. Local boards of education can exercise the same powers when proposing to delete courses of study from the curriculum. Taxpayer actions have challenged additions to the curriculum that have involved substantial expenditures of funds. This is especially true when the challenge attacks physical education programs, including the construction of stadiums and gymnasiums. In *McNair v. School District No. 1,* 288 P. 188 (MT, 1930), such action by the board of education was sustained.

Textbooks have been involved in no little controversy. The legal right of the state to prescribe textbooks was upheld in *Leeper v. State of Tennessee,* 53 S.W. 962 (TN, 1899), and in subsequent cases. The entire area of supplementary-textbook selection and instructional-material selection has been held to be within the implied powers of boards of education. Barring state mandates or constitutional restrictions to the contrary, boards of education cannot be compelled by the courts to offer particular instruction, to use a specific book in a particular way, or to remove a book from use in the curriculum.

In recent times, boards of education have been faced with challenges rooted in civil rights. In *Lau v. Nichols,* 414 U.S. 563 (CA, 1974), the Supreme Court of the United States held that non-English-speaking Chinese students in the San Francisco School District were entitled to relief as a class from the district's policy of providing special English instruction for only a portion of those who were eligible for such instruction. The court based its decision upon Title VI of the Civil Rights Act of 1964, which bars discrimination under federally assisted programs on a grounds of "race, color, or national origin." The regulations for the implementation of *Lau* became increasingly uncertain as proponents and opponents polarized in the early 1980s. The Tenth Circuit Court of Appeals held similarly to *Lau* for Spanish-surnamed students in *Serna v. Portales Municipal Schools,* 499 F. 2d 1147 (NM, 1974). However, not all litigation involving the necessity for a bilingual curriculum has had identical findings, as pronounced in *Guadalupe.*

Guadalupe Organization, Inc. v. Tempe Elementary School District, 507 F. 2d 1022 (USCA 9th, 1978)

GENERALIZATION

Local school boards must take affirmative steps to assure that school-children are not denied access to educational opportunities because they lack skill in English; however, this does not mean that boards must provide a curriculum to maintain or extend the non-English language skills of those students.

DESCRIPTION

This was an action to compel the board of the LEA to provide non-English-speaking children with a bilingual-bicultural education. The Guadalupe Organization was a nonprofit group formed to represent the interests of elementary school children of Mexican-American and Yaqui Indian origin. It was alleged that of the 12,280 children in the Tempe Elementary School District #3, approximately 18 percent were Spanish-speaking Mexican-Americans or Yaqui Indians, and that in one school, the Guadalupe Elementary, 554 of 605 students were Mexican-American.

Four discriminatory acts, violating Constitutional rights or civil rights, were charged: failure to provide bilingual instruction taking into account the special educational needs of Mexican-American or Yaqui Indian students; failure to hire enough teachers of Mexican-American or Yaqui Indian ancestry; failure to structure a curriculum that minimally takes into account the particular educational needs of the two ethnic groups; and failure to structure a curriculum reflecting some of the historical contributions of the ethnic groups to the state of Arizona and to the United States. At the same time, it was agreed by all that the school district did provide educational programs designed to cure existing language deficiencies of non-English-speaking students.

The court acknowledged cases from the United States Supreme Court, including *Keyes* from Denver, and *Lau* from San Francisco. It then declared that the LEA had fulfilled its equal-protection duty to children of Mexican-American and Yaqui Indian origin when it adopted a curriculum designed to cure existing language deficiencies of the non-English-speaking students. There was nothing in the equal-protection clause to impose on the district a duty to provide for a bilingual-bicultural education. Neither did the Civil Rights Act of 1964, Title VI, require the school district to provide non-English-speaking students with a bilingual-bicultural curriculum staffed with bilingual instructors. Providing adequate remedial instruction in English put the LEA in compliance with *Lau* and made available to those ethnic groups a meaningful educational opportunity.

Linguistic cultural diversity within the nation-state, whatever may be its advantages from time to time, can restrict the scope of the fundamental compact. Diversity limits unity. Effective action by the nation-state rises to its peak of strength only when it is in response to aspirations unreservedly shared by each constituent culture and language group. As affection which a culture or group bears toward a particular aspiration abates, and as the scope of sharing diminishes, the strength of the nation-state wanes.

The decision of this local school district to provide an educational plan that was predominantly monocultural and monolingual was a rational action, in harmony with a legitimate state interest. The court added that the Constitution neither required nor prohibited bilingual-bicultural education; that such a decision was a local matter and should be left to local boards of education.

The responsibility of the state to require students to pursue courses of instruction and to participate in activities that the state has considered to be essential to the educational development of the student is rational and reasonable. Balanced against that is the right of parents to guide the rearing of their children and to make a reasonable selection of courses for their children to pursue. It has been well established that the board of education has no legal power to force a student to take a particular subject or course or to participate in any activity that would violate the Constitutional right of the pupil or his parents. An area involving considerable controversy is that which sets the requirement that a student take a particular course or engage in an activity that collides with the religious belief of the child and his or her family. Unless the state or the local board of education can prove the participation is essential to citizenship, the courts are reluctant to abridge the student's Constitutional rights and generally have held that the school must excuse the student from those courses or activities.

The Board's Operational Procedures

THE CORPORATE NATURE OF THE BOARD

Boards of education are regarded as public or quasi-public organizations. This has been a consistent holding, and a good example of that judiciary attitude can be found in *Wilson v. Abilene Independent School District,* 190 S.W. 2d 406 (TX, 1945). Public school district boards of education have been referred to as municipal (see *Board of Education v. Stoddard,* 60 N.E. 2d 757 [NY, 1945]) or as quasi-municipal corporations (see *Rose v. Board of Education of Abilene,* 337 P. 2d 652 [KS, 1959]). Classifications of corporations are distinct and thus important. The statutes frequently confer specific powers and place certain limitations upon municipal corporations. Thus it is important to know the specific classification of a board of education to determine if it comes under the provisions of the statute.

Given a strict construction, the term *municipal corporation* is applied to a governmental unit that has been incorporated previously for purposes of self-government, and its status is, essentially, that of a local agency. This status enables citizens to govern their local affairs, and to do so, the corporation has been granted fairly extensive legislative and regulatory powers. On the other hand, the quasi municipal's primary function is to execute state policy.

Given these two definitions, and given the source of the board of education's powers and authority, there can be little doubt that the board of education is a quasi-municipal corporation. As such, its powers are limited to those that are conferred upon it by the statutes, either directly or by implication.

However, the issue is not as clear-cut as it may seem. The courts have consistently held that school districts and school boards are quasi-municipal corporations, and *Daniels v. Board of Education,* 158 N.W. 23 (MI, 1916), is a very clear statement on this matter. When interpreting certain constitutional provisions and statutory enactments, courts have decided that boards of education and school districts are, for these purposes, municipal corporations. It falls upon the court to determine if the intent of the framers of the statute in question meant to include quasi-municipal as well as municipal corporations within the body of the statute. As an example, in the case of *State v. Wilson,* 69 P. 172 (KS, 1902), the Supreme Court of the state of Kansas—in interpreting a statute providing that eight hours would constitute a workday for all laborers employed by the state of Kansas or by or on behalf of any county, city, township, or other municipality—held that, strictly speaking, cities were the only municipal corporations in the state but that the framers of the statute by the use of the word *municipality* intended to include school districts.

In the language of the three states included as examples in this chapter, the Code of Georgia Annotated, Section 32-902, holds that the county board of education is not a body corporate with authority to sue and be sued. The state of Georgia operates on the basis of a county school system, and the county board of education is merely the agency through which the county acts in school matters—54 App. 81—187 S.E. 601.

Article 2, Part 15, of the Michigan School Code of 1976, Section 380.1132 (1), states,

Each school district shall be a body corporate under the name provided in the act, may sue and be sued in its name, may acquire and take real and personal property for educational purposes within or without its corporate limits by purchase, gift, devise, or bequest, and may sell and convey the property as the interests of the district require.

Section 1701 of the New York Education Law defines the board of education of each union-free school district as a body corporate. The section furthermore stipulates that any liability created by a school is a liability of the corporation and not that of the members of the board as individuals. A school board is a continuous corporate entity and the legality of its contracts is not conditioned by the official life of its members.

It is clear from these illustrations that each state has provided statutory definitions of corporate status and powers of boards of education and that they vary, according to the state. A reading of the statutes of the state in which the reader is located will provide specific details on the corporate status of the local board of education.

BOARD MEETINGS

A local board of education is considered to be a legal entity only as a whole. Thus the board members must act as a board of education, through action taken at a meeting that is duly assembled, having been given proper notice in the manner prescribed by law, and by a present quorum of the membership, as prescribed by the statute, for the conduct of business. The statutes have established that the board of education's official acts and obligations are those of the district. Board decisions rest with the total board and not with individual members thereof, as characterized in *State v. Cons. Sch. District No. 3*, 281 S.W. 2d 511 (MO, 1955).

As a general rule, the legality of a meeting is determined by the manner in which it is called and the manner in which notice of the meeting is given to those who are entitled to receive it. It is required that board of education members be given the opportunity to deliberate on the matters before the board, and thus each member must receive due notice of the meeting in advance of the time at which the meeting is scheduled. In some states the time for notice is established by statute; in other states the board of education sets the time, day, and place of the meeting in accordance with its duly adopted procedures.

Many states—through their open-meeting laws—require publication of notice of board of education meetings to inform the public. Some states go so far as to require the publication of the agenda that is to be followed at the meeting. It is generally conceded that no state's open-meetings law is more demanding of rigid procedure than is Florida's.

One issue involved in notices is the waiver of notice. Courts are in general agreement that the rule regarding notification may be waived if all members of the board of education are present and all agree to act as in *Anti-Administration Association v. North Fayette County Community School District*, 206 N.W. 2d 723 (IA, 1973). It would be well for the clerk of the board of education to have waiver forms to be signed so that this record would be available in the event of a challenge to the legality of the meeting. In states allowing such waivers, two requirements must be met if the formal notice of meetings is to be waived. They are that all members must be present, and all members must agree to act. If a member is present, yet refuses to act, even though the remaining members are present and ready to act, the meeting may not be constituted, and no action may be taken.

There are several situations related to meetings that should be addressed. First, it is pertinent to discuss the "Sunshine Laws"—or the open-meeting laws. State statutes relating to open meetings require that public business be conducted in full view of the public. One should note that the public board of education meeting is a meeting of the board of education and not a meeting of the public (or a public hearing). Under these conditions, most boards of education have, in their rules of procedure, provided for members of the public who want to make a presentation to the board of education to be heard. Commonly, a place is made for such speakers on the agenda. Unless provided for and recognized by the presiding officer of the meeting, members of the public have no standing to participate in the meeting.

Second, questions about quorum frequently arise. State statutes define quorums and the requirements for voting. In the education section of the code of Georgia Annotated, Section 32-907 defines quorum as follows: "A majority of the board shall constitute a quorum for the transaction of business." The General School Laws of the state of Michigan provide that "a majority of the board shall constitute a quorum." In the state of New York, the General Construction Law, Section 41, controls and provides that a quorum is a simple majority (more than half) of the total number of board members. However, for final action to be taken on any proposition, an affirmative vote of a majority of the total members of the board is required. (If a board has nine members and a majority of five is present at a meeting, legal resolutions require all five votes—and a three to two or a four to one vote would not be legal). The number of members authorized by the statutes is the determinant of a quorum. A vacancy on the board of education does not reduce the number of members required for a quorum.

Third, executive sessions merit attention. Specific statutory provisions pertain to executive sessions. In general, three matters may be considered in executive sessions: purchase of real property, personnel matters, and discussions with the attorney who represents the board of education. Most statutory provisions stipulate that executive sessions are for discussion only, with formal action to be taken in open meeting. That is, voting may not be a part of executive sessions or must be disclosed publicly. Moving to an executive session shall be by a majority vote of the board of education. The purpose of the executive session must be stated in the motion. In the state of Georgia, when actions are taken in an executive session, the vote of each member shall be recorded in official minutes of the session and shall be open to public inspection.

Pointing out two situations dealing with executive sessions demonstrates some of the problems that arise in the interpretation of the statutory provisions for such sessions.

In *Karol v. Board of Education USD No. 1,* 593 P. 2d 649 (AZ, 1979), *rehearing denied,* April 24, 1979, a teacher challenged a board's action in executive session in Arizona. The board discussed personnel matters—termination and renewal of contracts of teachers—in the executive session. After meeting in this executive session, the board reconvened in open session whereupon it adopted a resolution approving contracts for certain teachers whose names appeared on a list; other names that were identified by asterisks were terminated, but those names were not read aloud. The entire list was attached to the official minutes of the open meeting and was subsequently made public. The court ruled in the board's favor, having found that the board's vote was within the law.

In *Hudson v. The School District of Kansas City, Missouri,* 578 S.W. 2d 301 (MO, 1979), the American Federation of Teachers alleged that the board of education of Kansas City, Missouri, violated the open-meeting law. The union sought injunctive relief from future executive sessions of the board and implementation of board action taken in the meeting. The issue turned on Missouri Laws 610.010, which allows closed meetings, closed records, or closed votes in "meetings relating to the hiring, firing, or promotion of personnel of a public governmental body." The board of education, facing a $7 million budget deficit, met in executive session to deal with personnel problems and the possibility of program reductions. The question that the court was to consider was whether a discussion of programs and finances was within the meaning of the open-meeting law exception. The court, in striking a balance of state and private interests, said that the discussion of programs and finances should have been done in open session and the discussion of reduction of personnel in closed session. However, the court denied the injunctive relief sought in holding that since reorganization was accomplished, it was not in the state's interest to have everything undone. It held, furthermore, that the board did violate the open-meeting law but handled teacher reductions and administrative demotions according to the law; therefore, on balance, the court found no error and found for the board of education.

Questions dealing with executive sessions tend to be somewhat complicated. Frequently, courts must weigh, as did the court in the previous matter, the balance between state and private interests.

Boards of education may convene in any of three types of meetings. The first is the regular meeting. This term is usually applied to a meeting of a board of education that is convened at a stated time and place in accordance with either the statutes or action of the board itself. With exceptions, which we will discuss later, the business of the school district is transacted at such meetings. These meetings are held under the open-meeting law provisions and are the official meetings of the board of education. Either by statute or board resolution, the day, time, and place of meeting are established at the beginning of the official year. Deviations from these specifications must be announced publicly and are restricted, very often, by statutory requirements.

Special meetings are those called for a special purpose. It has been argued that only the business that was included in the call for the meeting may be transacted. That is, special meetings are generally one-item agenda meetings; however, unless specifically limited to this proposition by statute or board policy, other matters may, with the consent of those present, be discussed. Under some statutes, decisions may be reached at special meetings. Special meetings, too, are subject to the open-meeting law.

The third type of meeting is the emergency meeting. Most states have statutes that permit boards of education to call emergency meetings subject to limiting the discussion to the emergency for which the meeting is called. The key is that a bona fide emergency shall exist. Waiver of notice of such a meeting is permissible if a true emergency does exist. An example of such an emergency would be the loss of a building through fire and the need to take immediate action to house the pupils and staff who were displaced.

Because the actions of a board of education are the legal bases under which the school district operates, meetings at which such actions take place are extremely important. In order for the board of education's actions to stand judicial scrutiny, the statutory requirements and the board's prescribed procedures for the conduct of meetings must be followed scrupulously.

BOARD MINUTES AND RECORDS

It is difficult to overemphasize the importance of maintaining an accurate and clear record of board of education proceedings. It has been held, consistently, that the board of education speaks through its minutes and records, which constitute prima facie evidence of the board's actions. *Lewis v. Board of Education of Johnson County,* 348 S.W. 2d (KY, 1961), is a good example of the value of accurate minutes.

Keeping proper minutes and records is important for taxpayer reference, reference of successor boards of education, updating of the policy manuals of the board of education, and—probably most important—to provide a legal record should actions of the board of education be called to bar for review in connection with an action or complaint. Statutes that require that records of board of education meetings be kept usually have been held to be directory in nature, and failure to keep such records under these statutes will not invalidate actions taken by the board of education, as was found in *School District of Soldier Township v. Moeller,* 73 N.W. 2d 43 (IA, 1955).

Board of education minutes should show what actions were taken by the board and should show that the board acted within the law. The actual vote on each proposal that is approved should be shown by recording the ayes and nays. Literally, this means that a statement that the vote was unanimous does not meet the requirements of a statute that requires the record to record the ayes and nays, as stated in *Potts v. School District of Penn Township,* 34 A. 290 (PA, 1937).

The board of education speaks through its records. They must be written and approved, and parol (word of mouth) evidence will not be permitted to alter the written record. However, courts, generally, have admitted parol evidence to supply omissions in the record, to provide information needed to reconstruct records that have been lost or destroyed, or to explain sections of the records that appear to be ambiguous. If an action was not recorded in the minutes, officially it never happened; thus the admission of parol evidence may remedy the omission, under certain circumstances.

Sufficient time should be provided to prepare the official record (minutes) of a board of education's actions. The courts have held, however, that these records should be available in a reasonable time. Thus unreasonable delay resulted in the finding in *Conover v. Board of Education,* 1 Utah 2d 375, that "It seems clear that final approval of the minutes at a board meeting is not a condition to the right of the public to inspect them, provided the board has had ample opportunity to take action on the minutes and has not done so."

Minutes can be amended, usually, to speak the truth of what happened at the meeting in question but may not be amended to reflect a change in mind—for such action might prejudice third parties who may have acted in reliance upon the minutes.

Judicial interpretation, more often than statutory specification, is called upon to determine what constitutes an official or public record. A case in point, here, is *Crabtree v. Board of Education, Wellston City School*

District, 270 N.E. 2d 668 (OH, 1970), in which the court held that although board minutes were not prepared by the person specified in state law, the minutes and proceedings were valid.

The "Right-to-Know" laws of many states permit copying and reproduction of board minutes (as public records) as well as inspection of the records at reasonable times and places. The cost of reproduction shall be a reasonable charge and shall be borne by the citizen requesting the copy.

BOARD HEARINGS

Boards of education are considered to perform duties of a quasi-judicial nature when holding hearings. Statutes frequently require boards of education to hold hearings on matters such as budgets, proposed bond issues, school district reorganization, termination of tenured personnel, pupil expulsions, and other matters where due process is involved—the right to a hearing before an impartial tribunal being one of the steps in due process. In such hearings, the board must adopt a judiciary stance and convene as an impartial tribunal.

Generally, the statutes specify that hearings must be held, but they may not prescribe the procedure to be followed. In *Board of Education v. Kennedy,* 55 S. 2d 511 (AL, 1951), the Supreme Court of Alabama made the following statement, which sets forth the generally accepted procedural requirements for a hearing—lacking specific statutory requirements. "No particular form of procedure is prescribed for hearings under the statutes here in question but of course due process must be observed."

Hearings before boards of education are not constrained by the usual formalities observed in court proceedings. Rules of evidence do not apply. However, the courts do agree that the right of a hearing includes the right to be represented by counsel. The question of swearing in witnesses has not been given a definitive answer, but in some states it is a statutory demand. It is very important that the board of education maintain an accurate record of the hearing. This is true, particularly, if the record is to be reviewed by a court in the event of an appeal. An appeal should be anticipated and planned for.

Where the statutes provide that board of education decisions may be appealed to a higher jurisdiction, generally, it is held that all administrative remedies must be exhausted before seeking judicial review. In cases that involve a question of law, the doctrine of exhaustion of administrative remedy is not applicable with respect to the board of education's decision.

Unless the courts can find that the board of education's decision was arbitrary, capricious, or unreasonable, the courts have been very reluctant to substitute their judgment for that of the board in educational matters. Thus the board of education should hold as its objectives good faith and fair dealing, basic components of the common law.

* * *

Local boards of education derive their powers from the state constitutions, state statutes, and court decisions. The Tenth Amendment to the United States Constitution reserves powers not delegated to the United States by the Constitution, or prohibited by it to the states, to the states respectively; thus education is provided by the constitutions of each of the fifty states.

Local school districts are creatures of the legislatures and have no power or authority except that which is provided through constitutional or legislative enactments for them. In each state a governing body at the state level is responsible for carrying out the constitutional and legislative mandate for providing public schools.

Intermediate school districts exist in many states. In general, they provide services that the component districts cannot efficiently or effectively provide for themselves. Generally, intermediate districts are service units.

Legislative enactments provide for the selection of local board of education members. The statutes of the fifty states establish the authority for acts, duties, and responsibilities of board members. Only the board of education can act for the school district and exercise the powers that have been granted by the statutes and the state constitution. Board members act in their official capacities only when meeting in a duly constituted meeting of the board of education.

Boards of education have three types of powers: *expressed,* which are conferred by constitution, statute, or court decision; *implied,* which are derived from the specifically stated powers; and *necessary,* which are required to carry out the operation of the school district.

Boards of education must comply with the common law principle that governs delegated powers; namely, a delegated power may not be further delegated by the body or the person to whom it was originally delegated. Based upon the continuing nature of a board of education, where statutory authority is granted to a board of education to undertake an action that will cover a period that extends into the future, that is, a capital construction program, and the board does so in good faith without intent to defraud another, succeeding boards will be bound by the action. It would be wise for any board of education that is considering entering into long-term commitments to seek legal advice on such contracts.

A board of education's primary functions are goal setting and policymaking. Written policies establish a legal base and carry the force of law. Policies must be consistent with and may not contravene the statutes.

Two types of actions govern a board of education's behavior. They are *discretionary,* which require the full consideration, counsel, and deliberation of the entire board of education, and *ministerial,* which are somewhat mechanical and do not require the board's discretion. Where boards of education operate on a committee system, it should be noted that these committees have no power to act; they may investigate a situation, report their findings, and make their recommendations to the entire board of education for consideration and action.

Boards of education have implied power to make and enforce *reasonable* rules and regulations for the efficient conduct of the schools. Such powers are not unlimited. If the rules and regulations conflict with existing statutes and/or constitutional provisions, they are invalid. Boards of education are obligated to provide due process to those to whom the rules and regulations will apply.

Boards of education are regarded as public or quasi-public corporations. They have been referred to as municipal or quasi-municipal corporations. Since the statutes frequently confer specific powers and place certain limitations upon municipal corporations, it is important to know the specific classification of a board of education in a particular state.

The local board of education is considered to be a legal entity only as a whole. Board members must act as a board of education, through action taken at a meeting that is duly assembled, having been given proper notice in the manner prescribed by law and by a present quorum of the membership, as prescribed by statute, for the conduct of business. Due notice of the meeting must be given to each member of the board of education. It is permissible to have a waiver of the notice of a meeting if the following two requirements are met: all members must be present, and all members must agree to act.

"Sunshine," or open-meeting, laws require that public business be conducted in full view of the public. The public board of education meeting is a meeting of the board of education and not a meeting of the public. Unless provided for and recognized by the presiding officer of the meeting, members of the public have no standing to participate in the meeting.

Quorum is determined by the statutes of the particular state in which the board of education is located.

Specific statutory provisions pertain to executive sessions. In general, these matters may be considered in such sessions: purchase of real property, personnel matters, and discussions with the board's attorney. State statutes prescribe procedures for executive sessions. These procedures vary from state to state.

Three types of open meetings exist: the regular meeting, which is the official meeting of the board of education; the special meeting, which is a called meeting to deal with a special purpose or situation; and the emergency meeting, which must be limited to the emergency for which the meeting has been called.

The board of education speaks through its minutes and records. Keeping proper minutes and records is important for taxpayer reference, future reference of successor boards of education, updating the policy manuals of the board of education, and providing a legal record. Such records shall be open to public view and shall be made available in a reasonable time following the meeting at which the action was taken.

Boards of education are considered to perform duties of a quasi-judicial nature when holding hearings. Statutes frequently require boards of education to hold hearings on matters such as budgets, proposed bond issues, school district reorganization, termination of tenured personnel, pupil expulsions, and other matters where due process is involved.

Where the statutes provide that board of education decisions may be appealed to a higher jurisdiction, generally, it is held that all administrative remedies must be exhausted before seeking judicial review. Unless the courts can find that the board of education's decision was arbitrary, capricious, or unreasonable, the courts have been very reluctant to substitute their judgment for that of the board in educational matters.

chapter 4

PARENTS' RIGHTS AND RESPONSIBILITIES

The nuclear family has prevailed in Western cultures for centuries. Prerogatives of deciding what is to happen to offspring have been held by parents. The latter part of the twentieth century is bringing a decrease in the decision-making span of parents, primarily because of new protections being conferred upon children. Nonetheless, it is still true that parental responsibility for the development and upbringing of children is a predominant aspect of American culture; it is true even in a time of decreasing family stability and strength.

Responsibility for the formal education of American children is shared between parents and agencies that function with state purposes, but especially, it is shared with public educational institutions. In response to the compulsory-education laws that prevail in all but two states, parents must respond and see to it that their children who are in the compulsory-education age range do attend school. Not to do so is to be in the role of contributing to truancy, a situation punishable by a fine and/or jail sentence in most states. Parents, then, are responsible for the regular and punctual attendance of their eligible children in school. Taken as a whole, parents have agreed to release their children into the care and custody of the schools, expecting that the pupils will be kept safe and will learn from what is being taught. It is a trade-off: a parental responsibility is accepted by the schools with a parental expectation of systematic development for the child by that release to the school. This is a condition of tension between the home and the school, for the parents' expectations may be high—sometimes even unrealistically high.

While the parent accepts this responsibility to relinquish some childrearing prerogatives and the child is in school, progress reports are regularly and periodically sent from the teacher to the parent. They are evaluative reports. When those reports contain good news, it is easy to convey the message, and it can be accepted with ease. When the reports contain news that the child is failing, that news is often received with an ear that is connected to a sensitized ego, with parents hearing the information as, in part, an evaluation of themselves, that is, they who had the child who failed.

Parents also have the responsibility to support the school. Aside from membership and work in service agencies of the school and community, this support is a part of the obligations of tax payment. Through property taxes, sales and income taxes, and other kinds of tax, too, parents function as school supporters—a responsibility that must be accomplished if schools are to be open to all and operating. These and other responsibilities represent the whole gamut of things that might be gathered together and labeled as school-patron responsibilities. Although parents may choose to enroll their child in a nonpublic school, they may not choose to avoid the obligations of taxes that are collected and spent for public education. In the educational concept, that is another condition of tension between some parents and schools, for many parents with children in nonpublic schools have sought relief from the tax obligations upon the premise that they are paying for their own educational costs. That feeling has provided much of the political support for the voucher plans that were proposed in the latter 1970s and early 1980s.

Once that small number of broad and general responsibilities has been enumerated, parents are into the realm of combined educational responsibilities and rights. For example, the Congress passed the Family and Educational Rights to Privacy Act (FERPA) in 1974. The act, also known as the Buckley Amendment, was a consequence of consideration of the legal and ethical aspects of record keeping in schools. The collection and use of information by schools about pupils—and access to that information by parents and qualified others—formed the basis for the political support to that act.

FERPA opened school records to parents. Because many public schools, until the time of this act, refused to provide open access to pupil records for parents, a modest amount of distrust developed from parents aimed at those schools. That is, were the schools hiding something from the parents? It is true that secrecy can lead to misuse. It can certainly lead to distrust. FERPA provided that school records should be open to parental scrutiny, an assurance to them. FERPA contained three key features:

1. Parents have the right to be informed about the whole school record of their child and to have some control over it.

2. In like condition, outsiders to the family do not have the right of access to a child's school record, except upon authorization.

3. Parents have the right to challenge information that, upon their reading it, appears to be misleading or incorrect.

It can be seen, then, that this act is a melding of rights into new responsibilities. Although it has carried its own cost for installation and operation through procedures that vary but little from state to state, LEAs have had no option but to shoulder those costs, providing a new service to parents. To have dropped the veil of record secrecy and to have provided formal procedures for examining records has surely had its own positive impact. It is a legal requirement upon schools that is also an opportunity to build improved school-home relationships.

Parents have been concerned about other aspects of the school, too, challenging the right of schools to develop curriculum, establish some courses as required of all students, maintain a curriculum of less than what might be offered under a broad construction of state statutes, and so on. Some of these challenges have found their way into court cases, because advocacy for parent and student rights in education has become an organized effort, involving issues such as suspension from school and educational opportunities for handicapped children. Parent advocacy groups that were prominent during the 1970s included Children's Defense Fund (in Washington, D.C.), Parent Union for Public Schools (in Philadelphia), and Chicano Education Project (in Denver). It is a characteristic of such groups to be aggressive and to move with speed and power against school practices seen as unproductive or harmful to children. These groups become involved of their own initiative, not waiting for invitations from school officials. They protest, testify, lobby, and sue—and their methods are likely to be abrasive, for their goal is to accomplish change toward their own views, quickly. Schools are not without problems and shortcomings, and parents have a large stake in school quality. Those two factors create a climate that is conducive to independent parent groups formed to protect their own interests, as they view them.

The Curriculum

When a school district offers a curriculum to be studied by the elementary and secondary students, that curriculum must meet the minimums established by state statute. However, this does not mean that the maximum program possible under state law must be offered. The governing board of an LEA may decide to offer less because of cost or other sufficient reasons. The case of *State ex. rel. Shineman v. Board, District #33,* 42 N.W. 2d 168 (NE, 1950), illustrated the power of a local board very well. Under the state constitution, the permissive attendance age for children was from age five; by statute, the mandatory minimum age for attendance was seven. Parents of several children age five contended that their children were ready for school and the board should establish and admit them to a kindergarten. There was no kindergarten and the board declined to establish one. Upon appeal to the state's supreme court, the decision of the LEA was upheld, because the Nebraska "Legislature did not undertake to say . . . that all schools should provide a kindergarten or a beginner grade" before first grade. General powers were statutorily placed with the LEA. There were no violations of department of education regulations. So the parents could not prevail, whatever could be said about the qualitative aspects of their arguments.

In the research literature on child growth and development aimed at the question of the most appropriate age to start formal schooling, there is conflict. Some findings point to the desirability of an early start; some findings have identified values of a less organized time as most helpful. Some individuals advocate for universal education for all three to four year olds. Equally vociferous advocates can be found contending that such early education, when organized and systematized, is harmful to children. Lacking a unified research base from which decisions might be made with confidence, but facing the necessity to decide cases in which parents have desired earlier start times, courts tend to adhere to legal mandates, incorporating only marginally the research results set forward to support an argument.

Beyond the questions of the most appropriate time to start formalized education, parents have been interested in questions of curriculum. That is, they have requested additions, deletions, and exceptions, and local schools that decide to proceed, insisting on their own plan, must be prepared to accept challenges in courts.

State ex rel. Kelley v. Ferguson, 144 N.W. 1039 (NE SC, 1914)

GENERALIZATION

There is a difference among the subjects that comprise the curriculum as between those that are required by statute and those that are required by the local board of education. Parents must agree to the registration of their children in the former but are entitled to consideration for exception from the latter group.

DESCRIPTION

Eunice Kelley had been advised by her father that she need not attend the classes in homemaking that were required by the local school district, but that were held in another building more than one mile from the building that she attended. Rather, he stipulated that his twelve-year-old daughter should use that time to study music, and he would pay the fees for private instruction. His request for her absence from the public school class to attend the private instruction was denied. He did not object to her study of any of the other courses required for sixth-grade students: reading, spelling, arithmetic, geography, drawing, writing, and general lessons. The question, then, not only included rights of parental control over the education of their children, but the rights of an LEA to add to the list of courses required by the state.

The right of the parent to make a reasonable selection from the prescribed course of studies which shall be "carried" by his child in the free public schools of the state is not limited to any particular school of that class or to any particular grade in any of such public schools. If the right exists at all, it exists at all times and in every grade.

In State v. Bailey the sole question involved was the constitutionality of a compulsory education act; one of the grounds upon which the act was assailed being that it was an unauthorized invasion of the natural rights of the parent. The court sustained the law and in support of its holding gave a very good discussion upon the duty and obligation of a parent to educate his child, and illustrated the fact that this duty the parent owes not only to the child but to the commonwealth. "If he neglects to perform it, or willfully refuses to do so, he may be coerced by law to execute such civil obligation. The welfare of the child and the best interests of society require that the state shall exert its sovereign authority to secure to the child the opportunity to acquire an education. Statutes making it compulsory upon the parent, guardian, or other person having the custody and children to send them to public or private schools for longer or shorter periods, during certain years of the life of such children, have not only been upheld as strictly within the constitutional power of the Legislature but have generally been regarded as necessary to carry out the express purposes of the Constitution itself.

"The matter of education is deemed a legitimate function of the state and with us is imposed upon the Legislature as a duty by imperative provisions of the Constitution.* * * The subject has always been regarded as within the purview of legislative authority. How far this interference should extend is a question, not of constitutional power for the courts, but of expedience and propriety, which it is the sole province of the Legislature to determine. The judiciary has no authority to interfere with this exercise of legislative judgment; and to do so would be to invade the province which by the Constitution is assigned exclusively to the law-making power.

"No parent can be said to have the right to deprive his child of the advantages so provided and to defeat the purpose of such munificent appropriations." In everything that is here said we heartily concur. Wherever education is most general, there life and property are the most safe, and civilization of the highest order. The public school is one of the main bulwarks of our nation, and we would not knowingly do anything to undermine it; but we should be careful to avoid permitting our love for this noble institution to cause us to regard it as "all in all" and destroy both the God-given and constitutional right of a parent to have some voice in the bringing up and education of his children. We believe in the doctrine of the greatest good to the greatest number, and that the welfare of the individual must give way to the welfare of society in general.

The state is more and more taking hold of the private affairs of individuals and requiring that they conduct their business affairs honestly and with due regard for the public good. All this is commendable and must receive the sanction of every good citizen. But in this age of agitation, such as the world has never known before, we want to be careful lest we carry the doctrine of governmental paternalism too far, for, after all is said and done, prime factor in our scheme of government is the American home.

Our public schools should receive the earnest and conscientious support of every citizen. To that end, the school authorities should be upheld in their control and regulation of our school system; but their power and authority should not be unlimited. They should exercise their authority over and their desire to further the best interests of their scholars, with a due regard for the desires and inborn solicitude of the parents of such children. They should not too jealously assert or attempt to defend their supposed prerogatives. If a reasonable request is made by a parent, it should be heeded. This court has expressly decided that the parent has a right to make such selection.

We think the action of the respondents was arbitrary and constituted an invasion of the relator's rights under the law. The judgment of the district court is therefore affirmed.

Although not a recent case, *Kelley* still stands as a good indicator of what a present school administrator might do when faced by a parental request for release from a class. This was not a request that the child should be released to get a headstart on an "every weekend at the family cabin" situation. It was a trade-off of one kind of instruction—selected and paid for by the parent—over one course within the whole curriculum, which was not on the state's required list. There is a limit to a board's discretion, which must be balanced against what a parent sees as desirable in the matter of educational development of the child.

Over the years of the twentieth century, several factors have converged to diminish the understanding of what should be widely accepted in regard to completing the curriculum. That is, what is the meaning of a high school diploma? Some of those impinging factors include social promotions, increased high school pupil-retention rates, and the mainstreaming of handicapped children. All three factors increase the span of meaning in a high school diploma. Many parents firmly believe that in some earlier time, high school graduation from an American high school stood for competency in academic accomplishment at some higher level than is presently true, and they decry the "lowered standards" for the accomplishment of those contemporary diplomas. In the best of the brief but politically potent tradition of consumerism, their critical interest is based upon the question, "Are we getting value received from the public schools?"

For some of those people, the answer to their problem has been to withdraw from public schools and to fashion their own, unique educational program. But such solutions carry many problems of their own. In *State ex. rel. Shoreline Schools v. Superior Court,* 346 P. 2d 999 (WA, 1959), the Washington Supreme Court addressed this very problem. That court established a three-part test as the necessary elements for a school: a qualified teacher, pupil(s) present, and a designated place to hold instruction. For that court, absence of any of the three was failure of the test.

The notion of quid pro quo—something received for something given—permeates American society. The concept of contract embodies that expectation. People who support schools, who send their children to schools, have an expectation that the schools will use their time and resources for the optimum development of the child. Upon graduation, some parents believe that schools may have done very well by their child; others believe the contrary.

Peter W. Doe v. San Francisco USD, 131 Cal 854 (1976)

GENERALIZATION

Although a child may spend the full complement of years in a school system as a student, the school is not liable for learning achievement at a level less than the parent thinks represents the true learning potential of that student.

DESCRIPTION

Peter W. graduated from the San Francisco public schools, receiving a diploma in 1972. He could not pass the test for enlistment into the armed forces. His reading ability was low, although his I.Q. was average. His parents sought damages of $500,000 from the LEA for the negligent work of the teachers who were employed in the school system. That is, their case rested on the development of a cause and effect relationship in which they attempted to establish that the cause of his low ability in reading rested with an ineffective curriculum and a deceptive grade-reporting system. The case was dismissed and appealed.

The novel—and troublesome—question on this appeal is whether a person who claims to have been inadequately educated, while a student in a public school system, may state a cause of action in a tort against the public authorities who operate and administer the system. We hold that he may not.

The appeal reaches upon plaintiff's first amended complaint (hereinafter the "complaint"), which purports to state seven causes of action. Respondent (San Francisco Unified School District, its superintendent of schools, its governing board, and the individual board members) appeared to it by filing general demurrers to all seven counts; we hereinafter refer to them as "defendants."

There were several causes of action set forward in behalf of Peter W. and the court examined each one. Attention to only a few can provide an understanding of the whole suit.

"XI. Defendant school district, its agents and employees, negligently and carelessly failed to provide plaintiff with adequate instruction, guidance, counseling and/or supervision in basic academic skills such as reading and writing, although said school district had the authority, responsibility and ability . . . [to do so] . . ."

In the closing paragraphs of the first count, plaintiff alleges general damages based upon his "permanent disability and inability to gain meaningful employment"; special damages incurred as the cost of compensatory tutoring allegedly required by reason of the "negligence, acts and omissions of defendants." . . .

On occasions when the Supreme Court has opened or sanctioned new areas of tort liability, it has noted that the wrongs and injuries involved were both comprehensible and assessable within the existing judicial framework. This is simply not true of wrongful conduct and injuries allegedly involved in educational malfeasance. Unlike the activity of the highway or the marketplace, classroom methodology affords no readily acceptable standards of care, or cause, or injury. The science of pedagogy itself is fraught with different and conflicting theories of how or what a child should be taught, and any layman might—and commonly does—have his own emphatic views on the subject. The "injury" claimed here is plaintiff's inability to read and write. Substantial professional authority attests that the achievement of literacy in the schools, or its failure, are influenced by a host of factors which affect the pupil subjectively, from outside the formal teaching process, and beyond the control of its ministers. They may be physical, neurological, emotional, cultural, environmental; they may be present but not perceived, recognized but not identified.

We find in this situation no conceivable "workability of a rule of care" against which defendants' alleged conduct may be measured, no reasonable "degree of certainty that . . . plaintiff suffered injury" within the meaning of the law of negligence, and no such perceptible "connection between the defendant's conduct and the injury suffered," as alleged, which would establish a causal link between them within the same meaning.

These recognized policy considerations alone negate an actionable "duty of care" in persons and agencies who administer the academic phases of the public educational process. Others, which are even more important in practical terms, command the same result. Few of our institutions, if any, have aroused the controversies, or incurred the public dissatisfaction, which have attended the operation of the public schools during the last few decades. Rightly or wrongly, but widely, they are charged with outright failure in the achievement of their educational objectives; according to some critics, they bear responsibility for many of the social and moral problems of our society at large. Their public plight in these respects is attested in the daily media, in bitter governing board elections, in wholesale rejections of school bond proposals, and in survey upon survey. To hold them to an actionable "duty of care," in the discharge of their academic functions, would expose them to the tort claims—real or imagined—of disaffected students and parents in countless numbers. They are already beset by social and financial problems which have gone to major litigation, but for which no permanent solution has yet appeared. The ultimate consequences, in terms of public time and money, would burden them—and society—beyond calculation.

The California court made it clear that the parents had not given over custody of the child to the school. Parents still had the responsibility, shared with the school, for the development of the child. Some observers might reasonably assert that low achievements such as were the accomplishments of Peter W. are as much, or more, the responsibility of the parents and the home environment provided by them than of the schools. At the same time, school administrators should take note of this case as a signal calling for the improved evaluation of students, where student achievement levels may be accurately determined and that information conveyed to parents with precision.

In a slight variation of the theme of negligence and liability, the New York court decided in *Donahue v. Copiague Schools,* 497 N.Y.S. 2d 874 (1978), that it was the duty of the schools to provide education but then also held that there was no clear basis upon which to claim an injury that was traceable to the schools.

On many other matters, courts have been inclined to embrace parental views. In *Jordan v. Erie School District,* 583 F. 2d 91 (1978), and other cases associated with it, the court set aside a negotiated contract between the district and the teachers that had stipulated how children with handicaps could be transferred from regular classrooms to alternative attendance centers. Agreeing with the mothers who had brought suit on behalf of their children, the court noted that the contract set forward a transfer routine that violated the due process requirements from pertinent Supreme Court decisions.

The stresses that parents face from their experiences with schools are several, then. To the extent that parents have felt shunted aside by an educational bureaucracy, an angry alienation is likely to be one result. When, additionally, they then see their children coming through a thirteen-year education experience with only modest academic achievements; or when they see their child placed for instruction in a manner to which they object, but for which they can discover no real recourse, frustration often drives them to ask, "What can I do to change the system?" Clearly, legal recourse comes forward as a possible solution, and many parents pursue it.

Extending this consideration of parent-school problems into the area of extracurricular activities, a key case came from Iowa, a case of disputed eligibility for participation. In *Bunger v. Iowa H.S. Athletic Association,* 197 N.W. 2d 555 (IA, 1972), a father sought to have set aside the rule of the state athletic association that addressed alcoholic beverages. The son was riding in a car during the summer months, and some occupants were drinking beer. When stopped by the highway patrol and brought into court, three youths pleaded guilty; Bunger pleaded not guilty and was found to be innocent. Yet when school officials applied the association's rule, Bunger was declared ineligible for football for six weeks in the fall semester. The Iowa Supreme Court set the rule aside, labeled it too sweeping, invalid, and unreasonable.

That is not to say that schools lack power to regulate the drinking of alcoholic beverages by students. Courts have recognized that schools have a valid interest in deterring the consumption of alcohol among students. In

Braesch v. DePasqueale, 265 N.W. 2d 842 (NE, 1978), parents were initially successful in their suit on behalf of their children who had, admittedly, been drinking alcoholic beverages. Eventually, the school district policy and the administration of that policy prevailed when the Nebraska Supreme Court set aside the injunction that had been issued against the school. Initially, the school had prevented the students from continuing in interscholastic sports, and the injunction had been issued at the instigation of parents. The state's high court held "that the rule prohibiting the use of alcohol and drugs by participants in the high school's interscholastic basketball program served legitimate, rational interests, and a penalty of expulsion for the season was not arbitrary or unreasonable" as one means to curtail the use of alcoholic beverages by high school students.

Parents of those children who have unusual athletic ability have a natural desire to secure opportunities for their children. Public performance is a strong motivator. Schools provide some of those opportunities by way of interscholastic sports, and denial of participation for rule breaking is a very serious consequence to visit upon a student. When participation is conditioned upon the student's meeting rules of good personal health and hygiene, and when those rules are reasonable, circulated to all participants, and when due process is afforded to any suspected offenders, parents must accept the consequences of offending behavior—even if it means that their children will be denied participation. On the other hand, the schools must accept such obligations as fairness, reasonableness, and advance notice.

Specialized aspects of curriculum have created problems for parents when, viewing the curriculum provided their children in light of civil rights legislation, they have concluded that the schools were not only shortchanging their children but were in violation of federal statutes such as the Bilingual Education Act of 1965 and the Civil Rights Act of 1964. Such a case originated in New Mexico.

Serna v. Portales Municipal Schools, 499 F. 2d 1147 (NM, 1975)

GENERALIZATION

Denial of special instruction in English to pupils who by national origin-ethnicity have a linguistic deficiency is a deficiency in educational program, violative of civil rights, generally, and of widely held educational goals.

DESCRIPTION

Statistical evidence indicated that many of the students knew very little English. They spoke Spanish at home and grew up in a Spanish-influenced culture. One consequence apparently was a lower achievement level than their Anglo-American classmates demonstrated and a higher percentage of school dropouts. Of the four elementary schools in the Portales Schools,

Lindsey School consisted of nearly 86 percent Spanish-surnamed children, and the ethnic composition of the students in the other elementary schools was 78-88 percent Anglo-American.

During an evaluation of the Portales Municipal Schools by the New Mexico Department of Education in 1969, the evaluation team concluded that the language arts program at Lindsey School "was below average and not meeting the needs of those children." Notwithstanding this knowledge of the plight of Spanish surnamed students in Portales, appellants neither applied for funds under the Federal Bilingual Education Act, 20 U.S.C. § 880b, nor accepted funds for a similar purpose when they were offered by the State of New Mexico. Undisputed evidence shows that Spanish surnamed students do not reach the achievement levels attained by their Anglo counterparts. . . . The Portales school curriculum, which has the effect of discrimination even though probably no purposeful design is present, therefore violates the requisites of Title VI and the requirement imposed by or pursuant to HEW regulations. Lau.

Appellants argue that even if the school district were unintentionally discriminating against Spanish surnamed students prior to institution of this lawsuit, the program they presented to the trial court in compliance with the court's memorandum opinion sufficiently meets the needs of appellees. The New Mexico State Board of Education (SBE), in its Amicus Curiae brief, agrees with appellants' position and argues that the trial court's decision and the relief granted constitute unwarranted and improper judicial interference in the internal affairs of the Portales school district. After reviewing the entire record we are in agreement with the trial court's decision. The record reflects a long standing educational policy by the Portales schools that failed to take into consideration the specific needs of Spanish surnamed children. After appellants submitted a proposed bilingual-bicultural program to the trial court a hearing was held on the adequacies of this plan. At this hearing expert witnesses pointed out the fallacies of appellants' plan and in turn offered a more expansive bilingual-bicultural plan. The trial court thereafter fashioned a program which it felt would meet the needs of Spanish surnamed students in the Portales school system. We do not believe that under the unique circumstances of this case the trial court's plan is unwarranted. The evidence shows unequivocally that appellants had failed to provide appellees with a meaningful education. There was adequate evidence that appellants' proposed program was only a token plan that would not benefit appellees. Under these circumstances the trial court had a duty to fashion a program which would provide adequate relief for Spanish surnamed children.

Serna, with only two languages in the school community controversy, was a comparatively simple case. That simplicity tends to obscure the fact that the American cultural and economic mainstream demands English proficiency. Educational efforts that fail to incorporate that goal are surely focused upon an extremely narrow interpretation of the role of the school.

Not all such cases have resulted in court orders to install new programs of language instruction (see *Guadalupe v. Tempe Schools,* 587 F. 2d 1022 [1978]). Yet it is still true that parents who see substantial deficiencies in a curriculum, deficiencies that do not promise to raise the English-language skills of their children to socially productive levels, may call for the legal rights of the children.

Curriculum and Religious Conflict

Many of the conflicts originating from within schools and focused upon religion have involved the rights of teachers—and what they may teach. Some have had characteristics that addressed the rights of many persons, teachers included. For example, *Meyer v. Nebraska,* 262 U.S. 390 (1923), not only touched upon the rights of teachers and pupils but also included the rights of parents in the selection of a school for their child—in this case, selection of a school where instruction in a foreign language was part of the schoolwork and desired by the parents.

More recently than *Meyer,* a parental sentiment has developed, and has seemingly swept across the nation, that might be described as a broad rejection of the public school curriculum. Parents who are avidly religious and who subscribe to beliefs that have been styled as Fundamentalist Christian, have withdrawn their children from public schools for registration in private schools sponsored by their own church. Or some have been withdrawn for instruction in a home tutorial setting or merely for separation from the public schools that they see as morally bankrupt and utterly lacking in ability to influence positively the educational development of their children.

An appeal was made in *Faith Baptist Church v. Douglas,* 207 Neb 802 (1981), to the U.S. Supreme Court, but the appeal was denied. The Nebraska court ruled that the private school that featured a curriculum integrally tied to the fundamentalist religious beliefs of the parents was, like public schools, subject to the compulsory-education laws of the state; that is, pupil-attendance records had to be reported to the state department of education (SDE). Moreover, the court supported teacher certification and curriculum minimums from the SDE, both of which had also been re-jected by the school at Faith Baptist. The state's court declared that the SDE rules were reasonable and related to the state interest in quality education and did not contravene the Constitutional rights of church-related schools. Similarly ruling in *State v. Moorehead,* 308 N.W. 2d 60 (IA, 1981), the Iowa court put the burden of proof upon the parents. It charged them to show that their children, registered in nonpublic unapproved schools, received an education that was the qualitative equivalent of public education. Not all states have held that public schools establish the standard to be met, and at least in Kentucky the powers of the SDE have been restricted, but most have followed that lead first enunciated in *Pierce v. Society of Sisters,* 268 U.S. 510 (1925).

Cude v. Arkansas, 377 S.W. 2d 816 (1964), is an example of an extremely difficult dispute between parent and school. The Cudes subscribed to a religious belief in which the body itself was a holy temple not to be violated. Vaccination was perceived as a violation, an insult to the body. School regulations forbade attendance of all who had not been vaccinated against smallpox, and that excluded three Cude children. The exclusion placed Archie Cude in a position of contributing to truancy, and he had been arrested and fined for it repeatedly. Finally, the question faced by the Arkansas Supreme Court was, should the children be taken from the parents by court order, placed in the custody of a social agency for a short while, and vaccinated? The ruling went against the parents. The court stated that parents lacked a legal right to prevent vaccination, that the risks to the child and the community in regard to a communicable disease exceeded the parental rights in the matter of the free practice of religious beliefs.

Inasmuch as there was doubt that the Cude children would be welcomed back into the household after the vaccination, because the purity of the body had been violated, this was a major question; that is, the permanent separation of children from their natural parents as the consequence of a court order. In a sociolegal conflict having no good resolution, the court opted for the legal side. Other states have commonly addressed the problem beforehand, providing in their vaccination statutes a waiver option to be selected by those parents who find themselves in religious opposition to the requirement. The Nebraska legislature, after mandating immunization, provided an option for "parents or guardians (who) shall object thereto in writing on the grounds that such . . . immunization is contrary to the religious tenets of an established church of which he or she is a member or adherent." Even more broadly, North Carolina provided exemption to "members of a religious organization whose teachings are contrary to [the obligation of immunization]." It is possible, then, to provide for religious freedom along with obligations for personal and community hygiene. Those states that provide exemption upon parental demand also stipulate new controls over school attendance; for example, in times of wide occurrence of a disease, uninnoculated children may be denied attendance.

Parents have been involved in many of the mandates issued to school districts about new and extended services, bringing suits in courts and lobbying in legislatures. Some observers have noted that the educational enterprise has extended far beyond the basic mission of schooling for children to embrace health care, medical care, nutrition, social welfare, and so on. There was a plethora of court decisions and statutes during the 1970s that altered the character of the public schools. The whole could be called special-service laws. The general direction has been to put new obligations on schools and remove from the home—from parents—some responsibilities. The percentage of school budgets supporting the primary mission of basic schooling decreased as special-interest mandates materialized, using the school as the organization to carry out their particular mission—all within the school's budget and its calendar. Although the role and function of public schools were expanded, the passage of that decade made it very apparent that all of the malaise of society could not be solved by even such a hardy organization. In the broader sense, these new obligations that were put upon schools must be seen candidly as privileged legislation, which is what they are. Public schools have become increasingly politicized agencies that respond to mandates for new kinds of services. The proportionate decrease of the public school effort in basic schooling has not only decreased some of its educational effectiveness but has also brought a new set of problems for educators, including disappointment with the academic accomplishments of children. Some parents have sought restrictions on the extent of the curriculum and some of those questions arose before the 1970s.

Board of Education v. Barnette, 319 U.S. 624 (1942)

GENERALIZATION

Even a curriculum that is broadly conceived by a state board of education must also recognize individual rights that are specified in the Bill of Rights, including freedom of religion.

DESCRIPTION

A religious denomination, the Jehovah's Witnesses, had developed through its church doctrine a patriotic position statement toward the United States of America. That position included statements of allegiance and obedience and also included a statement of respect for the flag, acknowledging it as a symbol of "freedom and justice for all." The doctrinal statements had been developed to set forward clearly its patriotic position, for its beliefs forbade participation in the flag salute ceremony itself.

Under statute, the West Virginia State board of education was charged to teach, foster, and perpetuate "the ideals, principles and spirit of Americanism" and to increase knowledge about both state and national government. In this context the state board stipulated that the "Flag is an allowable portion of the schools thus publicly supported." Continuing, then, the board resolved that the salute to the flag of the United States should become a regular part of the programs in public schools, and that all teachers and pupils should join in the salute, "honoring the Nation represented by the Flag." Refusal to join in the salute was defined as insubordination, and that led to expulsion, delinquency, fines, and jail terms. In effect and intent, it was a civics curriculum add-on.

In this setting of conflict the parents of children who had to reject some stipulation brought suit, seeking relief under the First Amendment and its application to the states through the Fourteenth.

Appellees, citizens of the United States and West Virginia, brought suit in the United States District Court for themselves and others similarly situated asking its injunction to restrain enforcement of these laws and regulations against Jehovah's Witnesses. The Witnesses are an unincorporated body teaching that the obligation imposed by law of God is superior to that of laws enacted by temporal government. Their religious beliefs include a literal version of Exodus, Chapter 20, verses 4 and 5, which says: "Thou shalt not make unto thee any graven image, or any likeness of anything that is in heaven above, or that is in the earth beneath, or that is in the water under the earth; thou shalt not bow down thyself to them nor serve them." They consider that the flag is an "image" within this command. For this reason they refuse to salute it.

Children of this faith have been expelled from school and are threatened with exclusion for no other cause. Officials threaten to send them to reformatories maintained for criminally inclined juveniles. Parents of such children have been prosecuted and are threatened with prosecutions for causing delinquency.

The Board of Education moved to dismiss the complaint setting forth these facts and alleging that the law and regulations are an unconstitutional denial of religious freedom, and of freedom of speech, and are invalid under the "due process" and "equal protection" clauses of the Fourteenth Amendment to the Federal Constitution. The cause was submitted on the pleadings to a District Court of three judges. It restrained enforcement as to the plaintiffs and those of that class. The Board of Education brought the case here by direct appeal.

The freedom asserted by these appellees does not bring them into collision with rights asserted by any other individual. It is such conflicts which most frequently require intervention of the State to determine where the rights of one end and those of another begin. But the refusal of these persons to participate in the ceremony does not interfere with or deny rights of others to do so. Nor is there any question in this case that their behavior is peaceable and orderly. The sole conflict is between authority and rights of the individual. The State asserts power to condition access to public education on making a prescribed sign and profession and at the same time to coerce attendance by punishing both parent and child. The latter stand on a right of self-determination in matters that touch individual opinion and personal attitude.

This case caused the Court to reconsider a 1940 decision in *Minersville School v. Gobitis,* 306 U.S. 604, another case from West Virginia with the same religious group and same point of contention. In *Barnette* the Court stated that the authorities in West Virginia had exceeded Constitutional limits on their power by compelling the flag salute. *Gobitis* and all other similar rulings were reversed, and the West Virginia regulations were enjoined. An excellent example of the balance of power between the parent and the schools was created. Incidentally, this is the most immediate reversal by the Supreme Court of the cases in school law that it had adjudicated.

Parents' Rights in Special Education

The enactment of P.L. 94-142 (The Education for All Handicapped Children Act of 1975) brought parents into a more responsible role with clearly defined rights. Congress, in the preamble to the law, set forth the purpose: to assure that *all* handicapped children have available to them "a free appropriate public education and related services designed to meet their unique needs."

The enactment of this law required that handicapped children must be provided a "free appropriate public education" in the "least restrictive" educational environment. Each state, in order to receive federal funds, was required to develop a plan for educating the handicapped. Included in such a plan are to be policies and procedures that, in safeguarding the rights of parents and children, must include at least the following:

1. Access to all relevant school records must be available.

2. Prior notice must be given to parents of any proposed change in their child's educational placement or program and a written explanation of the procedures to be followed in effecting that change.

3. All communications with parents must be in the primary language of the parents; testing of children must not be discriminatory, in language, race, or culture.

4. Opportunity for a fair and impartial hearing is to be conducted by the State Educational Agency (SEA) of local school district, *not* by the employee "involved in the education or care of the child." At any hearing, parents have the right to be represented by a lawyer or an individual trained in the problems of handicapped children; to present evidence; to subpoena, confront, and cross-examine witnesses; and to obtain a transcript of the hearing and a written decision by the hearing officer. Parents may appeal the decision to the SEA and, if they are still not satisfied, may appeal the SEA ruling in court.

5. The child has a right to remain in his or her current placement until the due process proceedings are completed. If the child is just beginning school, he or she may be enrolled in public school until then.

6. A "surrogate parent" will be designated for children who are wards of the state or whose parents or guardians are unknown or unavailable.

Parents have the right—and are required—to participate in the planning of the individualized educational plan (IEP) for their child. For the individual plan to be set in operation, the parent must sign it—thereby indicating approval and acceptance of the plan.

One of the major issues parents have faced is the issue of an "appropriate" education. One definition that is being used has emerged from the Rowley formula, which was developed by a federal district court and approved by the Second Circuit in *Rowley v. Hendrick Hudson Central*

School District, 483 F. Supp. 528 (E.D. N.Y. 1980), *aff'd* 632 F. 2d 945 (2nd Cir. 1980).

The *Rowley* case concerned the insistence of the parents of a deaf child that the school system provide a sign-language interpreter in the classroom. The parents contended that this was part of the free, appropriate public education to which the child was entitled. The district court judge stated the following formula:

An "appropriate" education could mean an "adequate" education—that is an education substantial enough to facilitate a child's progress from one grade to another and to enable him or her to earn a high school diploma. An "appropriate education" could also mean one which enables the handicapped child to achieve his or her full potential.

Judge Broderick, with the approval of the Second Circuit, came up with what he called an "extreme" in the middle that requires that

each handicapped child be given an opportunity to achieve his full potential commensurate with the opportunity provided to other children . . .

to achieve their full potential. Judge Broderick pointed out that

the difficulty with the standard, of course, is that it depends on a number of different measurements that are difficult to make. It requires that the potential of the handicapped child be measured and compared to his or her performance, and that the resulting differential or "short-fall" be compared to the "short-fall" experienced by non-handicapped children.

To apply the formula, then, you would have to select some or all nonhandicapped children and determine, in some way, a ratio of potential to performance and, then, compare that with the same ratio of the handicapped child in question. From that point one should be able to determine what special education or related services should be added to the handicapped child's side of the equation in order to balance it.

Neither the district court nor the circuit court applied the formula. Instead, they seem to have accepted a finding of fact by the district court that without a sign-language interpreter, only 59 percent of what transpired in the classroom was accessible to the deaf child, but 100 percent would be accessible to her with a sign-language interpreter. The district court also relied upon expert testimony that every deaf child fares better in class with an interpreter and concluded that the child's academic education would be "more appropriate" with, than without, an interpreter.

School Costs

Schools have never been *free.* Although that word is sometimes applied to public schools as a label indicating a difference between those schools and nonpublic schools, it may mislead as much as it informs. For many students in many public schools, there are costs involved in attendance and/or program participation that annually carry quickly into the hundreds of dollars levied back upon parents as fees. It is true, however, that parents have been active in keeping costs low and in distributing costs, diminishing the occurrence of large fees with a personal responsibility for their payment. This has been one of the true marks of difference between public and nonpublic schools, that is, distribution of the school costs over a wider population base.

When schools began programs that were auxiliary to the formal education endeavor, questions about those programs followed. Who should pay the costs of transporting children to the place where formal education occurred? Who should pay the costs of feeding the children after they got to the place where formal education occurred? Such questions are more than philosophical—for example, what is equitable?—and are fraught with operational complexities—what costs are politically acceptable?

In *Warren v. Papillion Schools,* 259 N.W. 2d 281 (NE, 1979), a question of school district-paid transportation arose. When school consolidation had occurred, it was understood by the parents who lived in the newly added school territory that bus transportation, paid by the district, was a part of the attraction to consolidate. By Nebraska statute, children living more than four miles from their attendance center had to be transported at public expense. The reason for the statute was to encourage regular attendance. However, the consolidated area was within the four-mile limit, and after providing transportation under their discretionary powers initially, the local board halted that service in 1976 and suggested a parent-pay bus service by neighborhood contract, should the parents want it.

The Nebraska Supreme Court ruled that even if some oral agreements had been made about pupil transportation, they were unenforceable, because the official public records of merged public school districts were not open to collateral attacks. The court pointed out that the Nebraska legislation contained a common element in transportation costs, that is, that children who lived near had no entitlement, but those who lived far away did. Proximity reduced entitlement, and the Nebraska statute provided relief only to those parents who lived four miles or more from where their child attended.

As LEAs make decisions on operations, they are often compromises between requests for programs and the operational funds that are available. In *Welling v. Livonia Board,* 171 N.W. 2d 545 (MI, 1971), the plaintiffs sought a court order requiring the local board to provide a full day of instruction for all students. Due to lack of funds, school was on half-day sessions and certain subjects were being taught on a compressed schedule. The state constitution conferred power to the state board of education to administer the public school system, but the SDE had no rule or regulation that prohibited the practices of the Livonia board, which was faced with a lack of funds.

No clear legal duty was shown on the part of Michigan LEAs. The SDE had not promulgated any regulations specifying the number of hours in a school day. The LEA was doing no more than exercising its reasonable discretion about the need to constrict or reduce a program, and with no state statute or regulation as mandate, LEAs were not required to provide a full day of instruction to certain students.

As alluded to earlier, and as evident in *Welling,* above, public school districts frequently have less than enough money to operate programs that are desirable and desired. This had led local boards to search for other revenue sources. A number of cases have indicated that public school districts are sharply restricted in fees that can be assessed against students, but the procedure goes on, and public schools engage in selling items, charging admissions, and organizing many programs so that students raise funds for operational costs themselves. All of those activities are endeavors to provide extended programs through funding that does not show in operational budgets or in tax levies. It is an operational mode in which there must be serious legal reservation.

Some states mandate that textbooks will be purchased by each LEA to rent, or offer free of charge, to students. Some states make that an option to each LEA. No state provides an option to its LEAs to engage in rental or sale of such basic items of the educational experience with the intention of making money from students. Short of that extreme, many LEAs have developed fee-charging systems.

In *Bond and Fusfeld v. Ann Arbor Schools,* 171 N.W. 2d 557 (MI, 1969), parents sought relief from the imposition of fees levied upon them that included the purchase of some books and supplies used in classwork. They sought refund of all such fees already collected as well. The court's decision was split, according to the items purchased. It was decided that school districts were not required to furnish books and supplies without any cost at all to students in elementary and secondary schools, for the Michigan constitution could not be so broadly construed—this, even though it included a section using the term *free education.* On the other question, the school was ordered to cease the assessment and collection of general fees and to discard the material ticket system, used for many of the laboratory classes. No order for refund by the district was issued, but that was only recognition of an administrative inconvenience, and it was a clear signal to other LEAs that if in the future they engaged in similar fee-collection practices aimed at children compelled by statute to attend and did not adhere to the ruling in *Bond,* refunds might be ordered.

* * *

The interest of parents and schools in the education realm is unified, but it is characterized by some ambiguities too. Parents may want more than schools can offer. They may think that more should be accomplished than is, in reality, possible when the constraints of "regular" public schools are superimposed against developmental patterns of children and consequences of socioeconomic classes. Sometimes, parental disappointments have created opposition to public schools and/or have caused parents to search for educational programs that are more harmonious with their own concept of education, generally nonpublic schools.

People who operate the schools—the teachers and administrators—have found that parents can be either allies or not, as they come to view the school where their child is assigned to attend. Consideration of the array of parental interests and the generally understood mission of the schools can be distinguished in the variety of cases brought by parents. The central thread of those cases is that parents want something seen to be advantageous to their child that is not being provided. Direction for every LEA can be seen in a thoughtful examination of those interests, and although not every interest can be satisfied, consideration of the interests is vital and necessary, for public schools cannot long endure without strong parental support.

Parents are responsible for sending children to school punctually and regularly. They also have certain rights in regard to that whole educational endeavor. The National Committee of Citizens in Education compiled a list of rights to which parents are entitled by either federal or state laws, and a selection of five specific items from that list is fairly representative of parental rights:

1. To take legal action against school officials in incidents of unreasonable physical force used as discipline

2. To appeal administrative decisions placing children in classes for students designated as troublesome or disruptive

3. To visit the child's classroom during the school day after notifying the school office

4. To request the absence of the child from studying subjects or joining activities objected to on religious, moral, or other reasonable grounds

5. To examine records and, upon cause, to challenge any record seen as unfair or untrue

chapter 5

CERTIFICATION, CONTRACTS, AND RETIREMENT

Certification

The schools employ several categories of professional specialized personnel. The standards of preparation for each type have evolved and now, approaching the end of the century, those standards are strikingly similar from one state to another, with only a few exceptions.

In the historical development of public school districts, a relatively simple system of identification of candidates and selection of applicants prevailed. The school districts of the latter nineteenth and early twentieth centuries were, typically, small. The geographical area was limited by district boundaries, and even though some of those districts were extensive, the population was small. The exceptions to that rule were the large city school districts, but there were not many of them.

Overwhelmingly, school districts were small, provincial, and personal acquaintance was common. School board members knew, personally, many of the candidates for positions as teachers. As time passed, conditions changed, and lack of personal familiarity enforced the proposition that all beginning professionals should have a credential attesting to minimum competence to teach children and likelihood of success as a starting teacher. Insofar as possible, uniformity within each state was also accepted as one goal for teacher certification. The certificate became that credential of uniform minimum competence. It has evolved in the direction of greater uniformity and enhanced competence. Certification has had the continuous support of the National Education Association (NEA) and the American Federation of Teachers (AFT).

There are several ways to develop a credential that will assure some minimum competence. With states in charge of certificate issuance, each has designed its own pattern. For some occupations, such as barbers, morticians, and engineers, states have generally opted for an examination following the completion of some academic program. Success in the examination is accepted as proof of competence, and a license is issued. The license allows the citizen to seek work in the specific occupational area. For those candidates who fail the examination, no license is issued. The effect is denial of the right to seek jobs in that occupational area. Success in the examination, and not in the academic program, is the indicator of whether a license should be issued. A license is not synonymous with a certificate, but they are parallel in that each is a necessary prelude to certain occupational settings.

Every professional working in a school must have a certificate. Aides do not need certificates; neither do secretaries, custodians, lunchroom workers, and so on. Such workers are integral to the operation of a school and may regularly be in contact with students, but they may not be in charge of students in an instructional setting. For every employee who has responsibility for some aspect of the instruction of a child, an appropriate certificate is a must.

Boards may not be held liable for payment for services to employees who have failed to obtain a proper certificate or who have obtained one through fraud. Boards of education cannot know personally the applicants for teaching positions, except in very small school districts. The unwavering demand that all applicants have, or be eligible for, proper certification provides a necessary protection for school boards and for the children who will receive instruction from the candidates finally selected. Local boards may add to the rigor of the certification requirements, enhancing teacher qualifications; they may not reduce them or set them aside.

All teachers must have certificates appropriate to the grade levels in which they will teach and/or to the subject area for which they will have responsibility. Specialized certificates must be possessed by other school employees, such as counsellors, principals, supervisors, librarians, and teachers of handicapped children. The certificate is a necessary part of the job seeker's credentials, for it is an acknowledgment from the state's department of education that a minimum level of competence is present. It is not an assurance of success in the job for which it specifies competence, but it does assure likelihood of success.

The certificates that might be sought as prelude to job search within a school system differ from licenses only in that their issuance is not generally dependent upon a score on an examination. Licenses and certificates are issued by state agencies and attest that the person named as recipient possesses certain professional competencies, and a confident expectation in his or her performance is reasonable. They are not assurances of absolute and perfect performance. A bridge built by a licensed professional engineer may collapse; a classroom where a certificated teacher has been assigned as instructor may turn to chaos. However, exceptions do not disprove the need for some basic indicator of competence in specialized occupational fields.

People who want to be teachers know that it is a lawful occupation, and they may, in freedom of choice, choose to be a teacher. The route to certification is through a bachelor's degree including certain specifics, according to the kind of certificate desired. Colleges and universities engaged in the preparation of teachers have designed programs containing courses and information appropriate to certain tasks in schools. Students who are in those institutions make choices and commit to one program rather than another. The institutions, through liaisons to their own state department of education (SDE) have gathered the necessary course work and information into programs of study for students. Once those programs are approved by the SDE, students may study in the programs, knowing that upon completion they will be eligible for a bachelor's degree from the institution and an appropriate certificate from the SDE. Issuance of the certificate after program completion is not a question. It will be issued upon application and evidence of completing an approved program. This procedure is used in some form in every state and is called the approved program procedure for certification. It is not the only approach. Current professional literature reveals some strong preferences in a growing number of states for certification upon examination during and after completing an approved program. Some statutory changes have been enacted, altering the pursuit of teacher certificates.

If there are mitigating factors, certificate issuance may not be automatic. For example, a student might have attended an institution lacking a teacher-preparation program approved in advance by the SDE; or the candidate might have a criminal record or lack some other statutory requirement. Such applications do not form a large group. Typically, certification is an entitlement upon evidence of accomplishment, and a chief state school officer may not deny a qualified applicant the appropriate certificate.

The entire teacher occupational episode is represented in the certificate-contract-job-performance-retirement timeline. Certificates are necessary for teachers, and even though, in a way, they represent a property interest for the teacher, certificates are issued by the state for its own convenience and may be subject to forfeiture. In *Hodge v. Stegall,* 206 Okla. 161 (1952), the Oklahoma Supreme Court upheld the state's commissioner of education in revoking a teacher's certificate for cause and with due process. That is, the certificate is not a contract between the teacher and the state, and when a teacher accepts a certificate, the issuance may be conditioned by the state and must be accepted by the teacher—or face loss of the certificate.

Cases that will follow and analysis of the certification-contract routines for teachers emphasize individual cases. Yet the same general principles apply to negotiated contracts for groups of teachers. Under the California Educational Employment Relations Act, the part-time teachers of the Santa Monica Community College organized and bargained for a contract. In *Santa Monica Community College District v. Public Employment Relations*

Board, 169 Cal. 460 (1980), the California Court of Appeals upheld a
Public Employment Relations Board (PERB) ruling that the part-time
teachers had been victims of an unfair labor practice when the employing
board granted pay raises to a full-time faculty but withheld pay raises for a
part-time faculty when the latter group declined to waive its right to
collective bargaining under California law. Boards may try to act in a
disciplinary mode that is less than nonrenewal.

For most teachers, who perform satisfactorily through an occupational
lifetime, retirement in accord with the statutes of each state tells what their
rights and obligations will be. In *Payne v. Board of Trustees of the
Teachers' Ins. & Retirement Fund,* 35 N.W. 553 (1948), the North Dakota
Supreme Court stated that the relation between teachers and the retirement
fund was contractual and that the state had created a trust fund from which
to pay annuity claims under the controlling statute—and that qualified
teachers could not be denied.

At one end of the employment continuum are certificates that are not
contractual. At the other end is retirement—a pension or an annuity—that
is contractual and cannot be denied or withheld from those who are
qualified to file against the fund.

Statutes and Teaching

Statutes from the many states are substantially uniform on how people
may come to be designated legally as teachers, counsellors, principals, and
so on. Excerpts from the three states of Oregon, Nebraska, and Connecticut
span the nation and reveal the similarities.

A teaching certificate provided for in this section shall qualify its holder to accept
any instructional assignment from preprimary through grade 12 for which he has
completed the professional requirements established by the rules of the Teacher
Standards and Practices Commission.

A basic teaching certificate shall be issued on application to an otherwise qualified
person who has completed an approved teacher education program and meets such
other requirements as the Teacher Standards and Practices Commission may consider necessary to maintain and improve quality of instruction in the public schools
of the state. Oregon Revised Statutes 342.135 (1) and (2)

No person shall be employed to teach in any public, private, denominational, or
parochial school in this state who does not hold a valid Nebraska certificate or
permit issued by the State Board of Education legalizing him to teach the grade or
subjects to which elected, except that no Nebraska certificate or permit shall be
required of persons teaching exclusively in junior colleges organized as part of the
public school system.

The State Board of Education may, for just cause, revoke any teacher's certificate
or administrator's certificate or suspend such certificate for such period of time as
the board, in its discretion, shall determine. Just cause may consist of any or more of

the following: (1) incompetence, (2) immorality, (3) intemperance, (4) cruelty, (5) crime against the law of the state, (6) neglect of duty, (7) general neglect of the business of the school, (8) unprofessional conduct, (9) physical or mental incapacity, or (10) breach of contract for teaching or administrative services. The revocation or suspension of the certificate shall terminate the employment of such teacher or administrator, but such teacher or administrator shall be paid up to the time of receiving notice of revocation or suspension. The board shall immediately notify the secretary of the school district or board of education where such teacher or administrator is employed. It shall also notify the teacher or administrator of such revocation or suspension and shall enter its action in such case in the books or records of its office; Provided, no certificate shall be revoked or suspended without due notice from the board and an opportunity given the teacher or administrator to explain or defend his conduct. Revised Statutes of Nebraska 79-1233 (1) and 79-1234

Any board of education may authorize the superintendent or supervising agent to employ teachers. Any superintendent or supervising agent not authorized to employ teachers shall submit to the board of education nominations for teachers for each of the schools in his jurisdiction and, from the persons so nominated, teachers may be employed. Such board shall accept or reject such nominations within thirty-five days from their submission. Any such board of education may request the superintendent or supervising agent to submit multiple nominations of qualified candidates, if more than one candidate is available for nomination, for any supervisory or administrative position, in which case the superintendent or supervisory agent recommends such candidates. If such board rejects such nominations, the superintendent or supervising agent shall submit to such board other nominations and such board may employ teachers from the persons so nominated and shall accept or reject such nominations within one month from their submission. The contract for employment of a teacher shall be in writing and may be terminated at any time for any of the reasons enumerated in subdivisions (1) to (6), inclusive, of subsection (b) of this section, otherwise the contract shall be renewed for a second, third or fourth year unless the teacher has been notified in writing prior to March first in one school year that such contract will not be renewed for the following year, provided, upon the teacher's written request, such notice shall be supplemented within five days after receipt of such request by a statement of the reason or reasons for such failure to renew. Such teacher may, upon written request filed with the board of education within ten days after the receipt of such notice, be entitled to a hearing before the board, or, if indicated in such request and if designated by the board, before an impartial hearing panel established and conducted in accordance with the provisions of subsection (b) of this section, but without the right to appeal provided in subsection (f) of this section, such hearing to be held within fifteen days of such request. The teacher shall have the right to appear with counsel of his choice at such hearing.

(b) . . . Employment . . . may be terminated at any time for one or more of the following reasons:

(1) Inefficiency or incompetence;

(2) insubordination against reasonable rules of the board of education;

(3) moral misconduct;

(4) disability, as shown by competent medical evidence;

(5) elimination of the position. . . ,

(6) other due and sufficient cause. . . .

(c) For the purpose of this section, the term "teacher" shall include each employee of a board of education, below the rank of superintendent, who holds a regular certificate issued by the state board of education.

(e) After having had a contract of employment as a teacher renewed for a fourth year in any one municipality or school district, any teacher who leaves his employment as a teacher in such municipality or school district, and is subsequently re-employed in such municipality or school district or who is subsequently employed in any other municipality or school district shall become subject to the provisions of subsection (b) of this section after eighteen months of continuous employment unless, prior to completion of the eighteenth month following commencement of the employment in such town, such teacher has been notified in writing prior to March first in accordance with the provisions of subsection (a) of this section that such contract will not be renewed for the following year irrespective of the duration of employment under the then existing contract beyond the date of said notification or unless, for a period of five or more years immediately prior to such subsequent employment such teacher has not been employed in any public school within the state. Connecticut General Statutes Annotated Title 10, sec 10-151, a,b,c, and e.

Some states, in considering what should be done about teacher certification, merely acknowledge that teachers must be certificated and then name an agency to develop standards and administer them. Typically, that agency is the state board of education, a subunit of it, or a commission on teaching competence. Other states have become statutorily specific about the criteria for certification, the methods for hiring, and the means for maintenance in position as a teacher. The point is that state legislatures are in command of the question "How can a teacher's certificate be obtained?" and may handle certification procedure any way they see fit.

In 1977 the Oregon legislature added a stipulation that every applicant for a teacher's certificate must "hold a recognized first aid card." Another add-on from that same era was the Oregon legislators' mandate that every teacher certificate applicant "demonstrate knowledge of Title VI of the Civil Rights Act of 1964" and other similar federal and state statutes aimed at the prohibitions of discrimination against protected classes of citizens. The legislature passed such substantive requirements along with the procedural aspects to the state's Teacher Standards and Practices Commission, specifying names and types of certificates. The tendency to modify requirements and make them more complicated or more rigorous, revealed in the Oregon example, is common among the states.

In this brief survey of certification statutes that apply to professionals in education, it is important to note that in an era that has seen *accountability* flourish as a catchword, the essence of that catchword has come to teacher certification. It has been the historical obligation to provide qualitative assurances through certification. Accountability continues that obligation but makes it individualized when testing of every candidate becomes one part of the requirements of the certificate. With a new statute in 1980, Oklahoma put a variety of tests and other rigorous accountability routines into one statute, along with minimum salaries, by academic degree level and years of experience. So long as the action is not arbitrary or discriminatory, the states may do what they deem best when setting forward the requirements for teacher certification.

National Education Association v. South Carolina (77-422 USSC, 1978), reported at 445 F. Supp. 1094

GENERALIZATION

States set the requirements for teacher certification. They may have to prove the direct relationship between their requirements and the job, if disproportionate numbers of applicants, separated by race, are disqualified at the point of meeting the requirements.

DESCRIPTION

The National Teacher Examination (NTE) results disqualified a substantially higher proportion of blacks than whites from among applicants for teacher's certificates in South Carolina. Among all who passed the NTE, a larger percentage of black than white teachers were placed in lower paying classifications as one consequence of their test scores. The record of the lower court was accepted and affirmed by the Supreme Court. The lower court noted that

The evidence in the record supports a finding that South Carolina officials were concerned with improving the quality of public school teaching, certifying only those applicants possessed of the minimum knowledge necessary to teach effectively, utilizing an objective measure of applicants coming from widely disparate teacher training programs and providing appropriate financial incentives for teachers to improve their academic qualifications and thereby their ability to teach. We conclude that these are entirely legitimate and clearly important governmental objectives.

In considering whether defendant's use of the NTE bears a fair and substantial relationship to these governmental objectives, we conclude that it does.

The record supports the conclusion that the NTE are professionally and carefully prepared to measure the critical mass of knowledge in academic subject matter. The NTE do not measure teaching skills, but do measure the content of the academic preparation of prospective teachers.

In any decision-making process that relies on a standardized test, there is some risk of error. The risk of excluding truly qualified candidates whose low test score does not reflect his or her real ability can be decreased by lowering the minimum score requirement. That also increases the risk of including an unqualified candidate whose low test score does reflect his or her real ability. The State must weigh many facets of the public interest in making such a decision. If there is a teacher shortage, a relatively high minimum score requirement may mean that some classrooms will be without teachers, and it may be better to provide a less than fully competent teacher than no teacher at all. But to the extent that children are exposed to incompetent teachers, education suffers. It may be that education suffers less than would be the case if classrooms were overcrowded due to lack of teachers. We think it is within the prerogative of the State to accept some unqualified teachers under circumstances where that is judged by the State to be on balance in the public interest, and that such an action by the State is not a violation of Title VII.

We also conclude that defendants' use of the NTE for salary purposes bears the necessary relationship to South Carolina's objectives with respect to its public school teaching force. Although the NTE were not designed to evaluate experienced teachers, the State could reasonably conclude that the NTE provided a reliable and economical means for measuring one element of effective teaching—the degree of knowledge possessed by the teacher. Having so concluded, defendants could properly design a classification system relying on NTE scores for compensating teachers and providing incentives for teachers to improve their knowledge in the areas that they teach.

We believe that a distinction for pay purposes between those who are qualified as well as between those who are not qualified survives the business necessity test. There appears to be no alternative available to the State, within reasonable limits of risk and cost, for providing the incentive necessary to motivate thousands of persons to acquire, generally on their own time and at their own expense, the necessary additional academic training so that they will be minimally competent teachers. Having made the investment of four years in an undergraduate education, it seems reasonable to try to upgrade the talent of unqualified teachers where possible, rather than rejecting them altogether.

Two justices took no part in this decision; two others, White and Brennan, dissented. With the acceptance of the district court's findings by a majority of the Supreme Court, South Carolina has continued to use testing as a way to differentiate between the most and least competent teachers and to indicate that difference, first, by the certificate itself and, second, by a rank system for the determination of pay.

Generally, the statutes not only set forward the procedures and qualifications for acquiring a certificate but also identify the agency responsible to carry out the legislature's bidding. That agency has wide latitude in how it provides for certification and how it creates eligibility for jobs in schools. The specific conditions of contract, including contract initiation, ratification, fulfillment, and termination, are addressed by the legislatures, so that teachers and boards may know the specifics of their labor relations.

Every state also has candidly recognized the possibility of failure or of trust misplaced, for certification is an indicator of trust conveyed from the state to a citizen. Certification can be suspended or revoked as a protection for children. It is the most drastic action that can be taken against a professional. For that reason, the professional needs the protection of both substantive and procedural due process. That is, the reasons for the consideration of revocation must be of importance, and those reasons must be examined, if requested by that teacher, by an impartial board or panel to determine that they truly exist. The conflicts of contract termination, continuation, and certificate revocation can be seen in the following case.

Richard Arlan Erb v. State Board of Public Instruction, 216 N.W. 2d 339 (IA SC, 1974)

GENERALIZATION

The duties of a teacher are limited in comprehensiveness. Challenges to a teacher's effectiveness on grounds of immorality must show an unfitness to teach.

DESCRIPTION

This was an appeal of a certificate revocation. Erb and another teacher in the same school formed an adulterous liaison. Her husband became aware of it, documented it thoroughly, and presented his findings to the local board of education with a demand for Erb's dismissal as morally unfit to teach. Erb offered to resign; however, because his teaching had been so effective, the local board declined to accept the resignation, an action in harmony with the superintendent's recommendation. At that time, the matter was brought to the attention of the Iowa Board of Public Instruction that convened, considered the situation, and voted five to four for certificate revocation.

Erb had never intended that an offer to resign should rise to certificate revocation, so he took his cause to the court and finally reached the Iowa Supreme Court. That court declared that a teacher's adultery was not sufficient grounds for certificate revocation, basing its decisions on reasons that were both substantive and procedural: Substantial evidence that Erb was morally unfit to teach was lacking; the conduct of a teacher away from the school has limited relevance in determining fitness to teach; there was a lack of evidence that retention of the teacher, as desired by the local board, would have an adverse effect upon the school; when sitting as a board of examiners, the board's power is specific to the protection from harm of a local school district; and it cannot be lawfully exercised for another purpose; the board of examiners failed to make findings of fact as a base for their decision; disapproval of the private conduct of a teacher by individual board members is not a sufficient base from which to call for certificate revocation, an extreme professional penalty.

We emphasize the board's power to revoke teaching certificates is neither punitive nor intended to permit exercise of personal moral judgment by members of the board. Punishment is left to the criminal law, and the personal moral views of board members cannot be relevant.

The board voted five to four to revoke Erb's teaching certificate and without making any findings of fact or conclusions of law, ordered it revoked. Revocation was stayed by trial court and then by this court pending outcome of the certiorari action and appeal. Trial court held Erb's admitted adulterous conduct was sufficient basis for revocation of his certificate and annulled the writ.

There was no evidence other than that Erb's misconduct was an isolated occurrence in an otherwise unblemished past and is not likely to recur. The conduct itself was not an open or public affront to community mores; it became public only because it was discovered with considerable effort and made public by others. Erb made no effort to justify it; instead he sought to show he regretted it, it did not reflect his true character, and it would not be repeated.

The board acted illegally in revoking his certificate. Trial court erred in annulling the writ of certiorari.

Although the court noted that an immoral act might be a basis for certificate revocation, in this instance the local school district board had decided that Erb's teaching was not impaired and had voted unanimously not to accept his tendered resignation. Immoral acts that lead to allegations of unfitness to teach must be examined by way of due process where certificate revocation is concerned.

Contracts

With a certificate in hand, a citizen is legally a teacher and may enter the job market. Eligibility for employment presupposes a certificate. That means that the person may become an applicant for a contract. Typically, contracts are written in a form prescribed by the SDE and include all of the elements of contract found in common law. Teachers are sellers and boards are buyers. There are five basic elements that describe contract as a condition: agreement is mutual, parties are competent, considerations are specified, subject matter is legal, and agreement is as required by law.

The first element pertains to the job description and compensation level that is agreed to by both parties. The second element specifies that the board is legally competent and that the teacher has—or will possess at an appropriate time to start work—the necessary certificate. The third element includes the job description and time of performance along with the total compensation for those professional services. The fourth element is a mutual assurance that the job and its performance will not be a violation of law. The fifth element is an assurance that the contract is in agreement with the statutory specifics of how a teacher's contract must be made in that state. The precise format for contracts may vary a little from state to state, but substantially they are the same, and in all states contracts must be written.

The contract is the document of proof that an agreement was reached between a teacher and a board of education. The teacher promises to deliver services within the certificated scope of competence for some term, that is, for some discrete period; the board promises to pay for those services at some rate.

Boards of education engage in such varied business that contracts become a common part of operating the school district. Here, the focus of attention has been on personnel and personnel contracts. The basic elements of contract, above, pertain not only to personnel contracts but to contract law generally and to all other aspects of contract in which boards normally engage. Several of those other aspects of school operation, in which contracting plays a key role, are treated elsewhere in this book, especially in Chapter 11, "Collective Bargaining," and Chapter 12, "Finance."

Initial employment for every teacher new to that particular job setting is the time when the characteristics of hiring and contracts are present distinctly. Subsequently, contracts for reemployment or contracts developed through collective bargaining may obscure some of the basic elements. When a teacher candidate is among the finalists for a job, and an interview with a school district's personnel officer is progressing happily, the job seeker is in final negotiations for the job. If agreement is reached, the job may be offered and a contract tendered. If the candidate signs the contract, he or she may leave the interview thinking that the job is secure, but strictly speaking, that is not so in most states. Connecticut is an exception and is one of the states where a superintendent acting as a personnel officer, with power to hire having been conveyed by the local board, can conclude the contract.

Legislatures have vested the hiring power in boards of education, and ordinarily, they cannot delegate that power to any of their officers or employees. Contract forms, signed by teacher applicants, go into a file for board action. In the natural order of events, and at the board's next regular meeting in a pro forma action, the board votes on the job candidates and ratifies the contracts. Legally, boards have the option to review and refuse applicants nominated or recommended for hiring; ethically, refusal would be another matter. After ratification, the contract becomes a firm and binding agreement for the services from the teacher and compensation from the board.

Contracts place a teacher in a job setting with an obligation to perform as instructional leader. Teachers generally want flexibility of assignment minimized; school administrators and boards generally want great flexibility in teacher assignment. This conflict, concerning place of assigned work and duties prescribed, gives rise to many problems, because each of them interprets the contract to serve his or her own cause. Extracurricular assignments have been frequent sources of misunderstanding between boards and teachers. Generally, contract forms are written to provide for some flexibility and include clauses such as, "and such other assignments as may be appropriate and in keeping with the policies of the board." Such a generic clause means that teachers may be assigned to supervise students in locations other than a classroom and to handle those extracurricular activities that harmonize with their teaching assignments. It does not mean that teachers are to be indiscriminately assigned to teaching duties for which they lack certification and in which their probability for success is low. The question cannot be finally and conclusively settled for every teacher for every year; some uncertainty must be accepted as a fact of the mix in the school. Accommodations must be developed that will withstand the reasonable-and-prudent-individual test.

Broken Contracts

Contracts can be broken. That is not to say that all parties to a contract will be pleased when it is broken. Displeasure may prevail. A broken contract may occur by mutual agreement to dissolve it or by a unilateral decision. When a contract is broken without mutual assent, it is breached. A teacher may breach a contract by declining to perform a specified service; a board may breach a contract by not paying for services rendered.

Historically, boards have seldom been in breach of contract. That is, design of curriculum, staffing for it, budget development, and tax-receipt systems are so closely aligned that boards typically hire the minimum staff necessary, have jobs for every person hired, and have money in the treasury for every position filled. When boards do breach a contract, it is for lack of money. More often than not, many teachers, rather than one, are involved. Boards might find that they are unable to pay all teachers at a regular payroll time and decide to pay none or all but one particular teacher group. In the 1930s, when large proportions of levied taxes were delinquent and uncollected, school board treasuries suffered. Many teachers were paid with promissory notes called "no-fund warrants." Occasional incidents of shortage of funds, especially in a few large city school systems, have recurred in the 1970s and 1980s. However, those incidents of breach by the board are rare, considering that in 1980 there were about sixteen thousand operating school districts.

Most contract breaches are committed by teachers. It is a part of American capitalism that every worker hunts for the best job to be found; for teachers, that generally means the job offering the most money. Just because most teachers work in the public sector does not mean that they are less interested in job improvement than other American job seekers. Teachers differ from other job seekers, though, in that they become parties to contracts for some term. Ordinarily, that term is for one year. What is a teacher to do when, after signing a contract with one district, another job—higher paying and more desirable—materializes with another school district or the job materializes in an entirely different work arena? That question cannot be treated here in its ethical dimension; here, the considerations are legality and practicality.

If the teacher writes a letter of resignation, requesting release from the contract, how can it be viewed by the board to which it is addressed: Is it a request or a fait accompli? Is it an item for pro forma acceptance by the board or an item for real discussion and action on its merits?

Legally, a letter of resignation may be refused. If the teaching labor pool is complete and balanced, if the area of performance is in short supply, if there is not enough time to find a replacement, or if other sufficient reasons exist, the board may hold the teacher to the contract and demand performance. Practically, there are problems in such board action, because even though teachers subscribe to and practice demanding professional ethics, many teachers' performances would slump if forced to stay where they did not wish to be. Practically, boards of education accept letters of resignation upon demand—in a real sense, a contract breach—because the alternative of an unhappy, dissatisfied teacher is not a good prospect for an outstanding instructional leader. The board, through practical action, relieves the teacher of the choice that might lead to an actual legal breach and identification as the defaulting party.

On the question of remedies for a contract breached by a board, affected teachers can pursue for money damages. Amounts of actual loss can be calculated and established. Recovery of money is the appropriate remedy, with the amount being equivalent to the amount lost by the board's breach. Not every denial of payment from a board is a breach. Other circumstances may have an overriding effect. Several specifics of contracts and breaches are well illustrated in the following cases.

Spence v. School District #3 of Arthur County, 236 N.W. 145
(NE SC, 1931)

GENERALIZATION

Boards of education enter into contracts on good faith that a teacher's certificate is valid. Boards are exempt obligation in situations of fraud. General rules of contract apply to public schools and protect boards of education and the public funds for which they have responsibility.

DESCRIPTION

Leroy C. Spence was a party to a contract in which he was obligated to teach school for nine months. After the contract had been ratified by the board, it was discovered that Spence's certificate would lapse and be invalid before the end of the school year. Spence had known that would happen at the time he signed the contract and later indicated that he would not do the things necessary to renew the certificate but would teach only until expiration occurred. The board wanted instructional continuity and directed that Spence could not and would not be paid.

Spence brought suit to recover all of the salary that would have been due him to the time when the certificate lapsed. The holding was in favor of the board, and no damages were allowed, largely because Spence had deprived the board of its discretion in hiring. By withholding information about his certification as teacher, the board had made its decision upon incomplete— effectively, false—information.

The plaintiff in this case contends that this contract cannot be voided by the district for that the district has not been prejudiced or injured by the fraud, but it is not necessary that the damage be monetary. We are of the opinion that the school district was prejudiced and injured in this case, in that they contracted with a teacher who represented himself to be qualified to teach the entire term, when as a matter of fact he was not. The board had a discretion as to whether or not they would hire a man under the circumstances, and they were deprived of the free exercise of that discretion by the misrepresentations and fraud of the plaintiff.

Questions of fact in this case were all submitted to the jury under proper instructions, and, there being no reversible error, the judgment of the district court is
Affirmed.

Rules that govern contracts, generally, apply to contracts in public schools. Contracts must be mutual, definite in the terms and provisions, and free from fraud. Boards may not be deprived of choice and discretion in hiring by incomplete or erroneous information, and action taken under those conditions may be rescinded.

Dorothy Meier v. Foster School District #2, 146 N.W. 2d 882
(ND SC, 1966)

GENERALIZATION

Inadequate planning for curriculum and staff by boards of education cannot be an adequate basis for teacher dismissal during the term of a contract. Lack of need for the services of a contracted teacher is not a sufficient basis for discharge.

DESCRIPTION

In a suit for damages, Dorothy A. Meier charged the board with breach of contract. Having been hired to teach home economics for a specified salary, Meier made visits to the homes of several prospective students before the actual school year began. She was paid a part of her contracted salary amount for that work and was notified when teachers were to report for work at their assigned building.

Later, she was summoned to a special meeting of the board of education. Occurring two days before her initial workday, she was informed that due to a low registration in home economics, all classes were being cancelled. The board asked for her resignation. She declined and declared herself ready, available, and qualified to teach as stipulated in her contract. The board then sent her a special delivery letter notifying her that there would be no home economics classes, that her contract was null and void, and that no money beyond that already paid would be paid.

We believe that it is immaterial whether a sufficient number of pupils were enrolled in the home economics courses in September 1958 to secure federal assistance for the home economics program for the 1958-1959 school year, because it is our view that the school district became obligated to pay Mrs. Meier the salary specified for the term specified when the contract was executed in February 1958. To hold otherwise would permit school districts to arbitrarily avoid commitments which teachers may have been induced to rely on to their detriment.

Generally, in the absence of any statutory or contractual provision to the contrary, the mere fact that a teacher's services are no longer necessary will not justify the dismissal of the teacher without further compensation prior to the expiration of his period of employment under a valid contract fixing a definite period of employment.

In action for breach of contract by a public school teacher, the measure of damages is the wages which would have been paid under the contract alleged to have been breached, less any sum actually earned or which might have been earned by the teacher by the exercise of reasonable diligence in seeking and obtaining other similar employment. . . .

We therefore conclude that Mrs. Meier is entitled to recover from the school district the amount of her salary less $267 paid to her, or a total of $4,183. The judgment of the trial court is reversed, and the case is remanded with instructions to the trial court to enter judgment in the sum of $4,183 plus interest thereon at the rate of four per cent per annum.

Ruling for Meier, the court agreed that the board had breached the contract and had denied compensation. A contingency about numbers of registered students could have been a part of the offered contract, but it was not. Neither was any board policy on minimum class size made a part of the contract. The board action was arbitrary, lacking any legislative or contractual base. Damages for the denial of employment can be determined. Having secured no alternative employment, Meier was entitled to the whole amount for the school year.

Contract Nonrenewal

Nonrenewal of teacher contracts is the area in which most disputes over contracts arise. Teaching has been a transient occupation in that many people who entered it did so with the full anticipation that they were passing through a time in their life that would lead them into another occupation. Well into the twentieth century large numbers of females taught until they married and left to become full-time homemakers. Many males taught while on the way to some other, more lucrative occupation. Such people had but limited interest in the protection of employment continuity.

The public nature of schoolteaching has provided a fertile ground for the development of pressures leading toward the dismissal of specific teachers. Teaching is not an occupation that has the protections that characterize civil service. Actually, many reasons could be identified that have contributed to relatively short terms for teacher employment, but from the viewpoint of teachers, the total remedy was to get more thoughtful control over the portion of contracts specifying the term, that is, the length of time of employment. One way to such control has been through legislated mandates about contracts and the structure of them.

American school years have never been calendar years. School years are shorter, with state legislatures specifying some minimum number of days. Typical school years are about 175-180 teaching days, and in interoccupational comparisons, it is a short workyear. Even for that very small group of school districts that demand a 200-day workyear, it is still, comparatively, a short year. That is a problem in equitable compensation, but it is only the first step to recognition of the larger problem: For how many years should a teacher be hired, and how much continuity of employment should be provided by the local public school district?

Boards of education want stability in the local teaching corps. One indicator of that desire can be seen in the historical term of the contract, that is, one contract has been for one year, not for one week or for one month. Education is an enterprise with a large call upon personnel; it is labor intensive. Traditionally, boards have made one grand effort each year to fill all of the teaching positions and then hoped that every position would be ably filled, with a high-quality performance for the school year. In its generic sense, the phrase "contract term" means any period mutually acceptable and stipulated in the contract. For teaching services, it has come to mean something specific. A teaching contract is for the term, for the school year. From the board's viewpoint, that length provides instructional continuity and still allows for personnel change when instructional effectiveness is questioned.

If boards have found a term contract to be a desirable length of time, teachers have, increasingly, found it to be too short. Much professional effort has been devoted to extending the time of the contract beyond one year. In state after state, legislatures have responded to the political action of teacher associations, providing for two developments in teacher contracts: continuing-employment contracts and tenure contracts. Teachers, wanting more job stability, have pursued it through statutory contract refinement.

Continuing contract provides that all personnel may assume continuation unless specifically notified to the contrary. Statutes specify a time when notification must occur, and if during that time there is no notification from the board to the teacher, continuation as an employee is automatic. There is also a time for information flow of an opposite nature, that is, resignation; and if no resignation is tendered during that time, a board may assume continuation as automatic for every employee who does not take the initiative to resign during that period. Both characteristics of continuing contract contribute to faculty stability.

Another word that has come to have a specialized meaning in teacher contracts is *tenure*. It means continued or permanent employment after a time of trial and probation. It means continued employment until death, retirement, dismissal for just and specified cause, or elimination of the position due to financial exigency. Probation periods are usually from three to five years, with designation as a tenured teacher coming after successfully completing the probationary period. Statutes in some states do not actually use the word *tenure* but describe a condition of permanent employment after a probationary period. With or without the name, statutory tenure has become common since state legislatures have described a condition of employment in local school districts having permanence and due process as integral characteristics. For teachers, it represents maximum security in harmony with academic freedom. For boards, it represents a reduction in personnel-management flexibility and increased burdens on administrations to prove instructional ineffectiveness of a high dimension if the teacher is to face the prospect of dismissal via a hearing. From the vast amount of litigation in the general area of contract management, including tenure, four cases in the area on nonrenewal have been selected as illustrative of important legal principles.

Barbara Boyce and Others v. Board of Education of the City of Royal Oak, 257 N.W. 2d 153 (Michigan Court of Appeals, 1977)

GENERALIZATION

Faced with financial exigency and within the statutes of the state, local boards may lay off probationary personnel on short notice when whole programs are eliminated.

DESCRIPTION

This board action for dismissal of teachers originally included some tenured teachers; eventually, only probationary teachers lost jobs. Five weeks before the layoff, the affected teachers received notification of dismissal and were told that programs and positions were being eliminated in the middle of the school year due to economic considerations. The contract for the year included the phrase that "The School District will not terminate . . . unless there is in the judgment of the Board of

Education . . . insufficient revenue during the school year to continue the payment of the salary called for in this contract.''

Ruling in favor of the board, the court noted that when economic conditions require it, a board can lay off tenured teachers as well as those on probation. The board was in compliance with the master contract provision and individual contracts and had acted in good faith. Although the contract called for fewer days of notice than the state statute demanded for tenured teachers, that did not apply to probationary teachers.

Spilman v. Board of Directors of Davis City Schools, 253 N.W. 593 (IA SC, 1977)

GENERALIZATION

Employees enjoy contract rights only according to their function, if that differs from their certification.

DESCRIPTION

D. Sue Spilman was certificated as both teacher and librarian; however, in the Davis City Schools she had been hired as a library clerk for the 180-day school year in 1973-74. She did not work as either a teacher or librarian. The contract designated her as ''library clerk,'' and she testified that at the time she signed the contract, she was aware of the differences between that employment category and that of ''librarian.'' Iowa statutes specify that all certificated employees are entitled to notice of nonrenewal of contract before termination. Spilman was terminated without prior notification from her position as library clerk.

The court found for the board, because Spilman had been hired as a library clerk, a position for which a state certificate was not necessary; and the statute was interpreted to apply to employees who by contract were designated as teachers or librarians. Schools employ many supportive personnel, but it is the category of employment that creates eligibility for statutory protection or lack of it. Employees who, coincidentally, also have a valid state certificate are not entitled to the benefits and provisions of the statute by virtue of that certificate. The termination of Spilman was in accordance with the practices and procedures for other support personnel.

Steven Ryan, et al. v. Aurora City Board of Education, 540 F. 2d 222 (USCA 6th, 1976)

GENERALIZATION

Practices and policies of local boards of education cannot exceed statutory grants of power, but boards can change their own policies. Teacher entitlement to continued employment is based in state statutes.

DESCRIPTION

Ryan and three other teachers had been employed by the Aurora, Ohio, schools for varying lengths of time, from two years to eight years. In common, all were labeled as nontenured teachers working under limited contracts, all of which expired in the spring of 1973. The local board, acting under the appropriate state statute, voted not to renew the contracts, after timely written notification to each teacher. No reasons for nonrenewal were given, and no requests for hearings were granted.

The teachers did not claim violation of statute, but based their claim to employment continuation on a portion of the board's 1965 policy manual:

1. Any teacher recommended for dismissal must have been clearly informed of his status by the superintendent and completely aware that such a recommendation is being made with definite reasons for the action.

2. Teachers who are not to be reappointed shall be given the reasons and notified in writing by the clerk-treasurer of the school district as confirmed by the board on or before April 30th.

The teachers contended that tenure, in the sense that it is continuous employment, was implied by board policy. Inasmuch as the board acted in accordance with the statutes, but not in accordance with its own policies, the teachers contended that the board had violated their civil rights and denied them the due process granted them under the Fourteenth Amendment.

Acknowledging that the local board acted within state statutes, the court tacitly agreed that board policy could be changed unilaterally by the board. The court also stated that nontenured teachers cannot lay claim to entitlement to continued employment, for to do so would, in effect, amend the Ohio tenure statute. Implied promises of contract continuation do not create a property interest for probationary teachers. Boards are not bound to give reasons why they decide not to renew contracts.

Frank Kibbon and Jane C. Akers v. School District of Omaha, 242 N.W. 2d 634 (NE SC, 1976)

GENERALIZATION

The contracts of probationary teachers lapse at the end of the term specified in the contract, and renewal is at the option of the employing board.

DESCRIPTION

Kibbon and Akers were teachers employed by the Omaha Public Schools. The school district is of a class in which teachers are identified as, initially, probationary and, later, tenured teachers. Both were probationary teachers, and at the end of the school year, each was notified that his or her contract would not be renewed for the next school year. Each requested the reasons for the decision, and each requested a hearing before the board of education, seeking protection under statutory treatment of the topics of contract termination, dismissal, just cause, and renewal. The board denied both requests.

The court examined the statutes of Nebraska and found that, really, a separate statute governed teacher employment in school districts of the class to which the Omaha Public School District belonged. That statute identified all beginning teachers as probationary. Under that statute, the employing district had the right to renew, or not to renew, at its option, probationary contracts and was not obligated to state any reasons for its actions or hold a hearing and provide due process for the affected teachers. In situations of statutory conflict, the special provisions on a particular subject will prevail over general statutory statements, thereby resolving the conflict.

To have held to the contrary would have, practically, eliminated the probationary class of teachers. It would have conferred upon every beginning teacher the rights of due process, as that teacher related to the employing board. Tenure is, really, procedural due process, so the teachers sought a kind of instant tenure. The court denied it.

When considered as a group, the four cases reveal that boards of education cannot exceed their grants of power from their respective legislatures, that teachers cannot create for themselves employment rights that exceed what has been provided by statute, and that both parties to the contract, board and teacher, must accept contractual limits that prevail in their state and for their type of school district. To some extent, labor relations in the elementary and secondary school sector have developed from, on the one hand, the political tension generated by teacher associations (unions) speaking their demands to legislators and, on the other hand, the messages of the associated school boards speaking different messages to the same legislators. Gradually, employment conditions are changing. Due process, just cause, and long-term employment are becoming much more prevalent conditions of teacher contracts.

Retirement

Sixty-five years of age has been the magic time when teachers and other workers are expected to have achieved enough financial independence to cut away from work and its attendant regular paycheck. American workers, through a wide spectrum of careers, accepted age sixty-five as the time to retire. Federal legislation for nongovernmental employees, including all of the social security statutes and amendments, harmonized on that age. With the expanded worker coverage of social security that has come with each decade since its passage, and its articulation with existing pension and retirement plans, that remained the accepted time for retirement through the middle of the twentieth century.

Increasingly, the appropriate time for retirement is becoming a more flexible concept—a more individualized choice—and at least three major factors have influenced the change. First, for those people who wanted to retire before age sixty-five, social security was altered, opening a choice for those who wanted it to initiate claims and retire at age sixty-two. Significant numbers of American workers, including teachers, have saved and invested so that even with the reduced claims that can be made against social security and retirement plans at age sixty-two, a sufficient financial independence exists to consider quitting work. Second, the time spent in retirement has become much more attractive than it was in the first half of the century. Retirees can do many things. Many opportunities have been developed expressly for the mature, retired adult. Things that take time demand that the people who do them be unhampered by work schedules. The prospect of an extended number of leisure years, including an acceptable level of financial support and excellent health services, have proved attractive to many Americans, and a tendency toward earlier retirement has occurred. Specifically for teachers, many school districts have attempted to grapple with the problems of declining enrollment by offering bonuses to teachers who would voluntarily retire at earlier ages, reducing the teacher corps by that technique. From a strictly legal viewpoint, money paid to teachers at the time of a voluntarily elected early retirement cannot be in the form of a bonus or labeled a bonus. The method of payment must be harmonized with the statutes declaring how boards of education can spend money for professional personnel services. A variety of formulas have been developed by which amounts of such early retirement money can be calculated and paid to professionals legally.

Third, an anomaly in retirement patterns has further contributed to the newly developing flexibility of age at retirement. Callously, but picturesquely, it is realistic to think of every worker as a cog in the nation's industrial machine. Cogs do wear out, and observations led to the conclusion that the productive capability of sixty-five-year-old cogs was on the downside. That is, the human physique and intellect passes a point of maximum capability and thereafter declines. Although this is a safe generalization, it is certainly not true for all individuals. If the generalization indicated the suitability of an arbitrary retirement age, sixty-five years, the exceptions indicated a need to consider an alternative for some American workers.

During the twentieth century, life expectancy has been continually extending. In 1977 life expectancy for American males was 69.3 years; for females, 77.1 years. For sixty-five-year-old males actuarial tables indicated another 13.9 years of expectation; for sixty-five-year-old females, another 18.3 years. Americans have been arriving at age sixty-five with increasingly hardy physiques. Now, the anomaly is that although some have opted to retire—even retire early—and enjoy time without the obligations of work, others have fought to preserve the right to work on the premise of adequate physical vitality. Others have opted for an extended work life, coupling that increased physical vitality with their desire to continue to build a retirement fund through those few additional years of work.

In 1978 Congress passed the Age Discrimination in Employment Act Amendments. That statute was in the heritage of the civil rights legislation of the 1960s and 1970s and extended the categories in which employment discrimination was unlawful to eight: race, color, religion, sex, national origin, physically handicapped, pregnancy, and age. Together with earlier statutes dealing with age and employment, the 1978 legislation contained a three-part intent on the part of Congress. First, it was the intent of Congress to assist older workers to keep or regain employment; second, to deter the establishment and continuation of upper age limits as disqualifications for work; third, to promote employment of older persons based upon what is known of their ability, rather than upon an arbitrary age-based decision. Now, employers may not discriminate against employees on the basis of age in areas such as hiring, promoting, transferring, or continuing. Although some employment categories are exempted—for example, state patrol officers—teachers and school districts are within the scope of the legislation. Protected citizens are those who are at least forty but less than seventy years of age. This statute complicated the intentions, procedures, and economics of retirement in public school districts.

Before 1978 school districts faced occasional suits from teachers who wanted to continue their professional life beyond age sixty-five, even in districts with policies mandating retirement at sixty-five. With that legislation as a watershed, what was appropriate on one side of it was not necessarily equally appropriate on the other side of it.

Goldie Monnier v. Todd County Independent School District, 245 N.W. 2d 503 (SD SC, 1976)

GENERALIZATION

When school policies concerning mandatory retirement are within the state and federal statutes, teachers cannot demand that the policies be waived.

DESCRIPTION

Goldie Monnier was sixty-seven years old and had taught for twelve years in the Todd County Schools. Local board policy stated that "Mandatory retirement of teachers at age 65 will become effective July 1, 1968 unless there is a specific request from the Principal or Director of Elementary

Education that the retirement age be waived with an annual review of each teacher receiving such a waiver.''

Monnier had received two one-year renewals. Approaching the end of the second renewal, it was recommended to the superintendent that she not be rehired and that she be retired in accordance with policy. She was informed by the superintendent that she would not be recommended for continued employment. The protection of the state's continuing contract law ceased at age sixty-five. She requested but was denied a hearing.

Faced with a policy that was complementary to the state's statutes, Monnier was left without an argument. The teacher was not entitled to a hearing or to due process generally. Contractual rights are not contractually abridged when a mandatory retirement coexists with state statutes.

Monnier occurred and was heard before the action of Congress in 1978 in which the forty to seventy age group became a protected group. Obviously, local school board policy cannot contravene federal statutes. Yet there is not any necessary contradiction, either, between statutes or policies that end tenure at some age such as sixty-five and the federal statute. If that condition prevails, it means that subsequent contracts would be offered for terms of one year, renewable upon satisfactory performance. Age could not be a reason for nonrenewal.

Retirement plans deserve the surveillance of the persons who expect to benefit from them. This is especially true if the plan does not vest in each individual for whom, eventually, there is an anticipation that the money will be paid. In *Dodge v. Chicago Board of Education*, 302 U.S. 74 (1937), the question of legislatively diminished retirement eligibility arose. In its original form, the teacher's retirement pension was for $1,500 per year. About two decades later, the legislature reduced the annual retirement amount to $500. The case traveled a usual appeal route, and the Supreme Court sustained lower courts, finding that the teachers, having not contributed to the fund, really had no annuity, no vested rights, no contract rights; rather, they had a pension, the annual amount of which had been set by the legislature. Therefore, it was appropriate for the legislature periodically to examine the pension payments and adjust them as deemed appropriate.

Americans are enjoying an extended vitality in their lives, and many are finding real physical vigor in those later years. From among them, many are choosing to remain active in their careers, into the latter sixties. It is their statutory right to defer retirement. To assure that children continue to receive high-quality instruction puts a new obligation on the shoulders of school administrators who conduct personnel evaluation. Complete personnel-evaluation systems must be in place and operational to assure necessary and fair scrutiny of those older teachers as they perform their roles of classroom instructional leader. Classroom effectiveness, instructional strategies, and job versatility provide indices of competence that should be evaluated before recommendations for renewal of one-year contracts. Assuming teaching competence, the earliest mandatory retirement age has become seventy years.

* * *

Professional careers in elementary and secondary schools now attract over 2.25 million persons. Teachers, principals, librarians, counsellors, and others must possess certificates attesting to minimum competencies for jobs. The fifty state departments of education issue certificates in correspondence to the academic programs completed by the applicants, and to a large extent, those certificates are transferable among the states. An increasing number of states demand some kind of examination for each applicant in addition to completing an approved academic program in teacher preparation.

With eligibility for a certificate, citizens can join the labor pool pursuing jobs in education. Certificates must come before contracts. Boards cannot be held responsible for contracts made with people who are not entitled to the job by virtue of lacking a proper certificate. All common law elements of contract exist in the contracts between boards of education and teachers. In over thirty states, contracts are bargained collectively, but that does not change the essence of a teacher's contract being an agreement of mutual assent, money for services, freely entered into by both parties.

Contracts are for specified periods. By mutual agreement between both parties, they can be terminated before their time; that is, employees may resign. Contracts can be broken arbitrarily, as one party refuses to continue to honor the contract; however, in the circumstances that constitute a breach of contract, the offended party may seek damages. Practically, boards of education have very limited recourse against teachers who unilaterally breach the teaching contract and physically relocate in another area or vocation. Refusal of boards to pay for services constitutes a kind of damage that is more nearly calculable and collectible.

A major source of contention has arisen from disputes about contract nonrenewal, teacher release, and teacher dismissal. Dismissal during the term of the contract can only be for verifiable cause. Questions about the obligations of boards and the rights of probationary teachers in states that have continuing contract laws have frequently risen to litigation. In questions about the suitability of release or nonrenewal, timing of the notification and contents of the notification have been exceedingly important. That is, boards must be in compliance with state statutes, or a question of procedure is opened for teachers whose contract is not renewed.

At career's end, employees look forward to retirement as a time in life to be free of the burdens of work-for-pay and to enjoy life in a leisurely fashion. That calls for adequate financial planning, and since teachers were included under federal social security eligibility in the 1950s, everyone now can have a plan in which the state's teacher or public employee retirement plan is correlated to social security. Each school district contributes to both state and federal aspects of the retirement system. Yet age is now a protected-citizen category, within the area of civil rights, and employees may not, any longer, be forced to retire at age sixty-five just because they have reached that age—another reason why personnel administration must include systematic performance evaluation.

chapter 6

ADMINISTERING STAFF PERSONNEL

State government is the repository of power under which public schools function. That power source is direct, mainly through Amendment X, which is the plenary power grant from the federal to the state governments; and through Article I, Section 8, of the Constitution, which calls for action to provide for the general welfare. In turn, as territories became states, state governments commonly made constitutional provisions of their own. Two states provide adequate illustrations. Article 9, Section 5, of the California constitution stipulates that "The legislature shall provide for a system of common schools by which a free school shall be kept up and supported in each district." The Nebraska constitution, Article VII, Sections 1 and 2, declares that "The Legislature shall provide for the free instruction in common schools of this state of all persons between the ages of five and twenty-one years. . . . The State Department of Education shall have general supervision and administration of the school system of the state." To consolidate those positions, the Nebraska Supreme Court enunciated a viewpoint shared widely with other states in *Kosmicki v. Kowalski,* 171 N.W. 2d 172 (1969), stating in no uncertain terms that "the state is supreme in the creation and control of school districts, and may, if it thinks proper, modify or withdraw any of their powers, or destroy such school districts.

School districts are political subdivisions of the state, sometimes called local education agencies (LEA). Governed by local boards of trustees, their function is to provide instruction for the local boys and girls. To discharge that function, teachers are hired and assigned to teaching posts. They are the instructional leaders, carrying the school board's charge directly into the classroom.

Historically, while the nation was developing, the number of such districts was large, the geographical territory in each district small, and the pupil registration, also, small. Through the latter nineteenth and the twentieth centuries changes have been at work in the opposite direction: the number of districts has decreased, geographical territories have enlarged, and pupil registrations, by district, have increased. (This is not a discussion of the consequences of reductions in the American birth rate; it is a general observation on the condition of public school districts.)

When districts were very small and the intellectual demands on teachers were much less than at present, boards could know, personally, many of the candidates for teaching positions. When, commonly, school boards had three-four-five persons in the entire membership, and that board operated a school district under the laws of its state with one or two teachers as the whole faculty, familiarity prevailed. Other reasons beyond size materialized to contribute further toward the likelihood that any board hiring a prospective teacher would have some personal familiarity with the applicant. Presently, with public school district faculties numbering into the hundreds as the rule, and some numbering into the many, many thousands being common, local district boards need help and some protection when applicants come forward, seeking to fill teaching vacancies. One such protection is teacher certification. In effect, it is a guarantee of some minimum performance level to be expected of that teacher by the board. Many people, aspiring to become teachers, do not, because they never qualify for the certificate. In a way, the certificate is a sorting device, a legal document attesting to certain professional skills.

To teach is to be a leader, to lead by professional skills toward some higher development. The teacher combines several uniquely cultured and developed abilities along with an intellectual capital in some academic area. For example, not only must the English teacher be knowledgeable in literature and in the skills of composition—the intellectual capital—but must also know the sociology and psychology that impinges upon learning, the technology and materials by which students can be better directed in their learning, and the organization of the curriculum in a fashion to optimize learning. The teacher must know the basics and refinements of pedagogy. In a sense, the operation of the local schools has not changed over the many decades, for the local boards still search for the highest competence that might be attracted to their particular school. Yet in another sense, a change has occurred that substantially affects how the teacher functions after having been hired. Typically, boards want to see evidence of continued professional growth.

Within the professional ranks of school administrators, it is widely conceded that personnel management is one of the tasks that is least well done. There are several contributing reasons. First, it is difficult for an administrator to observe a teacher in action and to conclude that the performance was so poor as to indicate incompetence; there is a wide range of quality, from clearly outstanding to barely acceptable, that is acknowledged as suitably competent. Second, and connected to the first, there are not many evaluative systems or instruments that are, themselves, acceptable by both teachers and principals. This lack of basic evaluation tools and techniques leaves the evaluator in a vulnerable position when an assessment is questioned. Third, there is no longer any appreciable academic distance to speak of between the evaluator—the principal or supervisor—and the person being evaluated—the teacher. For those decades in which principals were by statute or regulation demanded to have higher academic degrees than teachers, there was an academic leverage that supported the judgments of principals. Nowadays, the evaluation setting will typically involve people at academic parity, each of whom can claim a professional expertise couched in advanced university degree work as the adequate basis for doing what was done, whether as the teacher carrying out instruction or the principal carrying out evaluation. It is a kind of academic stalemate, centered upon the implied question, "Who are you to tell me that my teaching is faulty and should be changed?" Other observations could be made to show that personnel management in education is difficult. Suffice it to generalize, however, with the comment that teachers, who are trained for the necessity to make hundreds of independent professional decisions every working day, do direct a pressure back upon administrators who, observing teachers at work, proceed to make recommendations or directions for change.

That work environment and relationship is a far cry from the labor-management setting that typifies the private employment sector and much of the public sector other than schools. It is unique. It causes difficulties for personnel administration. The differences of opinion about the suitability and accuracy of professional assessment has stimulated a fairly large number of questions that, in turn, have become cases to be settled at court. When this unique aspect is added to such procedural techniques within the organization as teaching assignments, reduction in force, and so on, the administration of the personnel who constitute the professional faculty emerges as a large problem in school operation. Many of those same problems exist in the administration of classified personnel.

Administration Through Rewards and Penalties

To entice teachers toward higher levels of proficiency, boards may reward certain kinds of things or penalize for the lack of doing certain kinds of things. In other circumstances, teachers may earn certain rewards, as seen in the following cases.

Harrah Independent School District et al. v. Martin,
440 M.S. 194 (1979)

GENERALIZATION

Local boards of education may demand that teachers engage in some sort
of structured professional growth plan, including university course work.

DESCRIPTION

As one aspect of personnel development, the board of this LEA had
demanded that teachers should, periodically, return to school to earn appropriate additional college credits—five semester hours every three years.
Martin refused to return to college for additional work but had attained
designation as a tenured teacher under Oklahoma law.

Respondent, hired in 1969, persistently refused to comply with the continuing
education requirement and consequently forfeited the increases in salary to which
she would otherwise have been entitled during the 1972-74 school years. After
her contract had been renewed for the 1973-74 school term, however, the Oklahoma
Legislature enacted a law mandating certain salary raises for teachers regardless of
the compliance with the continuing educational policy. The school board, thus
deprived of the sanction which it had previously employed to enforce the provision,
notified respondent that her contract would not be renewed for the 1974-75 school
year unless she completed five semester hours by April 10, 1974. Respondent
nonetheless declined even to enroll in the necessary courses and appearing before the
Board in January, 1974 indicated that she had no intention of complying with the requirement in her contract. Finding her persistent noncompliance with the continuing
education requirement "willful neglect of duty," the Board voted at its April 1974
meeting not to renew her contract for the following year.

The school district's concern with the educational qualification of its teachers
cannot under any reasoned analysis be described as impermissible, and respondent
does not contend that the Board's continuing education requirement bears no
rational relationship to that legitimate governmental concern. . . . There is no
suggestion here that the Board enforced the continuing education requirement
selectively; the Board refuses to renew contracts of those teachers and only those
teachers who refuse to comply with the continuing education requirement. . . . That
the Board was forced by the state legislature in 1974 to penalize noncompliance
differently than it had in the past in no way alters the equal protection analysis of
respondent's claim.

With the legislature's action in 1974, the Harrah board was forced to shift
its ground if it wanted to keep in place its demand for academic renewal of
all teachers and to penalize those who failed to comply. The sanction
changed in severity, but the board was not precluded from the action that
was rationally related to the board's interest that teachers should accept an
obligation for continuing education and development. Martin's petition for
reinstatement was denied, and the circuit court of appeals was reversed as
the U.S. Supreme Court let the board policy and action stand.

Muriel Burnett et al. v. Durant Community School District, 249
N.W. 2d 626 (IA SC, 1977)

GENERALIZATION

In the endeavor continually to upgrade the performance of teachers, it is
reasonable and rational for boards of education to provide rewards or
remuneration for costs incurred by teachers as they pursue approved
graduate study.

DESCRIPTION

The board of the Durant schools contractually provided that teachers
could get tuition-cost reimbursements up to $320 if the teacher returned to
Durant as an employee in the next school year and if the courses taken were
approved in advance by the superintendent. Twenty-five teachers got such
approval, took their courses, and applied for reimbursement of costs in the
following school year. They were denied payment by the local board upon
the advice of the county attorney who stated that the board had exceeded its
authority and that part of the contract was void. To some extent, this
dispute hinged upon the question of timing, for the contract was made in
1971-72, and clarifying statutes were not enacted until 1976. The Iowa
Supreme Court held for the teachers and stated:

The 1972 Attorney General's opinion relied on by the county attorney in advising
defendant and by the trial court in its ruling had asserted school districts in Iowa
could not expend funds to pay teachers on sabbatical leave or reimburse them for
tuition for approved graduate studies. The trial court's decision upholding the
board's position was made in 1974, and the amendment was enacted in June, 1976
during the pendance of this appeal. It appears the amendment was enacted in
response to the attorney general's opinion and resulting controversy.
Considering these circumstances and the language of the affected statutes, we
think the amendment was enacted to clarify rather than change existing law.
We hold that defendant had authority to agree to reimburse plaintiffs for tuition
expense incurred by them in undertaking approved graduate studies in consideration
of plaintiffs' teaching services in the current and ensuing contract years. The trial
court erred in holding otherwise.
REVERSED.

U.S.D. #480 v. Lila Epperson and Oleta A. Peters,
551 F. 2d 254 (USCA 10th, 1977)

GENERALIZATION

Satisfactory performance by a teacher in a school district extending over
several years (here, seventeen and eleven years) can make of that job a
property right—this, without regard to whether the state has a tenure law
that demands procedural due process as a part of any dismissal proceedings.

DESCRIPTION

Peters and Epperson had taught in Unified School District #480, Seward County, Kansas, for eleven and seventeen years, respectively. In 1971-72 they were president and president-elect of the local unit of the National Education Association. Under Kansas law for continuing contract, they were timely notified that their teaching contracts would not be renewed for 1972-73. The reason for dismissal given by the board was budgetary cuts caused by decreased enrollments.

Peters and Epperson were of the firm view that the refusal of the school board to renew their teaching contracts was not really caused by budgetary problems, but on the contrary was in retaliation for the exercise by them of their First Amendment right to free speech in connection with their NEA activities. In any event, Peters and Epperson retained counsel, and asked the board for a hearing. The board, on advice of its counsel, refused this request for a hearing, believing that a teacher was not entitled to a hearing upon the refusal to renew a one-year teaching contract because of budgetary problems.

In a series of lawsuits and countersuits extended through several years, three substantive questions finally emerged for court action, and those questions were addressed by this court.

1. Did the school district board deny Peters and Epperson procedural due process?

2. Did that local school board qualify for the governmental immunity promised under the Eleventh Amendment?

3. Were the teachers due any money damages?

After citing references such as *Perry v. Sinderman* (1972) and *Wood v. Strickland* (1975), the circuit court examined Kansas statutes.

. . . we conclude that "on balance," School District No. 480 in Seward County, Kansas, and its school board members acting in their official capacity, are not the alter ego of the state, but are more like a municipality, for example, and hence do not enjoy Eleventh Amendment immunity.

And under Article 6, section 2(b) of the Kansas Constitution the State Board of Regents has "control," in addition to "supervision," over all institutions of higher learning. We know that a typical state board of regents really runs the state university, whereas the State Board of Education in Kansas merely "supervises" the local school districts with the latter having a high degree of autonomy.

In *Harris* we held that a local school district in Utah was an alter ego of the State of Utah. However, an influencing factor in that case was the possibility that a money judgment rendered in federal court against the school district might be paid, at least partially, out of state funds. In the instant case, as referred to above, it is agreed, and was so found by the trial court that any money judgment which might be entered in favor of Peters or Epperson against District No. 480 would be raised by special levy within the district, and would not come from the state.

The judgment is reversed and the case remanded to the trial court with direction that it determine the damages fairly attributable to the failure of the school board to afford Peters and Epperson their Fourteenth Amendment right to a pre-termination hearing. We recognize the damage question, and the extent of any such recovery, may itself be a troublesome one.

A local school district that dismisses teachers whose employment has been extensive enough to create a property right places itself in jeopardy by dismissing without a hearing. Although individual board members may not be liable, the district treasury itself must be the source of money to satisfy damages suffered from loss of the job.

In education, there is an observable tendency toward the all or none rule in personnel administration. That is, after teacher evaluation occurs, and administrative judgment is that the performance is incompetent or on the verge of incompetence, the tendency is for a recommendation of dismissal. Fines, suspensions without pay, extensions of probation, and similar management devices are used at minimum levels in school personnel relations. Incompetence, or instructional ineffectiveness, can be determined by low test results of pupil progress, as it was in *Scheelhaase v. Woodbury (IA) Schools,* 488 F. 2d 237 (1974). Another court also agreed with a board designation of incompetence in *Board of Sioux City v. Morz,* 295 N.W. 2d 447 (1980). There were fourteen specified deficiencies in four different performance categories. The board followed due process into a termination hearing and its decision to dismiss was upheld by the Iowa Supreme Court. Indicators of low pupil achievement and mediocre teaching performance were accepted by courts as sufficient evidence to support teacher dismissal upon charges of incompetence.

Constitutional Freedoms

Americans have certain rights and liberties that are protected in the Constitution. The Bill of Rights stipulates what those are. Yet they are not entirely clear when applied to specific situations. Some situational disputes cases are carried to courts for resolution. For teachers, the most important is the First Amendment and its applications to the states through the Fourteenth Amendment.

The First Amendment states that

Congress shall make no law respecting an establishment of religion, or prohibiting the free exercise thereof; or abridging the freedom of speech, or of the press; or of the right of the people peaceably to assemble, and to petition the government for a redress of grievances.

Although many controversies have developed from the portion dealing with the way public schools must address religion, that portion has not been often invoked for individual teachers. Individually, teachers are most interested in freedoms of speech, peaceful association and assembly, and the right to petition the government. In considering how teachers may act within these grants of liberty and freedom, many operational questions arise.

May a board of education curtail the things teachers say in classrooms—or in public? May teachers join some organization with impunity? If teachers see flaws in the operation of some government unit, may they become actively—even publicly—critical of it? Because it seems that American citizens want to maximize those liberties, to stretch them and make them personally comfortable, questions of propriety, ethics, practicality, and legality frequently come together in such cases.

As an occupational group, teachers have been held to a more rigorous code of conduct in their personal lives than has been demanded of other professional workers in American society. Now, in the latter twentieth century, there is a discernible trend to extend more freedom to teachers and to demand less of them as models. Still, teachers and administrators must be practical about their work setting and be ready to exercise some judicious restraint in their public behavior. In *Nicasio Board v. Brennan,* 95 Cal 712 (1971), a teacher provided an affidavit for a friend who had been arrested in which she said that she had used marijuana personally for several years and enjoyed its benefits. The affidavit became well publicized even though that had never been the intent of the teacher-author. She was dismissed, and the court upheld that board's action.

In *Muskego-Norway Schools v. Wisconsin Employment Relations Board,* 151 N.W. 2d 617 (1967), the superintendent engaged in thinly disguised intimidation of a teacher, Carston Koeller. Koeller was a primary author from the local education association of a proposal for faculty welfare. Although unqualifiedly recommended for rehiring, he was fired, and the superintendent offered to recommend him for a life teaching certificate only if he did not appeal his dismissal. He appealed. Finding for the teacher, the Wisconsin Supreme Court stated that his dismissal was based on his activities in the local education association, a Constitutionally protected citizen's choice.

In *Beilan v. Philadelphia Schools,* 357 U. S. 399 (1958), the Court found that Herman Beilan was not fired for being a member of certain political groups in the 1940s but rather evidenced his own incompetence when he refused to enter into conversation on this topic when it was raised by his superior, the superintendent of schools. That is, fitness to teach may be determined through inquiring conversations by an administrator, and refusal to speak and respond, in its own way, indicates incompetence.

So, legally, teachers may select their own associations, for that is a protected citizen's right. Practically, some associations may be so unwise, so troublesome, that to admit to membership may indicate incompetency of some sort by that teacher. At the same time, a teacher may not dodge legitimate inquiries about associations by an officer representing the local board of education, when the answers to such questions will play a part in determining fitness to teach.

Pickering v. Board of Education, District #205, 391 U. S. 563 (1968)

GENERALIZATION

Teachers are as free as any other citizens to participate in all aspects of democratic governments—including public criticism of governing boards—so long as that participation does not detract from their performances as instructional leaders in classrooms.

DESCRIPTION

Marvin Pickering was a teacher in the Township High School of Will County, Illinois, and was fired because he wrote to the local newspaper a letter that criticized the way in which the local board of education and the superintendent had spent money for the improvement of the school district's physical plant. A bond issue of over $5 million had been passed by the voters in 1961, and Pickering questioned several of the expenditures from that fund. The board held a full hearing and decided that his letter was "detrimental to the efficient operation and administration of the schools of the district." Pickering contended that his writing of the letter was a Constitutionally protected activity under the First and Fourteenth Amendments. The Supreme Court examined the Illinois statutes that applied, the manner of their application, and held that Pickering's "rights to freedom of speech were violated," reversing the Illinois Supreme Court.

The Board dismissed Pickering for writing and publishing the letter. Pursuant to Illinois law, the Board was then required to hold a hearing on the dismissal. At the hearing the Board charged that numerous statements in the letter were false and that the publication of the statements unjustifiably impugned the "motives, honesty, integrity, truthfulness, responsibility and competence" of both the Board and the school administration. The Board also charged that the false statements damaged the professional reputations of its members and of the school administrators, would be disruptive of faculty discipline, and would tend to foment "controversy, conflict and dissension" among teachers, administrators, the Board of Education, and the residents of the district. Testimony was introduced from a variety of witnesses on the truth or falsity of the particular statements in the letter with which the Board took issue. The Board found the statements to be false as charged. No evidence was introduced at any point in the proceedings as to the effect of the publication of the letter on the community as a whole or on the administration of the school system in particular, and no specific findings along these lines were made.

An examination of the statements in appellant's letter objected to by the Board reveals that they, like the letter as a whole, consist essentially of criticism of the Board's allocation of school funds between educational and athletic programs, and of both the Board's and the superintendents' methods of informing or preventing the informing of, the district's taxpayers of the real reasons why additional tax revenues were being sought for the schools. The statements are in no way directed towards any person with whom the appellant would normally be in contact in the course of his daily work as a teacher. Thus no question of maintaining either discipline by immediate superiors or harmony among coworkers is presented here. Appellant's employment relationships with the Board, and, to a somewhat lesser extent, with the superintendent, are not the kind of close working relationships for which it can persuasively be claimed that personal loyalty and confidence are necessary. . . .

The public interest in having free and unhindered debate on matters of public importance—the core value of the Free Speech Clause of the First Amendment—is so great that it has been held that a State cannot authorize the recovery of damages by a public official for defamatory statements directed at him.

In sum, we hold that, in a case such as this, absent proof of false statements knowingly or recklessly made by him, a teacher's exercise of his right to speak on issues of public importance may not furnish the basis for his dismissal from public employment.

With Pickering as a "trail blazer," it is now apparent that teachers may have substantial leeway in critical comments they may want to make about a public policy question and when the organizational distance—that is, from superintendent to teacher—is enough that the controversy will not impinge upon job performance by the teacher.

Perry v. Sinderman, 408 U. S. 593 (1972)

GENERALIZATION

When persons are successively employed on annual contracts that involve work evaluation and recommendations, competence must be deduced from those successive contracts. At some point, public employment-sector workers develop a property interest in a job as a consequence of time spent on the job and cannot be summarily fired. Rather, they are entitled to the procedural protections of the Fourteenth Amendment.

DESCRIPTION

Robert Sinderman taught in the Texas state colleges from 1959 to 1969. In 1965 he was appointed to the faculty at Odessa Junior College and received three successive renewals of his one-year contract. Although there was no systematic provision for tenure on that campus, the faculty handbook declared that each faculty member should feel that "he has permanent tenure as long as his teaching services are satisfactory." In May 1969 the regents voted not to renew Sinderman's contract.

During that year, as president of the Texas Junior College Teachers Association, Sinderman had made public statements and had given legislative testimony contrary to some stated positions of the regents. He was labeled insubordinate at the time of the regent's vote not to offer another contract and was not allowed any hearing to question the basis upon which his employment was terminated.

The Supreme Court decision, written by Justice Stewart, included the following comments.

For at least a quarter century, this Court has made clear that even though a person has no "right" to a valuable governmental benefit and even though the government may deny him the benefit for any number of reasons, there are some reasons upon which the government may not act. It may not deny a benefit to a person on a basis that infringes his constitutionally protected interests—especially his interest in freedom of speech.

. . . the respondent's allegations—which we must construe most favorably to the respondent at this stage of the litigation—do raise a genuine issue as to his interest in continued employment at Odessa Junior College. He alleged that this interest, though not secured by a formal contractual tenure provision, was secured by a no less binding understanding fostered by the college administration.

. . . the respondent offered to prove that a teacher, with his long period of service, at this particular State College had no less a "property" interest in continued employment than a formally tenured teacher at other colleges, and had no less a procedural due process right to a statement of reasons and a hearing before college officials upon their decision not to retain him.

A written contract with an explicit tenure provision clearly is evidence of a formal understanding that supports a teacher's claim of entitlement to continued employment unless sufficient "cause" is shown. Yet absence of such an explicit contractual provision may not always foreclose the possibility that a teacher has a "property" interest in re-employment.

Holding a much stronger view of the interests of the teacher, Justice Marshall dissented, stating that "every citizen who applied for a government job is entitled to it unless the government can establish some reason for denying the employment." To some extent, Marshall's view permeated the practical application of the decision, for *Sinderman* has made it necessary for any public board, acting to dismiss a tenured or long-term employee, to be ready to explain why that employment should not be continued. School administrators must be cognizant of where the burden of proof lies. That burden is not upon the affected employee.

Personnel Evaluation

When administrators function as evaluators of teachers and detect a performance that is unsatisfactory, they are not only obligated to point out what is below standard but also to specify what must be done to upgrade the performance. In *Sanders v. South Sioux Board,* 263 N.W. 2d 461 (1978), the Nebraska Supreme Court found that the local board had acted in an "arbitrary and unreasonable manner," dismissing Sanders when her current evaluation ratings were good, with a recommendation for renewal, and when there was no record of substantive stipulations for improvement having been given her by the administration.

There can be no doubt that performance accountability has risen to new levels of visibility. Yet that accountability is shared by teachers being evaluated on their teaching performance and by administrators engaged in the process of evaluation and development. When administrators find teachers performing below the standard for that school, those administrators must be prepared to enumerate—or demonstrate—with precision what the teacher must do to improve. The entire supervisory-evaluative episode must be documented.

Good documentation provides a baseline for tracing the degree of improvement. That is a practical and ethical minimum for both parties to the evaluation. It is also a legal necessity as the evidentiary base should some subsequent action be questioned in court. Lack of a systematic evaluation procedure and its documentation led the court to support Sanders, above, because the burden of proof rested upon the local board that had dismissed the teacher.

The words that describe the maximum punishment in personnel control are variable but include terms such as *fired, dismissed,* and *nonrenewed.* In effect, they mean the same, that is, termination of employment. Technically, they are slightly different and describe precise uses of state statutes. In part, the Nebraska statute states that the teacher's contract

shall be deemed renewed and shall remain in full force and effect until a majority of the members of the board vote on or before May 15 to amend or to terminate the contract for just cause at the close of the contract period. Revised Statutes of Nebraska 79-1254.

For probationary teachers, that statute stipulates that when a one-year contract has run its course of services for money, the obligations of both parties have ended. The board's minimum legal obligation is a timely notification of intent to terminate the contractual agreement. For ethical purposes, such boards may elect to specify causes, but to do so may open other legal questions about standards and judgments.

The practice in this book is to use the word *teacher* generically as well as specifically. That is, when conditions in schools are described that have application to all certificated employees, the word *teacher* has been used with a generic connotation. In those cases, it would include teachers, librarians, counsellors, and administrators—all of the job categories where a state-issued certificate is a preliminary to securing and holding the job. When that word *teacher* is used to describe the relationships in an employment hierarchy, it becomes narrower in meaning, for that relationship itself tends to separate teachers and counsellors from principals and principals from superintendents.

William Coe v. Paul M. Bogart, Superintendent of Schools, 519 F. 2d 10 (USCA 6th 1975)

GENERALIZATION

Local boards of education have latitude in involuntarily transferring their personnel to other assignments when demotions are not part of the transfer and when increased school effectiveness is an anticipated outcome.

DESCRIPTION

William S. Coe was transferred, against his will, from his position as principal of Sevier County High School, Tennessee. The transfer was made without Coe receiving any statement of charges against him or opportunity for a hearing before the county school board. Coe brought a civil rights action against that board, alleging that he was not given due process when he was transferred. The board contended that it had the right to transfer individuals within the system to increase efficiency.

He raised two questions: Does a local board and superintendent have the right to transfer a tenured teacher or principal from one location to another or from one job to another without due process? Was Coe, a tenured employee under Tennessee statutes, deprived of a property right within the meaning of the Fourteenth Amendment or of civil rights legislation?

The circuit court ruled in favor of the board of education, commenting:

This is an appeal in an action brought under 42 U.S.C., 1983 and 28 U.S.C., 1343 in which appellant William S. Coe alleged that he was deprived of procedural due process under the Fourteenth Amendment when he was transferred from his position as principal of Sevier County High School without being furnished any statement of charges against him or opportunity for a hearing before the County School Board. Coe had been employed in the county school system for 36 years, the last twelve of them as principal of its largest high school.

Following a trial on the merits, District Judge Robert L. Taylor . . . found that plaintiff was a tenured teacher with the Sevier County system within the meaning of Tennessee's Teacher Tenure Act T.C.A. 49-1401 et seq. He further found that the action of the defendant school board "constituted a routine transfer of personnel within a school system in the interest of administrative efficiency and did not amount to punitive demotion or a deprivation of property."

Our review of the trial record satisfies us that the findings of fact as reported by the trial judge are not clearly erroneous.

Tennessee tenure laws, like those commonly found in other states, did not entitle a teacher or principal to a specific job. The transfer of staff without notice or hearing constituted routine personnel administration. The transfer was motivated by a sincere belief that the effectiveness of that high school could be enhanced under different leadership. The transfer did not diminish the professional integrity of Coe or force him out of the system; neither did the transfer compel him to accept a demotion or lowered compensation. The transfer was a reasonable consequence of performance evaluation by the superintendent of schools.

In another Tennessee case, the same court spoke to two aspects of termination, also involving the Fourteenth Amendment. The court held that a probationary or nontenured teacher could be discharged at the end of the contract term without any reason being given for such termination of services. However, in *Kendall v. Memphis Board of Education,* 623 F. 2d 1155 (1980), the teacher evaluation revealed a performance that was so deficient that a decision was made to fire the teacher at once, that is, in midcontract. The court noted that she suffered two injuries, for she received no contract settlement, nor did she have opportunity for a due process hearing. The board was found liable for damages, the amount to be settled by the trial court.

In a California case, the transfer and reassignment of personnel came to the attention of a grand jury, *Calaveras School District v. Leach, Evans, et al,* 65 Cal. 588 (California Court of Appeals, 3rd, 1968). The reassignment of a principal as vice principal and a vice principal as teacher resulted in a court order for examination of personnel records by the grand jury. The superintendent appeared before the grand jury but refused to produce the records, and state statute supported his position, there being no criminal conduct involved.

The key point in personnel administration is that adequate records be kept. Although it is true that nontenured employees are not entitled to pretermination hearings, and that question was settled in *Bishop v. Wood,* 426 U.S. 341 (1976), when a probationary police officer was dismissed, good personnel records are still ethical and a minimum legal requirement. Boards cannot act with malice toward any employees, and records must be available to make it clear that fairness prevailed. Constitutional, contractual, and statutory protections must be met in any manipulation of the school district's labor pool, and those changes must have their base in an improvement of the educational setting.

Promotion and Tenure

Terms and conditions of employment, as well as the relative permanence of the job, have been concerns of workers since the world of work began to divide into two groups, employees and employers. Workers want to know if they are temporary or permanent. They want to know what must be done to change classifications from temporary to permanent, because Americans, fond of making long-range plans, cannot do so when they lack some basic economic understandings. For teachers, the words describing this critical aspect of work life are *probation* and *tenure.*

The underlying concept is that, when newly hired, too little is known about the professional performance characteristics to grant employment far into the future. Initial contracts are, typically, for one year. When after some time has passed, evaluations have been made, development has occurred, and evidence is available that the teacher is a dependable, effective professional, tenure may be granted. The time for that event, the statutory specifics that govern it, and the true consequences of conferring a status of permanent employment vary from state to state. The definitions, rights, and obligations are covered by statutes, as seen in the Oregon code.

"Permanent teacher" means any teacher who has been regularly employed by a fair dismissal district for a period of not less than three successive school years, whether or not the district was such a district during all of such period, and who has been reelected by such district after the completion of such three-year period for the next succeeding school year.

"Probationary teacher" means any teacher employed by a fair dismissal district who is not a permanent teacher. Oregon Revised Statutes 342.805 (4), (5)

In another place, a more complete description of the probationary teacher occurs.

Probationary teacher. The district board of any fair dismissal district may discharge or remove any probationary teacher in the employ of the district at any time during a probationary period for any cause deemed in good faith sufficient by the board. The probationary teacher shall be given a written copy of the reasons for this dismissal, and upon request shall be provided a hearing thereon by the board, at which time the probationary teacher shall have the opportunity to be heard either in person or by a representative of the teacher's choice.

The district board may, for any cause it may deem in good faith sufficient, refuse to renew the contract of any probationary teacher. However, the teacher shall be entitled to notice of the intended action by April 1, and upon request shall be provided a hearing before the district board. Upon request from the probationary teacher the board shall provide the probationary teacher a written copy of the reasons for the nonrenewal which shall provide the basis for the hearing.

If an appeal is taken from any hearing, the appeal shall be limited to:

(a) The procedures at the hearing;

(b) Whether the written copy of the reasons for dismissal required by this section was supplied; and

(c) In the case of nonrenewal whether notice of nonrenewal was timely given. Oregon Revised Statutes 842.835 (1), (2), (3)

From the same statutory source, a good, representative definition can be found.

Permanent teacher; permanent part-time teacher. (1) A permanent teacher shall not be subjected to the requirement of annual appointment nor shall he be dismissed or employed on a part-time basis without his consent except as provided in ORS 342.805 to 342.955. Oregon Revised Statutes 342.845.

Teachers move from one status to another by way of periodic evaluations done during the time they are classified as probationary teachers.

Teacher evaluation; form; personnel file content. The district superintendent of every school district, including superintendents of education service districts, shall cause to have made at least annually but with multiple observations an evaluation of performance for each probationary teacher employed by the district and at least biennially for any other teacher. The purpose of the evaluation is to allow the teacher and the district to determine the teacher's development and growth in the teaching profession and to evaluate the performance of the teaching responsibilities. A form for teacher evaluation shall be prescribed by the State Board of Education and completed pursuant to rules adopted by the district school board. Oregon Revised Statutes 352.850

Although the Oregon code differs from many other states in particulars, conceptually, it is a good example of how all states have acted to address the question of permanence in public school district employment.

The Nebraska statutes enumerate the specifics under which dismissal can occur, and they are strikingly similar to listings of cause for termination found in other states. The conditions of unsatisfactory performance are legislatively stipulated.

As used in this section and section 79-1254.02, the term just cause shall mean incompetency, neglect of duty, unprofessional conduct, insubordination, immorality, physical or mental incapacity, other conduct which interferes substantially with the continued performance of duties. Revised Statutes of Nebraska 79-1254

The passage from probationary to permanent—tenured—teacher is a critical time in a professional's life. It is a major decision for the employing board, for it signals the start of a long-term commitment, mutually shared. Teachers are anxious for accomplishment and designation as tenured. Boards are prone to painstakingly careful and thorough reexamination of all personnel coming to that point of long-term commitment. In *Holton Schools v. William Farmer,* 259 N.W. 2d 219 (Michigan Court of Appeals, 1977), Farmer was told that he would not be rehired at the end of his last year as a probationary teacher because of a program phase-out. He was not told that his work was unsatisfactory. Qualified by certification for four open positions in the school district, he applied but was not hired, being labeled as not best qualified. Although he had not achieved tenure, he had achieved some seniority, and the court supported his contention that he could not be denied employment until the local board of education comprehensively defined its term *qualified* and he could be identified as clearly outside of the group of qualified candidates.

Carolyn F. Robinson v. Jefferson County School Board, 458 F. 2d 1318 (USCA 5th, 1973)

GENERALIZATION

Even among those probationary teachers who are obviously intelligent and accomplished individuals, there is a necessity to accept and work within the policies and regulations of the employing school district.

DESCRIPTION

Carolyn Robinson was a first-year teacher in the Jefferson County, Alabama, schools, a probationary teacher. As a probationary teacher, she lacked a constitutionally protected property interest in continued employment, and the Alabama statutes empowered local boards to refuse reemployment to probationary teachers without a hearing. Upon allegations from the administration, she was dismissed by the school board for her use of profanity in the classroom, incompetency and inefficiency in the discharge of her daily duties, and inability to relate to ninth-grade students. Robinson, who defended herself, contended that she was not dismissed because of those reasons; rather, it was because the principal did not like her, or the way she graded, or the way she arranged her class. The circuit court stated:

The trial court found that the plaintiff was in fact dismissed because of her general ineffectiveness as a teacher. Upon a review of the record, we are unable to say that that finding was clearly erroneous.

In light of our holding, we deem it appropriate to make a few observations about the relatively unusual character of this case. The plaintiff appears in this court *pro se,* and she prosecuted her entire case below, through a substantial trial, in her own behalf. The appellant's briefs reveal an understanding of the law and an ability to make legal arguments rare in a layman. Apparently her performance in the trial court was equally impressive; the trial judge stated that he had "never had a case in which anybody has represented himself before in which the party doing so has operated as effectively as has the plaintiff in this case." Her performance led him to suggest that she might prefer the practice of law to returning to teaching. Ms. Robinson's performance as her own counsel leaves no doubt that she is an extraordinarily capable woman. In view of this, the record of this case is a troubling one. It describes the difficulties of an intelligent woman in her first year of teaching, whose ideas differed from those of her superiors in the school organization. We should have hoped that the principal of the school and school board officials and Ms. Robinson, a highly capable woman, could have found some amicable way to communicate and to work out their differences. But whatever may be said of this unhappy breakdown in communications and its cause, the County Board of Education did not violate the plaintiff's constitutional rights. That is all this Court holds.

Affirmed.

Robinson was an instance of regrettable but unreconciled conflict in which a district hired an aggressive, highly intelligent candidate as a teacher and then found that she was unable or unwilling to work within the confines of the organization. Intelligence must be prized among teachers; so, also, must organizational teamwork be prized—and local boards can demand that.

In *Brown v. Bathke*, 566 F. 2d 588 (USCA 8th, 1977), several questions arose, but primarily they were related to the facts that Barbara Brown was a first-year probationary teacher who had failed to provide an official copy of her college transcript as requested, was unmarried and pregnant, and did not—initially—request a hearing on the question of nonrenewal. The actions extended over five years as procedural questions were reviewed, along with questions of substance such as sex and race discrimination. Beyond the local board, commissions and courts heard appeals. In essence, the local board's action for dismissal was upheld.

Nancy Blurton v. Bloomfield Hills Schools, 231 N.W. 2d 535 (Michigan Court of Appeals, 1975)

GENERALIZATION

Boards are not at liberty to write clauses into contracts that violate state statutes, and teachers who accept and sign such contracts may not be bound by those invalid clauses.

DESCRIPTION

Blurton was employed by the Bloomfield Hills Schools on September 7, 1971, and began teaching without a contract as a permanent substitute. She taught fifth grade at one elementary school the entire fall semester of 1971. Near the end of that semester, she entered into a probationary teacher contract for the second semester, replacing a teacher who took a maternity leave. In the main body of the form contract, it was provided that the term of employment was for one year, starting on or about September 1. Typewritten at the bottom of her contract was the statement, 'Prorate from January 7, 1972. Contract to terminate at end of the school year, June 1972.'' Near the end of that school year, Blurton received notice that she would not be rehired for the next school year. She sought reinstatement as a teacher, stating that with the exception of three days in January, and permissible leave days, she had taught every day of the 1971-72 school year, and that upon that performance the Michigan teacher-tenure act stopped the district from discharging her.

Noting that, by statute, no teacher could "waive any rights and privileges under this act in any contract or agreement with a controlling board," the court made its own pronouncement.

By adopting a literal interpretation of the phrase "a full school year," the Legislature's purpose behind the teachers' tenure act would be frustrated. We hold that plaintiff's pleadings stated a cause of action. If plaintiff at trial is able to prove the facts alleged in her pleadings, we hold she would be entitled to the guarantees [provided in Michigan law].

The statute mandates that a probationary teacher or one employed on a noncontinuing contract must be informed that her work is or is not satisfactory and that she will not be rehired for the following school year at least 60 days before the close of the school year. Defendant contends that it was not required to inform plaintiff that her work was unsatisfactory. It contends it was wholly irrelevant under these facts. We do not agree.

It is our conclusion that a sufficient factual question exists for a trial on the merits of the cause. Reversed and remanded for trial. No costs, a public question being involved.

Although designation as a permanent teacher is a kind of employment security, it does not relieve teachers of the obligation to perform their professional tasks at high-quality standards. When performance falls, for any of the just causes enumerated in statutes, teachers may be dismissed—if their malperformance merits such an extreme penalty. Dismissal must follow correct procedure and rest upon evidence strong enough to convince a board of education, sitting as an impartial tribunal at a hearing devoted to that single question, that the board can by majority vote decide for dismissal.

Anita Louise Davis v. Callaway School District, 203 Neb. 1 (1979)

GENERALIZATION

When an administration brings to the board's attention a recommendation for teacher dismissal, testimony and documentation must be strong, or the board cannot act in harmony with the administration. The teacher is entitled to present as persuasive a case as possible, having equal rights with the charging administrators.

DESCRIPTION

Anita Davis was a tenured teacher in the Callaway Schools. That board terminated her employment in 1976 for "just cause" under Nebraska statutes. Evidence presented to the board of education consisted of testimony from the superintendent, the principal, three other witnesses, and a number of exhibits. The superintendent stated that in his opinion she should be terminated for just cause. The principal concurred with the superintendent's recommendation. Exhibits produced some conflicts. Other witnesses were favorable for retention. The Callaway board voted to terminate the contract of Anita Davis.

Appellant contends that the evidence was insufficient to support the action of the board of education in terminating her employment. The evidence presented to the board of education consisted of testimony from George Wright, the superintendent; David Weber, the principal; Anita Davis; Frank Swathel; Carolyn Kollmeier; and a number of exhibits. The superintendent testified he has observed the appellant and her class personally; student behavior was poor; appellant was too permissive; appellant lacked organizational control; and planning; and appellant did not motivate students. He stated in his opinion she should be terminated for just cause. The principal testified that he had taught for 10 years in the system; he personally observed appellant in her class; discipline was a problem; and appellant needed to improve organization and control. He concurred with the superintendent's recommendation for termination. The testimony of the other witnesses could be summarized as favorable for retention. The exhibits likewise produced conflicts either directly or in inferences to be drawn therefrom.

Appellant argues the decision herein should be controlled by the *Sanders* case. That case is not applicable here. In *Sanders* the expert witnesses charged with the duty of evaluating the performance of the teacher did not testify that her performance failed to meet the appropriate standard. Instead, they recommended to the board of education that the teacher be retained. The evidence, therefore, as a matter of law, did not establish "just cause" for terminating the teacher's employment. In the case now before us the testimony of the expert witnesses charged with the duty of evaluating the performance of the teacher was that her performance did not meet the appropriate standards. They recommended that her employment be terminated and the evidence, including the expert testimony, as a matter of law, was sufficient to support the action of the board in terminating her employment. The language in *Sanders* with reference to a standard of performance should not be interpreted to mean that in every hearing on termination before a board of education there must first be expert testimony establishing the appropriate and acceptable standard of performance before a board may consider whether particular conduct falls below that standard.

In an error, proceeding conflicting evidence will not be weighted and the order of an administrative tribunal must be affirmed if the tribunal has acted within its jurisdiction and there is sufficient competent evidence, as a matter of law, to sustain its findings and order.

The Nebraska Supreme Court held in favor of the local board, ruling that in Davis's dismissal the procedural and substantive obligations had been met.

Teachers who are tenured sometimes run afoul of board policies or regulations in ways that bring unexpected disputes to the fore. In *Rumph v. Wayne School District,* 188 N.W. 2d 71 (Michigan Court of Appeals, 1971), both teacher and board became involved in substantive errors. Having taught for nine years in Wayne, Rumph took a one-year traveling sabbatical leave at half pay, agreeing that he should file an interim and final report. Not receiving any interim report, the board suspended his salary and upon his return informed him that his breach of contract constituted grounds for dismissal. Bringing suit, Rumph won because the board's dismissal procedure was out of harmony with the state's teacher-tenure act; that is, it was procedurally defective. Discharge of a tenured teacher, then, may be made only for reasonable and just cause and only after such charges, notice, hearing, and determination by a board sitting as an impartial tribunal agrees that there is sufficient and persuasive evidence to call for dismissal. Administrators who bring charges against a tenured teacher must be confident of the grounds upon which they are acting and of the procedures followed in pressing those charges.

Just Cause and Due Process

In a sense, the entire structure of events and situations that must be met by a prospective teacher are protections for children. A teacher must be a college graduate, hold a valid teacher's certificate, apply for a job, and survive screening and consideration before the contract is offered and accepted. The whole structure is an attempt to assure high-quality instruction in every classroom. After accepting the job, actual performance as the appointed instructional leader for the students must be periodically evaluated and a judgment made.

Initially, teachers are hired on short-term contracts—normally, of one year's duration. State statutes may differ in particulars, but most states have a time specified when probationary teachers must be told what their future for employment may be. That is, by board decisions that very normally follow administrative evaluations and recommendations, teachers are offered successive contracts or are advised that another contract will not be offered. Unless the duty is mandated in statutes, boards are not legally bound to set forward any reasons why a successor-term contract is not to be offered, for the teacher-as-citizen has no constitutional entitlement to such information. On the other hand, boards are not forbidden to state, privately, the reasoning used in deciding not to offer a successor term contract. Substantively, the choice is up to the board; procedurally, the board must accommodate the statutes of the state.

Teacher-performance evaluation may lead an administrator to a decision to seek improvement by replacement. Most improvement is by development of the individual, responding to supervisory questions, recommendation, and directives. Teachers tend to stay on, working over several years, being regularly evaluated and demonstrating acceptable performance standards. Through such work-performance records clearly showing that acceptable standards have been met, teachers pass from the probationary class into the tenured class of employees. Tenured teachers are protected in their jobs from arbitrary actions of a local board of education and can be dismissed only for just cause and by way of due process if they choose to make use of that latter job-protection item.

Just cause means that there exists a reasonable, proper, and legal motive or reason as a base for some action against the teacher. When the action is so extreme that it may result in termination of a permanent, that is, tenured, teacher, that action must be based in the statutes of the state, for tenure is a condition of employment achieved under other, and equally potent, state statutes. Oregon's legislative treatment is typical.

Grounds for dismissal of permanent teacher. (1) No permanent teacher shall be dismissed except for:

    a. Inefficiency;
    b. Immorality;
    c. Insubordination;
    d. Neglect of duty;
    e. Physical or mental incapacity;
    f. Conviction of a felony or of a crime involving moral turpitude;
    g. Inadequate performance;
    h. Failure to comply with such reasonable requirements as the board may prescribe to show normal improvement and evidence of professional training and growth;
    i. Any cause which constitutes grounds for the revocation of such permanent teacher's certificate. Oregon Revised Statutes 342.865

The Nebraska statutes define *just cause* as consisting of most of those items in the Oregon code and extend it to include "other conduct which interferes substantially with the continued performance of duties." When teachers achieve permanent status in their local school districts, and can be dismissed only for just cause, there is very little chance that any dismissals will occur except for the welfare of the students. Some observers feel that the burden of proof—to discover and document just cause—has shifted too heavily upon administrators and boards and that tenure has protected too many mediocre teachers. No such intention can be discerned by reading the statutes, so if low-quality teaching performance is accepted in some specific situations or settings, it may indicate a lack of systematic, discriminating evaluation and appraisal by the administrators charged with that responsibility.

Due process derives from the Fourteenth Amendment and is a procedural protection that demands a slowed, conscientious, and considerate examination of the charges that may be brought against a teacher. For example, a teacher who is neglectful of a duty assignment, who has had that omission brought up for attention by a supervisor, and who has not remedied the deficient performance may be charged before the board in whatever way the statutes have provided for. Due process demands that an impartial hearing on the charges be allowed, if the teacher so chooses.

Suppose it is the teacher's view that the supervisor was prejudiced, withheld information, arbitrarily practiced the authority conferred upon the position as supervisor, and lacked substantial supporting evidence of the charge. Only through the exercise of due process could the truth be discovered. Many instances of teacher evaluation are controversial and can only be decided by local boards of education, sitting as impartial tribunals, hearing charges and countercharges, and, finally, making a decision based upon the evidence presented. In some states, such disputes may be referred to the commission established to examine questions of professional teaching practices. Some disputes are carried onward through appeals and become cases in courts.

Howard Cadell v. Ecorse Board, 170 N.W. 2d 277 (Michigan Court of Appeals, 1969)

GENERALIZATION

Boards of education may proceed against inadequate teaching performance when just cause is charged, and the whole employee-relations condition is carried forward within the structure of due process.

DESCRIPTION

Cadell was advised by the superintendent of schools that he was acting in violation of board rules and regulations, especially in regard to job absences, tardies, and falsified sign-in times. He was suspended, pending a due process hearing in which the superintendent would recommend for dismissal. The board, sitting as an impartial tribunal, found Cadell neglectful of his duty upon the facts presented by the superintendent. Cadell was dismissed and brought suit seeking payment of salary for the balance of the term contract or, lacking that, for the period from suspension to dismissal.

In the present case the grounds for plaintiff's dismissal from employment were absences from duty without properly reporting these absences; tardiness; and falsifying sign-in times. The circuit court concluded that the board's action was authorized by law. Plaintiff did not allege in his pleadings that this action was arbitrary, unreasonable, or beyond the scope of the board's authority. He did allege that his suspension was "without adequate cause or reason." However, the board's decision was a final dismissal from duty, not a suspension.

The circuit court correctly decided that the dismissal of the plaintiff was within the defendant board's statutory authority.

Although the Michigan court upheld the board's action, it did provide one remedy for Cadell. Inasmuch as he was dismissed while a valid contract was in effect, he was entitled to all salary that accrued from the time of his suspension until he was dismissed from employment.

Roger diLeo v. Richard Greenfield, Superintendent of Schools,
541 F. 2d 949 (USCA 2d, 1976)

GENERALIZATION

Tenured teachers may be dismissed for due cause, just cause, or sufficient cause—according to the statutes of an individual state—when dismissal procedures are also harmonious with obligations of due process.

DESCRIPTION

A junior high teacher had acquired tenure by way of teaching in the Bloomfield, Connecticut, school system for longer than three years. He was notified by the board that he would be terminated for exhibiting "improper conduct toward students," which was sufficient to constitute "due and sufficient cause" under the Connecticut statute that governed termination of teachers. That notification followed several meetings between school administrators and the teacher that had failed to relieve or improve diLeo's situation. A hearing occurred at which school administrators, parents, and students presented evidence regarding the teacher's misconduct as charged. Examples included failure to assist students with classwork, making statements with sexual connotations to students, failure to complete lesson plans as directed, and refusals to explain ambiguous textbook material to students. Following the hearing, the board of education officially terminated the tenured teacher's employment. DiLeo carried the dispute into the courts, contending that Connecticut's teacher-termination statute was unconstitutionally vague, allowing for violation of the rights of due process.

The Second Circuit Court of Appeals found for the local board and did not fault the Connecticut statute, noting that the challenged subsection of the statute, "other due and sufficient cause," was followed by five specific grounds for dismissal. All were clearly stated, each could be understood by a person of reasonable intelligence, and all related to the capacity of teachers to perform professional duties. The conduct of diLeo fell within the core of the statute's delineation of grounds for dismissal. He should have known that the conduct for which he was terminated constituted "due and sufficient cause" for dismissal under state law. Moreover, he was given generous notice by the board of the conduct violations it viewed as "other due and sufficient cause in the meetings and notices prior to termination."

Contracts protect teachers but do not relieve them of the obligations to perform at a high standard and in compliance with the reasonable rules of their employing board. In *Skeim v. School District 115,* 234 N.W. 2d 206 (1975), tenured Minnesota teachers were unsuccessful in their bid to recover salary withheld by the board. Board regulations had stipulated Columbus Day as a normal school day, but the teachers took it as a holiday. Along with some other punishments, the board was upheld in withholding one day's pay. Gradations of punishment for bad performance, less than dismissal, may be meted out to tenured teachers for just cause.

In *Zoll v. Allamakee Schools,* 588 F. 2d 246 (USCA 8th, 1979), a twenty-nine-year Iowa teacher was laid off with the reason being attributed to declining enrollments. Rose Zoll had written two letters critical of the schools to the local paper, and they were published. The court rejected the school's layoff procedure as subjective and biased. Zoll was awarded reinstatement, back pay, legal fees, and expenses as the court cited a "retaliatory motive" for her nonrenewal. Somewhat similarly, in *Givhan v. Western Line Schools,* 439 U. S. 410 (1979), the Supreme Court reversed the U.S. Circuit Court of Appeals, 5th Circuit, and ruled for the teacher Bessie Givhan. An eight-year teacher, Givhan was terminated after making candid, direct, and private criticisms of school policies to her principal. The high court ruled that, having allowed her into the office for discussion of school policies, the principal could not pose as a "captive audience" or "unwilling recipient of her views." The Court construed freedom of speech to include forceful, private expression of personal-professional views.

* * *

In the administration of personnel, the culturally based, widely accepted American concept of fairness must be present. Teachers may not treat children unfairly; neither can teachers be treated unfairly by administrators or employing boards of education. Reasonable people may view a single situation from different viewpoints, and it is from such divergence that many disputes arise. The disputes call for resolution within a system that is not vague. All parties are entitled to clarity in the statutes, rules, and regulations that will be used as a basis for judging standards of performance. Even with such a carefully laid base, and that presumed to be constitutionally harmonious, it is still possible, even inevitable, that all aspects of the operation of a school system will not be seen from identical viewpoints.

Disputes and disagreements create the environment in which due process becomes important. Administrators cannot allow a teacher to continue when students suffer from bad professional performance; neither can teachers become the objects of unreasonable or arbitrary judgments. The insistence upon constitutionally provided due process as the procedural arena in which performance problems can be examined after preliminary judgments have been made provides a margin of safety for all parties and creates an atmosphere of reduced hostility where questionable performance can be reviewed more objectively. Tenure laws were never intended to protect incompetence or to protect against any other just cause for dismissal. When just cause exists, it deserves to be exhibited before an impartial tribunal and, upon their awareness of it and agreement that it exists, becomes the base upon which to make even the most severe decisions affecting professional life.

chapter 7

ADMINISTERING STUDENT PERSONNEL

Schools exist for the purpose of educating the children within the community. Compulsory attendance is embodied in statutes that require boys and girls between certain ages to attend upon instruction. The several states have enacted specific legislation that grants the rights of children of specified ages to attend the public schools. The compulsory-attendance statutes are based upon the premise that the state is served by the development of an enlightened citizenry. Thus parents or guardians are compelled to see that their children are educated and are subject to penalties for noncompliance with the statutes.

Students' rights have been the subject of increasing numbers of cases being heard by the courts at all levels. As a result, we have seen a rather substantial change in the role of the school administrator. This school official is being called upon to serve as a pupil advocate. There are occasions when this role places the administrator in an adversarial relationship with the board of education. It thus becomes very important that the student of school law be very conversant with those rights that have been adjudged to be Constitutionally protected. Gone are the days when pupils were expected to leave their Constitutional rights outside the schoolhouse.

Tinker v. Des Moines Community School District, 393 U.S. 502 (1969)

GENERALIZATION

Students are "persons" under the Constitution. Action by school officials to limit student freedom is permissible only when that action can be defended as educationally necessary and when it is the least restrictive technique that can be used in the control of student behavior.

DESCRIPTION

Several children announced that they planned to wear a black armband to school on certain days. The armband was to express their opposition to the U.S. participation in the Vietnam War. It was their intention to make this passive protest by way of symbolic (but silent) speech. There was no demonstration or any disruption. The school administration feared demonstration, disruption, and confrontation and implemented a policy against such apparel, sending the offending children home.

The school officials banned and sought to punish petitioners for a silent, passive expression of opinion, unaccompanied by any disorder or disturbance on the part of the petitioners. There is here no evidence whatever of petitioners' interference, actual or nascent, with the school's work or of collision with the rights of other students to be secure and to be let alone. Accordingly, this case does not concern speech or action that intrudes upon the work of the schools or the rights of other students.

Only a few of the 18,000 students in the school system wore the black armbands. Only five students were suspended for wearing them. There is no indication that the work of the schools or any class was disrupted. Outside the classrooms, a few students made hostile remarks to the children wearing armbands, but there were no threats or acts of violence on school premises.

The District Court concluded that the action of the school authorities was reasonable because it was based upon their fear of a disturbance from the wearing of armbands. But, in our system, undifferentiated fear or apprehension of disturbance is not enough to overcome the right to freedom of expression. Any departure from absolute regimentation may cause trouble. Any variation from the majority's opinion may inspire fear. Any word spoken, in class, in the lunchroom, or on the campus, that deviates from the views of another person may start an argument or cause a disturbance. But our Constitution says we must take this risk, *Terminiello v. Chicago,* 337 U.S. 1 (1949); and our history says that it is this sort of hazardous freedom—this kind of openness—that is the basis of our national strength and of the independence and vigor of Americans who grow up and live in this relatively permissive, often disputatious, society.

In order for the State in the person of school officials to justify prohibition of a particular expression of opinion, it must be able to show that its action was caused by something more than a mere desire to avoid the discomfort and unpleasantness that always accompany an unpopular viewpoint. Certainly where there is no finding and no showing that engaging in the forbidden conduct would "materially and substantially interfere with the requirements of appropriate discipline in the operation of the school," the prohibition cannot be sustained.

In the present case, the District Court made no such finding, and our independent examination of the record fails to yield evidence that the school authorities had reason to anticipate that the wearing of the armbands would substantially interfere with the work of the school or impinge upon the rights of other students. Even an official memorandum prepared after the suspension that listed the reasons for the ban on wearing the armbands made no reference to the anticipation of such disruption.

Justice Fortas wrote the strong opinion for the court, elevating symbolic speech to a level of "pure speech," as the Des Moines schools lost the case.

The concept of legal rights of children has undergone substantial change during the past two decades. Many questions arise concerning these rights. How much freedom should be provided to children in school? Do schoolchildren have the right of self-determination in deciding what their behavior shall be? Are the rights of schoolchildren and adults identical? Are the rights of all children—regardless of age—identical? Undoubtedly, these and other questions of a legal nature will be the basis for court cases and appeals in the future. We are finding that boards of education must review their policies and school officials must review their procedures in an attempt to avoid costly and time-consuming litigation on the subject of student rights.

The days ahead will require changes in the operation of our schools; many of these changes will call for new, constrained approaches to pupils. The purpose of this chapter is to consider topics such as the admission and attendance of students, classification and instruction of students, and control of student conduct, activities, and rights.

Admission and Attendance of Students

A nation, if it is to prosper, must rely upon an enlightened citizenry. Education is to provide this enlightenment, and thus statutes have required compulsory attendance upon instruction. Courts have held that the several states have properly exercised their police powers in enacting compulsory-attendance laws and thus have denied the charges that these laws infringe upon individual liberties that have been guaranteed by the Constitution as noted in *Concerned Citizens v. Board of Education of Chatanooga,* 379 F. Supp. 1233 (TN, 1974).

In its decision in *Pierce v. Society of Sisters,* 268 U.S. 510 (1925), the Supreme Court struck down an Oregon requirement that, to comply with the compulsory-education statute, all children must attend the public school. Thus parents were assured of the right to direct the upbringing of their children and could send them to private schools, but the state could establish certain minimum standards of education for the schools, public and private.

Compulsory-attendance ages are established by state statute. For example, Michigan and New York require that parents or guardians having control and charge of a child from the sixth to the sixteenth birthday shall send that child to the public schools during the entire school year. For children who attend nonpublic schools, the requirement is that instruction given to the minor elsewhere than a public school shall be at least substantially equivalent to that given in a public school. (The state of Georgia requires pupils between the ages of seven and sixteen to be enrolled in a public or private school.) As a rule, the local public school superintendent is required to account for all resident children of compulsory-attendance age whether they are enrolled in public or private school, exempted from school attendance, or taught in the home.

There is one exception to the compulsory-education requirement. This was determined in 1972 when the Supreme Court held in *Wisconsin v. Yoder,* 406 U.S. 205 (1972), that the free exercise of religion clause of the First Amendment prevented a state from requiring Amish children to submit to compulsory formal educational requirements beyond the eighth grade. In the opinion of the Court, the Amish had been convincing in their argument that for almost three hundred years their sustained faith had prevaded and regulated their whole mode of life, and this would be seriously endangered, if not destroyed, by enforcement of the requirement of compulsory formal education beyond the eighth grade. Historically, compulsory age limits were related to child labor laws. These laws permitted earlier school-leaving ages for those entering agricultural employment. This, in effect, was what the Amish children were doing after the eighth grade.

An issue that surrounds the compulsory-attendance requirement is that of equivalent instruction. Generally, statutes require that if one elects not to attend public school, one must obtain equivalent instruction elsewhere. Parents and guardians have attempted to meet this requirement through private schools and home instruction. In *State ex. rel. Shoreline School Dist. No. 412 v. Superior Court,* 346 P. 2d 999 (1959), the Washington Supreme Court held that home instruction did not satisfy the law covering attendance at a private school. The court stated that there are three essential elements of a school: the teacher, the pupil (or pupils), and the institution (place). The test in this instance was that the arrangement did not meet the state requirements, because there was no qualified teacher. The family's argument that attendance at the public school conflicted with the religious beliefs of the family was unacceptable as the basis for noncompliance with the compulsory-attendance law.

Another issue that becomes entangled with the compulsory-attendance statutes is that of eligibility to attend school. It is held, generally, that eligibility to attend the public schools of a district tuition-free is extended by statute to those school-age youth who are residents of the district. We should distinguish between two terms that are applicable to this issue. *Domicile* is a place where one intends to remain indefinitely, and each person may have only one domicile. A minor child's legal domicile is that of his father except in special circumstances such as death of the father or separation or divorce of the parents, where custody of the child has been awarded to the mother or legal charge of the child is in the hands of the other persons. *Residence* is a factual place of abode, the place where one is, actually, physically living. It is held, generally, that a child has the right to attend the public school of a district in which he or she is living—unless the child is living in that district solely for the purpose of attending school there. This holding will be found in the *Fangman v. Moyers,* 8 P. 2d 762 (1932), and *Turner v. Board of Educ., North Chicago Community High School Dist. 123,* 294 N.E. 2d 264 (1973).

Children living in charitable homes, child-care centers, orphanages, or with court-appointed guardians are, in the absence of contrary statutory provisions, generally considered to be children residing within the school district for school purposes, and the public school system must accept the child tuition-free.

The right of a child to attend school in a district other than that in which he or she resides is dependent upon the statutes of the state in which the school district is located. Unless specifically barred by statute, school districts may accept pupils from other districts upon payment of tuition. Determination of the tuition is, generally, within the statutory authority of the board of education that is to provide the instruction. As a general rule, boards of education do not accept tuition pupils where the schools are already overcrowded, and these pupils would constitute an excessive burden for the receiving schools. Where school districts do accept tuition pupils, if a parent prefers to enroll a child in the schools of a district in which a child does not reside, the parent must pay the tuition. This is true even if the parent owns property and pays taxes in the receiving district, although some states, for example, New York, stipulate that the amount of the tax shall be deducted from the tuition due.

Instruction of Pupils

A variety of issues are found in this section. The courts have been called upon to rule on the issues that have evolved from rules and regulations of boards of education at all levels, legislative acts, and constitutional provisions.

The several states have established minimum lengths of school terms. Legislatures have exercised their authority in this matter. The state of Georgia requires a minimum of 175 days of attendance upon instruction, whereas the state of New York requires 180 days of instruction. When the legislature has been silent, however, local boards of education may determine the length of school term. Within the limits established by statutes or the constitution, local boards of education may exercise their discretionary powers in establishing the opening and closing dates of the school year.

Courses of study have been prescribed by state legislatures. Such authority has been assumed as being in the interest of the welfare and safety of the nation and its citizens. The courts have sustained such legislative acts, absent actions that are arbitrary, capricious, unreasonable, or in violation of state or federal Constitutions. Once the state has mandated—through legislative enactment and/or state board of education—that required courses of study be taught, the local board of education must comply with the mandate. Such mandates do not restrict the local board of education from instituting activities that exceed those that are required.

In enacting statutory provisions for the curriculum, the state may not circumscribe the rights guaranteed by the state or federal Constitution. Typical of this provision have been the attempts by states to prohibit the teaching of certain subjects. An illustration is found in *Mo Hock KeLok Po v. Stainback,* 336 U.S. 368, (HI, 1949), wherein the legislature attempted to prohibit the teaching of any language other than English to children who had not passed the fourth grade. This act was declared to be unconstitutional. In *State v. Board of Education of the City of St. Louis,* 233 S.W. 2d 697 (MO, 1950), the court held that where in the absence of mandatory statutes a board of education has complete discretion in determining what courses shall be offered, continued, or discontinued, its discretion will not be interfered with by the court.

Challenges have been made to the inclusion of certain specific topics in the curriculum. One of them that has been hotly debated in recent years is sex education. In *Hobolth v. Greenway,* 218 N.W. 2d 98 (MI, 1974), it was held that the offering of a course authorized by state statutes was not unconstitutional where attendance in a sex-education course was not compulsory, and it was held, furthermore, that the statutory authorization for offering this instruction was not an illegal delegation of authority. Generally, the courts will not interfere with courses of study that a board of education, acting within the scope of its authority, may prescribe as determined in *Ritz v. School District of Hazle Township,* 51, Luz. [Luzerne County] L. Reg. 269 (PA, 1961). There are specific instances, nonetheless, where the courts have required programs. They are found, primarily, where the courts have required remedial opportunities. In a recent decision in the matter of *Debra P. v. Turlington,* 474 F. Supp. 257 (FL, 1979), the court stayed the use of a minimum-competency test used as a graduation requirement for a four-year waiting period until the traces of a dual school system were gone and the students had been provided remediation for their deficiencies.

A broad construction of the term *curriculum* includes more than the usual academic subjects. In *Mathias v. School District of Trafford Borough,* 35 West [Westmoreland County] 143 (PA, 1953), the court held that organized sports could properly be included in the school program under the management of the board of education. Furthermore, the court, in *Woodson v. School District No. 26,* 274 P. 728 (KS, 1929), held that athletics were a part of the regular school program.

Questions have been raised about the authority of boards of education to require pupils to wear uniforms for physical education classes. In deciding this issue in *Mitchell v. McCall,* 143 So. 2d 629 (AL, 1962), the court held that required participation in physical education classes did not violate the student's constitutional rights so long as the student was not required to perform any exercise that would be immodest when performing in ordinary wearing apparel. The issue in this instance dealt with the requirement that pupils wear prescribed uniforms that were deemed to be immodest by them or their parents.

In many states the State High School Athletic or Activities Association prescribes rules that govern member schools. Among these rules are those that regulate the eligibility of the team members. One must remember that since many of these cases are decided in particular states, the statutes that govern are those of that state and are not applicable, universally, to all fifty states. In *Art Gaines Baseball Camp, Inc. v. Houston,* 500 S.W. 2d 735 (MO, 1973), the court held that the State Activities Association could lawfully impose a regulation that governed eligibility of secondary school students. In this instance, the provision was that a student who attended a summer camp specializing in one sport for more than two weeks would be declared ineligible to participate in that sport for the following year. One should note that not always have regulations of state athletic or activities associations been upheld. Prevailing opinion in this area is that a board of education cannot delegate its powers to make policy or rules to a state athletic association. An illustration of this application is found in *Bunger v. Iowa H.S. Athletic Association,* 197 N.W. 2d 555 (IA, 1972), where the court found against the state athletic association rule that made ineligible for athletic competition a boy who used or transported alcoholic beverages or drugs—or who had knowledge that they were being transported in the car he was riding in.

The Education Amendments of 1972, Title IX, Section 901, provided that "no person in the United States shall, on the basis of sex, be excluded from participation in, be denied the benefits of, or be subjected to discrimination under any education program or activity receiving Federal financial assistance." This provision, when applied by means of the regulations that were promulgated to put it into effect, led to considerable litigation. Furthermore, litigation on the extent to which girls may participate on boys' athletic teams was pursued under the civil rights laws. In the first instance, in *Brenden v. Independent School District,* 324 F. Supp. 1224 (MI, 1972), the court held that girls were entitled to participate in a boys' interscholastic athletic program, where it was shown that they could compete with equal ability and results on those teams and where there were no alternate competitive teams for girls. In the second instance, in *National Organization for Women Essex County Chapter v. Little League Baseball, Inc.,* 318 A. 2d 33 (NJ, 1974), the court held that Little League Baseball,

Inc., in refusing to permit girls to play on boys' baseball teams, discriminated against the girls and violated the nation's civil rights laws.

Organization of Instruction

Local boards of education have the authority to determine the grade levels to be maintained in the school district. The large majority of the schools in the United States are organized on a graded system. In *Ashton v. Jones,* 47 Lack. [Lackawanna County] Jur. 229 (PA, 1946), the court held that graded schools, being the preferred method, could stand, and it would not interfere when a board of education directed that instruction should be given by this method and children should be sent from a one-teacher school to a larger, graded school.

Boards of education, operating within statutory and constitutional requirements and limitations, shall determine what grades and schools are to be operated within the system. Furthermore, school boards are permitted substantial discretion in determining and adopting courses of study that respond to local conditions.

Each LEA possesses the authority to determine instructional levels and assignment of pupils to grades and classes. At the same time, assignment and promotion of pupils has been a source of considerable litigation, with parents at odds with the arrangements established by their own local board. In affirming the board's authority for placement of pupils, the court in *Isquith v. Levitt,* 137 N.Y. 2d 497 (1955), held that "A board of education is within its legal right in placing children in the kindergarten or 1st or 2nd or any other grade in accordance with its judgement based upon the mental attainment of the child." In this instance, parents had insisted that their son, being of appropriate age and having spent a portion of a year in school, be placed in the first grade. The board of education disagreed, basing its decision upon the fact that the boy's attendance in kindergarten could not be considered adequate; furthermore, the board had doubts that the son's scholarship was adequate for first-grade work.

Challenges to board authority in promotion, retention, and demotion have been numerous and are not new to the education scene. One, in particular, that affirms the board's right to determine methods of promotion—including permission to "skip" a grade—is found in *Sycamore Board of Education v. State,* 88 N.E. 412 (OH, 1909). A child had completed the sixth grade successfully. The parents provided tutoring during the summer so that he would be prepared to enter the eighth grade at the beginning of the next school year. In the fall, when he attempted to enter the eighth grade, his admission was refused, because there had been no authorization for him to "skip" the seventh grade. The parents sought a writ of mandamus, which the Ohio Supreme Court denied. In doing so, the court said, "Double promotion of a pupil from one grade to the second higher grade is discretionary with the board of education, and in the absence of evidence of permission by the board the court will not order it to be done."

The courts have been asked to rule on the use of grades as a part of the school's grading policy as a measure of disciplinary policy. In *Wermuth v. Bernstein,* 1965 S.L.D. 128, the New Jersey commissioner of education held that "the use of marks and grades as deterrents or as punishment is likewise usually ineffective in producing the desired results and is educationally not defensible. Whatever system of marks and grades a school may devise will have serious inherent limitations at best, and it must not be further handicapped by attempting to serve disciplinary purposes also." That is, grades should represent a professional assessment of the pupil's academic accomplishment during a discrete period—and not be diverted to another service.

Boards, in the absence of specific statutory limitations, may prescribe graduation requirements provided they are reasonable. Given the authority to prescribe reasonable graduation requirements, the board of education may deny graduation to students who for any reason fail or refuse to meet them. Once the student has completed the required courses and possesses the necessary qualifications to entitle him to a diploma, the board must perform a ministerial act that is mandatory and issue the student a diploma.

Participation in graduation exercises has been the subject of litigation. In *Valentine v. Independent School Dist.,* 183 N.W. 434 (1921), the court held that a student may not have his diploma withheld for refusal to wear a cap and gown at graduation exercises, but he may legally be denied the privilege of participation in the exercises of his Iowa high school. In a more recent holding, *Ladsen v. Bd. of Educ.,* 323, N.Y.S. 2d 545, the court overturned a superintendent's order to bar from the graduation ceremony a student who struck the school principal. The diploma was to be awarded privately. The court held that the power to discipline students did not embrace the power to exclude the student unless his presence would be disruptive. The principal had to seek other remedies to obtain redress for the student's act. In effect, what has been earned by the student, working in the school, cannot be denied.

Control of the Curriculum

The school system has the function and the professional staff has the authority to determine the proper mode of instruction for the students. Early in the history of American education, as noted in *Trustees of School v. People,* 87 Ill. 303 (1877), the court held that although the parent may make a reasonable selection of courses, this does not convey the right to the parent to insist that their child be taught courses not in the curriculum of the school. In another holding, *Wulff v. Inhabitants of Wakefield,* 109 N.E. 358 (MS, 1915), the court held that pupils may not refuse to study a subject because the parent objects to the method of instruction used by the teacher where that subject is a bona fide part of the adopted curriculum.

A study conducted by the National Institute for Education entitled *Study of State Legal Standards for the Provision of Public Education,* which summarized the law on public school curriculum, concluded that in all states the local public school district must offer a curriculum that the state prescribes. Furthermore, it was found that the degree of control exercised by each LEA differs from state to state. States do set guidelines within which local school districts must operate in establishing their curriculum. Some states are able to enforce their requirements by considering the district's curriculum a requirement for accreditation. Among the sanctions that may be applied for noncompliance could be the loss of state-approved status or the loss of state aid.

Curriculum is a word of extended definitions, a professional term also used widely by any persons speaking about the content of the schools. Taken in a narrow context, curriculum pertains only to courses that are given regularly for credit; the broader context would include all life experiences that are provided by the school. Generally, the courts have accepted the judgment of local school authorities about what subject matter is appropriate to public education, and what is intended as the curriculum in their schools.

With the expansion of school endeavors into areas that, formerly, had been reserved for other institutions—including the home—we have found increased legal conflict. We see an expression of this in *West Virginia Bd. of Education v. Barnette,* 319 U.S. 624 (1943), a landmark flag-salute case, when the Court said, "As government pressure toward unity becomes greater, so strife becomes more bitter as to whose unity it shall be." The Court allowed the pupils to choose whether to participate in the salute to the flag.

Local boards of education possess implied delegated powers to offer courses beyond those required by the state. Reviewing the many decisions dealing with the curriculum, we find quite liberal treatment by the courts of these powers. This treatment can be traced back to *Kalamazoo* (1874). There, the Michigan Supreme Court held that a local board of education did have the power to maintain a high school. The reverse is true, also, in that the courts have upheld the right of boards of education to drop a course or a portion of the curriculum that is not mandated by the state but that has been offered locally over a period of time. In supporting the right of the board of education to deal with curricular matters, the court, in *Jones v. Holes,* 6 A. 2d 102 (1939), recognized that it is an administrative function of boards of education and administrators to meet changing conditions and to create new courses, reassign teachers, and rearrange the curriculum.

Selection of textbooks, library books, and supplementary materials must be pursuant to statutes. Under New York statutes, a *textbook* is "a book which a pupil is required to use as a text for a semester or more in a particular class in the school he legally attends." Again, it is "a book which is selected and approved by the board of a school district and which contains a presentation of principles of a subject, or which is a literary work relevant to the study of a subject required for the use of classroom pupils" under the Michigan School Code. In the state of Georgia all textbooks purchased with state funds must be selected from a list approved by the state board of education.

Thus with respect to selection of textbooks, states fall into two categories. We have the "text-adoption" states, for example, Alabama, California, Georgia, North Carolina, Tennessee, Texas, Wisconsin (to name several), wherein the local board of education selects its textbooks from a list prepared by the state education agency; and the ones that are "local-adoption states," for example, Colorado, Iowa, Massachusetts, New York, Pennsylvania, and Wyoming, where the local board of education may adopt any textbook.

There is no question about the legal right of the state to prescribe textbooks or, through statutory enactment, delegate that responsibility to local boards of education. Supplementary books and instructional materials have been within the discretion of local boards to provide if these items are appropriate for the course or program being taught. Citizens cannot require a board of education to remove a book from use in the curriculum in the absence of proof that it is sectarian, "subversive," or "maliciously written" as affirmed in *Rosenburg v. Board of Education of City of New York,* 92, N.Y.S. 2d 344 (1949). More recently, in a conflict in West Virginia between patrons and the board that achieved national attention, the federal district court held in *Williams v. Board of Education of County of Kanawha,* 388 F. Supp. 93 (WV 1975), that the use of controversial textbooks does not violate the Constitutional principle of separation of church and state. Parents had objected to the books on the grounds that they discourage Christian principles and good citizenship. In its decision, the court said that the First Amendment "does not guarantee that nothing about religion will be taught in the schools." Furthermore, the court noted that material in some of these controversial textbooks was ". . . offensive to plaintiff's beliefs, choices of language, and code of conduct." Nonetheless, the court could find no cause for reversing the board of education's position.

In a related case, *Minarcini v. Strongsville City School District,* 541 F. 2d 577 (1976), the plaintiffs challenged the board of education's right to exclude certain books from its selection of high school texts and the right of this board of education to remove from the school library books that had been approved by a prior board. In the first instance, the court upheld the right of the board of education to refuse to approve new texts and, in the second instance, ruled that the board could not Constitutionally censor or remove books that had been lawfully placed in the library by a predecessor board. This finding lacks for administrative practicality and has not found widespread acceptance by other courts.

In recent years there has been an increasing number of challenges to the selection of text and library books. Somewhere in the United States, many of the literary works of importance in this century have been banned, according to a report from the American Library Association that appeared in the January 1975 issue of the *Phi Delta Kappan*. The books most often banned are Salinger's *Catcher in the Rye,* Steinbeck's *Grapes of Wrath,* and Vonnegut's *Slaughterhouse Five.* Among the other books that have been banned by schools somewhere are *Jonathan Livingston Seagull, Silas Marner, Moby Dick, Brave New World, 1984,* and *Fahrenheit 451.*

We do not find universal agreement on text and library book matters. Each state's court system will rule on complaints in the light of that particular state's statutes. In an attempt to prohibit the use of subversive textbooks in its schools, Section 118.03 (2) (1972) of the Wisconsin Statutes is specific in this instance and states: "No book shall be adopted for use or be used in any public school which falsifies the facts regarding the history of our nation, or which defames our nation's founders, or misrepresents the ideals and causes for which they struggled and sacrificed, or which contains propaganda favorable to any foreign government." Continued litigation with respect to text and library books seems likely. Boards of education and school administrators should consider, develop, and adopt policies governing the selection and review of complaints in this regard.

Tests have widespread uses in schools. Those tests that are used for placement of children are the subject of considerable litigation. Of concern to the courts are the outcomes that result from testing. Guidelines that schools should follow when administering tests that may discriminate against some of the children in their school are found in the Fifth Circuit Court of Appeals ruling in *U.S. v. Georgia Power Co.,* 474 F. 2d 906 (1973). First, the school must demonstrate that the test has separate validation scores for each minority group on which it is to be used. This is known as *differential validity.* It differs from *content validity*—the question of whether the test measures characteristics that are found among persons in a particular grouping—and *predictive validity*—the ability of scores on the test to relate highly to success in a school curriculum or on a job.

The second guideline deals with the level of confidence of the test. This should be at the 5 percent (0.05) level, meaning that the probability of obtaining the same test results through mere chance is no greater than one in twenty. The third guideline deals with statistical significance. Thus there should be a sample of sufficient size to be statistically significant. When given to a small group (sample) that may not be typical of a larger population, the results may be suspect and subject to being declared void. The fourth guideline requires that the test be administered to all testees under substantially similar circumstances as those pupils who were used in standardizing the test originally.

Grouping is a mode of operation in American schools; our economy precludes the ideal of one pupil per teacher. Thus it is incumbent upon each board of education to take the necessary steps to avoid discrimination and to assure that placement is fair at the same time that it is used as a matter of economical education. If that is done and if there are provisions for a periodic review of the policy, generally, the school district can withstand challenges to the testing and grouping system it employs.

In 1967 the grouping policies and practices in the Washington, D.C., school system were challenged. The charge was that the practices unconsitutionally deprived negro and other poor public schoolchildren of their rights to equal educational opportunity with majority and more affluent public schoolchildren. On the basis of examinations given early in the school career of each child, children were assigned to curricular tracks. There was no provision for compensatory education, and, once assigned to a track, it was difficult for a child to move to another track. In *Hobson v. Hansen,* 269 F. Supp. 401 (DC, 1967), the United States District Court found the concept used by the school system to be "undemocratic and discriminatory." The court thus barred the school system from using ability grouping that failed to include and implement a concept of compensatory education. On appeal, the United States Court of Appeals, D.C. Circuit, upheld the order that the track system of pupil classification be abandoned.

In *Larry P. v. Riles,* 343 F. Supp. 1306 (CA, 1972), *aff'd* 502 F. 2d 963 (1974), the Federal District Court for the Northern District of California on October 16, 1979, permanently enjoined the use of standardized intelligence tests in California for the purpose of identifying black schoolchildren for placement into classes for the educable mentally retarded (EMR). In its decision, the court noted that a clearly disproportionate number of black schoolchildren were represented in California's EMR classes. On the average, black schoolchildren made up 10 percent of the school-age population but represented 27 percent of the enrollment in EMR classes. The court's order enjoined the use of standardized I.Q. tests on black children for the purpose of determining EMR placement unless the court gives prior approval for the testing. Permission may be secured only if the defendants can demonstrate to the court's satisfaction that the test is not culturally or racially biased, that the test will be administered in a nondiscriminatory manner, and that the intended test has been determined to be reasonably accurate in its ability to diagnose mild mental retardation.

In *PASE v. Hannon,* 49 L.Wk. 2087 (1980), which is diametrically opposed to *Larry P. v. Riles,* Judge John Grady issued a 117-page decision in which he upheld the use of I.Q. tests, when used in conjunction with other criteria, for the placement of Illinois schoolchildren in special classes for the mentally handicapped. In acknowledging that the two children named in the suit were inappropriately placed, he said those mistakes were caused by misinterpretation of the tests, not their racial bias. He attributed differences in test scores between blacks and whites to differences in socioeconomic conditions, saying that "Plaintiffs' theory of cultural bias simply ignores the fact that black children perform differently from each other on the tests. It also fails to explain the fact that some black children perform better than most whites."

In *Peter W. Doe v. S.F. Unified School Dist.,* 131 Cal. 854 (1976), a high school graduate in San Francisco, who was graduated from high school with only a fifth-grade reading competency, sued the board of education for educational malpractice. An award of $1 million was sought. He charged that the district had failed to provide him with the basic academic skills and based his case on negligence and misrepresentation. In such a circumstance, with cause and effect very difficult to ascertain, both charges failed and the court found in favor of the school district.

The plaintiff in *Hunter v. Board of Education of Montgomery County,* 425 A. 2d 681 (1981), sued the board of education and three teachers for "educational malpractice," claiming that the defendants failed to teach him properly. The trial court held that the maintenance of such a suit would not be permitted in the state. On appeal, the trial court's decision was affirmed and the court said that public policy bars an action for educational malpractice. To allow such suits would require courts to sit in judgment not only of educational policies and matters entrusted by the legislature to each state department of education and to the LEAs, but also of day-to-day implementation of those policies as teachers function in their classrooms.

Handicapped Children

Title V of the Rehabilitation Act of 1973 reads "no otherwise qualified individual in the United States . . . shall, solely by reason of his handicap, be excluded from participation in, be denied the benefits of, or be subjected to discrimination under any program or activity receiving Federal financial assistance." Section 504, when added to Title VI of the Civil Rights Act of 1964 (which outlawed discrimination based on race) and Title IX of the Education Amendments of 1972 (which outlawed discrimination based upon sex), signaled a new era in protecting the rights of the handicapped.

The then Department of Health, Education, and Welfare, in promulgating guidelines for section 504, included these words:

Handicapped persons may require different treatment in order to be afforded equal access to federally assisted programs and activities and identical treatment may, in fact, constitute discrimination. The problem of establishing general rules as to when different treatment is prohibited or required is compounded by the diversity of existing handicaps and the differing degree to which particular persons may be affected.

The placement of children under Section 504 requires the board of education to defend its action in providing an education to the handicapped with proof that it was acting to fill a valid state purpose in its actions. Such proof should be demonstrable and rational. Mainstreaming or placement of a child in a segregated group of peers requires such a test. A school that receives federal financial assistance must ensure that no qualified handicapped individual is denied or excluded from participating in or benefiting from any program or activity because of inaccessibility of facilities. Furthermore, along with the Education for All Handicapped Children Act (P.L. 94-142) that was enacted in 1975, the federal government requires that to the maximum extent appropriate, handicapped children are educated with peers who are not handicapped and that only when the nature or severity of the handicap is such that education in the regular peer group cannot be achieved satisfactorily may special classes, separate schooling, or other removal of handicapped children from the regular school setting be permitted.

Under the terms of the Education for All Handicapped Children Act (EAHC) of 1975, funds to be used for special education flow from the federal government to the states. To receive these funds, each state was required to submit its plan for educating the handicapped to the federal government for approval. Each district must establish its plans for carrying out the provisions of EAHC (P.L. 94-142). Thus there does remain a modicum of local control, even though this must be consistent with the state plans and be subject to federal audit. Programmatically, this federal statute shifted responsibility away from the LEA; operational design and supervision remains with the local boards.

Parents, through the law's provisions, have the right to participate in the diagnosis, placement, education, and periodic reevaluation of their children. The provisions of the EAHC are specific and include the following rights for handicapped children:

1. The right to a free and *appropriate* public education if they are between the ages of three and twenty-one (effective September 1980)

2. The right to the same spread of programs and services, including nonacademic subjects and extracurricular activities, that are available to nonhandicapped children

3. The right to placement in the least restrictive learning environment, insofar as possible, with nonhandicapped children, and whenever possible, at the same school they would attend if they were not handicapped

4. The right to the availability of a number of alternative learning settings if attending a local public school is not possible

5. The right to have a person appointed to act as a surrogate parent, to be the child advocate, and to participate in meetings of the program and evaluation committees if the natural parents are unavailable or if the child is a ward of the state

6. The right to participate in the writing of their own Individual Education Program (IEP) where appropriate

7. The right to placement outside the local school district in another public or private school, at public expense, if local schools do not have an appropriate program

8. The right to testing for purposes of evaluation and placement that is free of racial or cultural discrimination

9. The right to an annual review of placement, based upon the IEP, and, at least, an annual review of that program before each school year begins and the right to review proposed changes in long-range and short-range program goals whenever this is appropriate

10. The right to remain in present placement during any administrative or judicial proceedings or the right to attend a public school if the complaint invokes an application for admission to public school

11. The right to privacy and confidentiality of all personal records

The school district is required to plan its program to meet the requirements of Section 504. Should there be discrepancies in the district model, the district should proceed first with remedial action to eliminate any violations with which it has been charged. Following that, the district should undertake voluntary action to eliminate any lack of accessibility to local programs by the handicapped. Finally, to carry out its full responsibilities, the district must establish and maintain a design that provides for continuous self-evaluation. To erase discrepancy, the district might consider a model that is closely allied to the scientific method. The steps in this model are determination of the need, setting of objectives, determination of the constraints that impact upon the objectives, development of alternatives, testing of the alternatives to determine "best fit," selection of the most appropriate alternative, implementation of the selected alternative, evaluation of the alternative, and feedback and modification, if necessary, of the alternative.

Pennsylvania Association for Retarded Children (PARC) v. Commonwealth, 334 F. Supp. 279 (PA, 1972)

GENERALIZATION

Children who are handicapped must be provided an educational opportunity, under the applicable statutes, that gives promise of enabling them to develop to the fullest possible extent.

DESCRIPTION

This case was brought as a class-action suit, seeking an order that public schools should place mentally retarded children in regular school classrooms to the greatest extent possible. It was contended that discrimination would be decreased in a mixed student setting.

Because of an absence of adequate resources, facilities and teachers as well as the lack of a structured plan, even those whom the State serves in its institutions (i.e., residential centers, hospitals, etc.) do not always benefit. For example, Dr. Edward R. Goldman, Commissioner of the Office of Mental Retardation, Department of Welfare, testified that there are presently 4,159 children of school age in state institutions. But only 100 of these children are in a full program of education and training; 1,700 are in partial but inadequate programs, and 3,259 are in no program of any kind. Moreover, the 1965 Pennsylvania Mental Retardation Plan reports that because of a lack of space, the State housed 900 mentally retarded persons at Dallas State Correction Institution, 3,462 at State mental hospitals and 104 in Youth Development Centers. And:

> Fewer than two percent of the residents of Pennsylvania's state schools leave the rolls each year; and half of those by death, rather than by discharge. A discharge rate of less than one percent has two implications: First, that beds are not opening up for persons in the community who need them; and second, that the state institutions continue to provide a program that barely rises above purely custodial care, if it rises at all.

Finally, the Report concluded:

> Nowhere is there a suitable commonwealth-supported local program for children of school age who are adjudged uneducable and untrainable by the public schools. Their normal fate is a waiting list for a state school and hospital, at which services do not conform to the spirit of the school code.

With these facts in mind, we turn to plaintiffs' equal protection argument. Plaintiffs do not challenge the separation of special classes for retarded children from regular classes or the proper assignment of retarded children to special classes. Rather, plaintiffs question whether the state, having undertaken to provide public education to some children (perhaps all children) may deny it to plaintiffs entirely. We are satisfied that the evidence raises serious doubts (and hence a colorable claim) as to the existence of a rational basis for such exclusions. See, e. g., Brown v. Board of Education, 349 U.S. 294, 75 S.Ct. 753, 99 L.Ed. 1083 (1955).

After examining evidence and declaring the state liable for whatever funds might be necessary to hire the extra personnel needed to raise the quality of education for handicapped children, the court pronounced a finding in which the obligations of the state to provide education for all handicapped children were ordered. Those obligations were stipulated in detail.

And now, this 5th day of May, 1972, it is ordered that the Amended Stipulation and Amended Consent Agreement are approved and adopted as fair and reasonable to all members of both the plaintiff and defendant classes.

It is further ordered that the defendants: the Commonwealth of Pennsylvania, the Secretary of the Department of Education, the State Board of Education, the Secretary of the Department of Public Welfare, the named defendant school districts and intermediate units and each of the school districts and intermediate units in the Commonwealth of Pennsylvania, their officers, employees, agents and successors are enjoined as follows:

(a) from applying Section 1304 of the Public School Code of 1949, 24 Purd. Stat. Sec. 1304, so as to postpone or in any way to deny any mentally retarded child access to a free public program of education and training;

(b) from applying Section 1326 or Section 1330(2) of the School Code of 1949, 24 Purd. Stat. Secs. 13-1326 and 13-1330(2) so as to postpone, to terminate or in any way deny to any mentally retarded child access to a free program of education and training;

(c) from applying Section 1371(1) of the School Code of 1949, 24 Purd. Stat. Sec. 13-1376, so as to deny tuition or tuition and maintenance to any mentally retarded person except on the same terms as may be applied to other exceptional children, including brain damaged children generally;

(e) from denying homebound instruction under 1372(3) of the School Code of 1949, 24 Purd. Stat. Sec. 13-1372(3) to any mentally retarded child merely because no physical disability accompanies the retardation or because retardation is not a short-term disability.;

(f) from applying Section 1375 of the School Code of 1949, 24 Purd. Stat. Sec. 13-1375, so as to deny to any mentally retarded child access to a free public program of education and training;

(g) to provide, as soon as possible but in no event later than September 1, 1972, to every retarded person between the ages of six and twenty-one years as of the date of this Order and thereafter, access to a free public program of education and training appropriate to his learning capacities;

(h) to provide, as soon as possible but in no event later than September 1, 1972, wherever defendants provide a preschool program of education and training for children aged less than six years of age, access to a free public program of education and training appropriate to his learning capacities to every mentally retarded child of the same age;

(i) to provide notice and the opportunity for a hearing prior to a change in educational status of any child who is mentally retarded or thought to be mentally retarded;

(j) to re-evaluate the educational assignment of every mentally retarded child not less than every two years, or annually upon the parents' request, and upon such re-evaluation, to provide notice and the opportunity for a hearing.

Litigation over handicapped children complaints is increasing as different kinds of programs are being examined in light of new legislation. In *Kruse v. Campbell,* 431 F. Supp. 180 (VA, 1977), the court held that a plan that picks up 75 percent of the cost of educating a handicapped child, leaving 25 percent for the parents to pay, discriminates against poor parents.

In *re Kirkpatrick*, 354 N.Y.S. 2d 499 (1972), the decision was that a school district may be financially liable for a handicapped child's education in a private institution even though the schools have a program that is otherwise suitable for a child with those handicaps.

In New Hampshire, *Doe v. Laconia Supv. Union No. 30,* 396 F. Supp. 1291 (1975), the state was challenged on its plan for allocating funds for the private education of the handicapped. The statutory requirement was for the state to pay any part of the tuition cost not paid by the local district. The state board of education lacked the funds to pay the costs of all programs. Thus the board established a priority list and funded the categories in that order. Under this system, no funds were available to fund the emotionally handicapped category. A student from that group charged denial of equal protection. The court disagreed with the action of the local board and said that the state was fulfilling a valid state purpose and need not consider the financial need of every LEA when meting out the state's benefits.

Shall the LEA provide an education beyond the length of the normal school year for handicapped children? In *Georgia Association of Retarded Citizens v. McDaniel,* 511 F. Supp. 1236 (1981), the court held that implicit in P.L. 94-142 and in Section 504 of the Vocational Rehabilitation Act of 1973 was the requirement that an education in excess of 180 days must be provided where it is determined by the IEP committee that it is necessary to meet unique needs of the child and that the policies and practices of the local and state board effectively limit the school year to 180 days in violation of these two acts; and that IEP committees from now on must be mindful of the law's requirements. Ironically, the court held, furthermore, that the plaintiffs had not carried their burden of proof in showing that a year-round program of education or any education in excess of 180 days was necessary for these particular children. In so ruling, the court denied the requested injunction for such a program. This case turned on the fact that the IEP committee, despite the objections of the parent, determined that an extended educational program was unnecessary in this instance. Even so, it seems clear that an entitlement for an extended school year is present in existing statutes and can be a part of any IEP if the professionals who develop that plan specify it as a necessary part.

Student Control

Questions over how schools can control student behavior continue to provide sources of litigation. The reasonableness of student searches on school premises is one such issue. The courts continue to use a lower standard when searches are performed by school personnel than for searches by law-enforcement personnel outside the school premises. A recent case has received considerable publicity. In *Doe v. Renfrow*, 475 F. Supp. 1012 (IN, 1979), an Indiana Federal Court upheld the use of dogs in a classroom as a means for detecting the presence of drugs on students and in their possessions. The plaintiff argued that her Fourth Amendment rights were violated through the use of the dogs and the search of her pockets and person. The court ruled that the use of the dogs, per se, did not constitute an unreasonable search, nor did the holding of students in their homerooms for one and one-half hours constitute a mass detention in violation of the Fourth Amendment. The court reasoned that the use of dogs was undertaken in accordance with the *in loco parentis* doctrine, and since the school officials had substantial evidence that the use of drugs had increased substantially before the search, there was reasonable cause to believe that school rules had been violated.

However, the judge did note that the searches undertaken that day were only for the purpose of determining violations of school rules. No criminal charges were filed, through a previous agreement with the participating police officers. The school district did mete out as penalties suspensions and expulsions from school, but no issues were raised in the case relative to the appropriateness or severity of these penalties. On the other hand, had criminal charges been filed, the "court's reasoning and conclusion may well have been different . . . the school may well have had to satisfy a standard of probable cause rather than reasonable cause to believe" that drugs might be found.

With respect to the nude search of the student following the dog alert, the court ruled that the search was unreasonable under the lesser standard of reasonable cause applied in the case. To make such a search permissible, there needed to be evidence that the student, in fact, did possess contraband. The court, in relying upon *Bellnier v. Lund,* 485 F. Supp. 47 (NY, 1977), noted that in determining reasonableness of the search, the following factors were important: the student's age, the student's history and record in school, the seriousness and prevalence of the problem to which the search is directed, and the exigency requiring an immediate warrantless search. The court could find nothing in the student's record that supported the reasonableness of this nude search. The court did, however, find that the school officials had acted in good faith and with a regard for the welfare and health of the plaintiff and, then, held the defendant school officials to be immune from liability in the case.

Locker searches require a lesser burden of reasonable cause than do searches of a student's person or effects. Lockers belong to the school and are merely loaned to the student, and this should be made clear in all communications to students. The courts do agree, generally, that a student can claim privacy in his locker with respect to other students but not against school officials. In meeting the test of providing a safe place, the principal has the right, even the duty, to search lockers for contraband so that the safety of the students might be protected. This right becomes a duty when there is a suspicion that contraband may be deposited in a locker.

The case *State v. Stein,* 456 P. 2d 1 (1969), *cert. denied,* 90 U.S. 966 (1970), dealt with a burglary. On the day following a burglary at a coin shop, two police officers appeared in the principal's office of this Kansas school and requested that the locker of a certain boy—a student at the high school—be opened. The boy consented to the opening of the locker. The principal opened the locker and found a key to a locker at the bus depot. The police officers, armed with a search warrant, searched the bus depot locker and found some of the stolen coins. As a result, the boy was found guilty of burglary. In upholding the conviction, the court held that the principal acted properly in searching the locker and, also, was not required to give a *Miranda*-type warning of citizen rights to the student in doing so.

The presence of student-operated vehicles on school property may bring them under the authority of the school official. It would appear that the best course of action by a principal who suspects that articles of a dangerous nature are concealed in a car would be to notify the police. Absent a search warrant, there is some doubt that the principal could search the car unless contraband was in plain sight or he had *probable* cause to suspect that the vehicle was being used for illegal purposes.

Boards of education and administrators should develop and put into effect policies governing warrantless searches. Specifically, such searches should not occur unless the administrator has a *reasonable* basis for believing that illegal contraband is secreted in a locker or unless the student has freely consented in writing to such a search. If a reasonable basis for a search does not exist, then consent must be obtained from individual students for each search. Thus such a policy should provide adequate authority to the school officials to keep dangerous contraband out of the school while, at the same time, giving students a small, secure place of privacy from peers that ought to be each citizen's right.

In order that teachers may teach and an appropriate environment be provided for learning, students in school are expected to conduct themselves in a manner that will not infringe upon the rights of others by creating distractions in the classroom. Educators do have considerable latitude in controlling student behavior. A legal term that defines the relationship of educator to pupil is *in loco parentis* ("in place of the parent"). Sir William Blackstone in his *Commentaries* explained it thus:

A parent may also delegate part of his parental authority, during his life, to the tutor or schoolmaster of his child; who is then *in loco parentis,* and has such a portion of the power of the parents *viz.* that of restraint and correction as may be necessary to answer the purposes for which he is employed.

Since Blackstone developed that definition, there has been much modification of the concept of *in loco parentis.* No longer can school authorities make arbitrary decisions about pupil behavior and discipline without facing some challenges. The courts have set conditions that boards of education must meet if they expect to have upheld their actions designed to control student behavior.

Corporal punishment in schools is the infliction of physical pain upon a student for his or her misconduct. The statutes of the particular states deal with this matter in unique ways. Some states authorize it, some states forbid it, and other states do not mention it but by implication authorize or allow it. New Jersey and Massachusetts forbid it by statute, and Maryland forbids it by a policy of its state board of education.

New York permits a teacher to administer corporal punishment unless there are local board regulations prohibiting it, that is, LEAs have the option. Corporal punishment as a means of discipline, however, must be reasonable in manner and moderate in degree (35.10—NY Penal Law). Under Section 3028 of the Education Law, all school boards must provide legal services and pay the fees and expenses where civil or criminal action is brought against a teacher based on disciplinary action taken against any pupil of the district while the teacher was in the discharge of his duties within the scope of his employment. This law does not require the board of education to pay a teacher's fine, should any such judgment come as a result of a verdict.

Section 380.1312 of the Michigan School Laws provides that:

(1) A teacher or superintendent may use reasonable physical force necessary to take possession of a dangerous weapon carried by a pupil, (2) A teacher or superintendent may use reasonable physical force on the person of a pupil necessary

for the purpose of maintaining proper discipline over pupils in attendance at school, and (3) a teacher or superintendent shall not be liable in a civil action for the use of physical force on the person of a pupil for the purposes prescribed in this section, except in case of gross abuse and disregard for the health and safety of the pupil.

The Code of Georgia is much more specific and provides as follows: Section 32-835, *Corporal punishment of students:* "All area, county, and independent boards of education shall be authorized to determine and adopt policies and regulations relating to the use of corporal punishment by principals and teachers employed by such area, county and independent boards." Section 32-836 provides the method of administering the punishment. It is quoted in its entirety to illustrate the procedural requirements of the law typically found in many other states. These requirements are the issues upon which cases have been tried.

Where so authorized, upon the adoption of *written policies, by an area, county or independent board of education* [emphasis supplied]; any principal or teacher employed by the board, in order to maintain proper control and discipline over pupils placed under his care and supervision, may, in the exercise of his sound discretion, administer corporal punishment on any such pupil or pupils, subject to the following requirement:

a. The corporal punishment shall not be excessive or unduly severe.

b. Corporal punishment shall never be used as a first line of punishment for misbehavior unless the pupil was informed beforehand that specific misbehavior could occasion its use; provided, however, that corporal punishment may be employed as a first line of punishment for those acts of misconduct which are so antisocial or disruptive in nature as to shock the conscience.

c. Corporal punishment must be administered in the presence of a principal, or assistant principal, or the designee of the principal or assistant principal, employed by the board of education authorizing such punishment, and the other principal or assistant principal, or the designee of the principal or assistant principal, must be informed beforehand in the presence of the pupil of the reason for the punishment.

d. The principal or teacher who administered corporal punishment must provide a written explanation of the reasons for the punishment and the name of the principal or assistant principal, or designee of the principal or assistant principal, who was present; provided however that such an explanation shall not be used as evidence in any subsequent civil action brought as a result of said corporal punishment.

e. Corporal punishment shall not be administered to a child whose parents or legal guardian have upon the day of enrollment of the pupil filed with the principal of the school a statement from a medical doctor licensed in Georgia stating that it is detrimental to the child's mental or emotional stability.

Section 32-837 provides for exemptions from legal action for principals and teachers who administer corporal punishment to a pupil or pupils under his or her care and supervision when that is in conformity with the policies and regulations of the area, county, or independent board of education employing him, and where the corporal punishment is administered in good faith and is not excessively severe.

In *Baker v. Owen,* 395 F. Supp. 294, *aff'd mem.* 423 U.S. 907 (1975), the court held that as long as the child knows beforehand what misconduct will result in physical punishment and is told why he or she is being punished, school officials may corporally punish pupils in the absence of a state law to the contrary. In addition, the court set forth generally the requirements that are expressed in Section 32-836 of the Georgia Code, above. The court held, furthermore, that the parent may not veto corporal punishment for his own child.

The second case, *Ingraham v. Wright,* 430 U.S. 651, 711 (1977), dealt with cruel and unusual punishment. In this instance, Ingraham was sent to the office to receive "licks," but he refused to assume the "paddling position." After this, two assistant principals held him over a desk while the principal administered twenty "licks" with a wooden board. As a result, Ingraham was severely bruised, suffered a hematoma, and required compresses, laxatives, sleeping pills, pain pills, ten days of rest, and suffered discomfort for three weeks.

In its *Ingraham* finding, the court held that the Eighth Amendment's prohibition of cruel and unusual punishment applies to criminals only and does not apply to children in school. Even though there may be a charge that the corporal punishment is cruel and unusual and even excessive, the proper relief should be sought in a state court under a charge of assault and battery.

Through the years, the courts have spelled out some general guidelines as to what constitutes *reasonable* corporal punishment. Generally, they are:

1. *It is consistent with the existing statutes.* Where corporal punishment is authorized by the statutes, and where boards of education have policies that are in compliance with the statute, or where corporal punishment is allowed by the statutes, the courts will—as a general rule—hold in favor of the board of education and its employees.

2. *It is a corrective remedy for undesirable behavior.* Occasionally, the teacher, like the parent, will need to resort to corporal punishment as the last means of correcting a child's errant behavior.

3. *It is neither cruel nor excessive.* The courts will weigh the evidence to determine if, in the face of the facts, the punishment was

excessive—not reasonably believed at the time to be necessary for the child's discipline or training. If it is found to be excessive, the school authorities who inflicted it may be held liable in damages to the child and, if malice is shown, they may be subject to criminal penalties.

4. *There is no permanent or lasting injury.* The implication here is that there may be a temporary injury that is insufficient to bring a finding against the school official.

5. *Malice is not present.* It is a standard rule of thumb that no punishment should be administered in a fit of anger on the part of the teacher or principal. Revenge is not a valid reason for administering corporal punishment.

6. *The punishment is suitable for the age and sex of the child.* The standard to be applied here is one of reasonableness.

7. *An appropriate instrument is used.* The courts will consider the appropriateness of the instrument when given the evidence in the case. Among the various types of instruments that have been considered to be reasonable are a wooden paddle and a twelve-inch ruler. The questionable factor is not the instrument used so much as the portion of the anatomy that is struck, the degree to which the instrument is used, and the end result of the corporal punishment.

We come now to an area that has received considerable attention since the decision in *Dixon v. Alabama State Board of Education,* 294 F. 2d 150 (1961), *cert. denied* 368 U.S. 930 (1961). This matter resided in the realm of higher education and centered around the expulsion or placing on probation of students for a sit-in at a lunch counter. These students were disciplined without any *notice* of charges and were not granted a *hearing.* The rights of notice and hearing are guaranteed and protected by the due process clause of the Fourteenth Amendment. Under the provisions of this amendment, a student is entitled to the names of witnesses against him, an oral or written report on the facts to which each witness testified, an opportunity to defend himself against the charges that have been filed, and an opportunity to call witnesses on his behalf.

Although *Dixon* dealt with students in the higher education area, it was not until the 1967 landmark case *In re Gault,* 387 U.S. (1967), that the applicability to the elementary- and secondary-age levels was clarified. When this case was decided, the Supreme Court held that a minor in juvenile court was entitled to the following protection under the Constitution: specific notice of the charges against him with time to prepare for a hearing; notification of the right to counsel or, if counsel cannot be afforded, the right to court-appointed counsel; privilege against self-incrimination; and right to confrontation and cross-examination of witnesses. The Supreme Court clarified the rights of children in exclusionary hearings.

Goss v. Lopez, 419 U.S. 565 (1975)

GENERALIZATION

Even in short-term suspensions, that is, less than ten days, a pupil is entitled to the rudiments of due process procedure: notice of charges against the student, an opportunity for denial, a statement of evidence school authorities possess, an opportunity to present the student version of the incident. All procedure should be accomplished as soon after the incident as is possible.

DESCRIPTION

A disruption of substantial dimensions occurred in the Columbus Public Schools. Several offending students were identified by school administrators and suspended in accordance with Ohio law. Although that state mandated free public education, ages six to sixteen, other statutes empowered school principals to suspend pupils for up to ten days in situations of misconduct. Different students seemed to get justice at different levels of sophistication.

Rudolph Sutton, in the presence of the principal, physically attacked a police officer who was attempting to remove Tyrone Washington from the auditorium. He was immediately suspended. The other four Marion-Franklin students were suspended for similar conduct. None was given a hearing to determine the operative facts underlying the suspension, but each, together with his or her parents, was offered the opportunity to attend a conference, subsequent to the effective date of the suspension, to discuss the students' future.

Two named plaintiffs, Dwight Lopez and Betty Crome, were students at the Central High School and McGuffey Junior High School, respectively. The former was suspended in connection with a disturbance in the lunchroom which involved some physical damage to school property. Lopez testified that at least 75 other students were suspended from his school on the same day. He also testified below that he was not a party to the destructive conduct but was instead an innocent bystander. Because no one from the school testified with regard to this incident, there is no evidence in the record indicating the official basis for concluding otherwise. Lopez never had a hearing.

Betty Crome was present at a demonstration at a high school other than the one she was attending. There she was arrested together with others, taken to the police station, and released, without being formally charged. Before she went to school on the following day, she was notified that she had been suspended for a 10-day period.

Because no one from the school testified with respect to this incident, the record does not disclose how the McGuffey Junior High School principal went about making the decision to suspend Crome, nor does it disclose on what information the decision was based. It is clear from the record that no hearing was ever held. . . .

On the basis of this evidence, the three-judge court declared that plaintiffs were denied due process of law because they were "suspended without hearing prior to suspension or within a reasonable time thereafter," and that Ohio Rev. Code . . . and regulations issued pursuant thereto were unconstitutional in permitting such suspensions. It was ordered that all references to plaintiffs' suspensions be removed from school files.

We stop short of construing the Due Process Clause to require, countrywide, that hearings in connection with short suspensions must afford the student the opportunity to secure counsel, to confront and cross-examine witnesses supporting the charge, or to call his own witnesses to verify his version of the incident. Brief disciplinary suspensions are almost countless. To impose in each such case even truncated trial-type procedures might well overwhelm administrative facilities in many places and, by diverting resources, cost more than it would save in educational effectiveness. Moreover, further formalizing the suspension process and escalating its formality and adversary nature may not only make it too costly as a regular disciplinary tool but also destroy its effectiveness as part of the teaching process.

Since suspension is normally defined as a temporary exclusion, not to exceed ten days from school, the Court held that the student must be given at least an informal notice of the charges against him or her and the opportunity for at least an informal hearing. (This process could occur as the teacher is escorting an obstreperous student from the room.) If the student denies the charges, the student must hear the evidence and be given an opportunity to respond to it and tell his or her side of the story.

In this instance the court ruled that the student does have a property right—which is protected by the Fourteenth Amendment—to an education. Thus if that right is to be removed, it can be done only through the application of procedural due process. (It should be noted, here, that there are two types of due process: *substantive,* which deals with the rights and authority of boards of education to act; and *procedural,* which refers to the process, or manner, in which due process is applied.) In school suspensions, due process can be flexible and its flexibility is determined by the nature of the transgression and the severity of the penalty that is assessed. It stands to reason, therefore, that the more serious the misconduct and the stricter the penalty, the higher the standard of due process that must be applied.

Expulsion is a much more severe punishment than is suspension and thus requires substantial due process before the actual expulsion can be carried out. Expulsion connotes exclusion from school for a period in excess of ten days and may go so far as to be permanent for the semester or school year.

A decision with a different twist but still dealing with expulsion was handed down in *Wood v. Strickland,* 420 U.S. 308 (1975). Two sophomore girls in the Mena, Arkansas, school brought suit against the board and the school district, including the superintendent, because they were expelled for spiking the punch at a school function in contravention of a board rule forbidding the use "of any intoxicating beverage" at such affairs. Although the board of education never really established that the students either possessed or used an "intoxicating" beverage, they did admit to the act, and the board expelled the girls for three months. The Court held that such a lack of evidence, and such precipitous action by the board of education in expelling the girls, amounted to a denial of their rights to due process of law. The decision in this case addressed the degree of immunity individual board of education members enjoy in the total conduct of their official duties and also to the standard of conduct that board members must meet in carrying out their official duties. In the language of the Court, the individual board of education member, to escape personal liability for violating the Constitutional rights of students or employees,

must himself be acting sincerely and with a belief that he is doing right, but *an act violating a student's constitutional rights can be no more justified by ignorance or disregard of settled, indisputable law on the part of one entrusted with supervision of students' daily lives than by the presence of actual malice.* To be entitled to a special exemption from the categorical remedial language of Sec. 1983 in a case in which the action violated a student's constitutional rights, a school board member, who has voluntarily undertaken the task of supervising the operation of the schools and the activities of the students, *must be held to a standard of conduct based not only on permissible intentions, but also on knowledge of the basic, unquestioned constitutional rights of his charges.* Such a standard neither imposes an unfair burden upon a person assuming a responsible public office requiring a high degree of intelligence and judgment for the proper fulfillment of its duties, nor an unwarranted burden in light of the value which civil rights have in our legal system. Any lesser standard would deny much of the promise of 1983 of the civil rights act.

Thus any individual board of education member who knows, *or should have known* in the eyes of a federal court, that he or she is violating the Constitutional rights of a student or employee may be held personally liable for such actions. This is known as the *knowledge-malice test.*

Fully developed and implemented, there are ten steps that must be followed in procedural due process. Some schemes portray more than ten, but these ten steps are a comprehensive pattern for procedural due process. It is imperative that school officials pay close attention to following these steps if they are to avoid losing cases because of defective procedures. Although requirements may vary from state to state and may vary according to the circumstances in a given situation, the following standards will, generally, apply and be sufficient:

    1. *Notice of Charges.* A statement of the violation, that is, notice of charges, must be given to the student. This notice may be oral if

there is no question or disagreement about the student clearly having been involved in the misconduct. Where a higher standard of due process is required, written notice is not only preferred but is essential. Such notice should state the specific charges against the student, school policy or rule that was broken, and date, time, and place of the hearing, at the student's choice. The student may waive the hearing and have an informal conference with the principal to dispose of the matter.

2. *Right to Counsel.* Although the courts are divided on whether or not the student is entitled to have counsel, it is common practice that whenever there is a hearing, the accused has the right to be represented. Some students of due process accept representation by parents to be sufficient where a lesser standard is required, that is, for a suspension in contrast to an expulsion. Absent a ruling to the contrary, representation by counsel may be permitted at a hearing.

3. *Right to a Hearing Before an Impartial Tribunal.* In this instance the hearing officer must not be involved in the situation. In larger school districts, usually, there is a permanent hearing officer who has been appointed by the board of education. Where the board of education is to be the hearing tribunal, care must be taken not to destroy its impartial status by briefing the board on the issues before the case is heard.

4. *The Individual Has the Right to Avoid Self-Incrimination.* The Fifth Amendment protection against self-incrimination does not apply to school disciplinary proceedings, it applies only to criminal proceedings. But if the testimony given by a student in a school disciplinary hearing is used later in a criminal proceeding, the student may then object to the use of statements made at the school hearing. The concept of double jeopardy is not applicable where school officials discipline a student for breaking a school rule, and the individual may then be tried for the same offense in a court of law. In a civil suit the jury may draw inferences from a refusal to testify.

5. *Evidence Must Be Presented Against the Accused.* It should be noted that the formal rules of evidence that govern a court trial do not apply in an exclusionary hearing. This was affirmed in *Boykins v. Fairfield Board of Education,* 492 F. 2d 697 (5th Cir., 1974), *cert. denied* 420 U.S. 962 (1975). However, before exclusion of students, a student should have the opportunity to examine the evidence against him, question the hearing officer, and refute the testimony of witnesses. Only when it can be determined that the charges are supportable by substantial evidence or guilt *beyond a reasonable doubt* should one be

declared guilty of the charges. That standard requires a higher degree of proof than the lesser one of circumstantial evidence or the preponderance of the evidence.

6. *The Accused Has the Right to Cross-Examine the Witnesses.* An element of due process is the right of the accused to cross-examine the witnesses. Although there is not full agreement in this respect, when in doubt, this right should be accorded any individual who is in danger of being excluded from attendance upon instruction. This right implies that an administrator may no longer take as an accepted or unquestioned fact the statement of a person reporting a student for violation of a school rule or regulation—especially, if the accused denies the accusation.

7. *Witnesses Are Compelled to Testify.* Recently, court decisions, for example, *Givens v. Poe,* 346 F. Supp. 202 (NC, 1972), have held that the right of a student to confront and cross-examine witnesses is fundamental. It is not universal that boards of education have the power of subpoena. In the few states where this power is present, witnesses are compelled to testify.

8. *There Is a Standard (Burden) of Proof on the Part of the Accused.* In criminal cases this standard is higher, and proof must be beyond a reasonable shadow of a doubt. This, too, is applicable in a hearing that may lead to the exclusion of a student from school. In civil cases a lesser standard is applied, and the proof may be by preponderance of the evidence.

9. *A Record of the Hearings Must Be Kept.* If there is to be any appeal from the decision of the hearing officer or board, it is essential that a record be kept. Although the courts are not in agreement about whether a student, as a matter of right, is entitled to a transcript of the proceedings, it would appear that the full provision of procedural due process would require this. Thus it would seem to be appropriate to provide the student with a transcript at his expense.

10. *The Accused Has the Right to Appeal.* In any hearing, full procedural due process requires that some procedure or mechanism be made available to the accused to appeal an adverse decision. In the case of a student, this may involve a series of steps terminating with the state department of education. In recent years students have chosen to go directly to the courts. Some courts have refused to hear such cases until the student has exhausted all administrative remedies. More recently, with increased frequency, students have resorted to federal rather than state courts and have argued for a reversal on the basis of a denial of due process under the Fourteenth Amendment.

Throughout the discussion of these several aspects of due process rights, two key elements—fairness and reasonableness—have been stressed. When boards of education and administrators have applied them, the courts have usually upheld them. Where these elements have been absent, the students have often been upheld.

With the passage of Public Law 93-380, The Family Educational Rights and Privacy Act, parents and students over eighteen years of age could no longer be denied access to the *complete* educational record of the student. Furthermore, P.L. 93-380 denied unauthorized third parties access to these records and imposed strict standards upon schools for the handling of student records.

What, then, constitutes a record? We should expect to see directory information, including student name, address, date and place of birth, dates of attendance, major and minor fields of study, and awards received, plus the academic record. In addition, there may be comments and descriptive evaluations of student personality, student discipline, student interests, and student attitudes.

Two categories of complaints relative to student records have arisen. The first deals with the access to confidential information by unauthorized third parties; the second charges that information contained in the record is unwarranted or that it is false and irrelevant. Usually, the latter complaint involves charges of defamation, and the complainant may seek damage awards.

It should be noted that despite increased statutory protection of student records by limiting access and by forbidding scrutiny to unauthorized third parties, school records are still open to inspection by persons who "have the right to know" what is contained in the record. School professional personnel do have protection available and are excused from liability when the statements made about the pupil are reasonable and true. Nonetheless, to avoid charges of defamation, certain precautions should be taken by school professional personnel.

1. Be certain that all statements made about a student and all evaluations of students are made by individuals whose professional status permits and may require such statements and/or evaluations.

2. Separate fact from fiction before placing a statement about a student in the record. Be objective.

3. Document the source and circumstance of each comment and evaluation.

4. Be able to demonstrate the direct connection between the statement or evaluation and the educational need and development of the student.

5. When in doubt about the need to record a particular bit of information in a student's record (other than those required to be kept), do not record that information.

Remember that the real purpose for which the schools exist is to educate young people. Records are a part of that process and material included in the record should be placed there to help students develop their educational potential.

Once information is recorded in a student's file, who shall decide what can be purged from that record? The principal has the ultimate responsibility for all things that occur in the school building. This includes student record keeping. Although this has been assumed to be the role of the principal in the past, currently, most laws, rules, and regulations require that a professional person in each school building be designated as the official custodian of the records.

Outdated, irrelevant, and inaccurate data should be removed from student records. Accordingly, it is the responsibility of school officials to subject such records to continuous examination and scrutiny. Parents (and students, where legally permissible) must be given opportunities to purge the child's school record.

To purge or expunge an item from the record is to remove, strike, or erase the item completely from the record. When the parent (or student) has required that an item be purged, and when the school officials have, with a valid reason, denied this request, and when all avenues of appeal have failed, the parent or student may place a statement of their position in the record.

Board of education policy statements on student records are one of the best guarantees of due process—both substantive and procedural—in this matter. Statutes on retention and destruction of records, records management, and requirements concerning retention/destruction vary from state to state. In several jurisdictions these decisions are left to local school districts. Generally, the entire student record is kept for a period, usually five years, following the student's graduation. After that time the academic record, dates of attendance, and directory information—including verification of birth—are retained (often on microfilm) as permanent records.

* * *

Schools exist for the purpose of educating the children within the community. Thus the several states have enacted statutes that grant the right and stipulate the requirement that children attend instruction. In that context, then, the administration of student personnel has a number of legal issues and implications that must be addressed. In recent years, the school administrator has been called upon to serve as a student advocate. There are times when this role has placed the administrator in an adversarial relationship with the board of education. A new, delicate balance has come to be a part of school administration.

Early, in the 1925 decision of *Pierce,* the U.S. Supreme Court ruled that students could comply with the compulsory-attendance law by attending private or public schools. The usual age requirement for compulsory attendance is from the child's sixth to sixteenth birthday, although this may vary in some states. An exception to the compulsory-attendance law was found in *Yoder,* wherein Amish children were not required to attend school beyond the eighth grade. The question of equivalent instruction was addressed by the Washington Supreme Court, which held that home instruction did not satisfy the compulsory attendance law. A few other cases have found to the contrary. Eligibility to attend tuition-free the schools of a public school district is extended to school-age youth who are residents of the district.

Instruction of pupils is determined by state statutes, state boards of education, and local boards of education. Courses of study are assumed to be in the public interest, and where the state board of education has mandated certain courses, the local board of education must comply with the mandate. The curriculum includes more than the usual academic subjects, that is, organized sports are often considered to be part of the curriculum. On the question of whether a state athletic or activities association may prescribe rules that are counter to LEA policies, rules, and regulations, a prevailing opinion is that a board of education cannot delegate its powers in this respect.

Local boards have the authority to determine the grade levels to be maintained in the school district. Boards of education, operating within statutory and constitutional requirements and limitations, shall determine what grades and schools are to be operated within the system. Each LEA possesses the authority to determine instructional levels and assignment of pupils to grades and classes. Generally, courts have held against the use of marks and grades for disciplinary purposes. Although boards may prescribe reasonable graduation requirements, they may not deny diplomas to students who have earned them. Participation in graduation exercises is controlled by the local board of education.

The LEA has the authority and the professional staff has the function to determine the proper mode of instruction for the students. Defining *curriculum* in a narrow context would indicate that the term applies only to courses that are given regularly for credit; in a broader context we would include all life experiences that are provided by the school. Local boards of education possess implied delegated powers to offer courses beyond those required by the state. Selection of textbooks, library books, and supplementary materials must be pursuant to statutes. There is no question about the legal right of the state to prescribe textbooks or, through statutory enactment, delegate that responsibility to local boards of education. There is not universal agreement in either statutory or case law on text and library book matters. We foresee continued litigation with respect to these books that are, in the eyes of some patrons, perceived as controversial or offensive.

Tests have widespread uses in schools. Those tests that are used for placement of children are the subject of considerable litigation. Four guidelines were stated in a Fifth Circuit Court of Appeals ruling. They required separate validation scores, the level of confidence of the test, statistical significance, and the administration of the test. Grouping, through the use of tests, has been the subject of a number of court tests. In one, ability grouping was found to be "undemocratic and discriminating"; in another, the court enjoined the use of standardized I.Q. tests on black children for the purpose of EMR placement; and in still another, the court approved the use of I.Q. tests, in conjunction with other criteria, for placement of children in special classes for mentally handicapped. Such judicial uncertainty tends to stimulate patrons to raise questions, and "malpractice" suits are beginning to emerge. Uniformly, courts have held in favor of the defendant boards of education.

Handicapped children are the subjects of recently enacted statutes and their accompanying regulations. The Education of All Handicapped Children Act (P.L. 94-142) spells out specific provisions guaranteeing certain rights for handicapped children. Mainstreaming is a means whereby handicapped students may attend upon instruction in the company of their nonhandicapped peers when possible. Litigation over handicapped children complaints is increasing. Finance continues to be a main consideration in the litigation. The question of whether a school district shall provide an education beyond the normal length of the school year for handicapped children was decided recently by establishing such a requirement if the IEP committee determines that it is necessary to meet the unique needs of the child.

Where school officials determine that there is substantial evidence of contraband being present, a search—including the use of dogs—may be conducted. Locker searches require a lesser burden of reasonable cause than do searches of a student's person or effects. Boards should develop and put into effect policies governing warrantless searches.

Educators have considerable latitude in controlling student behavior. There has been much modification of the *in loco parentis* doctrine. Corporal punishment has been the subject of considerable litigation. Two states, Massachusetts and New Jersey, prohibit corporal punishment by law. The Maryland state board of education prohibits, by regulation, the use of corporal punishment. Where permitted, boards of education should adopt and implement policies that are consistent with the state statutes. General guidelines about what constitutes *reasonable* corporal punishment require that it is consistent with the existing statutes, it is a corrective remedy for undesirable behavior, it is neither cruel nor excessive, there is no permanent or lasting injury, malice is not present, the punishment is suitable for the age and sex of the child, and an appropriate instrument is used.

Due process consists of two types—substantive and procedural. In a suspension (short-term exclusion) proceeding, a lesser standard is applied and consists of three requirements before suspension may be decreed: oral or written notice of the charges, an explanation of the evidence if the student denies the charges, and some kind of hearing that includes an opportunity to present the student's view of the incident. Expulsion (long-term or permanent exclusion) requires a much higher standard and due process, in this instance, consists of the following steps: notice of charges; right to counsel; right to a hearing before an impartial tribunal; right to avoid self-incrimination; evidence presented against you, if you are the accused; right to cross-examine the witnesses; compulsion of witnesses to testify; standard (burden) of proof on the part of the accuser; record kept of the hearing; and right to appeal. Throughout due process, two elements—reasonableness and fairness—must be present.

Records and record management have been the subject of increased litigation since the passage of Public Law 93-380, The Family Educational Rights and Privacy Act, also called the Buckley Amendment. Complaints concern access to confidential information by unauthorized third parties and false and irrelevant information being contained in the file. Records are a part of the educative process and material placed in the records should be there to help students develop their educational potential. Outdated, irrelevant, and inaccurate data should be removed from student records. Policy statements on student records are one of the best guarantees of due process—both substantive and procedural.

chapter 8

DISCRIMINATION AND EQUALITY OF OPPORTUNITY

Some Concepts of Equality

Discrimination involves choice—one thing or one person is chosen over another; one is selected while another is ignored; preference for one is accorded over another. Discrimination has come to have a socially and morally offensive connotation only recently, since adjectives have been attached indicating an unjustifiable discrimination or invidious discrimination. When some individuals or institutions in society act toward others of that society with bias, prejudice, malice, or hostility, an invidious discrimination is being practiced. For the past two to three decades, Americans have been at work identifying groups that have been victims of unjust discrimination and providing some remedies for those unjust actions.

Equality among the citizens of a society is a concept that was stated magnificently by Thomas Jefferson when he said, "We hold these truths to be self-evident; that all [people] are created equal." That is a reasonable starting point from which to try to grasp the meaning of *equality* in America. It is a word that has various meanings, and different aspects of the word are embraced as the whole truth by different segments of the American citizenry. In fact, it is a slippery concept, difficult to grasp, and if it is generally accepted as a minimum political birthright, it raises a whole host of new questions for the society conferring those rights of political equality on all citizens. No one has yet seriously argued that it means economic, psychological, or physiological equality, although some of those concepts can be seen in both statutory law and case law of the present. Surely, equality cannot prevail in an environment that allows discrimination. Upon recognizing and acknowledging the existence of discrimination, the continuing American move toward perfecting the ideal of equality demands conscious effort to eliminate social inequalities wherever they exist in society. Much of the effort expended over the past few decades to eradicate discrimination has involved the public schools. Initially concerned with racial discrimination, that focus has been enlarged to include discrimination on the basis of sex and several additional categories. Students and staff have been the objects of antidiscrimination efforts in schools.

When equality is accepted as a base for political opportunity, it means one thing. When accepted as a base for economic opportunity, it means something else. When accepted by one population segment to mean one thing and by another to mean something else, conflict is inevitable. In the American system where substantial liberties are guaranteed in law to individuals, equality cannot relate to effort or results. That is, equalized opportunity may be embraced at very different levels of effort, and rewards may be sharply unequal. An additional complication is that individual abilities are unequal—by a variety of measurements. Is it any wonder then that the concept of equality leads to unrealistic expectations, given the tensions and restrictions of opportunities in American society? It is a concept that can be more easily stated on paper than legislated and practiced in society.

For many Americans the disparity that occurs between expectations and socioeconomic positions is a reality contradiction, to some extent, of the whole notion of equality. But the facts of reality must include the characteristic of free American competition. The personnel marketplace responds to achievement; the payoff is for achievement as it is perceived to be valuable. Earnings may be spent without restriction. Some Americans earn and acquire; some do not. From an economic vantage point, inequality is surely as much the rule as is equality. It is an irrevocable irony resulting from the capitalistic system blended with the very substantial political liberties that are uniquely American.

The concepts embodied in equality gained a statutory voice immediately after the Civil War. It was the intent of Congress in the Civil Rights Act of 1871 to provide safeguards for those American black freedmen, who only a few years previously had been slaves. Section 1983 of that act is the least restrictive federal statute for rectifying violations of federally protected rights. Nearly one hundred years elapsed before the civil rights concept again came to the fore with comparable political emphasis. In 1964 Congress passed the Civil Rights Act. That statute, of several titles, was a culmination of the actual efforts calling for elimination of discrimination; at the same time, it was a starting point for the continuation of those efforts, providing a statutory base for litigation and further exploration of the meaning of the term *equality*. Part of that exploration has led toward the idea that for groups that can identify a place in the nation's history when that group was treated with inequality—penalized or stigmatized—some sort of compensation should be delivered. Briefly said, there are now three federal laws dealing with stigma that are primary concerns of school districts. Title IX deals with sex discrimination. Title VI deals with race discrimination. Section 504 deals with discrimination against the handicapped.

The essence of compensation is that injustices have been committed in times past when those groups were vulnerable, politically powerless groups. Furthermore, because of discrimination against the group, those injustices were not halted. Because the injustices caused suffering, compensation is due the victims. If this idea may be called the "principle of compensation," a number of problems spring from the principle, when it is examined. In American law and culture, there is a period in which an individual's guilt for injustices must be established or any claims against the accused forsaken. If one committed an act that might be considered a wrong, for how long a period would one be held accountable? On an individual basis, statutes of limitations speak to this, and a citizen may not be pursued, or held in potential guilt, except for a specific period. However, when compensation is addressed to acts committed in the far past, it is not addressed to an individual. It is addressed to groups, by groups.

In contemporary America, it is claimed by one group—the victims— against another group—the perpetrators. For example, American blacks may charge American whites with the circumstance of human slavery and establish an expectation of compensation upon that charge, which is historically verifiable, but which could not involve any of the persons who were actually parties to the slave-master situation. Likewise, American Indians could charge other Americans with fraud, misrepresentation, and a host of other unjust activities under which Indian territories were reduced, relocated, or lost and under which other Americans gained territory.

If articulated bluntly, on the current American political scene, the principle of compensation means, "You, or yours, took something from me, or mine, too cheaply. Now, it is time to pay up." There is an attraction for elected officials in that theme, for it has provided a rationale from which to design programs to help the downtrodden of our society. Americans have a history of altruistic help to the downtrodden. The principle stipulates that the disadvantaged in society should receive help from the more fortunate, and it is the corollary of that American cultural ethic that the strong should help the weak. The political manifestations of the principle of compensation provides for help from the stronger groups to weaker groups. Compensation is delivered on the basis of group membership, not on the basis of individual needs. Needs are assumed for all in the group, and compensation is a group entitlement.

Specifically, compensation has found legal expression in a number of antidiscrimination programs. Included would be legislation devoted to civil rights, equal educational and employment opportunities, salary restrictions calling for equal pay, and organizational obligations for affirmative actions with equalization of some sort as a goal. In the evolving American notion of a continually extending and expanding equality, a variety of laws have been passed to guide citizens toward accomplishing greater equality and toward reducing discrimination that rests upon bias or prejudice.

Civil Rights Legislation

More than any other single event that focused upon the shortcomings in American society to provide a nondiscriminatory environment for citizens, *Brown v. Topeka,* 347 U.S. 483 (1954), serves as the reference point from which to consider the civil rights movement. Along with three other similar cases, the Topeka board of education, under the laws of the state that made such an arrangement permissible, created public schools for black children only. They were segregated from white children, and the Supreme Court accepted the plaintiffs' claim that separate facilities were "inherently unequal," a violation of the Fourteenth Amendent. From this finding a new awareness of discrimination developed and found expression in several federal statutes.

1. The Civil Rights Acts of 1957 and 1960 were intended to enhance equality in voting rights and encourage school desegregation.

2. The Equal Pay Act of 1963 was intended to eliminate pay differentials among employees that were based solely upon sex.

3. The Civil Rights Act of 1964 was comprehensive, attending several problem areas of citizen inequality.

4. Other statutes of the 1960s and 1970s were devoted to topics such as voting rights, model cities, open housing, sex discrimination, and the rights of handicapped, pregnant, and aged citizens.

The civil rights thrust of the twentieth century got an initial impetus from the judiciary branch, which continued its interest after *Brown.* The energy of that original thrust was picked up in a long series of executive orders as one president after another issued orders extending the comprehensiveness of civil rights. Advocacy for civil rights was strong from within and from outside of government, and the Congress passed laws that had an accretionary effect, including more and more people under more and more varied social conditions. With all three branches of the federal government active in the civil rights effort, huge gains have been made by many of the groups that have come under special protective legislation.

In a legislative expression of clear political commitment to the disadvantaged, the Civil Rights Act of 1964 (P.L. 88-252) was passed with a comprehensive approach to the problems included in its several sections, called titles. The titles separately attended aspects of discrimination such as voting registration, community-relations services, judicial procedures in civil rights litigation, and opportunities for equal employment. Title VII of the Act, "Equal Employment Opportunity," provides definitions, accounts for state laws dealing with employment, and details how complaints should be investigated. Two portions bear so heavily upon school organization and administration that they merit extended examination.

DISCRIMINATION BECAUSE OF RACE, COLOR, RELIGION, SEX, OR NATIONAL ORIGIN

Sec. 703. (a) It shall be an unlawful employment practice for an employer—

(1) to fail or refuse to hire or to discharge any individual, or otherwise to discriminate against any individual with respect to his compensation terms, conditions, or privileges of employment, because of such individual's race, color, religion, sex, or national origin; or

(2) to limit, segregate, or classify his employees in any way which would deprive or tend to deprive any individual of employment opportunities or otherwise adversely affect his status as an employee, because of such individual's race, color, religion, sex, or national origin.

(b) It shall be an unlawful employment practice for an employment agency to fail or refuse to refer for employment, or otherwise to discriminate against, any individual because of his race, color, religion, sex or national origin, or to classify or refer for employment any individual on the basis of his race, color, religion, sex, or national origin.

(c) It shall be an unlawful employment practice for a labor organization—

(1) to exclude or to expel from its membership, or otherwise to discriminate against, any individual because of his race, color, religion, sex, or national origin;

(2) to limit, segregate, or classify its membership, or to classify or fail or refuse to refer for employment any individual, in any way which would deprive or tend to deprive any individual of employment opportunities, or would limit such employment opportunities or otherwise adversely affect his status as an employee or as an applicant for employment, because of such individual's race, color, religion, sex, or national origin; or

(3) to cause or attempt to cause an employer to discriminate against an individual in violation of this section.

(d) It shall be an unlawful employment practice for any employer, labor organization, or joint labor-management committee controlling apprenticeship or other training or retraining, including on-the-job training programs to discriminate against any individual because of his race, color, religion, sex, or national origin in admission to, or employment in, any program established to provide apprenticeship or other training.

Later, in the same title,

EQUAL EMPLOYMENT OPPORTUNITY COMMISSION

Sec. 705. (a) There is hereby created a Commission to be known as the Equal Employment Opportunity Commission, which shall be composed of five members, not more than three of whom shall be members of the same political party, who shall be appointed by the President by and with the advice and consent of the Senate. One of the original members shall be appointed for a term of one year, one for a term of two years, one for a term of three years, one for a term of four years, and one for a term of five years, beginning from the date of enactment of this title, but their successors shall be appointed for terms of five years each, except that any individual chosen to fill a vacancy shall be appointed only for the unexpired term of the member whom he shall succeed. The President shall designate one member to serve as Chairman of the Commission, and one member to serve as Vice Chairman. The Chairman shall be responsible on behalf of the Commission for the administrative operations of the Commission, and shall appoint, in accordance with the civil service laws, such officers, agents, attorneys, and employees as it deems necessary to assist it in the performance of its functions and to fix their compensation in accordance with the Classification Act of 1949, as amended. The Vice Chairman shall act as Chairman in the absence or disability of the Chairman or in the event of a vacancy in that office. . . .

(g) The Commission shall have power—

(1) to cooperate with and, with their consent, utilize regional, State, local, and other agencies, both public and private, and individuals;

(2) to pay to witnesses whose depositions are taken or who are summoned before the Commission or any of its agents the same witness and mileage fees as are paid to witnesses in the courts of the United States;

(3) to furnish to persons subject to this title such technical assistance as they may request to further their compliance with this title or an order issued thereunder;

(4) upon the request of (i) any employer, whose employees or some of them, or (ii) any labor organization, whose members or some of them refuse or threaten to refuse to cooperate in effectuating the provisions of this title, to assist in such effectuation by conciliation or such other remedial action as is provided by this title;

(5) to make such technical studies as are appropriate to effectuate the purposes and policies of this title and to make the results of such studies available to the public;

(6) to refer matters to the Attorney General with recommendations for intervention in a civil action brought by an aggrieved party under section 706, or for the institution of a civil action by the Attorney General under 707, and to advise, consult, and assist the Attorney General on such matters.

The statutes have been extended by subsequent legislation to include other groups. That is, in addition to the five citizen groups identified in 1964 as worthy of special protection, the categories of age, handicap, and pregnancy have been added. In some states, and under some negotiated contracts, an even longer list of specifically protected conditions or characteristics may pertain. The translation of those stipulations into operating public school programs has given rise to substantial concern in the area of school administration.

Race and Equal Opportunity

Initially, the litigation dealing with unequal opportunities that came from discrimination by one race against another was founded in that part of the Fourteenth Amendment that protects everyone, as citizens of the United

States, against the unnecessary or arbitrary discrimination of officialdom. That litigation also tended toward a simplified division of the American citizenry into black and white citizens. The entire situation is further complicated by the fact that *race*, when used as a term to identify certain groups of American citizens who are protected against present discrimination, is a political term. That is, it is a label that can be used for political purposes even though racial certainty, as determined by blood strain is only a myth. Americans have engaged in far too much intergroup procreation for the term to have any meaning beyond identification for political purposes. For the operation of the public schools, it has come to mean any of those people who are not white, and for whom there is either a history of discrimination in educational opportunities or a current condition that makes education a special problem for that group. Presently, the governmentally acknowledged categories of citizens, by race, are five: black, not Hispanic; white, not Hispanic; Hispanic; Asian and South Seas Islander; and American Indian and Eskimo.

Brown v. Topeka Board of Education, 347 U.S. 483 (1954)

GENERALIZATION

Local boards of education are obligated to provide educational opportunities of minimum-quality standards as set forward in the statutes of their state. They may not carry out those programs in facilities that are separated on the basis of pupil assignment by race.

DESCRIPTION

For several years preceding *Brown,* a series of cases had come before the Supreme Court questioning the lack of facilities, or their inadequacy, to care for the professional needs of black students from several states that did not allow qualified black students to attend postbaccalaureate programs in state universities. Holdings had consistently ordered their admission or the creation of equal educational opportunities, and in retrospect, those findings can be seen as indicators of what the Supreme Court might decide about elementary and secondary education. The arguments for and against in *Brown* were presented twice. First, they were heard by a Court chaired by Chief Justice Vinson. A year later, after his death, they were heard by a Court chaired by Chief Justice Warren, and he spoke for the Court.

These cases come to us from the States of Kansas, South Carolina, Virginia, and Delaware. They are premised on different facts and different local conditions, but a common legal question justifies their consideration together in this consolidated opinion.

In each of the cases, minors of the Negro race, through their representatives, seek the aid of the courts in obtaining admission to the public schools of their community on a non-segregated basis. In each instance, they had been denied admission to schools attended by white children under laws requiring or permitting segregation according to race. This segregation was alleged to deprive the plaintiffs of the equal protection of the laws under the Fourteenth Amendment. In each of the cases other than the Delaware case, a three-judge federal district court denied relief to the plaintiffs on the so-called "separate but equal" doctrine, announced by this court in *Plessy v. Ferguson,* 163 U.S. 537. Under that doctrine, equality of treatment is accorded when the races are provided substantially equal facilities, even though these facilities be separate. In the Delaware case, the Supreme Court of Delaware adhered to that doctrine, but ordered that the plaintiffs be admitted to the white schools because of their superiority to the Negro schools.

In approaching this problem, we cannot turn the clock back to 1868 when the Amendment was adopted, or even to 1896 when *Plessy v. Ferguson* was written. We must consider public education in the light of its full development and its present place in American life throughout the Nation. Only in this way can it be determined if segregation in public schools deprives these plaintiffs of the equal protection of the laws.

We come then to the question presented; Does segregation of children in public school solely on the basis of race, even though the physical facilities and other "tangible" factors may be equal, deprive the children of the minority of equal educational opportunities? We believe that it does.

We conclude that in the field of public education the doctrine of "separate but equal" has no place. Separate educational facilities are inherently unequal.

In a subsequent decision a year later, *Brown II,* the Court frankly addressed problems of implementation. At that time the Court directed that desegregation should occur "with all deliberate speed," a phrase that has continued to raise questions about how rapidly the changes should be accomplished.

After *Brown,* some school districts set out voluntarily to establish programs for the racial desegregation of their students, on the premise that, in a democracy, there are educational values in population mixes; that is, students gain more accurate pictures of "real-life" communities when they are in schools with students from other cultures and races. In *Van Blerkom v. Donovan,* 207 N.E. 2d 503 (NY, 1965), the courts refused to set aside efforts of the board of education to reduce de facto segregation. Declaring the question to be primarily educational, the court accepted the sociological and psychological rationale of the board as an adequate basis for the reassignment of student personnel upon racial identification.

Green v. New Kent County School Board, 391 U.S. 430 (1968)

GENERALIZATION

In the efforts to eliminate racially discriminative assignments of pupils, local boards have wide latitude in what may be done. However, whatever is done must show by results or fair promise that the segregation of pupils will be reduced inasmuch as segregation is the manifestation of unequal opportunity.

DESCRIPTION

New Kent County, Virginia, was a school district in a state that had statutorily demanded that local boards establish and keep a dual system in which some schools were for white, and some were for black, students. In the New Kent district, there were only two attendance centers, one for blacks and one for whites.

Evidence from the many cases that occurred between *Brown* and *Green*, since they had come from one of the other sixteen states with similar statutes, indicated that the facilities could seldom stand comparison for tests that they were, in fact, equal facilities. As viewed by the Court, not only were they inherently unequal, but they were literally unequal as well; the facilities with a primarily black student body were inferior.

The New Kent County board of education had responded to its obligation by describing and installing a freedom-of-choice plan. Citizens of the school district were both black and white, dispersed in a racial mix throughout the district but without attendance boundaries. One received all of the district's black pupils; the other received all of the white pupils. This meant that some pupils did not go to the school nearest their own home but rode buses to a more distant school. With the installation of the freedom-of-choice plan, it became possible for children of either race to elect to attend the other school. The board did not dictate attendance boundaries for its schools; did not demand that parents living in certain areas must, by the location of their residence, be bound to one school. What the board did was to make available an option that had not been available previously to patrons of that school district. However, in *Green* the Court chose to pass over evidence of effort and to ask, instead, for evidence that the effort was producing diminished discrimination against black students by segregating them in separate facilities. From the evidence, the Court deduced that the dual system persisted and that a unitary system had not been developed. Justice Brennan spoke for the Court.

New Kent County is a rural county in eastern Virginia. About one-half of its population of some 4,500 are Negroes. There is no residential segregation in the county; persons of both races reside throughout. . . . The segregated system (of schools) was initially established and maintained under the compulsion of Virginia. . . . The pattern of separate "white" and "Negro" schools in New Kent . . . established under compulsion of state laws is precisely the pattern of segregation to which *Brown I* and *Brown II* were particularly addressed. . . .

It is against this background that 13 years after *Brown II* commanded the abolition of dual systems we must measure the effectiveness of respondent School Board's "freedom-of-choice" plan to achieve that end. The School Board contends that it has fully discharged its obligation by adopting a plan by which every student, regardless of race, may "freely" choose the school he will attend. The Board attempts to cast the issue in its broadest form. . . . But that argument ignores the thrust of *Brown II.* In light of the command of that case, what is involved here is the question whether the Board has achieved the "racially nondiscriminatory school system" *Brown II* held must be effectuated in order to remedy the established unconstitutional deficiencies of its segregated system.

The New Kent School Board's "freedom-of-choice" plan cannot be accepted as a sufficient step to "effectuate a transition" to a unitary system. In three years of operation not a single white child has chosen to attend (the black) school. . . . In other words, the school system remains a dual system.

In *Green* the Court took a new direction and asked the very direct question, "Does the plan work?"

Swann v. Charlotte-Mecklenberg Board of Education, 402 U.S. 11 (1971)

GENERALIZATION

Boards of education should not hesitate to use a variety of techniques to overcome any vestige of a dual school system. Any obligation for local initiative cannot be set aside; if a local school district defaults in its obligations to eliminate discrimination, courts may intervene with detailed plans for its accomplishment.

DESCRIPTION

The Charlotte-Mecklenberg (North Carolina) School District was a large consolidated school. That board had proposed several plans for desegregating the schools, all of which had been rejected by a federal district court as inadequate. The Court was addressing segregation imposed by state law, that is, de jure segregation. It was stated that the local board had failed to initiate adequate plans for desegregation, and the Court cited four areas that demanded attention: racial quotas as targets or balances, one-race schools, alteration of school-attendance zones, and transportation of students.

At the same time that some of the questions about the Charlotte schools were settled, other questions, perhaps larger ones, arose. Population proportions have proved troublesome. The exceedingly fine line between an attendance quota derived from population proportions in a school district and an attendance target based on that same data has not been operationally helpful in addressing problems of racial desegregation. The same problem exists for the condition of population shifts that may occur in a school district after a court has ordered some sort of desegregation plan. In a decision that included a comment that boards in dual school systems had to carry the burden of proof to show that they were making racially nondis-criminatory pupil assignments, Chief Justice Burger also made a statement on the necessity for busing as a desegregation tool. It has become the most controversial of all techniques yet applied to reduce segregation by race.

No rigid guidelines as to student transportation can be given for application to the infinite variety of problems presented in thousands of situations. Bus transportation has been an integral part of the public education system for years. . . . Desegregation plans cannot be limited to the walk-in school.

An objection to transportation of students may have validity when the time or distance of travel is so great as to either risk the health of the children or significantly impinge on the educational process. District courts must weigh the soundness of any transportation plan in light of what (has been said, above). . . . The reconciliation of competing values in a desegregation case is, of course, a difficult task with many sensitive facets, but fundamentally no more so than remedial measures courts of equity have traditionally employed. . . .

After commenting on the general powers of district courts to carry out the sentiments and directives of the Supreme Court, and the inherent difficulties in achieving a balance on very controversial topics that would accommodate both equity and fairness, the Court concluded with a comment on the obligations that were left to a school district after a unitary school system began operation. It was a candid recognition of the phenomenon of resegregation.

It does not follow that the communities served by such (unitary) systems will remain demographically stable, for in a growing, mobile society, few will do so. Neither school authorities nor district courts are constitutionally required to make year-by-year adjustments of the racial composition of student bodies once the affirmative duty to desegregate has been accomplished and racial discrimination through official action is eliminated from the system. This does not mean that federal courts are without power to deal with future problems; but in the absence of a showing that either the school authorities or some other agency of the State has deliberately attempted to fix or alter demographic patterns to affect the racial composition of the schools, further intervention by a district court should not be necessary.

At the time of *Brown* seventeen states demanded racially segregated school systems, that is, dual school systems. Four other states had passed permissive legislation concerning pupil assignment by race in some of the school districts of these states. Other states had, or came to have, de facto segregation. In the latter circumstance, pupils were not assigned by race but by attendance boundaries. Given the social characteristic of like-type clustering, which is reinforced by economic status, that prevails in large city school systems, many schools have been nearly one-race schools, because the residents within that attendance area were of one race. It is a part of the cultural-economic phenomenon, seen long before the massive migrations of southern rural blacks to northern urban settings. Skin color added another factor to the affinity for clustering by like types.

It would be difficult to argue convincingly that racial prejudice has ceased to exist as a consequence of *Brown*. What has become apparent is that the racial desegregation of public schools, as a means to provide equal opportunity and to rid our society of discrimination, is difficult to accomplish. Court pronouncements are internalized by different citizens in different ways—and are rejected by some. There are several reasons, which are best expressed as questions:

1. How can it be determined when a school system is desegregated? How about a single school—an attendance center—within a large school district?

2. Should proportions of the five identified races be used in making pupil assignments to overcome segregation?

3. How can a school census be developed that will include stable and accurate labels of the student body by race?

4. When a larger proportion of one race is designated as gifted, has discrimination been involved? If a similar disproportion has been identified as handicapped, has discrimination been involved?

More questions could be developed, but that short list serves to point up the difficulty in addressing problems of racial discrimination. The questions, above, have all been limited to the pupil population; the necessary and suitable management techniques selected to deal with employee personnel by race—their hiring, placement, evaluation, and so on—pose yet another substantial organizational problem for public schools.

Over the years the difference between de facto and de jure segregation has diminished in the eyes of the Supreme Court. For example, the state constitution of Colorado specifically, and with strong wording, disallows any kind of dual school system. Yet a major case on this topic came from Colorado in 1973.

Keyes v. School District #1, Denver, 413 U.S. 921 (1973)

GENERALIZATION

Decisions made by boards about school-building locations, attendance boundaries, and curriculum are all affirmative actions; that is, they demand board initiative. Boards cannot allow that initiative to produce schools that tend to be racially segregated and that, thereby, produce "an unequal educational opportunity in violation of the Fourteenth Amendment equal protection clause.''

DESCRIPTION

Over the years the Denver School District grew in population, and new groups of Americans arrived as residents. In 1970 the racial and ethnic composition of the school district included significant numbers of whites, blacks, and Hispanics. Characteristically, those groups showed up as affinity clusters in the school district, not evenly dispersed through the territory of the district. The *Keyes* case brought to the fore several new aspects about racial segregation in schools, as noticed by the judiciary.

1. It was a northern school district.
2. It was in a state with a strong statement against dual systems.
3. It included three racial groups in substantial numbers.
4. Assignment of staff by race had occurred.
5. There was no cultural-racial curriculum designed to speak to minority interests.

Speaking for the Court, Justice Brennan stated, among other things, a new definition of a dual school system.

This is not a case, however, where a statutory dual system has ever existed. Nevertheless, where plaintiffs prove that the school authorities have carried out a systematic program of segregation affecting a substantial portion of the students, schools, teachers and facilities within the school system, it is only common sense to conclude that there exists a predicate for a finding of the existence of a dual school system. Several considerations support this conclusion. First, it is obvious that a practice of concentrating Negroes in certain schools by structuring attendance zones or designating "feeder" schools on the basis of race has the reciprocal effect of keeping other nearby schools predominantly white. Similarly, the practice of building a school—such as the Barrett Elementary School in this case—to a certain size and in a certain location, "with conscious knowledge that it would be a segregated school," . . . has a substantial reciprocal effect on the racial composition of other nearby schools. So also, the use of mobile classrooms, the drafting of student transfer policies, the transportation of students. . . .

In short, common sense dictates the conclusion that racially inspired school board actions have an impact beyond the particular schools that are the subjects of those actions. . . . We emphasize that the differentiating factor between de jure segregation and so-called de facto segregation to which we referred in *Swann* is purpose or intent to segregate. Where school authorities have been found to have practiced purposeful segregation in part of a school system, they may be expected to oppose system-wide desegregation, as did the respondents in this case.

The Court specified that the local board had to assume the burden of proof, that they had to explain any of their actions or district conditions to which the plaintiffs ascribed racially discriminatory motives.

In discharging that burden, it is not enough, of course, that the school authorities rely upon some allegedly logical, racially neutral explanation for their actions. Their burden is to adduce proof sufficient to support a finding that segregative intent was not among the factors that motivated their actions.

The ruling in *Keyes* greatly broadened the responsibility of all local boards in school districts with multiracial populations. With a new dimension established as the burden of proof to be assumed by any local board, findings were delivered in the form of court orders for desegregation in school districts of northern cities that had never explicitly advocated dual systems but that could not, during the 1970s and 1980s, meet the test stipulated in *Keyes* about why they did not have desegregated schools in the several forms also stated in *Keyes*.

Of all techniques that have been ordered by the courts to reduce segregation, busing pupils has been the most burdensome for school patrons. Magnet schools, clustered and paired schools, and other techniques have had, compared to busing, a ready acceptance. Citizens look critically at the time, effort, and money involved in busing for racial balance. It is also the technique that has been most shattering to some commonly held concepts of community that concern the neighborhood school. The patron who sees a school building one or two blocks away at the same time that his or her child is selected to attend a school eight or ten miles away is very likely to become personally and emotionally—but negatively—involved in the problem. Intense personal involvement in addressing large social questions is not a goal of every citizen who is caught up in the court orders for busing, so that many feel trapped and make judgments about the relative adequacy of the political system that demands their involvement. At least one implication that can be noted from this or similar orders imposed from without on an LEA is a loss of affection for the institution by the supporting citizen groups.

Technically, it is accurate to say that in each state where it has occurred, those states have been directly subject to the orders for desegregated schools. Practically, it is the private citizens who reside in the affected school district who become the subjects of that court order. Many citizens have refused participation in the large problem of racial separation and have elected to spend energy in solving their very personal part of that problem, acting to avoid the impact of the court orders—in effect, a kind of personal evasion. At least two discernible lines of reactionary avoidance have emerged since *Brown*.

In one such reaction, people merely remove themselves from the geographical territory encompassed in the court order and go to another place for their residence. Although it tends to include people of some socioeconomic homogeneity, this residence changing is often called "white flight." It iṣ the movement of whites—and others on a socioeconomic par—from school districts under a court order to desegregate their schools racially to some other area where the school district has no such obligation. Another reaction has occurred, primarily in several of those states that had dual school systems at the time of *Brown*. Private schools, or academies, were formed. Voluntary private schools burgeoned, both in numbers and in student registrations, until twenty-five years after *Brown*, many of the counties in those states had more than 25 percent of the whole student body registered in private academies offering elementary and secondary curriculums. Some academies are church related; some are not. Quality levels vary from place to place, partially a function of variable quality control from the SDEs in those several states. In the custom of American private education, these academies exercise selective admission and, as a matter of practice, register white children only. Both school settings, above, describe conditions in which court orders for racial desegregation in schools have been a prelude to resegregation.

Actually, resegregation may be a consequence of other actions that Americans are at liberty to take. There is an obvious tension between what the courts can order public institutions, such as schools, to do in regard to the education of their children and what citizens will accept as their reasonable obligation. If whites really constitute the group that the other four racial groups (the racial minorities) need to be protected from, the loss of wholehearted white support as a resource group in the entire public education endeavor is a loss that must be, at least sometimes, frankly discussed and calculated.

Manifestations of this tension were at work in two major school districts in 1981. In the St. Louis public schools, the resegregation phenonmenon developed through the 1960s and 1970s until it was contended that racial desegregation was not a possibility—only black students were left in the public schools. In 1981 it was proposed that only by busing black children from the St. Louis School District into several adjacent school districts, and busing white children from those districts into the St. Louis schools, could racial desegregation occur. The characteristic that every public school district ends at the boundary of another, and that each is responsible for its own concept of education—under state laws—is a characteristic that has not yet been argued to a conclusion, in terms of desegregation and equality of opportunity.

In the Los Angeles public schools, a busing order from a state court necessitated the transportation of over eighty thousand schoolchildren each day to achieve a desired racial balance. Strongly resisted by the local board and many school patrons, public school registrations dropped as children were transferred to private schools or parents moved to other school districts. Unique to California, that order had come from a state, rather than from a federal court. The citizens of the state passed at referendum a constitutional change that resulted in the withdrawal of the order, after there had occurred conclusive judicial tests of the amendment to the state's constitution.

The public school's portion of the problems of equality of opportunity by race is substantial. Even though great progress has been made in the American polity over the past two to three decades, the expectations of many minority groups in regard to progress toward equality have not been met.

Sex and Equal Opportunity

Masculinity has prevailed in social life, in the work world, and in politics. American society has been male dominated. The meanings of that short sentence are several, and a few examples can provide an explicit treatment of the meanings. Men have had much more locational flexibility than women. That is, when a man wanted to go to another place, he went, without any risk of a disapproving society. Men were decision makers, and in family households the "man of the house" decided where and when to spend money and, probably, how much money to spend. Not entirely irrelevant, it is fair to note that some observers have commented that conventional marriage is an institution that cannot function or endure when decisional equality exists, for with two equal partners no majority can prevail at times of disagreement, and disagreements become locked in. Men have been given preference over women in job selection upon the basis that the welfare of society was better served when the "head of the household"—the man—got the job. Whether true or false, that condition does not stand the test of equal opportunity, with sex an allowed factor for consideration. In the past there have been powerful American women, but they have been relatively few, so that, looking backward, one sees a "man's world."

Upon reflection, it is clear that sex identification has played a major role in American culture, a predetermination of what citizens could or could not do. These individual roles were based upon their biological identification as being of one, or the other, sex. The historical heritage includes a record of protection being afforded to females as the childbearers and especially providing protection and relief from exertion during pregnancy. In a postindustrial society with an extensive health-care industry, and with sociology bearing heavily upon the way the culture functions, pregnancy has ceased to loom as such a large health risk. Childbearing rates have decreased. New functions and new opportunities in society for females have had their origin in change patterns that are both biological and sociological.

In the administration of schools, it has become necessary for each local school district to be sure that it is in compliance with the various aspects of those federal laws dealing with civil rights. In focusing upon the Educational Amendments of 1972, Title IX, "Prohibition of Sex Discrimination," it is appropriate to examine the statute itself.

TITLE IX – PROHIBITION OF SEX DISCRIMINATION
Sex Discrimination Prohibited

Sec. 901. (a) no person in the United States shall, on the basis of sex, be excluded from participation in, be denied the benefits of, or be subjected to discrimination under any education program or activity receiving Federal financial assistance, except that:

(1) in regard to admissions to educational institutions, this section shall apply only to institutions of vocational education, professional education, and graduate higher education, and to public institutions of undergraduate high education:

(2) in regard to admissions to educational institutions, this section shall not apply (a) for one year from the date of enactment of this act, nor for six years after such date in the case of an educational institution which has begun the process of changing from being an institution which admits only students of one sex to being an institution which admits students of both sexes, but only if it is carrying out a plan for such a change which is approved by the Commissioner of Education, whichever is the later;

(3) this section shall not apply to an educational institution which is controlled by a religious organization if the application of this subsection would not be consistent with the religious tenets of such organization;

(4) this section shall not apply to an educational institution whose primary purpose is the training of individuals for the military services of the United States, or the merchant marine; and

(5) in regard to admissions this section shall not apply to any public institution of undergraduate higher education which is an institution traditionally and continually from its establishment has had a policy of admitting only students of one sex.

(b) Nothing contained in subsection (a) of this section shall be interpreted to require any educational institution to grant preferential or disparate treatment to the members of one sex on account of an imbalance which may exist with respect to the total number or percentage of persons of that sex in any community, State, section, or other area: *Provided,* that this subsection shall not be construed to prevent the consideration in any hearing or proceeding under this title to statistical evidence tending to show that such an imbalance exists with respect to participation in, or receipt of the benefits of, any such program or activity by the members of one sex.

(c) For purposes of this title an educational institution means any public or private preschool, elementary, or secondary school, or any institution of vocational, professional, or higher education, except that in the case of an educational institution composed of more than one school, college, or department which are administratively separate units, such term means each school, college, or department.

Statutory and case law since 1972 solidified the social views that work—in aspects such as hiring, placing, and compensating—should be equitable, without preference for one sex over the other. Those views have found expression in statements from employing organizations that they are equal-opportunity employers and that they carry on affirmative-action programs; that is, programs designed to discover, recruit, and place in employment more women than ordinarily would be true.

Under the principle of "comparable worth," females should be paid the same as males. That is, pay goes for the performance of a function. Sex, color, size, and so on of the performer are not pertinent. In education, that principle was the baseline for the single-salary schedule. For several decades, the single-salary schedule determined through a prearranged system that dollars were to be delivered for the function, by year and academic preparation. Sex has been an excluded variable. Within the single-salary schedule, it is even possible for a female to receive a higher salary than a male performing the same function—if the female is ahead in longevity and/or academic preparation. It is ironic, then, that after making such pioneering strides in salary-for-work that it is also true of the education profession that females do not have a high entry rate into the area of school administration. There are many reasons bearing upon that circumstance that have nothing to do with sex discrimination, but it is also related to the nation's cultural history, in many cases.

Actually, the question of discrimination by sex is one of degree that may occur at any point in the professional life, from time of first hiring to retirement. In *Rodriguez v. Eastchester Union Free Schools,* 620 F. 2d 362 (1980), the Second Circuit ruled that even though the teacher's transfer did not decrease her seniority or salary, the transfer did place her in a situation calling for radical professional change and constituted "interference . . . of employment adversely affecting her status within the meaning of (Title VII)." In *Dougherty Schools v. Harris,* 622 F. 2d 735 (1980), the Fifth Circuit stated that the secretary of Health, Education and Welfare had exceeded statutory and regulatory authority when she acted against and charged a local school board that paid a salary supplement to industrial arts teachers but not to home economics teachers when those salary funds were not from a federal source. In *Kunda v. Muhlenburg,* 621 F. 2d 523 (1980), a question of tenure arose. The plaintiff contended that she had not gotten the same counseling about the necessity for advanced degrees as had been provided to her male colleagues and had thereby lacked motivation to complete her studies. The circuit court agreed and accepted the ruling from the district court that she should be reinstated and given the opportunity to complete the academic work in a reasonable time. These cases indicate that substantial power has been placed in the federal government as that governmental entity views local schools. It is federal agencies that police alleged discrimination against females by school districts, but some of those cases also show that the power has limits that must be honored.

Pregnancy and the administration of pregnant employees in a school have raised many questions. Some rose to court challenges. The disputes that have surrounded pregnancy have been varied, and some of them are seen in the following questions.

1. At what time may a district demand that a teacher go on maternity leave?

2. What restrictions may a district place upon return from a maternity leave?

3. What may a district do in maternity leave policies that have conservation of funds as the rationale?

4. What may a district do in maternity leave policies that have protection of instructional integrity as the rationale?

5. At what level must a district continue to pay teachers who are on maternity leave?

Not all but several of those disputes have been heard in the federal courts. To provide an impression of the viewpoints held by court on pregnant school employees during the seventies, three cases have been selected and are presented chronologically. They reveal the judicial background from which came P.L. 95-555, passed by the United States Congress on October 31, 1978, and identified as an amendment to the Civil Rights Act of 1964, Title VII. The cases are *Green, Buckley,* and *LaFleur.*

In *Green v. Waterford Board of Education,* 473 F. 2d 629 (1973), the Second Circuit ruled for the Connecticut teacher. It declared that the time picked for unpaid leave, that is, four months before the expected delivery, was arbitrary. Agreeing with the board's contention that continuity of instruction was an important concern, the court noted that continuity was not dependent upon a particular start date for a substitute teacher. The board had also argued that uniform maternity leaves reduced the work load for administrators, an argument that the court acknowledged might be real but was insufficient. In *Buckley v. Coyle Public Schools,* 476 F. 2d 92 (1973), the Tenth Circuit Court addressed the question, "Did board policy violate any Constitutionally protected rights?" Ruling for Buckley, the answer was yes, because although there existed no Constitutional right to the job as a teacher, there did exist the right to be free of unconstitutional restrictions placed upon that employment. This Oklahoma board presented no compelling reasons for its arbitrary rule of termination for pregnancy.

The court also reasoned that marriage and procreation are essential to the extension of humanity and should not be the objects of punishing regulations levied upon women, that is, women who became pregnant. The signal case in pregnancy and teacher leave was *LaFleur.*

Cleveland Board of Education v. LaFleur, 414 U.S. 632 (1974)

GENERALIZATION

Arbitrary leave dates may not be established in advance. They must be established on an individualized basis and in response to the pregnant female's physical condition, as attested by a physician.

DESCRIPTION

LaFleur and her colleagues were married teachers who did not want to take unpaid maternity leave during the time stipulated by board policy. The policy stated that pregnant teachers had to take leave beginning five months before the "expected date of the normal birth of the child." The teachers took leave in March but under duress, for they had wanted to teach the remainder of the semester. Policy also fixed the date of return as being no earlier than the beginning of the semester following the child's age of three months. Practically, the policy excluded the possibility of a teacher delivering a child at any time during the summer and not being forced to miss some work. The rationale for the policy was stated as being twofold: continuity of instruction and protection of the health of the parent and the child.

The United States Supreme Court addressed the question, "Did the policy violate the due process clause of the Fourteenth Amendment and/or civil barriers to the deprivation of rights?" Ruling for LaFleur, the Court answered that arbitrary termination dates had no "rational relationship to the valid state interest of preserving continuity of education." Medical evidence, not rigidly predetermined dates, was identified as the appropriate informational source for decision making in matters of personal health, at the same time, the Court noted that pregnancy put upon the employee the responsibility for substantial advance notice to the administration. With ample time for planning, personal health and classroom continuity could both be accommodated, the Court declared.

Justice Stewart, speaking for the Court said,

This Court has long recognized that freedom of personal choice in matters of marriage and family is one of the liberties protected by the Due Process Clause of the Fourteenth Amendment . . . there is a right "to be free from unwarranted governmental intrusion into matters so fundamentally affecting a person as the decision whether to bear or beget a child."

By acting to penalize the pregnant teacher for deciding to bear a child, overly restrictive maternity leave regulations can constitute a heavy burden on the exercise of these protected freedoms. Because public school maternity leave rules directly affect "one of the basic civil rights of man,". . . the Due Process Clause of the Fourteenth Amendment requires that such rules must not needlessly, arbitrarily, or capriciously impinge upon this vital area of a teacher's constitutional liberty. The question before us in these cases is whether the interests advanced in support of the rules of the Cleveland and Chesterfield County School Boards can justify the particular procedures they have adopted.

The school boards in these cases have offered two essentially overlapping explanations for their mandatory maternity leave rules. First, they contend that the firm cut-off dates are necessary to maintain the continuity of classroom instruction, since advance knowledge of when a pregnant teacher must leave facilitates the finding and hiring of a qualified substitute. Secondly, the school boards seek to justify their maternity rules by arguing that at least some teachers become physically incapable of adequately performing certain of their duties during the latter part of pregnancy. By keeping the pregnant teacher out of the classroom during these final months, the maternity leave rules are said to protect the health of the teacher and her unborn child, while at the same time assuring that students have a physically capable instructor in the classroom at all times.

It cannot be denied that continuity of instruction is a significant and legitimate educational goal. Regulations requiring pregnant teachers to provide early notice of their condition to school authorities undoubtedly facilitate administrative planning toward the important objective of continuity. But, as the Court of Appeals for the Second Circuit noted in *Green v. Waterford Board of Education,* 473 F. 2d 629, 635:

> Where a pregnant teacher provides the Board with a date certain for commencement of leave, however, that value (continuity) is preserved; an arbitrary leave date set at the end of the fifth month is no more calculated to facilitate a planned and orderly transition between the teacher and a substitute than is a date fixed closer to confinement. Indeed, the latter . . . would afford the Board more, not less, time to procure a satisfactory long-term substitute. [Footnote omitted.]

Thus, while the advance notice provisions in the Cleveland and Chesterfield County rules are wholly rational and may well be necessary to serve the objective of continuity of instruction, the absolute requirements of termination at the end of the fourth or fifth month of pregnancy are not. Were continuity the only goal, cut-off dates much later during pregnancy would serve as well or better than the challenged rules, providing that ample advance notice requirements were retained. Indeed, continuity would seem just as well attained if the teacher herself were allowed to choose the date upon which to commence her leave, at least so long as the decision were required to be made and notice given of it well in advance of the date selected.

In fact, since the fifth or sixth months of pregnancy will obviously begin at different times in the school year for different teachers, the present Cleveland and Chesterfield County rules may serve to hinder attainment of the very continuity objectives that they are purportedly designed to promote.

Under the Cleveland rule, the teacher is not eligible to return to work until the beginning of the next regular school semester following the time when her child attains the age of three months. A doctor's certificate attesting to the teacher's health is required before return; an additional physical examination may be required

at the option of the school board. . . . To the extent that the three months provision
reflects the school board's thinking that no mother is fit to return until that point in
time, it suffers from the same constitutional deficiencies that plague the irrebuttable
presumption in the termination rules. The presumption, moreover, is patently unnecessary, since the requirement of a physician's certificate or medical examination
fully protects the school's interests in this regard. And finally, the three month
provision simply has nothing to do with continuity of instruction, since the precise
point at which the child will reach the relevant age will obviously occur at a different
point throughout the school year for each teacher.

Thus, we conclude that the Cleveland return rule, insofar as it embodies the three
months age provision, is wholly arbitrary and irrational, and hence violates the Due
Process Clause of the Fourteenth Amendment. The age limitation serves no
legitimate state interest, and unnecessarily penalizes the female teacher for asserting
her right to bear children.

The two cases, from Ohio and Virginia, epitomized that surge of activity
during the 1960s and 1970s as employees in many occupations, but certainly
including teachers, moved to test local rules and regulations against
Constitutional and statutory benchmarks. Those tests were initiated to
secure more latitude for the employee, and that included new degrees of
freedom for females. *LaFleur* and *Cohen* did not release pregnant
employees from the control of boards of education but did alter the
management processes, linking them to facts of health. Together with
similar cases from many other sections of the economy, a politically
persuasive influence developed, and the Congress passed P.L. 95-555,
entitled "Pregnancy Sex Discrimination Prohibition."

The act provided 180 days (until April 29, 1979) during which employers
could bring fringe benefit or insurance programs into conformity—or
longer if a negotiated contract were in force until some later time.
Substantially, the act stipulated:

The terms "because of sex" or "on the basis of sex" include, but are not limited
to, because of or on the basis of pregnancy, childbirth, or related medical
conditions; and women affected by pregnancy, childbirth, or related medical
conditions shall be treated the same for all employment related purposes, including
receipt of benefits under fringe benefit programs, as other persons not so affected
but similar in their ability or inability to work, and nothing in section 703(h) of this
title shall be interpreted to permit otherwise . . . nothing herein shall preclude an
employer from providing abortion benefits or otherwise affect bargaining
agreements in regard to abortion.

The liability of public schools has been expanded as a consequence of
cases brought, recently, under the nation's civil rights legislation. Many of
those alleged wrongs committed by public schools are in the area of sex
discrimination. Teachers have sought relief from many of the customary
personnel-management processes, such as hiring, transfer, leave,

promotion, and demotion, in instances where discrimination has been perceived. Affected employees—primarily, teachers—have sought court relief in forms such as damage awards, injunctions, and court orders for appointment or reinstatement.

Title VII of the Civil Rights Act of 1974 prohibits discrimination based on color, race, national origin, religion, and sex. Title IX of the Education Amendments of 1972 prohibits sex discrimination against the beneficiaries of any educational program that is receiving federal financial assistance. Coupled with the equal-protection clause of the Fourteenth Amendment to the Constitution, there now exists a formidable array of legal protection against sex-based discrimination. The Equal Employment Opportunities Commission (EEOC) is the agency charged with the Administration of Title VII, and the EEOC has periodically issued statements of condition and position as well as regulations for the accomplishment of the legal mandates of Title VII.

A source of current debate is the question whether Title IX protections cover only those students in schools that receive some federal funding, or whether those protections extend to all employees as well. This question was first addressed in *Romeo Community Schools v. HEW*, 438 F. Supp. 1021 (1977), and has since been raised in several circuit courts. The original ruling was that Title IX did not apply to teachers, that they could not seek the protection of that law, and that the HEW had overstepped its own bounds in the development of unlawful regulations. Most of the circuit courts of appeal have agreed. The U.S. Office of Civil Rights has refused to accept the court opinion that Title IX does not cover teachers. The resolution of this argument will be by way of Supreme Court decision.

Finally, two other areas in the whole realm of discrimination by sex seem necessary to point up for school administrators. In 1980 the EEOC defined sexual harassment as

unwelcome sexual advances, requests for sexual favors, and other verbal or physical conducts of a sexual nature . . . when (1) submission to such conduct is made either explicitly or implicitly a term or condition of an individual's employment; (2) submission to or rejection of such conduct by an individual is used as the basis for employment decisions affecting such individual; or (3) such conduct has the purpose or effect of unreasonably interfering with the individual's work performance or creating an intimidating, hostile, or offensive working environment.

Given the predominantly female work force of the public schools, it is an appropriate obligation for each LEA to take affirmative action to prevent sexual harassment from ever occurring by developing a program of information before incidents and accusations occur.

Second, many of the questions about discrimination by sex have involved the restricted access to extracurricular activities, where female students have ordinarily had fewer opportunities than have their male counterparts.

Charges have been brought against local school districts and state activities associations when either had rules that disqualified females from non-contact sports. (In fact, some courts have ordered local schools to allow females to participate in coed football, a contact sport. See *Clinton v. Nagy,* 411 F. Supp. 1396 (1974). In *Brendan v. Independent School District,* 477 F. 2d 1292 (1973), the Eighth Circuit ruled that where a school did not provide teams for females in tennis, skiing, and running, qualified females could compete with males, and a rule to the contrary was unenforceable. Qualified females may not be deprived of opportunities to participate, and such a provision may exist as equivalency in girls' teams or in invitations into coed activities. In either case, the initiative is the responsibility of the local education agency. In *O'Connor v. School District #23,*101 S. Ct. 72 (1980), Justice Stevens pointed up a very pertinent problem in this whole area when he said, "Without a gender based classification in competitive contact sports, there would be a substantial risk that boys would dominate the girls' programs and deny them an equal opportunity to compete in interscholastic sports." That is, sports opportunities, classified by gender, increase the opportunities for participation for girls.

Yellow Springs Schools v. Ohio Athletic Association, 443 F. Supp. 753 (1978)

GENERALIZATION

Local schools cannot be bound to the rules of state associations when those rules include unconstitutional denials of rights.

DESCRIPTION

The Yellow Springs High School was a member of the Ohio High School Athletic Association, a nonprofit organization of over eight hundred high schools. The association administered interscholastic athletic programs through its functions of rules making and scheduling of events.

The activity which forged this dispute occurred in 1974. Two female students, who were enrolled in a school within the Boards' jurisdiction, competed for and were awarded positions on the school's interscholastic basketball team. Because of their sex, the Board excluded them from the team and, instead, created a separate girls' basketball team on which they could participate.

By so doing, the Board complied with Association Rule 1, § 6, which prohibits mixed gender interscholastic athletic competition in contact sports, such as basketball. A failure of such exclusion would place in jeopardy membership in the Association and would exclude the basketball team from interscholastic competition.

The Association's exclusionary rule deprives school girls of liberty without due process of law. Freedom of personal choice in matters of "education and acquisition of knowledge," *Meyer v. Nebraska,* 262 U.S. 390, 400, 43 S. Ct. 625, 67 L.Ed. 1042 (1923), is a liberty interest protected by the Due Process Clause of the Fourteenth Amendment. By denying all girls the chance to compete against boys for positions on teams which participate in interscholastic contact sports, that right may be permanently foreclosed. The Due Process Clause permits such a deprivation only when it is predicated upon a sufficiently important governmental interest.

Two governmental objectives could be proffered to support the Association rule. First, the State arguably has an interest in preventing injury to public school children. Second, the State could contend that prohibiting girls from participating with boys in contact sports will maximize female athletic opportunities. Both are palpably legitimate goals. To achieve these goals, however, the State must assume without qualification that girls are uniformly physically inferior to boys. The exclusionary rule, as it related to the objective of preventing injury, creates a conclusive presumption that girls are less proficient athletes than boys. However, these presumptions are in fact indistinguishable since both posit that girls are somehow athletically inferior to boys solely because of their gender.

A permanent presumption is unconstitutional in an area in which the presumption might be rebutted if individualized determinations were made. *Cleveland Board of Education v. LaFleur,* 414 U.S. 632, 94 S. Ct. 791, 39 L.Ed 2d 52 (1974); *Vlandis v. Kline,* 412 U.S. 441, 93 S. Ct. 2230, 37 L.Ed. 2d 63 (1973); *Stanley v. Illinois,* 405 U.S. 645, 92 S. Ct. 1208, 31 L.Ed. 2d 551 (1972). The athletic capabilities of females is such an area. Although some women are physically unfit to participate with boys in contact sports, it does not "necessarily and universally" follow that all women suffer similar disabilities. *Vlandis, supra,* at 452. Babe Didrikson could have made anybody's team. Accordingly, school girls who so desire, must be given the opportunity to demonstrate that the presumption created by the rule is invalid. They must be given the opportunity to compete with boys in interscholastic contact sports if they are physically qualified.

Handicaps and Equal Opportunity

In 1975 the Congress passed P.L. 94-142, the Education of All Handicapped Children Act, amending the earlier Education of the Handicapped Act. In 1973 Congress had passed the Rehabilitation Act (more familiarly known as Section 504). The implementing regulations for that act became effective in 1977. Taken together, these two federal statutes constitute the substantial statement of the federal government about the necessity for improved educational programs as a basic effort to help handicapped children move nearer to a kind of equality in society. Subsequent state and local actions on subprograms have been harmonious with these federal statutes. Some educators have observed that P.L. 94-142 is really a kind of parents' "bill of rights," stating in great detail what must be done to educate handicapped children, binding LEAs into a rigid acceptance of court interpretations of parts of the bill, and having been passed by the Congress only after a majority of the states had renewed their own statutes dealing with special education for handicapped children.

The statutes are replete with definitions and lists of qualifications. P.L. 94-142 identified handicapped children as those who are hard of hearing, speech impaired, visually impaired, mentally retarded, emotionally disturbed, orthopedically impaired, or suffering from some specific learning disabilities. Section 504 defined a handicapped person as anyone having a physical or medical impairment that creates a substantive limit on one or more major life activities, and they include walking, seeing, hearing, breathing, learning, working, and self-care. Section 504 includes all of the handicaps in P.L. 94-142 and is even more extensive, including persons addicted to the use of drugs or alcohol. Both laws are aimed against the warehousing of children. Together, the laws mandate that local schools must provide a free appropriate education to a person who has a qualifying handicap and who falls within the age range for public education as set forward in the laws of the individual states.

The prime social areas for litigation in the wide realm of discrimination were for race in the 1950s, 1960s, 1970s; for sex in the 1970s; for the handicapped, it apparently will be in the 1980s. Office of Education rulings and policy letters on the interpretations of P.L. 94-142 numbered into the hundreds by the 1980s—a good indication of the high-quality level of litigation so likely to materialize in the decade.

In *Concerned Parents and Citizens v. New York Board of Education,* 629 F. 2d (1980), the Second Circuit upheld the transfer of 185 handicapped children from one school to others, because it found no substantive change in the IEP's that were, in the first instance, adequate. In *Hines v. Pitt City Board*, 497 F. Supp. 403 (1980), funds were not available in the local board's treasury, or in the state department of education to pay for the private school special-education program of a boy suffering from a personality defect. Finding the private school placement suitable and necessary, the court ordered the state to pay for that education, even though that cost might run as high as $1,850 per month.

Two of the cases that were most instrumental in laying the political groundwork for P.L. 94-142 occurred in 1972. In *Penn. Ass'n. Ret'd. Child v. Commonwealth of Pa.,* 343 F. Supp. 179 (1972), the district court decided that handicapped children were less the custodial responsibility of the state's welfare department and more the responsibility of the education department. That view has prevailed in other courts. The second case developed from the Washington, D.C., public schools, and from that case District Judge Waddy emerged as a staunch advocate for increased educational opportunities for the handicapped.

Mills v. Board of Education, Washington, D.C., 348 F. Supp. 866 (1972)

GENERALIZATION

Even though children may be labeled as behavioral problems after intense observation and testing, local school boards are not free to exclude such children from access to free public education.

DESCRIPTION

It is reasonable to test children and to find that most appropriate place for them in the array of educational programs that exist in a school district, or in some other institution, if the local board assumes the cost of that placement. The seven plaintiffs in this case were all black, some male and some female, and they suffered from a variety of handicaps. The judge made extended comments on the obligations of a local public school district, detailed the necessary due process protections, and set down some very conclusive orders for that board. The following judgment was entered.

No child eligible for a publicly supported education in the District of Columbia public schools shall be excluded from a regular public school assignment by a rule, policy, or practice of the Board of Education of the District of Columbia or its agents unless such child is provided (a) adequate alternative educational services suited to the child's needs, which may include special education or tuition grants, and (b) a constitutionally adequate prior hearing and periodic review of the child's status, progress, and the adequacy of any educational alternative.

The defendants, their officers, agents, servants, employees, and attorneys and all those in active concert or participation with them are hereby enjoined from maintaining, enforcing or otherwise continuing in effect any and all rules, policies and practices which exclude plaintiffs and the members of the class they represent from a regular public school assignment without providing them at public expense (a) adequate and immediate alternative education or tuition grants, consistent with their needs, and (b) a constitutionally adequate prior hearing and periodic review of their status, progress and the adequacy of any educational alternatives; and it is further ORDERED that:

The District of Columbia shall provide to each child of school age a free and suitable publicly-supported education regardless of the degree of the child's mental, physical or emotional disability or impairment. Furthermore, defendants shall not exclude any child resident in the District of Columbia from such publicly-supported education on the basis of a claim of insufficient resources.

Defendants shall not suspend a child from the public schools for disciplinary reasons for any period in excess of two days without affording him a hearing and without providing for his education during the period of any such suspension.

Defendants shall provide each identified member of plaintiff class with a publicly-supported education suited to his needs within thirty (30) days of the entry of this order. With regard to children who later come to the attention of any defendant, within twenty (20) days after he becomes known, the evaluation (case study approach) called for in paragraph 9 below shall be completed and within 30 days after completion of the evaluation, placement shall be made so as to provide the child with a publicly supported education suited to his needs.

In either case, if the education to be provided is not of a kind generally available during the summer vacation, the thirty-day limit may be extended for children evaluated during summer months to allow their educational programs to begin at the opening of school in September.

Defendants shall cause announcements and notices to be placed in the Washington Post, Washington Star-Daily News, and the Afro-American, in all issues published for a three week period commencing within five (5) days of the entry of this order, and thereafter at quarterly intervals, and shall cause spot announcements to be made on television and radio stations for twenty (20) consecutive days, commencing within five (5) days of the entry of this order, and thereafter at quarterly intervals, advising residents of the District of Columbia that all children, regardless of any handicap or other disability, have a right to a publicly-supported education suited to their needs, and informing the parents or guardians of such children of the program.

Battle v. Pennsylvania, 629 F. 2d 269 (1980)

GENERALIZATION

The Third Circuit Court of Appeals ruled that handicapped children are entitled to a free appropriate public education, and that a statutory limitation of the school year to 180 days was incompatible with federal statutes designed to extend new opportunities to the handicapped.

DESCRIPTION

The state of Pennsylvania set the length of the school year at 180 days. The state and political subdivisions (local public school districts) budgeted accordingly. The plaintiffs contended that for some handicapped children, a school year of 180 days was not appropriate and that a lack of program continuity contributed to the regress of certain pupils. They sought to have the state rule set aside, so the IEPs that included attendance year-around could be developed in every case where that seemed appropriate. The plaintiff class in this case was generally composed of children identified as severely and profoundly impaired and the severely emotionally disturbed, many having an I.Q. of less than 30.

The court heard testimony from experts on the educational progress—and regress—of both normal and handicapped children and the relationship of those characteristics to the 180-day rule.

We recognize that by this decision we may merely be postponing the inevitable. The statute provides for federal and state judicial review of individual educational programs which have been appealed through the statutory procedure. Thus it is quite possible that, in the future, we will be called upon to evaluate the substantive content of educational programs developed under the Act. We are hopeful, however, that prior to that day the states, in cooperation with the Commissioner of Education will establish acceptable guidelines to aid in that most difficult decision. Until we are presented with that case, however, "this (c)ourt's lack of specialized knowledge and experience counsels against premature interference" with educational policy decisions.

We therefore conclude that inflexible application of a 180 day maximum prevents the proper formulation of appropriate educational goals for individual members of the plaintiff class. Because our reasoning differs from that of the district court, some of its orders may require modification. However, because of the multiplicity of factors involved, we believe these modifications are best undertaken by the district court on motion of the parties. In the interim, these orders will remain in force. The case will be remanded to the district court for further proceedings consistent with this opinion.

Concurring with the majority opinion, Judge Van Dusen nonetheless wrote a more specifically limiting statement, seeming to express concern over the call on the state's financial resources that would result with a too general application of the decision.

I agree with Judge Hunter's opinion that under the Education For All Handicapped Children Act, 20 U.S.C. §§ 1401-1420 (1976), it is up to the states, not Congress, to establish educational goals for handicapped children. I agree also that the inflexible application of a 180-day maximum in every instance, regardless of the needs of the child or resources available, violates the Act by preventing the proper formulation of appropriate educational goals for individual members of the plaintiff class. I write separately, however, to emphasize what I perceive to be the limited nature of our holding in this case. I believe that the class before us is narrow in scope, and that the Act, while placing numerous requirements on recipients of federal funds, makes accommodation for legitimate financial concerns of the states.

The cases dealing with the rights of handicapped children to equal education have involved instances where one student was involved, either as an individual or as a representative of a class of similar persons. Those cases have also included questions arising from masses of data, when that data has indicated disproportions that need to be questioned or explained.

Larry P. v. Riles, 495 F. Supp. 926 (1979)

GENERALIZATION

When children are identified and classified into areas of handicaps by testing, and when those classifications are greatly disproportionate to the racial make-up of the population from which the children come, it is reasonable to question the accuracy of the placement procedure. Cultural and racial bias must not be a part of the testing-identification-placement.

DESCRIPTION

These black children challenged the method by which the state of California identified them as educable mentally retarded (EMR). The state used (after 1975) individually administered intelligence tests, and those tests were a primary deciding factor in identifying students who were not capable of mastering educational tasks beyond a very minimum level and in placing them in programs for the EMR. The state's school population was 10 percent black; the state's EMR pupil population was 25 percent black. The court examined research and enrollment data, heard expert testimony on placement decisions and patterns, and conducted a partial item analysis of the tests that were commonly used.

Courts cannot solve our educational problems, but they played a part in the incremental effort to improve those aspects of our educational systems that effectively deny minorities an equal opportunity to succeed. In particular, the phenomenon of special education such as that for the "mentally retarded" has not yet been subjected to much judicial scrutiny. We have been forced in this case to enter that complicated area, and it raises special problems for court intervention. . . . A principal focus of this litigation is on testing—on the use of individual I.Q. tests—to classify black children and assign them to EMR classes.

Fortunately, the "scientific controversy" surrounding the I.Q. tests has not materialized to the extent that might have been expected. The experts have tended to agree about what I.Q. tests can and cannot do, even if they disagree about the utility of I.Q. testing for EMR placement. Our decision, therefore, rests more on a consensus than on the testimony of any one line of experts. Given that consensus, coupled with the other factors present in this case, there is no choice but to invalidate California's present system of classification of black children for EMR classes. The bases for this ruling, both statutory and constitutional, will be explained in detail below, but it may be helpful to summarize them briefly at the outset before proceeding to the main body of the opinion.

This court finds in favor of plaintiffs, the class of black children who have been or in the future will be wrongly placed or maintained in special classes for the educable mentally retarded, on plaintiffs' statutory and state and federal constitutional claims. In violation of Title VI of the civil Rights Act of 1964, the Rehabilitation Act of 1973, and the Education for All Handicapped Children Act of 1975, defendants have utilized standardized intelligence tests that are racially and culturally biased, have a discriminatory impact against black children, and have not been validated for the purpose of essentially permanent placements of black children into educationally dead-end, isolated, and stigmatizing classes for the so called educable mentally retarded. Further, these federal laws have been violated by defendants' general use of placement mechanisms that, taken together, have not been validated and result in a large over-representation of black children in special EMR classes.

Defendants' conduct additionally has violated both state and federal constitutional guarantees of the equal protection of the laws. The unjustified toleration of disproportionate enrollments of black children in EMR classes, and the use of placement mechanisms, particularly the IQ tests, that perpetuate those disproportions, provide a sufficient basis for relief under the California Constitution. And under the federal Constitution, especially as interpreted by the Ninth Circuit Court of Appeals, it appears that the same result is dictated.

The named plaintiffs, including Larry P., are black children who attended elementary schools in the San Francisco Unified School District and were placed in special classes for the educable mentally retarded. Their scores on individual standardized I.Q. tests contributed to the placement decisions, which plaintiffs contend were erroneous.

Defendant Wilson Riles has been the Superintendent of Public Instruction for the State of California since the inception of this lawsuit. He has overall responsibility for administering California'a public educational system, including classes for the mentally retarded. Defendants Marian W. Drinker, Michael W. Kirst, James W. Dent, John R. Ford, Louis Honig, Jr., Patricia D. Ingoglia, Virla R. Krotz, Lorenza C. Schmidt, and Tony N. Sierra are members of the California State Board of Education. The Board is empowered to set the policies that the Superintendent executes.

The United States is participating in this lawsuit as *amicus curiae* pursuant to a motion granted in August, 1977. As *amicus curiae* the United States was given the right to present expert witnesses, file briefs, and make oral arguments to the court. . . .

While we have followed many of the suggestions in plaintiffs' proposed remedy memorandum, we have not opted for as broad a remedy as was there advocated. Two examples merit particular attention. First, plaintiffs proposed that the court correct any disparities in "EMR pupil identification," even if the identification does not result in placement in a special class. The court will obtain data on those identifications, and it may be that at some future time further court action will be warranted, but at present it would not be appropriate to intervene with a relatively rigid requirement. The I.Q. tests that necessarily lead to such disparities have been enjoined, and the remaining problems resulted largely from the particular nature of the EMR classes. On the facts now before the court, it would not be useful to go beyond testing and EMR classes to regulate conditions of "mainstreamed" EMR students about whom we know very little.

Second, plaintiffs sought a court order mandating supplemental assistance to black disadvantaged children who are now in regular classes. While we recognize that California's educational system is failing to educate adequately a vast number of minority and disadvantaged students, that matter is not before the court. It is not the role of the court to reach out to order what would amount to a massive expenditure of funds for supplemental assistance. As we have noted several times in this opinion, educational reform of that scope will depend on action by other branches of government.

The remedy in this case, therefore, has been confined to the facts and issues found at the trial. The injunctive relief will place some burdens on defendants, but those burdens should not be difficult to meet. Defendants have already survived for several years without the use of I.Q. tests for EMR placement . . . and the remedy to correct the disproportionate enrollment of black children is very similar to that voluntarily accepted for Hispanic children as result of the *Diana* settlement in the early 1970s. We are thus confident that defendants can comply with the remedy, conform their EMR system to applicable law, and get on with the task of providing a quality education for all of California's children.

This court has been forced to intervene in a complex and controversial area.

Despite the prodding of a preliminary injunction, California state defendants have not been willing to remedy the problems of EMR classification and placement addressed by this litigation. Nevertheless, we should recognize that other changes are taking place that may ultimately soften the impact of this court's order.

It may be that EMR classes and the philosophy underlying them are educational anachronisms. They focus on a label—retardation—derived for the most part from arbitrary cut-off scores on standardized I.Q. tests, and that label is used to justify academic isolation in special dead-end classes.

* * *

As America has consciously moved toward an increasingly egalitarian position, the public schools have become the primary agency for the accomplishment of those goals. People of rational viewpoints differ about whether that is an appropriate performance burden to be given to and accepted by the public schools of the nation. Some persons contend that a too broad mission has been put upon the schools, given their history, personnel, funding, and so on. However, it is true that in the latter half of the twentieth century, public schools have extended their programs very substantially, trying to provide adequate—equal—educational opportunities to a student population that is much more diverse than was the population in those same schools during the first half of the century.

Requests for educational programs differing from the norm, from community cultural patterns, and from a century of tradition have been supported by statutory and case law, since both the legislative and judicial branches have been active. Actually, the nation's executive branch has been very active in this whole endeavor too, for the executive orders of the Presidents of the 1960s and 1970s often set the pattern for the legislation that followed. For example, that was true of the developing concept of equality of educational and employment opportunity and its research and enforcement branches.

Now, the nation has codified in statutes from the legislative branch, opinions from the judiciary, and regulations from administrative agencies a vast array of statements about how people can—and cannot—be treated. Primarily, all of this activity in law has been designed to provide protections for groups of citizens who can be identified as having been extended a lesser opportunity than was offered to other citizens and whose relative position in society reflects that lack of opportunity. The protected groups include members of racial minorities, females, handicapped persons, the aged, those of national origin other than native-born American, and people of unusual political and religious views.

The public schools (LEAs) are obligated to accommodate all of those protected groups. That protection must be available to pupils as well as employees. It calls for ingenuity and care in the development and operation of educational programs, and the disputes over suitable curricula addressing cultural and language problems are, even after many years, unsettled. That obligation for protection demands a new perspective in personnel search and hiring, and it may necessitate for many of the nation's nearly sixteen thousand LEAs an identification of new or different characteristics when attempts are made to select the highest quality from among several applicants. Some affirmative-action plans have necessitated such revisions in which the realities of the labor market play a much decreased role in recruitment and hiring.

In many ways, the public school is American society in microcosm. The American social condition is characterized by increased tension that has matched the movement of that society through the twentieth century. For school administration, the condition demands an awareness that is visible and a performance that is balanced. School administrators must know of the real pressures from diverse agencies such as the Leadership Conference on Civil Rights, American Civil Liberties Union, and Office of Civil Rights. Representing a much wider spectrum of advocacy and enforcement agencies, the sentiments of those agencies have been in the forefront to secure new rights for new groups by way of legal demands for new performances in each LEA.

All of that action is indicative of a free, inventive, and lively society. It puts upon every LEA a very basic problem, that is, where to get the money to fund the new programs. It is a condition of tension, and some groups in the entire clientele of public schools want to move at a much more rapid pace of change than do others. Schools are left to cope with many ambiguous areas. It is surely fair to speculate that the tension will continue, and that clashes will continue to arise to the courts of the nation as people seek the service of the judiciary to resolve perceptions of inequalities in public schools.

chapter **9**

INJURY AND NEGLIGENCE

Injuries incurred by persons range in severity from an inconsequential level to one so serious as to cause death. They may be the result of negligent actions or may be the result of purely accidental circumstances. The damages that come from some injuries are very apparent; others are less so. For example, when a student falls on the playground and breaks a bone, the injury is obvious or will become so. Eventually, the medical costs of that injury can be totaled. The pain and suffering from the injury may have been quite real but cannot be set forward as an actual, unquestioned total number of dollars. The injury may have caused a loss of services from the student to the parents, but that, too, is a type of claim from which it is very difficult to develop a reliable total cost. Therefore, the least disputable costs of physical injuries are the medical costs consequent to that injury; yet other costs may be claimed in a suit and may be awarded, depending upon the facts of an individual case.

In other words, the consequences of an injury may be complex and pervasive, and it is those characteristics that lead to litigation, for if an injury has been caused by negligence, a damage award may follow. There is a duty of care imposed upon public school districts, demanding that the responsibility for the safety of the students and employees be accepted and fulfilled. School boards can fulfill a part of that responsibility through regulations for the control and operation of the school. Ordinarily, injuries that are the result of purely accidental situations are not actionable for damages.

Actions seeking damages for injuries coming from attendance in public schools do not have a long history because such schools were protected from suit under the common law concept of sovereign immunity. Literally, that concept meant that the king could do no wrong, that whatever a king did, as the head of government, was right. Altered slightly to fit the

American governmental patterns, the concept was expressed as governmental immunity, meaning that the people controlled the government process and had never acted explicitly to make their governmental agencies liable for the negligent acts of their employees even though those acts might have contributed to accident and/or injury. This all began to change with the pronouncement in *Molitar v. Kaneland Community School,* 18 Ill. 2d 11 (1959). Speaking for the Illinois Supreme Court, Justice Klingbiel noted that the sovereign-immunity concept was first extended to a political subdivision in England in 1788. A century later that concept of immunity was reversed in England but continued to prevail in America, leaving American citizens with no protection from unjust and negligent acts of governmental units that could lead to injury. That court refused to accept the arguments supporting school-district immunity as out of phase with the times, as excluding school districts from their appropriate civil responsibility, and reversed the lower court, ruling for Thomas Molitar, who had been injured in a school bus accident.

The arguments for governmental immunity are several:

1. Legislatures, as representatives of the people, can set aside governmental immunity by statute.

2. The treasuries of political subdivisions should not be spent to satisfy a claim, for the taxes were not collected for that purpose. Neither should public properties be sold to satisfy a claim.

3. Public quasi corporations, such as school districts, are not perfectly comparable to private corporations.

4. Allowance of damage claims creates budgetary unpredictability.

5. Public endeavors should not be endangered by individuals claiming damages for injury at a cost to the public treasury.

The list could be extended, but the circumstance has been that, in state after state, the legislatures of the 1960s took their cue from *Molitar* and acted to set aside governmental immunity. Such actions made school districts and other political subdivisions liable for the negligences of their employees. Injury, negligence, and damages go together. Injury in a setting of obvious attention to care for the welfare and safety of schoolchildren is not likely to produce awards for damages, even in those states that statutorily set aside governmental immunity.

Governmental immunity is not a constant, either in its elimination or maintenance. In *Jones v. State Highway Commission,* 557 S.W. 2d 225 (MO, 1977), the Missouri Supreme Court set aside governmental immunity for the political subdivisions and the agencies of the state. At the same time, the court, acknowledging the legislative function, specified that the state legislature cou¹ ' reinstate the immunity by specific statute if it chose to do so, and it did. (In this case, the Missouri Supreme Court followed the pattern of the Wisconsin Supreme Court when, in 1962, it ruled similarly but gave the legislature a period to prepare for the financial ramifications of the loss of immunity.) There is not a perfect understanding, either, of who fits within the shield of governmental immunity. In *Webb v. Hennessy,* 257 S.E. 2d 315 (GA, 1978), the Georgia Court of Appeals ruled that immunity from suit provided to the governing boards of Georgia school districts did not necessarily include the employees of the board and found a school principal negligent of performing certain basic duties.

One consequence of enveloping school districts into the group of social organizations subject to suit for injury has been a new budget cost. Schools have purchased insurance to protect the district treasury from a disastrous claim and to protect the trustees of the governing board from claims against them as individuals. Such an insurance program is nearly universal among school districts in states that have set aside governmental immunity. Likewise, many local schools and/or the local education associations have secured liability insurance for the administrators and teachers. As a "cost of doing business,"liability insurance has become a recent addition—but a very necessary one—to LEA budgets. Although some observers have claimed that such insurance protection had led LEAs to a more casual view of their obligation to provide reasonable care for the protection of students, there is a lack of research evidence to support the claim, and the ethics of the obligation to care for children compelled by law to attend schools has in no way changed.

Schools owe to the students and to the parents of those students the exercise of reasonable care in accepting the children as students. If the students are injured by wrongful acts of the professional adults in whose care they are, penalties may be imposed by law upon individuals or the whole organization. A tort is a wrong committed against the person, reputation, or property of another. It has three elements: the generally understood duty, a breach of that duty, and the extent of damage consequent of that breach. Students who are injured and who seek restitution through an award for damages generally base that claim on some point of negligence, that is, a failure to exercise the necessary and prudent degree of care. From that concept, a civil action may be brought against a board of education, administrators, teachers, or whatever party or parties are alleged to have caused or contributed to the injury. School districts are not necessarily exempt from liability resulting from the negligence or tortious action of employees as they perform their duties. Neither are they automatically liable for such injuries. Liability can be deduced only from the facts of a given situation.

Liability of Teachers and Administrators

Each teacher is the instructional leader for the assigned students and stands as the professional representative of the board's responsibility to provide safe instruction to every child. If a student is injured while under the supervision of the teacher, it is natural to follow with questions to determine who was responsible for the injury. While in the classroom, the teacher stands in place of the parent, a position of special responsibility that articulates with the position of professional responsibility. The teacher must always act in such a way as to prevent, or minimize, injury to the student. Teachers not only instruct; they also supervise, plan, intervene, reward, punish, and engage in other actions appropriate to a professional in a position of trust. Their scope of employment is broad, necessitating thoughtful consideration of what should be done—or not done—to provide protection for the students, especially against bodily injury. To the degree that teachers cannot produce evidence of such a high level of job performance, they increase the likelihood that, as one consequence of injury to a student, civil suits for the recovery damages will be successful.

To say that students do get injured in school is no detraction from the preponderant evidence that schools are safe places. Yet some students are injured; some even die from the injuries. Others are injured in school-related incidents. In *Tinkham v. Kole,* 110 N.W. 2d 258 (IA, 1961), Marius Kole disciplined a student by striking him about the face and ears, and as a result the student suffered a punctured eardrum. Considering the student's misconduct, the Iowa Supreme Court stated that a teacher's right to use physical punishment is limited, was excessive in this case, and was the direct cause of the injury to the student Michael Tinkham. In *Wire v. Williams,* 133 N.W. 2d 840 (MN, 1965), suit was brought against an elementary physical education teacher. While Diane Wire, a second grader, was jumping rope, one end was held by Patricia Williams, the teacher. The rope, which had a wooden handle, was jerked from her hand and struck the student in her upper front teeth. The court found that the teacher was using proven equipment as part of a well-planned curriculum and attributed the injury to an unavoidable accident. In *Cook v. Crain,* 288 N.W. 2d 609 (MI, 1980), suit was brought by the parents of an injured child against both a teacher and a principal. The injury occurred at recess on a day when the teacher was not present and a substitute teacher was in charge. The court found that the absent teacher had no liability; likewise, the substitute teacher and the school district were exonerated. However, the court found that the principal had broad supervisory powers that she exercised in such small degree that she did not minimize potential injury to pupils in her building, and that such an omission was neglectful performance of her duty. In *Lake County School Board v. Talmadge,* 381 So. 2d 698 (FL, 1980), a teacher was judged negligent upon an act of commission. There, the teacher physically placed a student upon a trampoline over the objections of that student and then forced the student to perform. The student complied and fell, injuring himself.

Teachers should be advised by administrators not to leave a classroom unattended. An adult presence, as instructional leader, is part of any school's safety program. In *Segermann v. Jones,* 259 A. 2d 794 (1969), a Maryland teacher left her fourth-grade class for about five minutes. Before leaving, the teacher instructed the class to do physical exercises, and the class had started the exercises, with recorded music to give rhythm to them. During her absence, and while the class was exercising, one pupil was hit by another in such a way that two of her front teeth were badly chipped. When the case was appealed to the Maryland Supreme Court, strict tests for negligence were applied, and the teacher was exonerated because the accident might have occurred in the teacher's presence, and the teacher had very carefully prepared the class for the exercise. Despite this finding, teachers are ill advised to leave the classroom unattended, except for emergencies.

A small number of states have provided a statutory protection under which teachers and administrators are protected and indemnified from judgments rendered in school-connected injuries. Such statutes are referred to as save harmless laws. The prevailing condition, however, is that as adult professionals, certificated school district employees are responsible for the consequences of their acts and must answer for injury to students.

Lutterman v. Studer et al., 217 N.W. 2d 756 (MN SC, 1974)

GENERALIZATION

When injury to one student results from the action of another student, the actions of the injured student and the actions of the teacher in charge must also be considered before any action for fixing negligence and awarding damages can be made.

DESCRIPTION

John Lutterman was a student in Independent School District #456. He was injured by a baseball bat, released by another student during a supervised batting practice, and through his father brought suit for damages against Wayne Studer, the boy who released the bat; Douglas Ringnell, the coach; the Gopher Athletic Supply Company, seller of the bat; the Hillerich and Bradsby Company, manufacturers of the bat; and the public school district. Lutterman was a student in the school but not a member of the group designated to practice batting on the day of the accident. He had, however, come into the school gymnasium to watch the practice, for it had been moved inside because of inclement weather.

The students participating in a simulated batting practice were lined up in five columns, the columns consisting of five students, extending in a north-south direction. All participants wore baseball helmets. Studer was in the front row of either the first or second column numbered from the west. The distance between Ringnell and Studer was approximately 20 feet. Ringnell would simulate pitching a ball, and as he announced its location over an imaginary homeplate, the students would swing their bats in the area where the ball would cross homeplate. Plaintiff, a nonparticipant, stood at a distance of 30 or 40 feet watching the drill. During the drill the bat slipped out of Studer's hand and struck plaintiff on the left side of his head.

Plaintiff was standing in front of a batting machine when the track coach entered the gymnasium and spoke with one of the baseball players. This player went to the weight room leaving by the door at the northwest corner of the gym. Plaintiff watched this player leave the gym, turning his head from the batting drill for approximately 1 minute. He was struck as he was turning back to watch the batting practice again.

(1) Plaintiff contends on this appeal that Studer was negligent as a matter of law and that the negligence of Ringnell, as a matter of law, was direct cause of the injury. We find no support in the circumstances of the case for plaintiff's position that Studer was negligent as a matter of law.

(2) Plaintiff contends more strenuously, however, that Ringnell's negligence was, as a matter of law, the proximate cause of the injury. The applicable legal principles, which are not disputed by either side, are captured in the following statement from Pluwak v. Lindberg, 268 Minn. 524, 528, 130 N.W. 2d 134, 138 (1964):

"Proximate cause, like negligence and contributory negligence, is a fact question which ordinarily must be left to the jury, and we have frequently said that it is only where different minds can reasonably arrive at only one result that fact issues become questions of law.

"Even where there is a finding of negligence, proximate cause usually presents a jury issue. Infrequently cases do arise where a person's negligence is of such a nature that proximate cause becomes a question of law. Cases also arise where negligence is not the proximate cause."

. . . (4,5) Let it be assumed only for the purpose of this consideration that the jury would have been justified under the evidence finding that plaintiff had permission to be in the gymnasium during the practice. Plaintiff was knowledgeable of dangers connected with baseball. Additionally, he failed to keep a proper lookout during the drill. Admittedly, he was aware that his fellow students were swinging 25 to 30 bats in his direction. He was aware of the possibility of flying bats. The evidence sustains the jury's finding of his negligence. It may be that the jury's finding that his negligence was not a direct cause of the injury to him is more difficult to follow. This court's statement in Seivert v. Bass, 288 Minn. 547, 466, 181.

"We cannot agree with plaintiffs' contention that the record compels a conclusion that the conduct of defendant (Ringnell) was a proximate cause of the accident as a matter of law. The facts herein are not susceptible to a single inference. It was for the jury, in the exercise of its broad powers with respect to the drawing of inferences from the evidence, to determine the issue of causation. Ordinarily, that issue is for the jury, and its determination must stand unless manifestly and palpably contrary to the evidence viewed as a whole and in the light most favorable to the verdict. It is only in those cases where the evidence is so clear and conclusive as to leave no room for differences of opinion among reasonable men that the issue of causation becomes one of law to be decided by the court."

The facts present a combination of circumstances without which the accident would not have occurred. Had the coach been more careful in surveying the area and the boy more alert to the danger in which he placed himself, the accident would not have occurred. Neither the failures of the coach not the acts of the boy standing alone were sufficient to lodge legal liability. This combination of the acts of both very probably was the basis for the jury's verdict. The facts did not establish a situation where, as a matter of law, the court could determine the issue of causation. The answers to the interrogatories by the jury can be reconciled and are consistent with the evidence.

Affirmed.

Lutterman points up two important aspects of litigation seeking damage awards. First, when the plaintiff decides to launch the suit, and if the defendants are not clearly identifiable and isolatible, there may be an inclusive list of defendants, lest a decision be made that negligence caused the injury, but the negligent party may not be among the named defendants. Originally, there were five defendants named in *Lutterman.* Second, contributory negligence is one defense against a charge of negligence. Persons who suffer injuries have some responsibility for their own welfare, and if they expose themselves needlessly to danger, they must be willing to accept some of the consequences. In this case young Lutterman was experienced in batting practice and positioned himself in a dangerous place on his own choice, taking some risk himself.

Rixmann v. Somerset Public Schools et al., 266 N.W. 2d 326 (WI SC, 1978)

GENERALIZATION

When teachers are confronted with emergency situations created by students, they must act. When that action is reasonable, even though it may be ineffective, that teacher cannot be held liable for negligence.

DESCRIPTION

This action for damages came from an incident in a laboratory experiment being conducted in a high school science class. Harold Ammerman was the teacher and one of the defendants. Other defendants were the school district, insurance company, and two students who shared the laboratory station with Ronald Rixmann.

Ammerman had demonstrated the experiment the previous day. The experiment involved heating a beaker of water and beaker of alcohol on an electric plate and using these liquids to remove starch from a leaf. Because alcohol is flammable, the students were instructed to have no open flames near the experiment.

The class was divided into two groups for the purpose of conducting the experiment. Ronald, the defendants-respondents, Thomas LeMire and Robert Kieckhoefer, and three other students were in one group. During the course of the experiment, Kieckhoefer used a plastic spoon to pour a small puddle of the heated alcohol onto the table for the purpose of lighting it with a match. LeMire then set fire to the puddle with a match furnished by Ronald. Eventually, the spoon itself caught fire. Kieckhoefer, in an attempt to extinguish the burning spoon, waved it in the air. He then proceeded to place the spoon in the beaker of water, but in so doing ignited the fumes from the beaker of heated alcohol.

Ammerman, who was at that time with the other group of students, saw the beaker on fire and attempted to extinguish it by placing a notebook over its mouth. The alcohol beaker tipped over, spilling the flaming liquid onto Ronald. He was severely burned.

On an amended complaint, this action was maintained against the school district, the district's liability insurer, LeMire, Kieckhoefer, Ammerman and his liability insurer. The case was tried to a jury and during the course of the trial the plaintiffs proffered a document under which Ronald's father's health insurer, Guardian Life Insurance Co., purported to assign to him any interest it might have by reason of payments made for medical expenses arising out of this incident. The trial court, however, ruled that Guardian Life had no interest to assign to the father, and that his recovery for medical expenses would be limited to that amount which had not been covered by the insurance.

At the close of the evidence, the trial judge granted the plaintiffs' motion for a directed verdict holding Ammerman negligent as a matter of law, but reserved ruling on the plaintiffs' motions for directed verdicts against the other defendants.

The jury returned a verdict finding only the school district and Ammerman causally negligent, and apportioned 40% of the causal negligence to the school district and 60% to Ammerman. The jury awarded the plaintiff $656.33 for past medical expenses (the amount set by the trial court to reflect the unpaid portion of those expenses); $8,400 for future medical expenses, and $25,000 for past and $30,000 for future pain, suffering and disability.

(3) It may be true, as the trial court stated, that these students "weren't the brightest." But all three of the students were bright enough to know that alcohol was flammable and that they were not supposed to have open flames near it. On the basis of these admitted and undisputed facts, we conclude that the students, by collaborating to set fire to the puddle of alcohol on the table, did not conform their conduct to that which would be expected of a similarly situated child of the same age and with the same capacity, discretion, knowledge and experience in creating the initial fire. The evidence does not reasonably admit an alternate conclusion. Thus, the trial court erred in not holding these students, Ronald included, negligent as a matter of law.

The plaintiffs also contend that the trial court erred in not finding as a matter of law the students' negligence a cause of Ronald's injuries. The concept of causation as it pertains to negligence cases in this state has been described as follows:

"In this state negligence is causal if it is a substantial factor in producing the injuries or death complained of. The cause of an accident is not determined by its most immediate factor. The doctrine of proximate cause in the strict sense of that term has been abandoned for the substantial-factor concept of causation to properly express "cause" or "legal cause." Consequently, there may be several substantial factors contributing to the same result. The contribution of these factors under our comparative negligence doctrine are all considered and determined in terms of percentages of total cause. It follows that, in resolving questions as to causation in the case before us, we will apply what this court has termed ". . . the substantial-factor concept of causation, under which there may be several substantial factors contributing to the same result. . . ." *Sampson v. Laskin,* 66 Wis 2d 318, 325-26, 224, NW. 2d 594, 597 (1975).

(4) The defendants, LeMire and Kieckhoefer, contend that the acts of the teacher, Ammerman, constituted a superseding cause of Ronald's injuries.

After exploring the legal concepts of "superseding cause" and "intervening force" and their relationship to negligence and liability, the Wisconsin court made its pronouncement.

It does not shock the conscience of this court to hold the defendant students liable for their negligence; indeed, it would be shocking if the court were to relieve them of liability.

Therefore, on the basis of this record, we hold that the negligence of the students—Kieckhoefer, LeMire, as well as Ronald himself—was a substantial factor in bringing about Ronald's injuries. These three, to various degrees, joined forces to create an open flame in the proximity of a heated beaker of alcohol. Once this condition was created, none of the boys alerted Ammerman to the danger, nor did Ronald take even the most elementary steps to remove himself from the scene. Rather, Kieckhoefer increased the danger by setting fire to the spoon and then to the beaker of alcohol. Though Ammerman's negligence intervened at this juncture, it did not supersede the boy's negligence in bringing about Ronald's injuries.

Because liability must be reapportioned in light of our conclusions above, we reverse and remand this case for a new trial on this as well as the damage issue. In view of the above, we do not reach the remaining issues concerning the constitutionality of sec. 895.43 Stats.

Judgement reversed and remanded for further proceedings not inconsistent with this opinion.

Meyerhoffer v. East Hanover School District, 280 F. Supp. 81 (PA, 1968)

GENERALIZATION

School districts engage in both governmental functions and proprietary functions. Although they may have immunity for tort liability for the governmental functions, they do not have such immunity for those proprietary functions they may undertake.

DESCRIPTION

Rae Ann Meyerhoffer was struck by a school bus owned by the East Hanover schools. The driver of the bus was Lloyd H. Umberger, also a defendant in the suit. Plaintiffs alleged that the bus driver, an employee of the school, operated the bus in a negligent manner and sought to recover actual medical costs in an amount less than $10,000. To bring the case

before a federal court for such a small amount, an out-of-state guardian—
Jean M. Loughridge from Michigan—was appointed for Rae Ann Meyerhoffer.

It is well established in Pennsylvania that a school district is immune from tort
liability arising in the performance of a governmental function. Plaintiffs assert,
however, that the transportation of children by bus is not a governmental function
but a proprietary one, and it is also well settled Pennsylvania law that a municipal
corporation is liable in tort for acts committed in the course of a proprietary
function.

The already difficult task of determining whether a given municipal operation is a
governmental or proprietary function is made even more so by this court's obligation
to decide the issue as it would be decided by the Pennsylvania state courts. The law
in this area, as enunciated by the Pennsylvania courts, is far from clear.

Judge Follmer considered the complexities that entered into distinguish-
ing between proprietary and governmental functions, the small amount of
damages sought, and ruled for the school district, dismissing the suit against
it.

I therefore hold that in the instant case on behalf of a minor wherein our
jurisdiction is based on the foreign citizenship of the minor's guardian, this court
does not have pendent jurisdiction over the claim of the minor's parent whose
citizenship is not diverse from that of the defendant. Alternatively, if it be ruled on
appeal that this court does have the power to entertain the parent's claim under the
doctrine of pendent jurisdiction, then, in the exercise of my discretion I decline to do
so.

The fourth ground for dismissal raised by defendants, that the court lacks
jurisdiction of the claim of plaintiff Franklin O. Meyerhoffer, Jr., because the
amount of damages which he seeks to recover is less than $10,000.00, need not be
considered because of this court's decision on the third ground raised by defendants.

Accordingly, the motion of defendant school districts to dismiss the complaint as
to them will be granted and the motion of all defendants to dismiss the claim of
Franklin O. Meyerhoffer, Jr., will be granted. The complaint of Rae Ann
Meyerhoffer, a minor, by her guardian, Jean M. Loughridge against Lloyd H.
Umberger remains.

There is some risk attached to attending school in that there is a risk
attached to participation in society in any way. Yet by the use of police
powers, every state compels the attendance of children for some time.
Teachers and administrators are responsible for the instructional programs
that will encourage educational growth but also must act to protect the
students from harm. Lack of such thoughtful, affirmative action in the face
of injuries may leave any school employee open to charges for negligence.
This is true for physical injuries, where damage is most obvious. It is also
true of psychological, reputational, and emotional injuries, to the extent that

they become known and that their occurrence may be presented before a court in a reasonable way.

Liability of School Districts

As the political subdivision charged in each state to carry out, at the local level, the state responsibility for education, each district is also responsible to provide a safe, clean, supervised environment for that education. Boards of education may not allow their physical facilities to fall into disrepair and endanger the well-being of the students (nor of the teachers, for that matter). Parents must have confidence that the local board will keep a safe place, and that is as true for the routines of the school's operation as for the facilities where the child must go, under the compulsory-education statutes of each state. Courts will not accept a plea that for lack of funds, a local board operated a dangerous school. Simply, each local board must find the necessary funds. Practically, the necessary funding situation is much more complex when consideration is given to the fact that funds come from various sources, often with maximum dollar limits and with yearly vacillation in amounts and sources. All of the complexities of securing adequate funds for the operation of each local school district and doing so without evidence of neglect is part and parcel of the obligation upon the governing board of each of the nation's nearly sixteen thousand public school districts.

With substantial case law and statutory law to indicate the liability of each board for its potentially injurious acts, it is now common practice for local boards to carry liability insurance—on the board itself to protect the district's treasury and on individual members of the board to protect their personal wealth from adverse judgments. Inevitably, schoolchildren will get injured; parents or guardians may seek damages through litigation; liability insurance should be in force to cover such claims as may be awarded. Although considerations of circumstances in which such protection would be most needed would lead toward protection from physical injury, other kinds of liability protection should be sought too. In *Wood v. Strickland,* 420 U.S. 308 (1975), suit was brought against some members of the local board of education and two administrators by two suspended students, Peggy Strickland and Virginia Crain. The girls contended that by their suspension for a relatively small matter, some board members acted inappropriately and denied them basic Constitutional rights. The Court discussed standards of conduct, degrees of governmental immunity, and stated that ". . . in the specific context of school discipline, we hold that a school board member is not immune from liability for damages under §1983 if he knew or reasonably should have known that the action he took within his sphere of official responsibility would violate the constitutional rights of the students affected, or if he took the action with malicious intention to cause a deprivation of constitutional rights or injury to the student.''

In *Wong v. Waterloo School District,* 232 N.W. 2d 865 (IA SC, 1975), Peter Wong was enrolled in a summer swimming class held at a public school and supervised by school employees. Evidence presented in court included the plans for the instruction, statements on the abilities of the instructors, and the condition of the pool and led to a decision that the local district was not liable, for it had engaged in reasonable and careful planning. This was so, even though Wong's parents sought damages upon his death by drowning during the last session of the swimming class. In *Stevens v. St. Clair Schools,* 115 N.W. 2d 69 (MI SC, 1962), action was brought, declaring that injuries sustained to the plaintiff while playing on a school playground occurred because the playground was unsafe. Lacking proof of any breach of duty, the Michigan court ruled that the declarations against a school district (even though it carried liability insurance) were insufficient to entitle the plaintiff to prosecute, given the defense of governmental immunity. In *Brahatcek v. Millard Schools,* 202 Neb. 86 (1979), David Brahatcek was injured and died as a result of being struck in the head by a golf club during a physical education class. In the class were fifty-seven students, supervised by one teacher and one student teacher. The Nebraska Supreme Court, citing failure to follow existing procedures and a lack of adequate supervision, granted a total damage award of $53,370.06 as an indication of the school district's liability for the malperformance of its employees.

Keiffer v. Southern Pacific Transportation and Corrigan-Camden Schools, 486 F. Supp. 798 (TX, 1980)

GENERALIZATION

States may statutorily set aside the common law doctrine of governmental immunity. When that occurs, political entities are liable for any of the activities and the limits generally specified in law.

DESCRIPTION

The Texas legislature had passed the Texas Tort Claims Act. James Keiffer represented that class of parents and children who brought a suit for damages against Southern Pacific after a collision between a school bus and a train. The railroad filed a third-party claim, bringing in the school district, on the grounds that it was the owner of the vehicle that was operated by one of its employees. The school district asked to be released from the suit, but that request was denied by the court.

Traditionally, a political entity such as a local school district is immune from liability in tort so long as it acts in its governmental, rather than proprietary, capacity. This is the rule adopted by Texas, and, without more, it blankets the

School District with a cloak of immunity 844, 846 (Tex. 1978) ("an independent school district is an agency of the state and, while exercising governmental functions, is not answerable for its negligence in a suit sounding in tort").

Texas, however, has chosen to partially shed this immunity and has done so by enacting the Texas Tort Claims Act. Under the Act, a school district is liable for money damages for personal injuries or death when proximately caused by the negligence or wrongful act or omission of any officer or employee acting within the scope of his employment or office arising from the operation or use of a motor-vehicle . . . under circumstances where such officer or employee would be personally liable to the claimant in accordance with the law of this state, . . . Liability hereunder shall be limited to $100,000 per person and $300,000 for any single occurrence for bodily injury or death.

At the outset, it is clear that the Texas Tort Claims Act may be used by a third-party plaintiff to implead a third-party defendant for a claim of contribution or indemnity ("the right of indemnity is available under the [Texas Tort claims] Act even though [the third-party plaintiff] suffered no personal injuries"). Accordingly, any argument of the School District that the third-party claim for contribution under the Act fails to state a claim upon which relief can be granted is without merit.

Larson v. Independent School District #7314, 289 N.W. 2d 112 (MN SC, 1979)

GENERALIZATION

School districts hire professionals to carry out the mission of the school. When injury occurs through their negligence, the local district may not be held responsible to indemnify any judgment for damages made against them.

DESCRIPTION

Steven Larson was injured in a physical education class at a time when one teacher had just left and another teacher, Lundquist, had been hired to take his place. It was determined by a jury that the new teacher and the principal, Peterson, were negligent and an award, plus other costs, was made in the amount of $1,013,639.75 to Steven. Substantial expert testimony about the teaching of physical education and the adequacy and intent of Minnesota's curriculum guides was taken.

Because of Lundquist's inexperience, the jury could reasonably have believed that Peterson should have exercised closer supervision over planning and administering the physical education curriculum by specifically instructing Lundquist to refer to Curriculum Bulletin No. 11, by instructing an experienced physical education instructor like Embretson to closely plan the curriculum and submit a detailed report, or by requiring detailed written plans from Lundquist. It could also have believed that Peterson should have more closely supervised the transition between Embretson and Lundquist by formulating definite goals and requiring detailed reports. The jury's finding that Peterson was negligent is supported by the evidence.

The crux of plaintiffs' position is that Curriculum Bulletin No. 11 established mandatory activities and courses of study which could not be departed from in a physical education curriculum. At the time of the accident, Minn. Reg. Edu. 162(b) provided:

"(b) Secondary school course. There shall be taught in every Secondary school the prescribed course of study prepared and published by the commissioner of education in accordance with M.S. 121.11, Subd. 7 and M.S. 126.02, which is Curriculum Bulletin No. 11, 'A Guide for Instruction in Physical Education, Secondary School, Grades 7-12, Boys and Girls,' . . . Plaintiffs contend this regulation demonstrates that Curriculum Bulletin No. 11 established mandatory affirmative duties for physical education instruction. We disagree.

Lundquist and Peterson also argue that any liability on their part for Steven's accident is precluded by the common-law doctrine of discretionary immunity. Under the doctrine of discretionary immunity state officials and employees are not absolutely immune from suit but ordinarily may be held liable only in the performance of ministerial rather than discretionary duties. As we observed in *Susla v. State* 247 N.W. 2d 907, 912 (1976), "It is settled law in Minnesota that a public official charged by law with duties which call for the exercise of his judgment or discretion is not personally liable to an individual for damages unless he is guilty of a willful or malicious wrong."

Discretionary immunity must be narrowly construed in light of the fact that it is an exception to the general rule of liability. Because of the special protection that the law affords school children, Spanel v. Moundsview School Dist. No. 621, 264 Minn. 279, 291, 118 N.W. 2d 795, 802 (1962), failure by Peterson, in this case, to adequately supervise the planning and administering by Lundquist of the physical education curriculum cannot be considered decision-making that the doctrine of discretionary immunity is designed to protect. We therefore hold that Peterson's liability is not precluded by the doctrine of discretionary immunity.

Peterson also argues that his liability should be less than the amount determined by the trial court. He argues, and we reject, that (1) his liability is limited to the insurance coverage prescribed by Minn. St. 1971, § 466.04, and (2) that he is entitled to indemnity from the school district.

Peterson is not entitled to indemnity from the school district. His attempt to obtain indemnity is barred by governmental immunity conveyed to the school district under § 466.12 subd. 2. The limited waiver of immunity provided in § 466. subd. 3a, was the result of the legislature's desire that persons injured by the negligence of a school district's employee have recourse to the school district's insurance coverage. Peterson does not come within the class to whom waiver of the school district's governmental immunity has been granted. His quest for indemnity is therefore barred by c. 466. Furthermore, Peterson was found personally negligent, and he may not seek indemnity from his employer, whose only liability to plaintiffs in this case is vicarious.

Affirmed.

Larson is a good illustration of the manner in which school district treasuries are protected in states that have set aside governmental immunity. In instances of large dollar awards, both the plaintiff and the defendant may seek to shift the responsibility for payment. Unless Peterson, personally, had an unusually large liability insurance policy, all of his assets could have been liquidated and, still, the award for damages not be paid in full. So he would have sought the financial protection, by way of employee indemnification, of the school district's liability insurance under state statutes. Likewise, the plaintiff would have sought incorporation of the school district into the liable group as a much larger source of money from which to satisfy the damage award. However, when negligence is strictly attributable to the poor performance of employees, the school district may be exonerated, as it was.

Strictly speaking, groupings of private schools do not comprise school districts. Each school is separate and unto itself. Because the school-student relationship is a private contractual one, nonpublic schools are seldom sued, but in *Haymes v. Catholic Bishop of Chicago* (IL SC, 1968) an injury to a student in a private school was litigated. A seventh-grade student was injured in a cloakroom incident, sustaining a fractured hip. Negligence was established, and in an initial suit, a damage award was made for $10,000 on the basis that Illinois statutes limited action against nonprofit private schools to that amount. The Illinois Supreme Court classified the statute as violative of the Illinois constitution and directed a retrial on the issue of the amount of damages.

* * *

Largely as a matter of convenience, this discussion of injury and negligence has focused upon injuries to schoolchildren. Injuries can occur to other persons, including employees and patrons, who might subsequently have an interest in attempting to prove negligence as a basis for an award of damages. The focus has also been upon physical injury. Many other kinds of injuries may have their origin in schools or school-related activities, but the vast preponderance of injuries are physical and involve children.

School boards must answer strict tests of responsible action when called upon to explain injuries that occur to children in their schools. Boards, and their professional employees, stand *in loco parentis;* although that concept is not so literally applied as it was in the first half of the twentieth century, it still pertains. The obligation of a local school board to provide a safe place can hardly be overemphasized. It is a legal understanding with strong and widely spread roots in the ethics of American culture: adults are responsible for the care and protection of children.

Employees of school districts must accept their professional responsibilities without reservations. Neither can they expect their own school to indemnify them for their own inattention to the job. Just like school-board members are obligated to fulfill their official duties in good faith, without malice, and with appropriate attention to the overall operation of the school district, teachers and administrators are similarly obligated. In addition, it is the professionals who are entrusted with the supervision of students on a daily basis, and a high standard of performance will be demanded from them by any court.

chapter 10

RELIGIOUS INFLUENCES
AND PUBLIC SCHOOLS

Beliefs and American Society

People having a religious faith have subscribed to some more or less orderly theological system. It includes the relationship between persons and the Divinity. The faith also includes a belief in that higher being, the Divinity; the kind and amount of influence exerted by the Divinity upon the lives of humans; and a denial of the necessity for the Divinity to engage in unequivocal self-revelation. Religious faith is detached from commonly accepted and logical systems of proof. That is, if God exists and the believers have faith in that existence, there is no need for proof. Religious faith has high overtones of emotional attachment, since each believer accepts and embraces all of the incidental items that mark one religion as different from another. No believer wants to have his religion assailed, and ordinarily, believers would like to have other citizens join them, sharing their beliefs.

For most religious denominations or sects, new members are actively sought by existing members. Each tends to think that his or her own religion includes the most important and the best beliefs. Other religions are viewed as less satisfactory and less accurate representations from the basic scriptures or holy books. For example, Christians base their beliefs on the old and new testaments of the Holy Bible, identified as important or unimportant.

Attempts to define *religious* legalistically and, by inference, the characteristics of people who have religious faith is not a very promising intellectual exercise. Theology is the proper source from which to define *religious beliefs,* and theologians are the persons most competent to develop those definitions if they are to be both comprehensive and accurate. Yet the churches, as units of organized religious believers, have had such a pervasive influence on elementary and secondary education in America that it would be, plainly, a mistake not to provide a systematic, if primary, description of the church-state-school relationships in a book devoted to school law. Therefore, this brief but systematic description is included as a necessary reference point from which to approach some of the church-state arguments.

Churches are units in which believers meet to share aspects of their faith with other believers. For each church there are two audiences, the groups attending and those who might be persuaded to join. Some of the church's efforts are directed toward this second group. Much of the controversy that has been so extensively litigated in the church-state arena has its origin in two approaches to the question, "How can the tenets of this religious faith be extended so that others may accept it?"

Relationships between a public school district—a tax-collecting agency—and the sectarian-private schools within the district are variable. Philosophical viewpoints vary. Some public school boards, viewing the public service role of the sectarian schools, proceed to deliver all support services that can legally be given to the children attending private, fee-charging, sectarian schools. Other boards, viewing the sectarian characteristic and denominational influence, refuse to deliver any services other than those that have been demanded of the local educational agency by the legislature.

Although sectarian schools represent one answer to the question, above, another approach is to create a religiously neutral educational setting. Public schools are commonly seen in this light. No single church can dominate the public schools, and no single set of religious beliefs can be extolled over any other sect. There is an aspect of fair play at work. To preserve the freedom of choice in religious beliefs, the secular public school does not have a curriculum that includes the religious tenets of any church, for to do so would bring to bear an undue influence upon the children in each school. They could be proselytized by teacher-believers who would have nearly unrestricted access to them.

Theoretically, the secular school has been sanitized of religious beliefs. Practically, the problem is not that neat and clean. Many religious beliefs are pervasive in social behavior. Most organized religions include ethical and moral systems, and since schoolchildren form their own values in the secular school, the separation of those value systems from any and all religions is not so easy, if at all possible. Moreover, the moral and ethical values of some churches are unique and recognizable as based in the religious tenets of one certain church. When coupled to the fact that many parents want their children to be exposed to, to learn, and to accept religiously based moral systems—the protective shroud of secularism may be penetrated from several directions.

Another approach to the question has problems of its own. In this other approach, a candidly biased religious setting is also the place where the child is educated. Churches sponsor private elementary and secondary schools, also called sectarian or parochial schools. The legality of such schools has been questioned, and it was settled in *Pierce v. Society of Sisters,* 268 U.S. 510 (1925). In *Pierce* the Supreme Court established several principles. First, it was decided that states could not use the police power to compel students into public schools exclusively. Other principles of school law included the right of parents to enter into decision making about where their child would attend school; the power of the state to regulate private schools was reiterated, as an assurance of a minimum acceptable curriculum; and the right of private groups, including churches, to own property, hire personnel, and establish schools that might include both secular and sectarian components in the education was stipulated.

Private schools, sponsored by churches, may exist. In most states the SDE is responsible to regulate quality in private as well as public schools, providing an assurance to all parents that schools in the state meet some standards of minimum quality. Religion can be studied as a part of the curriculum or as a pervasive influence spread through the entire endeavor of the school or both. Commonly, it is both. The church that has been most aggressive in establishing elementary and secondary schools is the Roman Catholic Church. Although some other churches, such as the Lutheran, Baptist, and Seventh Day Adventist, have also established elementary and secondary schools, no group is a close second to the Catholics in this endeavor. In 1980 over 80 percent of the children who attended church-sponsored nonpublic schools were in Roman Catholic schools.

To the extent that the church-sponsored school openly teaches the specific religious beliefs and accompanying system of morality, the desires of parents to see their offspring grow and mature in that church are satisfied. Not everything in this plan is satisfying, however. Although public nonsectarian schools are tax supported, the private sectarian schools may not receive tax funds, lest they be in violation of the clause from the First Amendment that forbids government support for the establishment of a religion. Patrons of those schools pay the taxes levied by the public school district where they reside and also pay tuition or fees to the private school they have selected. Fees paid directly or through contributions to their church are still educational costs over and above local taxes paid to support public schools.

Each school type, the secular public or the sectarian private, leaves parents less than entirely satisfied. From time to time, parents of children in public schools have attempted to get incorporated into that curriculum various religious aspects, including Bible reading and prayer. On the other side of that dissatisfaction question, parents of children in sectarian private schools have attempted to get tax money for the support of their schools. Viewed in the short term, the American system that calls for separation of church and state does not fit the desires of either parent group. It does provide for a distribution of dissatisfaction that meets certain tests of fair play, however, and that is no small accomplishment for any political system.

In the United States Constitution, the First Amendment states, "Congress shall make no law respecting an establishment of religion, or prohibiting the free exercise thereof." The clause contains two prohibitions: Congress shall not establish a religion, and Congress shall not forbid citizens to exercise freedom of choice in religion and worship. The first is called the establishment clause; the second is called the free-exercise clause. The prohibitions were made applicable to each state through the Fourteenth Amendment. State constitutions have followed the federal lead, and their terminology has been at least as strong in describing the separation between church and state that must be maintained. The Nebraska constitution is representative of a few with unusually strong wording, stating that "Neither the State Legislature . . . or other public corporation shall ever make any appropriations from any public fund" to any church-related enterprise.

Nonpublic Sectarian Education

A historical examination of sectarian schools reveals that the large-city school districts, as they were forming in the latter part of the nineteenth century, also became the locales in which large numbers of Catholic-sponsored elementary and secondary schools first flourished. Upon the rationale that the church should be a dominant force in the education of the young, the movement spread. Even very small parishes started schools. Many failed, but many prevailed too. Parents were proud of their schools, and in the pattern of extensive parental involvement in schools, many other religious denominations have entered the schooling arena. If those latter efforts are not as apparent, it may be largely because of the comparatively large number of Catholic schools in the United States. A church with a large membership, families that have been atypically large, and, originally, a strong teaching group in religious orders produced a very visible "system" of church-dominated elementary and secondary schools.

The efforts of other churches have been more recent. Christian schools and academies, especially, have flourished in the 1970s. Groups that might be generically described as Fundamentalist Christians have moved toward supporting their own schools and have also fostered systematized, centrally directed home tutorials. Questions of state control over those schools, and of exceptionality from compulsory-attendance laws for children in home tutorials, are now before both federal and state courts.

Questions of educational obligation have arisen. Must sectarian schools fulfill all obligations that are put upon public schools? Answers to this question have varied from state to state, but in *State of Ohio v. Whisner*, 351 N.W. 2d 750 (1976), that court stipulated a differential test for public and private schools. The state could require of (church-sponsored) private schools only those programs and procedures necessary to assure that students would get an education leading to economic self-sufficiency and performance as socially responsible persons upon reaching adulthood—a lesser demand than that imposed upon the state's public schools. Some states have demanded that church-sponsored schools be comparable to public schools.

The term *church* has only been defined here by implication. The situation of church-sponsored schools has been viewed from the larger perspective. Specific and local questions have been omitted. The consideration has been specific only in that Christian churches have been the sponsoring churches. Other religious beliefs have secured the support of members toward the establishment of their schools too. Jewish and Islamic schools and several church schools that relate to Asiatic religions were among the many church-sponsored elementary and secondary schools on the American educational scene by 1980. Churches are groups of believers who accept a set of tenets in common. Those groups, large or small, may set out to establish sectarian private schools for the education of their children.

Those schools are a different kind of educational setting from the home tutorial in which a parent has chosen to teach his or her child at home. Both are private, and even though that choice for the home tutorial may have been motivated in part by religious beliefs, a home tutorial is not a school. Instruction in isolation from other children is, in many ways, the opposite from a school. Presently, states do not provide for any kind of financial relief for the home tutorial. Neither has there surfaced any concerted political drive to get such an advantage through legislation, unless it would be provided through some kind of educational voucher. Nonpublic sectarian education is schooling that is church sponsored, fee supported, and with selective admissions.

The principle that education could meet the demands of the state and still be strongly sectarian was enunciated in *Pierce* in 1925. As stated earlier, the U.S. Supreme Court struck that Oregon statute demanding that all students in the compulsory-education age range had to attend public schools and established the Constitutionality of attendance at academically equivalent private schools, sectarian or nonsectarian. Viewed in retrospect, a rather systematic sequence of cases followed slowly. The "child-benefit theory" was discussed in *Cochran v. Louisiana State Board of Education,* 281 U.S. 370 (1930), as the high court allowed public school districts to furnish textbooks to pupils in nonpublic schools. *Everson v. Board of Education of Ewing Township,* 330 U.S. 1 (1947), followed, and no conflict was found between the New Jersey statute that directed local school districts to pay the school transportation costs incurred by parents, even when those children were attending sectarian schools. That is, transportation was described as a service lacking in any aspects of religiosity. In both cases there was a judicial differentiation between aid to children and aid to the schools they attended. An aid, or a benefit to a schoolchild, was not seen as aid to a sectarian school—which would have been unconstitutional.

The selected cases that follow are representative of current judicial thinking and are also in a direct logical line following precedents set by those earlier Supreme Court decisions above.

American United, Inc. as Protestants and Other Americans United for Separation of Church and State, et al. v. School District #622 Ramsey County, 179 N.W. 2d 146 (MN SC, 1970)

GENERALIZATION

Local boards of education can pay the transportation costs for children in sectarian schools, if the legislature has empowered them to do so and if the state constitution does not forbid it.

DESCRIPTION

A census revealed that in School District #622 there were 13,600 school-children of elementary and secondary age, and that of that total, 2,000 were enrolled in sectarian schools during the 1969-70 school year. At a mid-summer meeting of the local board, it was voted to pay the costs for transporting these children who lived in the district and who attended sectarian schools in the district. The resolution was a benefit to about 1,200 children, all of whom attended schools that conformed to minimum standards promulgated by the Minnesota Department of Education. The cost was $70,200, with nearly half of that to come from state aid.

The court noted that any support that came to private education by way of public payment for pupil transportation was incidental. Citing *Everson v. Ewing Township,* the state court showed that the question of violation of the U.S. Constitution was settled and followed with the conclusion that there was no prohibition in the state constitution. With an enabling state statute, it was appropriate to use public funds to pay for the transportation costs of all schoolchildren. Transportation was construed as a kind of general welfare, similar to other services such as streets, sewers, sidewalks, and fire and police protection. Transportation is secular. Such services are available to all citizens without reference to any religious inclination or lack of it.

Religious sects may hold schools that are academically equivalent. They are free from interference in conducting such schools, even when they are heavy with doctrinal teaching. Lacking evidence to the extent that would have proved beyond a reasonable doubt that the Minnesota statute was unconstitutional, the validity of the law was upheld.

*William D. Gaffney and Mary A. Gaffney v. Nebraska State
Department of Education,* 220 N.W. 2d 550 (NE SC, 1974)

GENERALIZATION

What is allowable as aid to the schoolchildren in one state may not be allowable in another. The wording of the statute and of the state's constitution become critical in resolving church-school disputes.

DESCRIPTION

The Nebraska court stated that the "granting of free textbook loans to a parochial school student lends strength and support to the school, and, although indirectly, lends strength and support to the sponsoring sectarian institution."

The legislature had passed the Nebraska Textbook Loan Act, LB 659, in 1971. It provided that public school districts should purchase textbooks and loan them, upon request, to students who attended private secondary schools. Requests were made to the Omaha Public School District, and they were denied. The county court ruled in favor of the plaintiffs, but the Nebraska Supreme Court reversed, with two dissents.

The majority opinion cited Article VII, Section 11, of the Nebraska constitution, which says in part, "Appropriation of public funds shall not be made to any school or institution of learning not owned or exclusively controlled by the state or a political subdivision thereof." Seeing in the statute an attempt by the legislature to circumvent the constitutional mandate, the court stated that such aid was only a conduit to aid the school indirectly and that, in effect, there was an ultimate benefit from public funds to schools not owned or controlled by the state.

Two dissenting justices accused the majority of ignoring Article I, Section 4, a comprehensive statement in that same constitution. That section called for the legislature to enact laws to protect "religious denominations in the peaceable enjoyment of its own mode of public worship, and encourage schools and the means of instruction." Moreover, the dissent stated that private schools served a public purpose and were a part of the state's whole educational system in the largest sense.

The question of using tax funds to reimburse certain educational costs incurred by parents who choose to enroll their children in private schools is not entirely settled. In regard to payment for transportation costs, most states allow recovery of those costs or mandate that local districts provide transportation without regard to whether the student goes to a private or public school. However, the question of providing textbooks for all students is not so clear. The Constitutional question was resolved in *Cochran,* above, and reiterated in *Board of Education v. Allen,* 392 U.S. 236 (1968), when the U.S. Supreme Court by a six to three vote held true to the "child-benefit theory" and ruled that New York schoolchildren could borrow, upon request to their local public school district, suitable secular textbooks for their grade and subject. The question in the case was whether the statute conflicted with the First and Fourteenth Amendments, and the ruling was that it did not. When state constitutions contain sections forbidding such action, as is the case in Nebraska, it cannot be done, even though there is no federal conflict.

Two cases came before the Supreme Court in the 1970s through which this question was addressed: "What can be purchased or funded from public school tax funds that would enhance the education of schoolchildren in private schools?"

The Committee for Public Education and Religious Liberty, et al. v. Nyquist, Commissioner of Education of New York et al., 413 U.S. 756 (USSC, 1976)

GENERALIZATION

Under the U.S. Constitution, aid that may be extended by a state legislature to families with children in nonpublic schools is sharply restricted in both the specific items and the procedure for such aid.

DESCRIPTION

New York's Education and Tax Laws were signed by the governor in May 1972 and established three financial-aid programs for nonpublic schools and parents of children in those schools. The first section provided aid for the maintenance and repair of nonpublic schools that served a high concentration of low-income families. Thirty dollars per pupil was set aside for buildings constructed within the last twenty-five years, and $40 per pupil was set aside for those buildings over twenty-five years in age. Section 2 established tuition reimbursement for parents of nonpublic schoolchildren. The rate was $50 for each elementary child and $100 for each secondary child. The reimbursement could not exceed 50 percent of the total tuition cost. Other sections established income tax relief for parents of children in nonpublic schools. Incomes from $5,000 to $25,000 were made eligible for tax credits on the state income tax return. The amount that could be claimed was established in graduated amounts and linked to their ability to pay tuition costs. A schedule for calculating amounts was included in Section 5 of the statute. The legislation was challenged by the plaintiffs as a violation of the establishment clause of the First Amendment. In the state of New York, about 700,000 to 800,000 students, or about 20 percent of the entire elementary-secondary student population, attended nonpublic schools.

After examining the statute, the Supreme Court ruled that Section 1 was direct payment to a sectarian institution. Ample precedent disallowed such action. Monetary reimbursement to parents may represent a kind of enhanced freedom of choice, but that money obviously found its way as direct support to the sectarian institutions. Other sections encouraged the excessive entanglement between church and state.

Most of the cases coming to this Court raising establishment-clause questions have involved the relationship between religion and education. Among these religion-education precedents, two general categories of cases may be identified: those dealing with religious activities within the public schools and those involving public aid in varying forms to sectarian educational institutions. Although the New York legislation places this case in the latter category, its resolution requires consideration not only of the several aid-to-sectarian-education cases but also of other educational precedents and several important noneducation cases. The now well-defined, three-part test that has emerged from our decisions is a product of considerations derived from the full sweep of the establishment-clause cases.

To pass scrutiny under the establishment clause, legislation must do three things: It must clearly reflect a secular legislative purpose. Its primary effect may be neither to advance nor to inhibit religion. It must avoid excessive entanglement with religion.

Justice Powell wrote the opinion of the Court, stating that although *Everson* and *Allen* did aid parents of nonpublic schoolchildren, they did not directly aid the school, because the school could have avoided the transportation and textbook costs by placing the burden directly on the parents' shoulders. In contrast, he pointed out that any assistance such as tuition, reimbursements, or tax credits does eventually find its way back as financial support to nonpublic schools.

In the six to three decision, Chief Justice Burger dissented along with Justices Rehnquist and White. As support for his position, he pointed out that there was no restriction of federal monies provided for education under the G.I. Bill of Rights. He maintained that if the money is well spent on quality education, it doesn't matter which schools receive it. In his view, parochial schools serve a public purpose. Justice White pointed out that if the nonpublic schools closed, the public schools would receive an overwhelming burden. He also pointed out that parents desiring a secular and religious education for their children might find it unaffordable, placing them under an undue strain of conscience and violating their freedom of choice.

Meek v. Pittenger, Secretary of Education, 421 U.S. 349 (USSC, 1975)

GENERALIZATION

When a legislature passes an omnibus bill with many kinds of aid to children attending nonpublic schools and to the instructional effort of such schools as well, each part of that bill will be scrutinized for Constitutionality.

DESCRIPTION

"The commonwealth of Pennsylvania was authorized to provide directly to all children enrolled in nonpublic elementary and secondary schools meeting Pennsylvania's compulsory-attendance requirements 'auxiliary services' (Act 194) and loans of textbooks (Act 194)" with those textbooks being made available by purchase through publicly collected taxes. "The auxiliary services include counseling, testing, psychological services, speech and hearing therapy, and related services for exceptional, remedial, or educationally disadvantaged students." In that same act was a provision for the loan from public to nonpublic for materials and equipment to be used directly in the instructional endeavor. The plaintiff questioned the Constitutionality of both acts in which the instructional materials included periodicals, photographs, maps, charts, recordings, and films. The equipment, itself, included things such as projectors, recorders, and a variety of laboratory paraphernalia.

The justices examined all parts of each act. Not all were in agreement on which parts were Constitutional and which were not. That is, some justices were in the majority on some aspects and in the minority on others. Nonetheless, their decision was so organized that it provided very good guidance about what services, materials, and equipment may be purchased by public funds and provided to nonpublic schoolchildren.

First, Act 194 violated the establishment clause, because the auxiliary services were provided at predominantly church-related schools. The district court erred in holding that such services were permissible, because they are only secular, neutral, and nonideological. Excessive entanglement would be required for Pennsylvania's department of education to be assured that public school professional staff members providing those services would not advance the religious mission of the church-related schools in which they might be assigned.

Second, the direct loan of instructional materials and equipment to nonpublic schools authorized in Act 195 had the unconstitutional primary effect of establishing a religion, because 75 percent of the nonpublic schools in Pennsylvania that qualify for aid were church related or religiously affiliated. With aid that was neither indirect nor incidental, it was clear that religious establishment would be enhanced by that aid.

Third, Part III of Act 195—the textbook-loan provision—was limited to textbooks acceptable for use in the public schools and was Constitutional. It merely made "available to all children the benefits of a general program to lend books free of charge," and yielded a financial benefit that was not to the schools but rather was to the children and their parents.

Finally, Act 194 and all but the textbook-loan provisions of Act 195 violated the establishment clause of the First Amendment as made applicable to the states by the Fourteenth Amendment.

In *Wolman v. Walter,* 433 U.S. 229 (1977), the Supreme Court examined another omnibus bill, this time passed by the Ohio legislature. Noting the great preponderance of Catholic sponsorship among private schools in Ohio, Justice Blackmun wrote a badly split decision for the Court. In general, the decision was harmonious with *Meek* and stipulated that the provisions for textbooks loaned from public agencies to children attending any school—public or private—were Constitutional, and that diagnostic and therapeutic services to certain handicapped children enrolled in private schools could be supplied by public agencies.

Public Funds for Public Schools of New Jersey v. Brendan T. Byrne, Governor, 590 F. 2d 514 (USCA 3rd, 1979)

GENERALIZATION

State income tax relief grants will not be allowed as a way to meet the costs of tuition and fees to assist parents who have children in nonpublic schools.

DESCRIPTION

In 1976 the state of New Jersey passed its first general income tax law, which included tax relief to parents of children attending nonpublic schools. Other exemptions included those for taxpayers or spouses who were sixty-five years of age or older, blind, or disabled and dependents of the taxpayer who attended a college or university—either private or public—and received from the taxpayer at least half the cost of tuition and maintenance. Personal deductions of $1,000 against gross income would be allowed for each child attending any nonpublic elementary or secondary school on a full-time basis. Plaintiffs objected to this tax measure as advancement of religion, because 714 of 753 nonpublic schools in the state were religiously affiliated.

The Third Circuit Court affirmed a district court ruling that the statute was unconstitutional and stated several reasons for its position. The New Jersey statute violated the First Amendment in that the exemption had as a primary effect the advancement of some religion. The court acknowledged the fact that the government should not have excessive entanglement in dealing with religion. The state must be neutral in its relationships with religion. The money involved represented a charge made upon the state for the purpose of religious education. That is, a special tax exemption is, in effect, a charge made against the state. Parents supporting children enrolled in public schools were denied the additional benefit of the challenged exemption. The statute did not encompass a comprehensive system of education exemptions; rather, its effect was preferential and selective.

The New Jersey statute was a substantial change of existing tax laws and was required to initiate this new method of finance for the educational system of the state. The plaintiffs contended that this statute violated the First Amendment, because it helped those parents who sent their students to nonpublic schools that were sectarian. The defendants' position was that these parents were helping the state and alleviating the true cost factor by sending their children as students into nonpublic schools. Thus a partial reimbursement was merited, in their argument. The court held to the contrary and ruled against the defendants.

This contention over funding is one of the recurring themes in a troublesome area. Early on in the nation's development, Thomas Jefferson admonished that there should be a "Wall of separation between church and state." The court called up the three standards enunciated during the 1960s by the Supreme Court for dealing with cases that may violate the establishment clause and reiterated them. To satisfy the Constitution, a challenged law

1. Must have a secular legislative intent
2. Must have, as its principal or primary effect, neither the advancement nor inhibition of religion
3. Must avoid excessive entanglement between government and religion

Court decisions have indicated a line of allowable support. Specifically, that is support to the citizens involved in nonpublic education, parents, and their children. At the same time, those decisions have indicated that support aimed directly at nonpublic institutions is not allowable.

Every institution is financially dependent. Said another way, when an institution's money source is halted, the institution halts too. There is a direct relationship between money flowing to an institution and the establishment. They are the same, and both violate the establishment clause when the flow is tax money to sectarian schools.

Incidentally, it is pertinent to identify some organizations that have as their mission the thwarting of legislative attempts to divert public tax funds to the support of nonpublic education. One is the Public Funds for Public Schools of New Jersey, above. Others are the Committee for Public Education of New York and the Americans United for the Separation of Church and State. There are many others. Still other organizations, such as the American Civil Liberties Union, approach such questions of religious freedom from a broader viewpoint, but when all such organizations are considered, there emerges a formidable citizen force that frequently engages in litigation to test statutes enacted by legislatures in response to political pressures for new considerations to children enrolled in private schools. The phenomenon provides an excellent example of the power balance that exists in the American system as the judiciary is used by some citizens who find the legislative branch oppressive—and that, without regard to whoever might prevail in court decisions. The American system provides the opportunity for challenge on both sides of the several church-state questions and does not foreordain the winner. Totally, it is a picture of the fair play that is central within a political system of checks and balances.

Curriculum Disputes

Even though curriculum constriction is under the purview of the states, curriculum disputes involving some aspects of religion provide an ongoing story in litigation. In *Ring et al. v. Grand Forks Public Schools,* 483 F. Supp. 272 (1980), the district court declared unconstitutional a North Dakota statute stating that every public school board "shall cause a placard containing in the Ten Commandments of the Christian religion to be displayed in a conspicuous place in every school room, classroom or other place where classes convene for instruction." The court ordered the placards removed, as being in violation of the establishment clause. That legislative effort is a good reminder of the constant desire of some people to integrate into publicly supported education some basic religious tenets as among the foremost part of a program of study.

Similar desires have been evidenced in legislative activity within the federal Congress. Although some congressmen have spoken out against religion in public schools, declaring the public schools cannot—by both definition and function—train children either in piety or morality, others disagree. In 1980 both senators and congressmen were actively pursuing means by which federal court jurisdiction in school-prayer cases could be ended. Typically, federal statutes that have been proposed and resolutions in committees describe a need for public schools to set aside a short period for silent prayer, meditation, or contemplation.

The question is not new. Its difficulty is extended by the fact that religion, as practiced in the United States, lacks commonality. What is a religious exercise for one has nothing of religiosity for another. In *West Virginia Board of Education v. Barnette,* 319 U.S. 624 (1943), the Supreme Court protected the religious integrity of students who saw, in the flag salute, a violation of the biblical admonition that believers should not bow down to a graven image. Those affected schoolchildren were excused from the state requirement that all students should stand and salute the flag in a daily routine.

Zorach v. Clauson, 343 U.S. 306 (USSC, 1952)

GENERALIZATION

If schoolchildren are released from school classes to go to another location for religious instruction, there does not seem to be a conflict with either religious clause of the First Amendment.

DESCRIPTION

New York City has a program that permits its public schools to release students during the school day so that they may leave the school buildings and school grounds and go to religious centers for religious instruction or devotional exercises. Students are released on written request of their parents. Those not released stay in the classrooms. The churches make weekly reports to the schools, sending a list of children who have been released from public school but who have not reported for religious instruction.

This "released-time" program involved neither religious instruction in public school classrooms nor the expenditure of public funds. All costs, including the application blanks, are paid by the religious organizations.

Zorach and Gluck were taxpayers and residents in the New York City Public School District, and they attacked this released-time program as violating the provisions of the First Amendment, which, as embodied in the Fourteenth Amendment, prohibits the states from establishing religion or prohibiting its free exercise.

The court viewed this as a narrow question, whether the New York schools prohibited the free exercise of religion or created a system "respecting the establishment of religion," as depicted in the First Amendment. The Court paid scant attention to factors such as the degree to which the state's compulsory-attendance laws influenced children to attend religious classes or the role of teachers who received parental excuses for each child. Although three justices—Black, Frankfurter, and Jackson—dissented, the majority stated, "We cannot read into the Bill of Rights such a hostility toward religion."

Several reasons were set forward to support the decision. First, no one was forced to attend the religious instruction, and no religious instruction was brought into the public schools. Second, the religious program required no expenditures from public funds. Third, school authorities were neutral in regard to the program, and no attempt was made by the staff to persuade or coerce students into participating in the religious instruction. Fourth, the First Amendment reflected the philosophy that church and state should be separated; however, it did not say that in every and all respects there must be a separation of church and state. Finally, the Court declared that the history of the First Amendment did not reveal that religion and the state shall be aliens to each other—hostile, suspicious, and unfriendly.

The establishment of religion clause of the First Amendment means at least this: Neither state or federal government can set up a church; pass laws that aid one religion, aid all religions, or perfer one religion over another; force or influence a person to go to or to remain away from church against his or her will or force a person to profess a belief or disbelief in any religion; punish a person for entertaining or professing religious beliefs or disbeliefs or for church attendance or nonattendance; levy a tax to support any religious organizations or groups and vice versa; finance religious groups, undertake religious instruction, blend secular and sectarian education, or use secular institutions to force some religion on any person.

Preceding *Zorach* had been *McCollum v. Board of Education,* 333 U.S. 203 (1948). In that case, Vashti McCollum, a resident of the school district, was successful in her efforts to end religious instruction that was delivered on public school premises by ordained clergymen of various denominations. Although attendance was voluntary as it was in *Zorach,* the place of attendance was the critical factor, and the Champagne, Illinois, board of education was ordered to halt its on-premises religious instructional program.

In *Holt v. Thompson,* 225 N.W. 2d 678 (1975), the Wisconsin Supreme Court ruled on the Released Time for Religious Instruction Act. In that law the Wisconsin legislature stipulated the procedures for pupil flow, their accounting on attendance rolls, and the number of instructional minutes per week (60-180) that could be allotted to religion. The statute provided that such instruction was at the discretion of each local school board and, upon testing, was declared in harmony with the state's constitution.

Several cases have arisen concerning prayer and Bible reading in public school classrooms. In *State v. Sheve,* 91 N.S. 946 (1902), the Nebraska Supreme Court ordered that daily readings from teacher-selected Bible verses should halt, being forbidden by the state constitution. Occurring early in the twentieth century, that case was not very influential, even in the schools of the state where it was pronounced. More recently, similar cases have found their way into federal courts. *Abington School District v. Schempp* and *Murray v. Curlett,* 347 U.S. 203, came before the Supreme Court in 1963. In one, the Court ruled against students reading from various versions of the Holy Bible and piped through the school's loudspeaker system. In the other, the Court ruled against teacher-led prayers in the Baltimore public schools.

Engle v. Vitale, 370 U.S. 421 (USSC, 1962)

GENERALIZATION

Local or state boards of education may not write prayers and order that they must be said by all schoolchildren each day. In fact, writing of prayers by boards of education is an inappropriate function.

DESCRIPTION

The New York State regents recommended a daily procedure that included this prayer: "Almighty God, we acknowledge our dependence upon Thee, and we beg Thy blessings upon us, our parents, our teachers, and our Country." Not surprisingly, this came to known as the *Regent's Prayer* case.

The Union Free School District #9, New Hyde Park, initiated the prayer, to be said aloud by all students. The parents of ten pupils brought this action, "insisting that use of this official prayer in the public schools was contrary to the beliefs, religions, or religious practices of both themselves and their children." They challenged the Constitutionality of the state enabling law and the local school regulation ordering the recitation of this particular prayer and alleged that it violated the establishment clause of the First Amendment. The Court reviewed history and especially those times when people found the church in ascendency over the political state. This led to a declaration on the importance of religious liberty, and that value was what led James Madison to write the First Amendment as he did. That is, only when there is protection against the political ascendency of religion can there be freedom of religion. The Court also pointed out that although some might see hostility toward religion in a decision setting aside the Regent's Prayer, the decision was really one of friendliness toward all religions but preference for none. Prayer, then, to any deity cannot be a part of the instructional routine of a public school, for it would amount to the state establishing a religion.

Two other cases, from among several, demonstrate still other aspects of the church-state conflict as it arises in public schools. When there is honest dispute among citizens on some unsettled point in the spectrum of human knowledge, can a public school follow a theological interpretation of that problem? When national holidays and religious holidays coincide, must public schools ignore the religious aspects of those days, even when they are deeply ingrained in the nation's culture?

Epperson v. Arkansas, 303 U.S. 97 (USSC, 1968)

GENERALIZATION

A legislature cannot dictate an exclusive treatment of a questionable and controversial subject for the public schools, when that treatment adheres to some religious belief and excludes all other considerations on the subject.

DESCRIPTION

Susan Epperson was a teacher with a master's degree, employed by the Little Rock Public Schools to teach biology in 1964-65. Arkansas law made it unlawful for any public schoolteachers "to teach the theory or doctrine that mankind ascended or descended from a lower order of animals." The statute had been passed in 1925 and seemed to have been, and apparently was, one product of an upsurge of religious fervor at that time. It was derived from Tennessee's "monkey law," a law that gained some fame in the celebrated *Scopes* case of 1927.

After one successful year, in the fall of 1965, Susan Epperson was assigned to teach from a new text. That new text contained a chapter adapting much of the essence of Darwin's theory of the origin of species. Her dilemma was either to skip that chapter or to teach it and face possible criminal prosecution and dismissal. (The record indicated that Epperson was also interested in bringing the Arkansas statute into a Constitutional test, to the end that it would be set aside.)

The Supreme Court of Arkansas sustained the statute as an exercise of the state legislature to control the schools and specify the curriculum. The Supreme Court recognized that the Arkansas law demanded a curriculum that was attuned to a literal interpretation of the Book of Genesis as the adequate and exclusive explanation for the presence of life. Noting that the First Amendment "does not tolerate laws that cast a pall of orthodoxy over the classroom," the Court specifically observed that Arkansas "has sought to prevent its teachers from discussing the theory of evolution."

Speaking for the Court, Justice Fortas stated:

Judicial interposition in the operation of the public school system of the Nation raises problems requiring care and restraint. Our courts, however, have not failed to apply the First Amendment's mandate in our educational system where essential to safeguard the fundamental values of freedom of speech and inquiry, and of belief. By and large, public education in our Nation is committed to the control of state and local authorities. Courts do not and cannot intervene in the resolution of conflicts which arise in the daily operation of school systems and which do not directly and sharply implicate basic constitutional values. . . .

In the present case, there can be no doubt that Arkansas has sought to prevent its teachers from discussing the theory of evolution because it is contrary to the belief of some that the Book of Genesis must be the exclusive source of doctrine as to the origin of man. No suggestion has been made that Arkansas' law may be justified by considerations of state policy other than the religious views of some of its citizens. It is clear that fundamentalist sectarian conviction was and is the law's reason for existence. Its antecedent, Tennessee's "monkey law," candidly stated its purpose: to make it unlawful "to teach any theory that denies the story of the Divine Creation of man as taught in the Bible, and to teach instead that man has descended from a lower order of animals" . . . there is no doubt that the motivation for the law was the same: to suppress the teaching of a theory which it was thought, "denied" the divine creation of man.

Arkansas' law cannot be defended as an act of religious neutrality. Arkansas did not seek to excise from the curriculum of its schools and universities all discussion of the origin of man. The law's effort was confined to an attempt to blot out a particular theory because of its supposed conflict with the Biblical account, literally read. Plainly, the law is contrary to the mandate of the First, and in violation of the Fourteenth Amendment to the Constitution.

The decision was that Arkansas's statute was not one of religious neutrality and the state supreme court decision was reversed.

Roger Florey et al. v. Sioux Falls Schools, 619 F. 2d 1311 (USCA 8th, 1980)

GENERALIZATION

Some aspects of our culture such as music and painting are so permeated with religious themes that to avoid scrupulously every such composition or work of art would be to present an art curriculum with terrible voids; however, schools cannot teach such subjects in a way that gives aid to any religion.

DESCRIPTION

In a pattern not terribly different from previous years, two kindergarten classes in the Sioux Falls public schools prepared a program for parents during the Christmas season of 1977. It contained substantial religious content. Upon receiving complaints, the superintendent of schools called for the establishment of a citizen's committee to study the church-state issue as related to school functions. A recommendation from the committee became board policy in 1978 as a guide to Christmas season programs. Plaintiffs alleged that the new policy still violated the establishment clause of the First Amendment.

The policy was a substantive change from previous guidelines. If the policy had been in place in 1977, the two kindergarten programs that originally caused the complaint could not have been done. The new policy stated that schools could observe holidays having both religious and secular importance, such as Christmas; that schools could present holiday programs containing religious art, literature, and music; that such materials had to be displayed in a prudent and objective way; that religious symbols having deep cultural significance could be displayed as part of such programs if pertinent.

The district court ruled that the new board policy was not in violation of the establishment clause. The circuit court of appeals upheld that ruling. The boards' policies did not result in any relationship between the schools and any religious authority; hence there could be no excessive entanglement. The policies represented a substantial change from a previous posture by the local school board. From the evidence describing the 1978 presentations, the courts found no aid to religion or to any religious institution.

The school district made a substantial change in both policy and practice between 1977 and 1978. Justice Jackson's comment from *McCollum* was quoted by the district court, and it is pertinent:

Music without sacred music, architecture minus the cathedral, or painting without scriptural themes would be eccentric and incomplete, even from a secular point of view. . . . The fact is that, for good or for ill, nearly everything in our culture worth transmitting, everything which gives meaning to life, is saturated with religious influences, derived from paganism, Judaism, Christianity—both Catholic and Protestant—and other faiths accepted by a large part of the world's people.

Without Constitutional violation and lacking any historical basis for hostility, the efforts of the local school district were allowed to stand by the courts.

Finance and Organization

Can a church own property? Can a church own property and have it exempted from local property taxation? Can a local school district rent space for instructional purposes? Can such a rental include space owned by a church? Can students enrolled in a church-sponsored nonpublic school attend any classes in public schools, if they live in that school district? When does excessive entanglement occur?

The questions that arise upon sober reflection over how to keep church and state separated are both many and complicated. In part, this is true because the questions are part of a never-ending parade of questions—new ones and refinements of old ones that are constantly arising. No sooner is one question settled by a court decision than another one arises, because many Americans are not satisfied with the conditions of no public funds for private education and no religious activities in public education. Given the American characteristics of aggressiveness and inventiveness, new proposals will doubtless continue to flow as citizens seek ways to accomplish Constitutionally the goals they deem to be important.

The professionals in educational administration have seen all of this activity. Many administrators have played active roles in some of the controversies. Yet there is very little evidence of any long-range planning within the professional fraternity in regard to some of the basic questions of the church-state controversy. With compulsory-education laws in every state, the public schools are the organizations that must receive all who are qualified to attend. This is one of the differentiating characteristics between public and private schools that merits thoughtful organizational planning from school administrators before some court decision is made that private schools—sectarian or not—perform such a pervasive public service that they are entitled to support from public tax funds. In fact, there are at least three critical areas in the realm of money and organization that deserve such extended professional attention. If, in any fashion that may be invented, more tax money is to flow to students in private schools or to the schools themselves,

1. Who should control the curriculum and hire the faculty in the private schools?
2. Who should own the physical plant and the instructional equipment in the private schools?

3. Who should set standards and control admission and assignment of students in private schools?

Without attention to those matters, and a very few other similarly basic questions, court decisions on the larger question of money support may very likely have an adverse effect on education, generally, if in no other way than by the sundering of community support for the whole concept of elementary and secondary education for all.

Walz v. Tax Commission of New York City, 397 U.S. 664 (USSC, 1970)

GENERALIZATION

Property owned by a church and used for religious or educational purposes can be exempted from property taxation by state constitution or statute, for such a practice is not in violation of the U.S. Constitution.

DESCRIPTION

The appellant property owner unsuccessfully sought an injunction to prevent the New York Tax Commission from granting property-tax exemptions to buildings used for religious worship. The state constitution and statutes provided for tax exemptions for property used for religious, educational, or charitable purposes. It was argued that tax exemption as applied to religious bodies violated the provisions prohibiting the establishment of religion under the First and Fourteenth Amendments. The First Amendment to the Constitution provides in part that "Congress shall make no laws respecting an establishment of religion, or prohibiting the free exercise thereof," and the Fourteenth Amendment made that provision binding on all of the states.

In essence, the contention was that since all taxes were public funds, and since the constitution prohibited the use of public funds for religious purposes, the state was indirectly requiring Walz to make contributions to religious bodies.

To understand the First Amendment means that a person must understand the times in which it was written and the historical antecedents that caused Madison and Jefferson to dwell on it. The establishment of religion at that time connoted active involvement of the sovereign in religious activity, as was the case in England. There, the church of England was established, sponsored, and financed by the crown. Exemption from property tax for the church under provisions of the U.S. Constitution and its First Amendment does not, and cannot, mean establishing, sponsoring, or financing the church by the state out of public funds. It is an act of benevolent neutrality that enhances the Constitution by granting the church the freedom of existence and exercise without interference. Also, it frees the government from certain obligations and commitments to the church.

The Constitutional purpose of the property-tax exemption is neither sponsorship nor hostility but respect for peaceful coexistence of church and state and a recognition of the religious nature of the American people. Government derives its main support from tax money. Receiving tax from the church puts the issue the other way around—the church supporting the state—and tends to tie the two together, rather than separating them. Property-tax exemption for the church's property by the state is no more or less an aid, in principle, than is the federally granted exemption of contributions to churches from income taxes.

The church, through its program of health, education, and other social welfare services to a large population of the community, relieves the government of such burdens that would have consumed a reasonable proportion of the nation's tax money. Tax exemption, equated with subsidy, and used this way, has not promoted religion; rather, it has promoted secular and social services by the churches for the community. Churches not only provide for religious experiences but also carry on many secular services. Absolute separation or noninvolvement between church and state, which is pursued in this case, does not exist and cannot exist. The ruling was for continuation of the exemption.

In *Walz*, a long-time practice in the United States was reaffirmed, verifying that churches by their mission, and through the use of their property, serve a secular purpose. In *Hartington,* which follows, the question was much more specific.

School District of Hartington v. Nebraska State Board of Education,
195 N.W. 2d 161 (NE SC, 1972)

GENERALIZATION

To carry out a part of an instructional program, local boards of education may need to rent additional space. When designed especially to qualify for federal funding, the program may need to include students who live in the school district and who attend private school, and the space may be rented in church-owned property, with certain qualifications.

DESCRIPTION

The Hartington School District applied for a grant of federal funds to provide instructional activities and services to meet special education needs of children identified as educationally deprived. The application was not approved by the state board of education or the Nebraska Department of Education, because it revealed that the public school district intended to lease needed space from Hartington Cedar Catholic, a parochial school, to conduct the program. It also revealed that the instructional program would be made available to the parochial school students who needed special education.

The *Hartington* case involved Constitutional questions at the federal and state levels. The First Amendment of the Constitution provides that "Congress shall make no law respecting an establishment of religion, or prohibiting the free exercise thereof." The right of a public school district to use or lease all or part of a church or other sectarian building for public school purposes has been upheld in a number of earlier cases. As long as the leased are under the authority, control, and operation of the public school district, and a secular instructional program is carried on, there is no establishment of religion. The instruction must be nonsectarian with no religious pictures or symbols on the leased site. These are the conditions that must be met, and the Nebraska court found, in a four to three decision, that there was no excessive entanglement between government and religion.

The second constitutional question arose from the Nebraska constitution, which provides that "no religious test or qualification shall be required of any student for admission to any public school." The court reasoned that an attempt to prohibit a student enrolled in a parochial school from participating in a program conducted by the public schools, solely because the student was enrolled in a parochial school, violated this provision with attendance at a nonpublic school being the test. A concurring opinion pointed out that the special-education classes in question were a result of a federal act that provided services for children enrolled in any kind of school, as long as they were under the direct supervision and control of the public school during the offering of that program. The Elementary and Secondary Education Act of 1965 had not been found to be in violation of the Constitution. The leasing of classrooms by a public school district from a parochial school for special-education programs funded by the United States government, then, must not be unconstitutional.

The Nebraska constitution is strongly separatist and states that "Neither the state legislature nor any county, city, or other public corporation shall make any appropriation from any public fund, or grant any public land in aid of any sectarian or denominational school which is not exclusively owned and controlled by the state." It was on this unusually strong language that the dissenting justices based their decision. However, their view did not prevail. The classes in question were conducted by the Hartington Public School and were free of religious entanglement.

* * *

In candor, it is a very narrow line that separates support given to children attending private schools as Constitutional while declaring as unconstitutional support that goes to the school itself. If parents find relief from the costs of books and transportation, for example, they are surely in better financial shape to face the tuition and donations paid by them to the private school. Yet the line is discernible, and the fact that it is a narrow line does not make it any the less legal or socially acceptable.

From court tests of state and federal statutes, it is now clear that if state constitutions do not preclude it, several kinds of support from public funds to children attending nonpublic church-sponsored elementary and secondary schools are Constitutional: bus transportation (or transportation costs), secular textbook loans, health services, psychological services, reimbursements on a per-pupil-cost basis for the administration of state-mandated standardized tests, tests for speech and hearing defects, and remedial help for the handicapped. Assistance from public funds, aimed specifically at the children who will benefit from that assistance, has been the guiding rule since about 1930.

Some kinds of support from public funds have been consistently ruled unconstitutional: salary supplements to parochial teachers, direct money grants to nonpublic schools, and tax credits or exemptions to parents of parochial school students.

The question of prayer and meditation, as kinds of religious expression in public schools, is not so clear. The religious beliefs of schoolchildren deserve extended protection and yet not to the extent that they should be exempted obligations for vaccination—unless statutes provide exemption for people holding religious tenets against medical practices such as vaccination. Can children pause in the school day for silent meditation but not for silent prayer? Children can be released from public schools to go to another location for instruction in a religious denomination. In some states shared-time enrollment or dual enrollment can be carefully structured and meet tests of constitutionality. But that is determined by state, for what proved to be acceptable in Nebraska proved to be unacceptable in Michigan. With so many unsettled questions about the church-state relationships in education, it will continue to be a frequently litigated area.

chapter 11

COLLECTIVE BARGAINING

The decade of the sixties witnessed substantial growth in collective bargaining in public education. Emerging from a time when initial efforts by teachers to organize and bargain collectively met with public criticism, more than 90 percent of today's teachers in the United States are covered by a contract that is the result of collective bargaining. Semantic terms —*collective negotiations, collective bargaining,* and other terms—are used in several states. For our purposes we refer to *collective bargaining* as the process through which the parties (the board of education and the employee organization) reach an agreement.

At last count—and this number has been changing—over forty states provide for some form of collective bargaining by school employees. Six of them approved teacher collective bargaining in the sixties; the remaining states granted statutory approval in the seventies and eighties.

It must be recognized, however, that because of the very nature of the employment relationship, there are substantial differences between the rights of employees in the public sector compared to the rights of employees in the private sector. One of the major issues that has not yet been resolved satisfactorily is the right of public employees to strike.

Federal legislation has had an impact upon all states with regard to organized labor. In 1935 the Wagner Act (which established the National Labor Relations Board [NLRB]) provided employees the right to organize and bargain. Furthermore, this act granted the employees the right to strike and picket. The Constitutionality of the act was upheld in *National Labor Relations Bd. v. Jones and Laughlin Steel Corp.,* 81 *L.Ed.* 893 (1937). This act specifically excluded workers in public employment, but it established a political tone in labor relations.

Believing that there should be a better balance between labor and management, the Congress enacted the Taft-Hartley Act of 1947. Section

14-b of this act, known as the "right-to-work" provision, set the stage for states to adopt legislation that grants employees the right to work whether or not they join a labor union.

With that very brief acknowledgment of federal statutes that changed the government's position toward bargaining, let us examine a landmark case that deals with the issue of sovereignty of the board of education and with the issue of strikes by public employees. It came from Norwalk.

Norwalk Teachers' Association v. Board of Education, 83 A. 2d 482 (CT SC 1951)

GENERALIZATION

In the American system of government, sovereignty is inherent in the people. The people can delegate this sovereignty to a government that they create and operate by law. Persons employed by such a government are agents who are to carry out the government's task. The status of these persons is different from that of persons in the private sector; that is, they serve the public welfare. The profit motive of free enterprise is absent. To say that persons in the public employ, absent statutory authority to do so, have the right to strike is the equivalent of saying they can deny the authority of government and contravene the public welfare.

DESCRIPTION

In April 1946 there was a dispute between the parties over salary rates. After protracted negotiations, 230 of the approximately 300 members of the teachers' association rejected the individual contracts tendered to them and refused to return to their teaching duties. The governor and the state board of education entered the negotiations and finally a settlement was reached. This was carried forward through the school year 1950-51. Doubt and uncertainty arose concerning the rights and duties of respective parties, the interpretation of the contract, and the construction of the state statutes relating to schools, education, and boards of education. The parties joined in an action to seek judicial determination of their respective rights, privileges, duties, and immunities. Questions were raised about the right to strike, the right to organize as a labor union, the right to demand recognition and collective bargaining, and the question of whether collective bargaining between the plaintiff and the defendant was permissible.

The court first held that teachers did not have the right to strike.

Questions (a) and (b) related to the right of the plaintiff to organize itself as a labor union and to demand recognition and collective bargaining. The right to organize is *sometimes* [emphasis supplied] accorded by statute or ordinance. . . . The right to organize has also been forbidden by statute or regulation. In Connecticut the statutes are silent on the subject. Union organization in industry is now the rule rather than the exception. In the absence of prohibitory statute or regulation, no good reason appears why public employees should not organize as a labor union. . . . It is the second part of the question (a) that causes difficulty. The question reads: "Is it permitted to the plaintiff under our laws to organize itself as a labor union for the purpose of demanding and receiving recognition and collective bargaining? The question is phrased in a very peremptory form. The common method of enforcing recognition and collective bargaining is the strike. It appears that this method has already been used by the plaintiff and the threat of its use again is one of the reasons for the present suit. As has been said, the strike is not a permissible method of enforcing the plaintiff's demands. The answer to questions (a) and (b) is a qualified "yes." There is no objection to the organization of the plaintiff as a labor union, but if its organization is for the purpose of "demanding" recognition and collective bargaining, the demands must be kept within legal bounds. What we have said does not mean that the plaintiff has the right to organize for all of the purposes for which employees in private enterprise may unite, as those are defined in Sec. 7391 of the General Statutes. Nor does it mean that, having organized, it is necessarily protected against unfair labor practices as specified in Sec. 7392 or that it shall be the exclusive bargaining agent for all employees of the unit, as provided in Sec. 7393. It means nothing more than that the plaintiff may organize and bargain collectively for the pay and working conditions which it may be in the power of the board of education to grant.

Questions (c) and (d) in effect ask whether collective bargaining between the plaintiff and the defendant is permissible. The statutes and private acts give broad powers to the defendant with reference to educational matters and school management in Norwalk. If it chooses to negotiate with the plaintiff with regard to the employment, salaries, grievance procedure and working conditions of its members, there is no statute, public or private, which forbids such negotiations. It is matter of common knowledge that this is the method pursued in most school systems large enough to support a teachers' association in some form. It would seem to make no difference theoretically whether the negotiations are with a committee of the whole association or with individuals or small related groups, so long as any agreement made with the committee is confined to members of the association. If the strike threat is absent and the defendant prefers to handle the matter through negotiation with the plaintiff, no reason exists why it should not do so. *The claim of the defendant that this would be an illegal delegation of authority is without merit.* The authority is and remains in the board. This statement is not to be construed as approval of the existing contracts attached to the complaint. Their validity is not an issue.

As in the case of questions (a) and (b), (c) and (d) are in too general a form to permit a categorical answer. The qualified "yes" which we give to them should not be construed as authority to negotiate a contract which involves the surrender of the board's legal discretion, is contrary to law or is otherwise ultra vires. For example, an agreement by the board to hire only union members would clearly be an illegal discrimination. . . . Any salary schedule must be subject to the powers of the board of estimate and taxation. "The salaries of all persons appointed by the board of education . . . shall be fixed by said board, but the aggregate amount of such salaries . . . shall not exceed the amount determined by the board of estimate and taxation."

This case, for many years, set guidelines on the right of the board of education to negotiate with teachers. The following precedents were established by the decision in this instance:

1. Absent a statute or regulation to the contrary, public employees may organize as a labor union.

2. The board of education may recognize the union as the bargaining agent for the teachers and, having done so, may bargain collectively for pay and conditions of employment that may be within the power of the board to grant.

3. Even though the board of education has recognized the union and agreed to bargain collectively with it, the board may not abrogate its right to have the last word in the bargaining process.

4. Public employees may not strike, individually or collectively, to enforce their demands.

5. Upon reaching an impasse, the parties may agree, legally and voluntarily, to arbitration of specific issues with the proviso that the board may not surrender its power to have the last word; these same provisions apply to fact finding and mediation.

6. The board—throughout the collective bargaining process—may not delegate its statutory and/or constitutional powers to other parties.

States that have provided a limited right to strike to teachers are Alaska, Hawaii, Minnesota, Montana, Oregon, Pennsylvania (reference is made to *Butler Area S.D. v. Butler Educ. Assoc.,* 97 LRRM. [Pa. 1978]), Vermont, and Wisconsin.

Elements of Collective Bargaining

There is no Constitutional right to bargain; each state legislature establishes that right through its enactments. These statutes will vary from state to state even as the application of the statutory provisions will vary from school district to school district within the state. However, although a court decision is based upon an interpretation of the language of a particular state's collective bargaining act and the language of a specific school district's contract, this may or may not be controlling in another jurisdiction.

Where states have enacted collective-bargaining statutes, formal bargaining is the generally accepted practice. These statutes call for the formal pattern but not necessarily the full content of federal labor laws. The major topics that are included in these statutes include the bargaining unit and representation, processes for resolving disputes, rights and security of the bargaining representation, handling of unfair labor practices, and the creation of state boards and agencies to administer the statutes. Minus the exceptions noted above, these collective-bargaining statutes contain prohibition against strikes by public employees.

Designation of the Bargaining Unit and the Bargaining Representative

The first step in the process is the designation of the bargaining unit. There is no clear-cut universal definition of such a unit; the guidelines to determine the "appropriate bargaining unit" vary and are subject to the provisions of particular state statutes. Generally, the following criteria are controlling:

1. There should be as few bargaining units as possible to represent the membership.
2. The units should include members who have a "community of interest" in the same collective-bargaining procedure. (Wis. Stat. Ann., Sec. 14.70 [4] [d] 2.)

It should be readily apparent to the reader that having employees with conflicting interests and duties in the same bargaining unit would be counter-productive and would, thereby, tend to defeat the purpose of the collective-bargaining process—the fair representation for all employees in the unit.

Although most statutes do provide wide latitude in determining the appropriate bargaining unit, certain state statutes place restrictions on bargaining-unit composition. For example, Connecticut, Delaware, and Hawaii require separation of certificated employees according to their certification classes or administrative duties (Conn. Gen. Stat. Ann., Sec. 10-1536; Del. Code Ann., Tit. 14, Sec. 4001 [5]; Haw. Rev'd Stat. 89-6 [a] [5-8]) and the Minnesota statute requires that all teachers be placed in the same unit (Minn. Stat. Ann., Sec. 17963, Subd. 17). One of the more difficult problems to be resolved in determining the composition of the bargaining unit is the placement of supervisors and administrative personnel. The New York State Civil Service Laws, Section 207(1), leave the inclusion of such personnel in a teachers' unit to the discretion of the Public Employees Relations Board (PERB). New Jersey and Pennsylvania statutes place supervisors in units that are limited to supervisors, and Rhode Island and Wisconsin prohibit any representation of supervisors by any labor organization. (R.I. Gen. Laws, Sec. 28-9.3-2; Wis. Stat. Ann., Sec. 111.81(12).)

Where the statutes are unclear and/or where the particular circumstances with a school district create some doubt about the proper placement of employees, expert legal counsel should be sought before bargaining units are designated for specific groups of employees.

After the bargaining unit is established, the bargaining representative is selected in accordance with the provisions of the statute(s) of the state within which the unit is located. For the most part, states have authorized the organization that receives the majority vote of the unit members to act as the *exclusive* bargaining agent for all unit members—including those who have elected not to join the union or association. There is very little provision for proportional representation. It should be noted that in any election to determine the bargaining representative, not only should the ballot contain the names of competing organizations, but, also, it should contain a provision whereby the members of the bargaining unit may elect not to be represented by any bargaining agent.

Several interesting cases on recognition of bargaining units were decided during the late seventies. In *Crestwood Educ. Assoc. v. Michigan Employment Rel. Comm.,* 276 N.W. 2d 592 (Mich. Ct. of App., 1979), replacement teachers were hired to replace teachers who were dismissed following an illegal strike, and they were given the right by the appellate court to vote in a representative election that excluded the discharged teachers. In *Northwest Arctic Reg. Educ. Attendance Area v. Alaska Pub. Serv. Employees, Local 71,* 591 P. 2d 1292 (AK, 1979), the Alaska Supreme Court applied NLRB doctrine regarding successor employers. In this instance legislatively created school districts replaced a state corporation that administered public education systems in unorganized boroughs. The court held that the new entity was a successor employer that remained essentially the same and was, therefore, obliged to continue recognition of, and to bargain with, the union that had represented the noncertificated employees of the former employer. In *Nebraska Assoc. of Pub. Employees v. Nebraska Dept. of Education,* 281 N.W. 2d 544 (NE, 1979), the Nebraska Supreme Court held that those who objected to and moved to set aside an election had the burden of proof, and that only when a preponderance of the evidence indicated that material misrepresentations of relevant facts were made in campaign statements, and that such misrepresentations had a substantial impact on the outcome of the election, would the election be set aside.

The United States Supreme Court, in *Abood v. Detroit Board,* 431 U.S. 209 (1977), found that the granting of exclusive bargaining rights to a certified union or association, by statute, was Constitutional. In this case a group of teachers was challenging the validity of an agency-shop clause in a collective-bargaining agreement between the Detroit board of education and the Detroit Federation of Teachers. Under the agency-shop provision, the Michigan statute required that teachers who did not become a union member within sixty days of their employment had to pay the union an amount equal to the regular dues or face discharge. The nonunion teachers cited their opposition to collective bargaining and their disapproval of a number of the union's political activities (for example, support of political candidates) that were unrelated to the collective-bargaining process. They then asked the Court to declare the agency-shop clause unconstitutional and argued that their Constitutional right to freedom of association, under the First and Fourteenth Amendments, had been violated. The Court ruled that the agency-shop clause was Constitutional and noted that a previous labor-relations decision in the private sector held that such arrangements were viable in that bargaining activities benefited all employees, and, therefore, all employees should help defray the union's expenses in negotiations. Citing a union-shop arrangement, the court reasoned that agency-shop arrangements were valid for public employees in that a "union shop arrangement has been thought to distribute fairly the cost of these activities among those who benefit, and it counteracts the incentive that employees might otherwise have to become 'free riders'—to refuse to contribute to the union while obtaining benefits of union representation that necessarily accrue to all employees."

In *Abood* the Supreme Court ruled that it was in violation of the First Amendment to require a public employee to be forced to pay dues to support a union's political activities. However, the Court did not define "political activities" and noted, instead, that there would be "difficult problems in drawing lines between collective bargaining activities, for which contributions may be compelled, and ideological activities unrelated to collective bargaining, for which such compulsion is prohibited."

Rights and Obligations of Exclusive Bargaining Representatives

Several recent cases deal with the rights of the bargaining agent. Once granted exclusivity, the union does acquire certain rights, standing as the recognized representative of the teachers in the district.

In a lower New York court decision, *Maryvale Educators Association v. Newman,* 416 N.Y.S. 2d 876 (App. Div., 1979), the exclusive bargaining agent was granted access to faculty mailboxes denied to a minority union, since this status "was rationally related to the valid state objective of ensuring labor stability."

The Minnesota Supreme Court—in deciding a case in favor of the state teachers' association local affiliate—held that the parent body (the state teachers' association) "served only as a resource and supporting organization." The state organization had joined the local association in filing an unfair labor-practice charge and did not agree when the local association agreed to dismiss the charge against the board of education. (*Minnesota Educ. Assoc. v. Ind. School Dist. #404,* 287 N.W. 2d 666 [MN, 1980].)

An element of union security, related to *Abood,* above, is the requirement for identifying membership or nonmembership. Precise identification is by way of these three terms:

1. *Closed shop* is an arrangement whereby the management employs, and retains in employment, only those persons who are members in good standing of a specified labor union. This is the most extreme of all the "union-security" arrangements.

2. *Union shop* is an arrangement under which an employer may hire a nonmember of a union with the understanding that the new employee shall join the union within a specified period; failure to do so will result in the termination of the new employee's employment.

3. *Agency-shop* employees are not required to join the union but must pay, as a condition of their employment, an "agency" fee for being represented by the bargaining agent; failure to pay the fee will result in the employee's discharge.

When the New York legislature extended its agency-shop provisions for another two years, it continued a law that requires that when the agency shop is negotiated, it shall be accompanied by a procedure to refund, upon request, the employee's pro rata share "in aid of activities or causes of a political or ideological nature only incidentally related to terms and conditions of employment." A local teachers' union argument that this applied only to funds retained by the local organization and did not apply to the portion that was transmitted to the state and national organizations was rejected by the court, which explained that such procedures could be subverted by a reallocation of the dues. The court ruled against the union's refund requirement that the objections to expenditures be specific rather than general. (*Warner v. Board of Gates Chili School,* 415 N.Y.S. 2d 939 [1979].)

The Oregon law permits an employee who objects to joining a union due to "bona fide religious tenets or teachings of a church or religious body of which such employee is a member" to pay the agency-shop fee to a nonreligious charity. ORS Sec. 243, 666 (1). However, there must be a showing of the nexus between the objector's beliefs and his or her unwillingness to join or pay dues to the union. (*Gorham v. Roseburg,* 592 P. 2d 228 [OR, 1979].)

The employee organization that acts as the exclusive bargaining agent also has the legal duty to represent all teachers in that bargaining unit. Such "duty of fair representation" requires that there be no discrimination against any of its members in negotiating and administering collective-bargaining agreements. Furthermore, this duty requires that the union represent the interests of all members of the bargaining unit in the negotiation process—even those who are not union members. Although this requires the union to be "honest and fair," it does not deny the union the use of its discretion in deciding its negotiations strategy with the board of education or in handling grievances. Unless it can be shown that the union has acted in "bad faith," the union can take positions with which some members disagree, or it can decide to settle a grievance that may not be to a unit member's satisfaction. It is, after all, a unit, represented in some central "steering" committee that is not obligated to the individual inclinations of all teachers in the unit—members or not.

In *Offutt v. Montgomery Board,* 404 A. 2d (Md. App., 1979), a group of "twelve-month" teachers, counsellors, librarians, and athletic coaches attempted to invalidate an agreement the union made terminating the program that called for twelve-month assignments and placing all faculty on a ten-month basis. The court held that the employees did not have the right to bypass the authority of their designated bargaining representative and secure for themselves benefits directly from the employer, notwithstanding the school board's failure to bargain in good faith. *Offutt* is a good illustration of the inability of the bargaining unit to represent adequately the views of all unit members.

In an instance where the collective-bargaining agreement specified that sick leave would not apply to disability resulting from pregnancy, the Massachusetts Supreme Judicial Court upheld the order of the State Commission Against Discrimination that a teacher is entitled to sick leave arising out of her absence due to pregnancy. The court reasoned that although a union has the power to waive statutory rights related to collective action, rights of a personal, and not merely economic, nature are beyond its ability to bargain away. (*School Comm. of Brockton v. MA Comm. Against Discrimination,* 386 N.E. 2d 1240, 1244 [MA, 1979].) The New York Appellate Division held that pregnant teachers had the right to take sick leave to the same extent as if they were suffering from some other physical ailment and stated, "When a union . . . permits an employer to discriminate against union members, it has discriminated against them as surely as if it proposed the inequitable agreement and is equally liable... (*Div. of Human Rights v. Sweet Home Schools,* 423 N.Y.S. 2d 748 [NY, 1979].)

The Bargaining Table

Usually, the physical setting for collective-bargaining sessions includes a table at which the parties are seated and across which they conduct their bargaining session. There is a figurative sense to the table also. In collective bargaining the parties are assumed to come to the table as equal partners who have equal powers. Labor legislation requires that the parties bargain in good faith. The parties meet at reasonable times to present and receive proposals and counterproposals. The parties are to try honestly to reach agreement on the issues. There is nothing in the law that requires either party to agree to any demand. Good-faith bargaining requires the practice of the art of compromise and includes a need for invention and substitution.

Although the United States Supreme Court has interpreted the requirements of "good-faith bargaining" in a number of cases drawn from the private sector, these same standards have been cited, frequently, as the standards that should be applied in public sector collective bargaining. An illustration of that is found in *San Juan Teachers v. San Juan Schools,* 118 Cal. 662 (CA, 1975), in which the California Court of Appeals, relying upon the holding in a case decided under the Labor Management Relations Act, outlined the school board's obligations with regard to good faith bargaining as follows:

> The statutory duty to bargain collectively . . . imposes upon the parties the obligation to meet . . . and confer in good faith with respect to wages, hours and other terms and conditions of employment with a view to the final negotiation and execution of an agreement. The statute states specifically that this obligation "does not compel either party to agree to a proposal or require the making of a concession." Thus the adamant insistence on a bargaining position is not necessarily a refusal to bargain in good faith. "If the insistence is genuinely and sincerely held, if it is not mere window dressing, it may be maintained forever though it produces a stalemate." . . . The determination as to whether negotiations which have ended in a stalemate were held in the spirit demanded by the statute is a question of fact which can only be answered by a consideration of all the 'subtle and elusive factors' that, viewed as a whole, create a true picture of whether or not a negotiator has entered into discussion with a fair mind and a sincere purpose to find a basis of agreement.

There is a principle at stake that declares, in effect, that there is to be something for something (quid pro quo) wherein those who present demands should be willing to give something in return. These items are known as *trade-offs.*

At a point in time when the bargainers have decided that they have made all concessions that they can and have not reached agreement on all issues, they have reached an impasse. There are three major methods of breaking an impasse. They provide for intervention of a third party who must be neutral and impartial.

The first is *mediation.* This process calls for a mediator who will attempt, through an advisory process, to bring the parties back to the bargaining table. The mediator usually will meet with the parties separately to determine if there might be some movement toward a resolution of the conflict. Typically, the mediator moves back and forth between the separated parties, carrying ideas and seeking new views on the disagreement.

The second method is *fact finding.* Each side will present its factual information to the fact finder. In some states it is a team of fact finders. After reviewing this information, the fact finder will verify the facts and, then, will recommend a solution based solely upon the facts that have been presented to the impasse. That recommendation(s) flows back to the board and the teachers. If accepted by both parties, settlement occurs, and the impasse is broken.

The third method is *arbitration*. There are two forms of arbitration—advisory and binding. In *advisory arbitration,* the arbitrator attempts to advise the parties on what the arbitrator considers to be an equitable solution—based upon the arbitrator's analysis of the impasse, the positions of the parties, and the evidence that has been gathered. Note that this arbitrator's report is advisory, only, and will not be binding upon either party. The hoped-for effect of advisory arbitration will be that once this has been made public, pressure will be brought to bear upon the parties, and they will agree upon a settlement. The second form—*binding arbitration*—requires that the parties abide by the decision of the arbitrator; it is binding upon both parties. This form of arbitration may raise some questions of constitutionality when a duly constituted public body is required to surrender to a third party duties and responsibilities specifically charged to the board of education by the constitution, statutes, and/or decisions of the high state court. At the same time, in some states, binding arbitration is the statutorily mandated last effort when impasse has not been resolved by any other method.

The parties must agree upon the procedures they will follow in the bargaining process. One question that needs to be addressed at the outset of bargaining deals with the procedures in handling news releases. In some instances this is determined by statute as in the California Government Code, Section 3547a, which reads as follows: "All initial proposals of exclusive representatives and of public school employers, which relate to matters within the scope of representation, shall be presented at a public meeting of the public school employer and thereafter shall be public records." There is no set pattern for the conduct of the bargaining sessions or for determinining the composition of the bargaining team. News releases that come as surprises to the other party detract from the desired level of trust and tend to increase the difficulty level of bargaining. The bargaining process usually begins when either party drafts a contract proposal or a set of demands. As a rule this process is initiated by the union and presented to the employing board of education.

Scope of Bargaining

The several states have enacted statutes that determine what can be included in the bargaining process. These laws vary widely. Some laws are very broad and permit school boards and teachers' unions to bargain "in respect to rates of pay, wages, hours of employment or other conditions of employment, and shall be so recognized by the public employer" (State of Michigan, Gen. Sch. Laws, Sec. 423.211). Other state laws are more restrictive and specific (as provided in Tenn. Code Ann., Sec. 49-5510 [Cum. Supp. 1979]).

The board of education and the recognized professional employees' organization shall negotiate in good faith the following conditions of employment:

  a. Salaries or wages
  b. Grievance procedures
  c. Insurance
  d. Fringe benefits, but not to include pensions or retirement programs of
     the Tennessee consolidated retirement system
  e. Working conditions
  f. Leave
  g. Student discipline procedures
  h. Payroll deductions

Nothing shall prohibit the parties from agreeing to discuss other terms and
conditions of employment in service, but it shall not be bad faith as set forth in this
chapter to refuse to negotiate on any other terms and conditions. Either party may
file a complaint in a court of record of any demands to meet on other terms and
conditions and have an order of the court requiring the other party to continue to
meet in good faith on the required items of this section only.

The collective-bargaining process between boards of education and
teachers' unions may occur under one of several conditions. One such
condition is mandatory bargaining, which requires a board of education to
negotiate with the representative teachers' union. The second condition is
prohibitive bargaining, which may forbid bargaining completely or, if not
completely, may restrict bargaining to certain specified subjects and
prohibit the inclusion of others. Where the statutes are silent on bargaining,
the board of education is not required to enter into any collective-
bargaining agreement. The third condition is permissive bargaining. If the
board of education agrees to permissive bargaining, it shall bargain on
those items until an agreement is reached and shall be bound by the
agreement that is reached. In those states where the board of education
agrees to meet and confer, usually, the board is not bound to bargain to the
extent that it shall reach an agreement—although that impasse, appealed
into the state court system, may produce a decision that is, in effect, an
agreement through binding arbitration.

Defining the subjects for bargaining has created many difficulties. Where
the language of the statute is general, this has precipitated court cases
seeking a determination of obligations. Some courts limit mandatory
subjects of bargaining to those that are directly or significantly related to
wages, hours, and other conditions of employment; other courts are more
flexible and limit mandatory subjects of bargaining to matters materially
related to wages, hours, and other conditions of employment. In the latter
instance, the courts apply a test of balance to determine if the impact of the
bargaining subject outweighs its probable effect on the school system's
basic policy and by determining the relationship and possible impact of the
bargaining subject(s) on wages, hours, and other conditions of employment.

Seward Education Assn. v. School Dist. of Seward, 188 Neb. 722
(NE SC, 1972)

GENERALIZATION

If continuity of the educational program is to be promoted and strikes by teachers averted at times of disputes in labor relations, some procedures and/or agencies must be available to make final decisions and impose those on both the teachers' union and the local board of education. By state constitution or statutes, such agencies can be identified and procedures set forward.

DESCRIPTION

The union and the local board had agreed on all aspects of the contract for 1970-71 except salary. While in that impasse, the parties had appeared before the commission (then, court) of Industrial Relations (CIR), which, in Nebraska, is the agency designated to settle disputes in the public employment sector. Its money settlement was not acceptable to the Seward board, and an appeal was made from the CIR to the state supreme court. The appeal contended that the commission had violated both statute and constitution when, by its ruling, it had imposed new budgetary consequences upon the local board. Initially, the board had declined to bargain on any item and had done so only upon an earlier order from the CIR but had been unable to reach settlement on matters of salary.

The supreme court first addressed the questions of constitutionality and statutory authority of the CIR. Support for its creation was found in several places in the Nebraska constitution. The court could find no violation by the CIR as it implemented its statutory authority and addressed the impasse in the Seward schools. Then, assessing the statutes under which teachers and boards bargained in Nebraska, the court made a helpfully clarifying statement, providing answers to questions about topics that boards were obligated to bargain.

The next question raised involved an interpretation of the language "conditions of employment." While the issue may be moot because the parties did reach agreement on all points referred except wages, we do feel some observations are pertinent. Generally, teacher organizations have given the term "conditions of employment" an extremely broad meaning, while boards of education have tried to restrict that term to preserve their management prerogatives and policy-making powers. While there are many nebulous areas that may overlap working conditions, boards should not be required to enter negotiations on matters which are predominately matters of educational policy, management prerogatives, or statutory duties of the board of education. Kansas, by statute, has defined conditions of employment to include hours of work, vacation allowances, sick and injury leave, number of holidays, and wearing apparel. K.S.A. 1971 Supp., § 75-4322(5). Without trying to lay down any specific rule, we would hold that conditions of employment can be interpreted to include only those matters directly affecting the teacher's welfare. Without attempting in any way to be specific, or to limit the foregoing, we would consider the following to be exclusively within the management prerogative: The right to hire; to maintain order and efficiency; to schedule work; to control transfers and assignments; to determine what extracurricular activities may be supported or sponsored; and to determine the curriculum, class size, and types of specialists to be employed. The public policy involved in this legislation is expressed in section 48-802, R.R.S. 1943. With this public policy in mind, school districts and teacher associations should negotiate in good faith within the ambit of their respective responsibilities.

In *Beloit School Bd. v. WERC and Beloit Educ. Ass'n.,* 242 NW 2d 231 (WI, 1976), the Wisconsin Supreme Court held that not only should the board of education bargain over matters related, primarily, to wages, hours, and other conditions of employment, but, also, the board of education was required to bargain on the impact of its policy that affected wages, hours, and other conditions of employment.

To illustrate the differences that exist from state to state, we cite *Byram Township Bd. v. Byram Township Educ. Ass'n.,* 377 A. 2d 745 (NJ, 1977), where the appellate court held that the duty-free lunch period is not a subject for mandatory negotiations; it is a prerogative of management, whereas Section 3029 of the New York State Education Law requires that where a teacher's duty hours are in excess of five, a period of at least thirty minutes must be free from duties of any nature, and it must be scheduled as far as practicable during the hours normally allowed for pupils' lunch periods. The same New Jersey appellate court held that the board of education did not have to negotiate on the qualifications of personnel to fill vacancies. Furthermore, the court did hold that the following four issues were mandatory bargaining items: length of the teachers' workday, teachers' workload, pupil contact time, and teachers' facilities.

In two other New Jersey decisions, the first being *Red Bank Bd. v. Warrington,* 351 A. 2d 778 (NJ, 1976), mandatory bargaining was required over the assignment of elementary schoolteachers to an additional period of teaching to replace a free period they previously had. In the second case, the court dealt with a topic that is becoming increasingly more important—reduction in force (RIF). In *Union City H.S. Bd. v. Union City Teachers' Ass'n.,* 368 A. 2d 364 (NJ, 1976), the court agreed with the board of education's position that it was not required to negotiate the criteria or guidelines that would be used in selecting those teachers whose contracts were nonrenewed due to a reduction in force. The court held, furthermore, that the board of education was not required to negotiate over the future employment rights of the nonrenewed teachers. Compare this with Sections 2510 and 2585 of the New York Education Law, which require that if a position is abolished, the teacher with the least seniority within the tenure area of that position, in that school system, must be the person dismissed (only after determining that this teacher does not possess certification and training in another area where a teacher with less seniority may then be dismissed). The dismissed teacher's name then must be placed on a preferred eligible list and is entitled to reinstatement whenever, within four years, a vacancy in a similar position occurs.

Those subjects that are, for all intents and purposes, managerial prerogatives may be prohibitive subjects. Many of the court decisions in this area have involved the nonrenewal of teachers' employment. Generally, the courts have ruled that the procedural questions on staff nonrenewal are subject to bargaining: substantive questions are not. Three recent cases dealt with substantive aspects of bargaining issues. They were *Board of Educ. v. Areman,* 394 N.Y.S. 2d 143 (NY, 1977), in which the appellate court held that the board of education could not bargain away, counter to public policy, its right to inspect teacher personnel files; *Board of Educ. v. North Bergen Fed'n. of Teachers,* 357 A. 2d 302 (NJ, 1976), where the court held that a decision to or not to promote was a managerial prerogative and, therefore, not subject to collective bargaining; and *School Comm. of Hanover v. Curry,* 325 N.E. 2d 782 (MA, 1975), in which a Massachusetts appellate court held that the decision to abolish the position of music supervisor was a matter of educational policy and, thus, was a management prerogative.

The greatest conflict in rendering decisions comes in the area of permissive bargaining. There is a very wide range of permissive subjects. This might be illustrated best by citing *Morris v. Board of Educ.,* 401 F. Supp. 188 (DE, 1975), which was based upon a Delaware statute that provided that the employer and employee are required to negotiate about salaries, benefits, and working conditions *but* allowed agreements on other subjects as long as they were consistent with state law. The federal district court, relying upon that statute, held that the board of education was not prohibited from bargaining over a proposal by the teachers' union that called for prior notice of administrator-board of education meetings in which discussions would be held that might adversely affect a teacher's employment. One would hope that writers on school law could provide a comprehensive list of specific subjects for public sector collective bargaining. But since such a list is not feasible, one would be well advised to consult the state statutes in one's state of residence to determine those subjects. Litigation more frequently occurs over the phrase "terms and other conditions of work." To some, this generality means "everything."

The courts have held, generally, as in *Bd. of Educ. v. Yonkers Fed. of Teachers,* 383 N.E. 2d 569 (NY, 1976), that unless permissive bargaining is contrary to public policy, agreements are legal and enforceable. We find that cases from the industrial sections of the country show a trend toward including in permissive bargaining any item that is not explicitly and definitely prohibited by statute.

School management is bound in conflict between the provisions of labor statutes and education statutes. It remains for the courts to determine which statute shall prevail. It is not uncommon for opposite findings to be held in different states as is found in Conn. Gen. Stat. Ann., Sec. 7-474 (f) (Supp. 1969) where the court decreed that the terms of the lawfully bargained agreement "shall prevail" over any conflicting law or regulation, but in Massachusetts General Laws, Chapter 150 E., Section 7, the holding was that the terms of prior laws prevailed over later inconsistent labor laws.

"Terms and conditions" finally reduce to some very specific items, but they are troublesome to operationalize.

Courts have not reached unanimity about whether or not class size is a mandatory item for negotiations. Boards of education, to provide justification for not negotiating this item, should make their position very clear and should provide a rationale that will support their position. In *West Irondequoit Teachers' Ass'n. v. Helsby,* 346 N.Y.S. 2d 418 (NY, 1973), the court held that the board of education was not required to negotiate on this subject. In this instance, the board of education justified its position that this issue was not a bargainable issue, because it claimed the need for program flexibility and innovation. The teachers' union demanded different classes with varying numbers and no exceptions beyond those that were mutually agreeable to the teacher and the principal. Within the same state, in *Susquehanna Valley Central School Dist. v. S. V. Teachers' Ass'n.,* 376 N. Y. S. 2d 427 (NY, 1975), another court held that since the subject of class size was not forbidden by statute, it was arbitrable. A third court in the same state, one year later, held in the matter of *Board of Education v. Greenburgh Teachers' Fed'n.,* 381 N.Y.S. 2d 517 (NY, 1976), that the board of education was not required to bargain on class size, but it could do so voluntarily.

In *Pennsylvania Labor Relations Bd. v. State College Area School Dist.,* 337 A. 2d 262 (PA, 1975), the Pennsylvania Supreme Court remanded this case for a specific resolution of the question about whether class size was a mandatory or permissive issue. By definition, it was ruled that items were mandatory if they were of fundamental concern to the employee's interest in wages, hours, and other conditions of employment, even if the issues impinge upon basic policy. The balance-of-interests test applied here and the issue became mandatory where the impact of the issue on the employee in wages, hours, and other conditions of employment outweighed its probable effect on the basic policy of the school system as a whole. On the other hand, items are permissive where the impact on the basic policy of the school system as a whole outweighs the impact of the employee's interest.

Another area concerned financial benefits. Where the statutes have provided for collective bargaining—either mandatory or permissive—there is no question but that teachers' salaries are a negotiable item. The question, then, concerns other financial matters that may be negotiated.

One is reminded that decisions handed down in one state will not, necessarily, prevail in another state, and it is important to review the statutes and decisions of a particular state to determine the suitability of certain fringe benefits as bargainable items. For example, in *New Jersey Civil Service Ass'n. v. Mayor and City Council of Camden,* 343 A. 2d 154 (NJ, 1975), the court upheld collective bargaining on a dental plan. Similarly, a Massachusetts court, in *Allen v. Town of Sterling,* 329 N.E. 2d 756 (MA, 1975), upheld collective bargaining on sick leave.

Once granted, controversy has grown out of proposed adjustments to fringe benefits. In *Fitchburg Teachers Ass'n. v. School Comm.,* 271 N.E. 2d 646 (MA, 1971), the court upheld an agreement under which the school committee and the teacher's association had agreed to an adjustment in salary for persons nearing retirement. The auditor refused to approve payment to a teacher, but the court disagreed and ordered the payment. Generally, when contracts have expired, there is no legal obligation upon the board to continue paying them.

In the very sensitive area of reduction in force, boards of education are not required to bargain over their authority to employ and dismiss personnel. The matter of *Board of Education v. Lakeland Fed'n. of Teachers,* 381 N.Y.S. 2d 515 (NY, 1976), based upon Sections 2510 and 2585 of the New York State Education Law, above, did not prohibit the board of education and the teachers' association from bargaining on a definition of seniority to include past nonconsecutive service. In another aspect of dismissal, *Carmel School v. Carmel Teachers Ass'n.,* 348 N.Y.S. 2d 665 (NY, 1973), and *Schwab v. Bowen,* 363 N.Y.S. 2d 434 (NY, 1975), made it very clear that the board of education could not give up its authority to abolish teaching positions in the collective-bargaining process. The release of the plaintiff teachers in these cases was simply due to the abolition of positions, and no charges were brought against the teachers nor had they been disciplined in any way.

Although RIF is not a mandatory item of collective bargaining, there are some considerations to which boards of education must pay attention. Although one should first seek answers to legal questions regarding employee layoffs in the state statutes, board policies, and collective-bargaining contract provisions, the statute and/or contract very often is silent or unclear. The major question to be answered is "who" is to be riffed. Most school districts, in their RIF policies, either follow a strict seniority rule (last in-first out) or give greater weight to seniority when making a decision about who is to be released. Both the American Federation of Teachers and the National Education Association strongly support the seniority principle and make this one of their cornerstones on staff reduction in their labor contracts with boards of education and in lobbying for statutes that govern RIF.

There is substantial difference between discharge for cause and reduction in force. Most state statutes list incompetence, neglect of duty, insubordination, failure to comply with school laws and/or reasonable requests, immorality, and conviction of specified crimes as causes for discharge. Note that each of these things relates to a teacher's behavior or failure to act. On the other hand, RIF is related to external forces such as lower student enrollments, reduced turnover among teachers, shifts of pupils from public to private schools, reduced mobility among teachers, change in program, reduced funds available because of inflation, voter-imposed tax limitations, and reduction in local, state, and federal funding. Thus the board of education has a heavier burden of proof when it seeks to terminate an employee for cause than when it faces RIF.

Boards of education, administrators, and board attorneys must examine state statutes, board regulations, or collective-bargaining contracts to determine the procedural safeguards. A few of them require that discharge and RIF be treated alike. A case in point is the state of North Carolina, where the teacher-tenure statute requires the same procedure for discharge for cause as it does for RIF due to declining enrollments or district reorganization. The parties responsible for the delivery of educational services should have a carefully considered and developed policy on RIF in operation and one that is harmonious with the statutes of the state.

Another area, work load, does not command universal agreement that it should be an item for negotiations. Here the courts are divided as can be shown in two decisions that were handed down in New Jersey. The first, *Dunellen Board v. Dunellen Educ. Ass'n.,* 311 A. 2d 737 (NJ, 1973), involved a school district's attempt to consolidate department chairmanships. The board and association differed over whether this was a policy decision or whether it was subject to arbitration as part of a negotiated contract. The state's supreme court determined that it was a management decision and that it was not related, directly, to terms of employment. The second, *Board of Education v. West Orange Educ. Ass'n.,* 319 A. 2d 776 (NJ, 1974), considered as assignment of homerooms to be an extension of work load, and, thereby, such assignment was a negotiable issue since the matter was tied so closely to wages, hours, and conditions of work. It is important to note in these instances that the court made the determination based upon its interpretation of contract terminology. This principle imposes a duty on the parties to develop clarity of language in the contracts.

The school calendar and length of school day are other areas on which the courts are divided. There is more agreement on the length of school day being subject to negotiation than for the school calendar to be so classified. In *New York City School Bds. Ass'n. v. Board of Education,* 383 N.Y.S. 2d 208 (NY, 1976), the court held that the board of education was free to negotiate on the subject of the length of the school day, absent statutory prohibition or countervailing public policy. A New Jersey court, three years previously in *Board of Educ. v. Englewood Teachers Ass'n.*, 311 A. 2d 729 (NJ, 1973), held that the extension of the school day related directly to financial and personal considerations and was, thereby, a proper subject of negotiations.

On the school-calendar issue, a Missouri school district modified the school calendar by scheduling additional days and adding them to the calendar after distributing a calendar to the teachers with their contract. In *Adamich v. Ferguson-Florissant School District,* 483 S.W. 2d 629 (MO, App., 1972) the court held in favor of the board of education, ruling that the board did possess unilateral power to fix three designated days not originally listed since the board had initially contracted the right to fix the number of teaching days and the school calendar was not a part of the contract.

A Connecticut court demurred from designating the school calendar as a mandatory subject of bargaining. In *West Hartford Educ. Ass'n. v. DeCourcey,* 295 A. 2d 526 (CT, 1972), the court said that "The significance of calling something a 'condition of employment' is that it then becomes a mandatory subject of collective bargaining. . . . The duty to negotiate is limited to mandatory subjects of bargaining." At least one state has taken the opposite view. In *Board of Educ. v. Wisconsin ERC,* 191 N.W. 2d 242 (WI, 1971), the Wisconsin Supreme Court held that the school calendar was a condition of employment and, thereby, subject to negotiations. State statutes govern negotiability of many aspects of employment.

A final specific subject for discussion is academic freedom. Normally, this issue is not a subject for negotiations; it is covered under an individual's Constitutional right under the First Amendment of the United States Constitution and is seldom surrendered to a negotiated contract. Two cases are cited here dealing with this topic. In the matter of *Los Angeles Teachers' Union v. Los Angeles City Bd.,* 74 Cal 461 (CA, 1969), a teacher's freedom of speech was involved. The teachers' union sought to circulate within the schools a petition on school finance. The signed petition was to be forwarded to the governor, state superintendent of public instruction, and the city board of education. The California court held that this action amounted to political activity and, thus, had no place within the school. Consequently, the court ruled that the board of education could restrict the teachers' freedom of speech as a collective endeavor at their place of employment.

The *City of Madison Joint Dist. v. WERC,* above, 1976, dealt with First Amendment rights of teachers to speak out on public issues. The Court held that the teachers, who were speaking at a meeting of the board of education, were presenting the results of a survey on an issue being negotiated to the board of education. These teachers were not attempting to bargain on an issue nor were they the union representatives who were empowered to speak out on matters of negotiation but were only citizens speaking out at a public meeting.

Grievances

A grievance dispute is one in which the school district and the bargaining agent disagree upon the meaning or performance of a collectively bargained contract. The grievance must be filed with respect to a provision of the contract, for it is the administration of the contract that is being questioned.

Labor statutes, as a general rule, provide a technique of dispute resolution within some form of arbitration. A number of state laws mandate arbitration of grievances over the meaning and performance of outstanding collectively bargained agreements. When the item in dispute is genuinely negotiable, the board of education must, generally, enter into arbitration with the teachers' union if the collective-bargaining agreement calls for arbitration of such disputes.

When arbitration does take place under these conditions, a number of states have held that arbitration awards are presumptively valid, absent a challenge that shows them to be illegal. Courts will not uphold arbitration awards that are prohibited by the statutes or principles of judge-made law, that is, the rule against a board of education's delegation of discretionary duties that are vested exclusively in the board. This was illustrated in *Port Jefferson Station Teachers v. Brookhaven Comsewague Union Free Sch.,* 411 N.Y.S. 2d 345 (NY, 1978), in which the court set aside, as unenforceable, an agreement to arbitrate board decisions on selecting promotion candidates and a second agreement to pay sabbatical salaries greater than those specified in the statutes.

Most problems that are handled through formal grievance procedures originate from teachers' associations, but that is not a necessary limitation, and *Minneapolis Ass'n. of Administrators v. Minneapolis School District #1,* 311 N.W. 2d 474 (MN, 1981), is a case in point. In that case declining enrollments indicated the reasonableness of a reduction in the number of administrative positions. Along with the reductions, job consolidation led to a plan for the elimination of seven positions. The plan had been developed without consultation with the association, and an unfair labor practice was filed against the board, asking for a court order to stop the plan and for damages. Appealed by the board from a district court decision, the Minnesota Supreme Court split but ruled in favor of the board. The court noted that the seven employees were not fired; their job scope was reduced. That reduction was, by its nature, not of a kind mandated by statute for bargaining. Finally, the court found a necessity for local school districts to be able to delegate duties and to have some discretion in determining the structure of the organization and the positions necessary for its operation, saying, "defendant may not be required to meet and negotiate with the plaintiff concerning the method of determining which positions to divest of administrative functions."

There have been marked differences about what may be classified as matters subject to arbitration. State courts in New York, Oregon, and Pennsylvania have held that teacher ratings were subject to grievance arbitration once school boards had agreed to arbitrate teacher evaluations. The question of termination and nonrenewal of teachers was addressed in *Board of Education v. Niagara Wheatfield Teachers,* 388 N.Y.S. 2d 459 (NY, 1976), where the court held that teacher termination was subject to grievance arbitration when "just cause" was specified in the collective-bargaining agreement as the limitation for termination. In another New York decision, *Morris Cent. v. Morris Ed. Ass'n.,* 388 N.Y.S. 2d 371 (NY, 1976), the court refused to enforce an arbitration award under a collective-bargaining agreement limiting nonrenewal to "just cause." Some courts have refused to grant to arbitrators the power to order boards of education to reinstate teachers who were terminated through violation of agreed-upon evaluation procedures; the arbitrators were permitted to award the teachers monetary forms of relief. In states that provide comparatively wide opportunities for negotiation, both teachers and boards need to search for precise terminology that will clearly convey their intentions lest misunderstandings arise at the point of contract administration.

Ultimately, the legality of arbitration awards will turn on the court's interpretation of the awards' consistency with related state statutes. Courts refuse to substitute their judgment for that of the board of education unless the board's judgment has been patently in violation of the statutes. In instances that involve grave consequences, such as requiring a school district to grant tenure even to a teacher who was dismissed improperly, courts have been very hesitant to sustain arbitration awards that ordered such requirements. This was the holding in the *Bd. of Trustees v. Cook Cty. College Teachers Union,* 318 N.E. 2d 202 (IL, 1974).

With the increase in collective-bargaining agreements and the demands for review of the awards, the courts have been limiting their review to very narrow grounds. One explanation for this can be found in *Sergeant Bluff-Lufton Educ. Ass'n. v. SBL Comm. School,* 282 N.W. 2d 114 (IA, 1979), in which the Iowa Supreme Court described judicial involvement in the arbitration process as follows:

Arbitration is a faster process, draws on the expertise of persons in the field and is less expensive. To allow a court to "second guess" an arbitrator by granting a broad scope of review would nullify those advantages. Most important, limited judicial review gives the parties what they have bargained for—binding arbitration, not merely arbitration binding if a court agrees with the arbitrator's decision.

Some courts have used the "essence test" in reviewing arbitration awards. In *Hazleton Area School v. Hazleton Area Educ. Ass'n.* 408 A. 2d 544 (PA, 1979), the Commonwealth Court declared its compliance with this test under which a court must uphold the arbitrator's interpretation of the agreement if it can in any rational way be derived from the language and content of the agreement. The court added this language, "It is not our province to prove the mental processes of an arbitrator and to determine what role a piece of evidence or a brief might have played in an arbitrator's decision." Two related precepts have been added in other courts. The first held that the court's power to intervene is even more restricted when the arbitrator's interpretation of the agreement resolves the question that was submitted and not merely one aspect of the dispute. The second held that an arbitrator's resolution of substantive law or fact is not judicially receivable in the absence of prejudicial misconduct. Thus in this case the court held that the arbitrator could use, properly, past practice in interpreting the meaning of "Attendance Days."

In reviewing the decision in *Board of Charles Cty. v. Education Ass'n. of Charles Cty.*, 408 2d 89 (MD, 1979), the Maryland Court of Appeals affirmed the lower court decision and rejected the board of education's contention that when a court is asked to enforce an arbitration award that was concerned with the legality of the underlying contract, the court cannot be bound by the arbitrator's determination of that issue but must itself determine the contract's legality. That is, the court upheld the decision of the arbitrator that the local board had wanted to set aside.

One of the major areas to be considered in a standard of review of arbitrators' decisions is an examination of whether an arbitrator exceeded his or her authority. In *Milwaukee Bd. of School Dirs. v. Milwaukee Teachers' Educ. Ass'n.*, 287 N.W. 2d 131 (WI, 1980), the Wisconsin Supreme Court stated that "an arbitrator is confined to interpretation of that contract (from which he obtains his authority), and he does not sit to dispense his own brand of justice." In this case, the arbitrator was held to have exceeded his authority when he was authorized by the parties to resolve grievances arising out of a 1974 contract, and he then proceeded to render an award that affected teachers hired in 1975 or 1976 and found that the board of education's violation of the contract was a continuing one and that the contractual provision had not been altered by subsequent contracts. Another instance in which an arbitrator exceeded his authority was found in *School Comm. of Holyoke v. Duprey*, 391 N.E. 2d. 925 (MA, 1979), where he ordered the city to pay in excess of 50 percent of the teachers' health insurance premiums, which was prohibited by law unless the city enacted enabling legislation to permit payment of higher contributions. Arbitration will generally be upheld in court tests; however, awards in excess of statutory or contractual language will not be supported. When boards are directed to pay awards that come out of bad contract language, those awards will stand—the board must accept responsibility for its own contractual laxity.

The Right to Strike

The ultimate weapon that may be used by employees to obtain concessions from an employer is the strike. This is permissible in the private employment sector but is denied, generally, to teachers and other public employees. Eight states, previously listed in this chapter, permit a limited right to strike. The most recent state—Minnesota—to grant teacher unions the right to strike legally if mediation efforts fail experienced more teacher strikes in the fall of 1981 than in the previous nine years combined. Twenty-one strikes occurred, and the majority of the public school districts were working without contracts.

Not all concerted refusals to work are unlawful. Courts may be asked to determine what constitutes an unlawful strike. The mass refusal of teachers to sign new individual contracts for the coming school year has been held to be a lawful means of expressing their collective demands as are mass teacher resignations, if submitted without conditions and in proper form to terminate the teachers' employment, since the individuals who presented them are no longer employed and are no longer involved in collective bargaining. However, those resignations that are submitted to become effective only if their bargaining representative fails to achieve a satisfactory settlement have been considered to be an illegal strike as determined in *Bd. of Education v. Shanker,* 283 N.Y.S. 2d 548; *aff'd.* 386 N.Y.S. 2d 543 (1967).

Forms of work interruption—slowdowns, "work-to-rule," mass "sickouts," cancellation of all extracurricular volunteer assignments—if used as a weapon in the collective-bargaining process may be considered to be a form of strike pressure. The Pennsylvania Statutes Annotated, Title 45, Section 215.1, shows a broad definition of a strike:

Strike means concerted action in failing to report for duty, the willful absence from one's position, the stoppage of work, slowdown, or the abstinence in whole or in part from the full, faithful and proper performance of the duties of employment for the purpose of inducing, influencing, or coercing a change in the conditions or compensation for the rights, privileges, or obligations of employment.

One of the hazards in "work-to-rule" (performing only those duties that are specified in written contracts) is that courts have held teachers to be in breach of contract and thus subject to dismissal for failure to perform duties that are implied even though they have not been reduced to writing. Contracts for professional work in public school districts have both specific and implied duties. In *Warren Ed. Ass'n v. Adams,* 226 N.W. 2d 536 (MI, 1975), the court held that illegal concerted activities—regardless of by which name they are called—are subject to injunctive relief and such penalties as the court may prescribe.

There are limitations on the statutory right to strike. In states permitting strikes when negotiations have reached an impasse, usually the requirement that the parties exhaust statutory settlement remedies, that is, third-party intervention such as mediation or fact finding, must be satisfied before a strike may occur. Statutes that permit strikes provide, also, for the termination of the strike by court injunction where it has been determined that the strike poses a clear and present "danger or threat to the health, safety, or welfare of the public," as found in the Oregon Revised Statutes, Section 243.725(6). The courts must determine the kinds and degrees of dangers to public health, safety, and welfare. In *State v. Delaware Ed. Ass'n.,* 326 A. 2d 868 (DE, 1974), mere inconvenience will not satisfy the requirement for injunctive relief. In some states, for example, Pennsylvania, the courts cannot grant an injunction where no actual strike is in progress, but in other states, for example, New Jersey, the threat of a strike is sufficient grounds for the issuance of an injunction. Then, too, if the court feels that the public interest is best served by promoting good-faith bargaining and third-party intervention procedures and is of greater importance than the temporary interruption of public education, it may refuse to enjoin even a harmful strike.

Teachers, or labor unions, that willfully disobey a court injunction may be held in contempt of court. Punishment for contempt may be in the form of fines assessed against individuals and/or the union or imprisonment of individuals or both. Some statutes require specific sanctions. An illustration is Article 14 in the New York Civil Service Law, the Public Employees' Fair Employment Law, commonly referred to as the Taylor Law.

That law provides two types of penalties against employee organizations that participate in a strike: If an employee organization violates a court injunction against striking, the organization may be fined for criminal contempt (Sec. 751 of Judiciary Law), and if there has been a strike, the Public Employee Relations Board (PERB)—or in some instances a court—may suspend the striking employee organization's right of dues check-off, after a hearing, to determine the extent of the organization's responsibility for the strike. In each case the amount of the fine and the period of suspension of the right of check-off depend in part on whether the public employer committed acts of extreme provocation so as to diminish the organization's responsibility for the strike. Any employee who participates in a strike or a slowdown will lose two days' pay—one day's pay for the pay not earned and one day's pay as a penalty—for each day of such participation. In addition, the attorney general has ruled that an employee placed on probation by reason of a Taylor Law violation is to be treated as any other probationer, for layoff purposes—and probationers must be laid off *before* tenured employees.

Section 433.202 of the state of Michigan General School Laws prohibits strikes using the following language:

No person holding a position by appointment or employment in the government of the state of Michigan, or in the government of any one or more of the political subdivisions thereof, or in the public school service, or in any public or special district, or in the service of any authority, commission, or board, or in any other branch of the public service, hereinafter called a "public employee," shall strike.

Elsewhere, that same law provides, in part, that days lost because of strike or teachers' conference, so that the minimum of 180 days of student instruction is not met, shall not be counted as days of student instruction.

What remedies are available to a board of education for unlawful work stoppage? The most stringent is discharge for cause. Cause may be breach of contract, unauthorized absence, insubordination, or a statutory penalty. Such dismissal occurred in *Hortonville,* and the Court ruled (426 U.S. 481 [1976]) in favor of the board.

Hortonville Jt. Sch. District No. 1 v. Hortonville Jt. Sch. District No. 1 Ed. Assn., 426 U.S. 481 (1976)

GENERALIZATION

By virtue of the law that governs the actions of boards of education, those same boards have the power to employ and dismiss teachers and other employees. Can a board, vested with the power to employ or dismiss, but consistent with the due process clause of the Fourteenth Amendment, dismiss teachers engaged in a strike prohibited by state law? The Court found that the state has an interest in maintaining the allocation of responsibility for school matters as established by statute, and absent a showing of personal, financial, or antiunion bias, the court must hold with the presumption of impartiality on the part of the board of education.

DESCRIPTION

The teachers in the Hortonville School District worked under a master collective-bargaining agreement during the 1972-73 school year; even though there was no contract for the 1973-74 school year, the teachers continued to work while negotiations proceeded. Finally, on March 18, 1974, the members of the teachers' union went on strike. This was in direct violation of the Wisconsin law. On March 20 the superintendent of schools, by letter, requested the teachers to return to their classrooms; a few complied. A second letter was sent on March 23 in which the superintendent requested that the striking teachers return to work and reminded them that they were in violation of the law. The board of education, having operated the schools using substitute teachers, decided to conduct disciplinary hearings for each of the teachers on strike, as required by law. Thus individual notices were sent to each teacher setting hearings for April 1, 2, and 3. On April 1 most of the teachers appeared before the board with their counsel who indicated that the teachers did not want individual hearings but preferred to be treated as a group.

Although admitting that the teachers were on strike, counsel argued that the board was not sufficiently impartial to hear the case and that the due process clause of the Fourteenth Amendment required an independent, impartial decision maker. Counsel made an offer of proof to demonstrate that the board's contract offers were unsatisfactory, that the board used coercive and illegal bargaining tactics, and that teachers in the district had been locked out by the board. Counsel further requested permission to cross-examine the board members individually. The board refused this request but did permit counsel to make the offer of proof.

The board then, on April 2, voted to terminate the employment of the striking teachers and advised them to that effect by letter. This same letter invited the striking teachers to reapply for teaching positions; one did, and the board filled the remaining positions with replacements.

The Wisconsin Supreme Court held, in favor of the teachers, that the board was biased and thereby lost its statutory power to determine that the strike and persistent refusal to terminate it amounted to conduct serious enough to warrant discharge of the strikers. The school district, the seven members of the board of education, and three administrative employees of the district petitioned the United States Supreme Court to grant certiorari.

Reversing the state court and ruling for the board, Chief Justice Burger delivered the opinion of the Court:

The sole issue in this case is whether the Due Process Clause of the Fourteenth Amendment prohibits this School Board from making the decision to dismiss teachers admittedly engaged in a strike and persistently refusing to return to their duties. The Wisconsin Supreme Court held that the State Law prohibited the strike and that termination of the striking teachers' employment was within the Board's statutory authority. We are, of course, bound to accept the interpretation of Wisconsin law by the highest court of the State. The only decision remaining for the Board therefore involved the exercise of its discretion as to what should be done to carry out the duties the law placed on the Board.

Respondents' argument rests in part on doctrines that have no application to this case. They seem to argue that the Board Members had some personal or official stake in the decision whether the teachers should be dismissed, and that the Board has manifested some personal bitterness toward the teachers, aroused by teacher criticism of the Board during the strike . . . the teachers did not show, and the Wisconsin courts did not find, that the Board members had the kind of personal or financial stake in the decision that might create a conflict of interest, and there is nothing in the record to support charges of personal animosity. . . .

The only other factor suggested to support the claim of bias is that the School Board was involved in the negotiations that preceded and precipitated the striking teachers' discharge. Participation in those negotiations was a statutory duty of the Board. The Wisconsin Supreme Court held that this involvement, without more, disqualified the Board from deciding whether the teachers should be dismissed.

Due process, as this Court has repeatedly held, is a term that "negates any concept of inflexible procedures universally applicable to every imaginable situation." Determining what process is due in a given setting requires the Court to take into account the individual's stake in the decision at issue as well as the State's interest in a particular procedure for making it. Our assessment of the interests of the parties in this case leads to the conclusion that . . . the board's prior role as negotiator does not disqualify it to decide that the public interest in maintaining uninterrupted classroom work require that teachers striking in violation of state law be discharged.

The teachers' interests in these proceedings is, of course, self-evident. They wished to avoid termination of their employment, obviously an important interest, but one that must be examined in light of several factors. Since the teachers admitted that they were engaged in a work stoppage, there was no possibility of an erroneous factual determination on this critical threshold issue. Moreover, what the teachers claim as a property right was the expectation that the jobs they had left to go and remain on strike in violation of law would remain open to them.

State law vests the governmental, or policymaking, function exclusively in the School Board and the State has two interests in keeping it there. First, the Board is the body with overall responsibility for the governance of the school district; it must cope with the myriad day-to-day problems of a modern public school system including the severe consequences of a teachers' strike; by virtue of electing them the constituents have declared the Board members qualified to deal with these problems, and they are accountable to the voters for the manner in which they perform. Second, the state legislature has given to the Board the power to employ and dismiss teachers, as a part of the balance it has struck in the area of municipal labor relations; altering those statutory powers as a matter of federal due process clearly changes that balance. Permitting the Board to make the decision at issue here preserves its control over school district affairs, leaves the balance of power in labor relations where the state legislature struck it, and assures that the decision whether to dismiss the teachers will be made by the body responsible for that decision under state law.

Respondents have failed to demonstrate that the decision to terminate their employment was infected by the sort of bias that we have held to disqualify other decision-makers as a matter of federal due process. A showing that the Board was "involved" in the events preceding this decision, in light of the important interest in leaving with the Board the power given by the state legislature, is not enough to overcome the presumption of honesty and integrity in policymakers with decision-making power. Accordingly, we hold that the Due Process Clause of the Fourteenth Amendment did not guarantee respondents that the decision to terminate their employment would be made or reviewed by a body other than the School Board.

Reversed and remanded.

* * *

Collective bargaining is the process through which the board of education and the employee organization reach an agreement. This process has undergone substantial growth during the decades of the sixties and seventies, with a major case in 1951 to set the pace. The *Norwalk Teachers' Association v.*

Board of Education, 83 A. 2d 482, (CT, 1951), with respect to the issue of bargaining by public employees, included items that have become standard for schools.

1. Absent a statute or regulation to the contrary, public employees may organize as a labor union.

2. The board of education may recognize the union as the bargaining agent for the teachers and, having done so, may bargain collectively for pay and conditions of employment that may be within the powers of the board to grant.

3. Even though the board of education has recognized the union and agreed to bargain collectively with it, the board may not abrogate its right to have the last word in the bargaining process.

4. Public employees may not strike, individually or collectively, to enforce their demands.

5. Upon reaching an impasse, the parties may agree, legally and voluntarily, to arbitration of specific issues with the proviso that the board may not surrender its power to have the last word; these same provisions apply to fact finding and mediation.

6. The board—throughout the collective-bargaining process—may not delegate its statutory and/or constitutional powers to other parties.

Eight states—Alaska, Hawaii, Minnesota, Montana, Oregon, Pennsylvania, Vermont, and Wisconsin—have provided a limited right to strike to teachers.

The first step in the bargaining process is the designation of the bargaining unit. Once this unit has been established, the bargaining representative is selected in accordance with the state's statutory provisions. Where the union has been granted exclusivity, it does acquire certain rights such as access to faculty mailboxes and, in those states that permit it, agency-shop provisions. Another element of the bargaining process is the bargaining table where, figuratively, the parties are assumed to come as equal partners who have equal powers. Coming to the table requires that the parties bargain in good faith, which furthermore requires that the parties meet at reasonable times to present and receive proposals and counterproposals. There is nothing in the law that requires either party to agree to any demand, although, for practical purposes, the development of a contract does involve compromises and agreement.

Failure to reach agreement creates an impasse. There are three methods for resolving impasse. *Mediation* involves an attempt by a mediator, through an advisory process, to bring the parties back to the bargaining table. In *fact finding,* a fact finder attempts to verify the facts presented by both parties and then recommends a solution to the impasse, based solely upon the facts that have been presented. Finally, *arbitration,* whether advisory or binding, involves a third party or a third-party panel that will recommend (advisory) a resolution to the impasse or that will decide (binding) the resolution of the impasse that shall, then, be binding upon both parties.

The scope of bargaining may occur under one of several conditions. One is *mandatory bargaining,* which requires a board of education to negotiate with the union on issues that are considered to be mandatory; another is *prohibitive bargaining,* which forbids bargaining on items that are reserved exclusively to the board of education; the third condition is *permissive bargaining,* where once the board of education has agreed to bargain on certain items, bargaining shall proceed on those items until an agreement is reached. State statutes frequently define those items that are mandatory, prohibited, or permissive subjects for bargaining. Usually, the terms *wages, hours,* and *conditions of employment* are found in the statutes. "Conditions of employment" has been interpreted differently in the various states. Among these items may be found subjects such as class size, welfare items or financial benefits, reduction in force, work load, school calendar and length of school day, and academic freedom.

A *grievance dispute* is one in which the school district and the bargaining agent disagree about the meaning or performance of a collectively bargained contract. Usually, grievances are resolved through arbitration, when and if the collective-bargaining agreement calls for this procedure.

In the private sector, the strike is the ultimate weapon that may be used by an employee to obtain concessions from his employer. However, except for the eight states in which there is a statutorily granted limited right to strike, the use of the strike is an illegal activity that may result in severe penalties, including dismissal, fines, and/or imprisonment. The right of a board of education to dismiss striking employees, even though the board must, ultimately, act upon the collectively bargained agreement, was upheld in *Hortonville.*

Collective bargaining in the public sector requires a thorough understanding of the statutes of the particular state in which the school district is located. Above all, those who represent the parties should recognize their obligations, under the statutes, and should conduct themselves in such a manner as to arrive at an agreement that will permit the school district to discharge its primary function—the education of boys and girls.

chapter 12

FINANCE

Public schools are creatures of state and local governments. Forty-nine of the fifty states provide funds for education from state and local sources. The proportions of state and local funds vary. The fiftieth state—Hawaii—operates a state school system and funds this completely at the state level. The basic support for most public schools comes from tax dollars. The major producer of these dollars at the local level is the *ad valorem property tax,* that is, a tax levied against some proportion of the actual value of the property in the district. Some jurisdictions provide for other sources of taxation including, but not limited to, the local income tax, a utilities tax, and the tax used most frequently as a property-tax alternative—the sales tax. The use of the property tax has received much attention, has been labeled an oppressive and regressive tax, and has led to a number of court cases when citizens have sought relief from it.

The general argument advanced by the opponents of the present finance system is that reliance upon local property-tax revenues has caused wide discrepancies in the funding of educational programs not only when one state is compared with another but, also, when comparing one public school system with another within the same state. Additionally, some fault it as an inequitable tax upon those who pay it. The property tax—the main support for public schools—is a controversial tax.

Since many of the court challenges to public school financing programs attack the Constitutionality of such programs—usually under the equal-protection provision of the Fourteenth Amendment of the United States Constitution, the Constitutional aspects of public school district finance merit attention.

Constitutional Freedom and the Federal Role in Educational Finance

Amendment X of the United States Constitution reads: "The powers not delegated to the United States by the Constitution, nor prohibited by it to the States, are reserved to the States respectively, or to the People. " There is no reference to education in the Constitution, and education is, thereby, reserved to the several states. The 1945 Georgia State constitution reads: "The provision of an adequate education for the citizens shall be a primary obligation of the State of Georgia, the expense of which shall be provided for by taxation." That constitutional statement typifies what is said in the other forty-nine states.

Even though the federal government is not charged with the direct financing of education, federal funds are made available through various Congressional enactments. The basis for such funding is, generally, derived from the general-welfare clause found both in the Preamble of the Constitution—"We the People of the United States, in order to form a more perfect Union . . . promote the General Welfare . . . do ordain and establish the Constitution of the United States of America"—and in Section 8—"The Congress shall have the power to lay and collect Taxes, Duties, Imposts, and Excises, to pay the debts and provide for the common Defense and general Welfare of the United States." In *United States v. Butler,* 297 U.S. 1 (1938), the Court addressed the question of the meaning of Section 8 (Article I). In a six to three decision, the Court declared that this clause did not merely refer to other enumerated powers of Congress but actually conferred a new and separate power. With that clarifying case, Congress secured the power to tax and to appropriate "limited only by the requirement that it shall be exercised to provide for the general welfare of the United States." Comparatively, that could be described as a broad construction of the Constitution and, inasmuch as public education can be rationally described as within the rubric of general welfare, provided a case-law basis for federal participation in local educational costs.

One other basis that is cited, frequently, as a justification for federal support of education is the child-benefit theory. This concept, enunciated in both statutory and case law, is based upon the argument that the aid benefits the child directly even though there may be indirect and incidental aid to the school, public or nonpublic, that the pupil attends.

In 1785 the Congress of the Confederation authorized grants of public lands for maintenance of the public schools. This was followed, in 1787, by the Northwest Ordinance, under which federal land was granted for education—the sixteenth section of each township being reserved for schools. Additional land was reserved for a university. Thus began the complex current pattern of federal support for education. This pattern established the concept of categorical aid, whereby funds are appropriated for specific purposes and restricted to those purposes, alone. Following is a selected list of federal legislation that supports educational activities and that can be taken as exemplary of the federal involvement in education.

1862—First Morrill Act—Authorized public land grants to the states for the establishment and maintenance of agricultural and mechanical colleges.

1890—Second Morrill Act—Provided money grants for support of instruction in the agricultural and mechanical colleges.

1917—Smith-Hughes Act—Provided for grants to states for support of vocational education.

1935—Agricultural Adjustment Act (P.L. 74-320)—Commodities purchased under this authorization began to be used in school lunch programs in 1936.

1943—School Lunch Indemnity Plan (P.L. 78-129)—Provided funds for local school lunch food purchases.

1946—National School Lunch Act (P.L. 79—396)—Provided assistance through grants-in-aid and other means to states to assist in providing adequate foods and facilities for the establishment, maintenance, operation, and expansion of nonprofit school lunch programs.

1950—Financial Assistance for Local Educational Agencies Affected by Federal Activities (P.L. 81-815)—Provided assistance for construction—and (P.L. 81-874)—provided assistance for operation of schools in federally affected areas ("Impact Aid").

1954—School Milk Program Act (P.L. 83-690)—Provided funds for purchase of milk for school lunch programs.

1958—National Defense Education Act (P.L. 85-865)—A Sputnik-inspired program that was designed to provide assistance to state and local school systems for strengthening instruction in science, mathematics, modern foreign languages, and other critical subjects; improvement of state statistical services; guidance, counseling, and testing services and training institutes.

1963—Vocational Education Act (P.L. 88-210)—Increased federal support of vocational schools, vocational work-study programs, and research, training, and demonstrations in vocational education. Funds could be used on a 50-50 basis for constructing and equipping vocational school facilities.

1964—Civil Rights Act of 1964 (P.L. 88-352)—Authorized the

commissioner to (1) arrange through grants or contracts with institutions of higher education, for the operation of short-term or regular-session institutes for special training to improve quality of elementary and secondary instructional staff to deal effectively with special-education problems occasioned by desegregation; (2) make grants to school boards to pay, in whole or in part, the cost of providing in-service training in dealing with problems incident to desegregation; and (3) provide school boards, technical assistance in desegregation and required nondiscrimination in federally assisted programs.

1965—Elementary and Secondary Education Act (P.L. 89-10)—Provided large-scale direct federal aid to elementary and secondary schools. The act specifically prohibited federal control of education. It authorized aid to children attending parochial schools but placed control of the expenditures with the public school agencies.

The act authorized grants for elementary and secondary school programs for children of low-income families; school library resources, textbooks, and other instructional materials for schoolchildren; supplementary education centers and services; strengthening of state education agencies; and educational research and research training.

1972—Emergency School Aid Act—Designed to meet the special needs incident to the elimination of minority-group segregation and discrimination among students and faculty in elementary and secondary schools; to encourage the voluntary reduction, elimination, or prevention of minority-group isolation in such schools; and to aid schoolchildren in overcoming the educational disadvantages of group isolation.

1975—The Education of All Handicapped Children Act (P.L. 94-142)—Intended that a free and appropriate education and related services be provided to all handicapped children.

Taxes and Taxing Authority

Even though there is this evidence of the federal incursion into educational finance, it remains that school districts are, in fact, instrumentalities of the state that have been created by legislative enactments to carry out the constitutional mandates for providing educational opportunities for the children in that state. Having been charged with these mandates, school districts must develop financial plans for implementing them. These plans, too, commonly find their basis and boundaries in state statutes.

Students of educational finance recognize that the school budget is the financial statement of the educational program for the school district. Once the expenditure side of the budget has been determined, it remains that the revenues to support these expenditures must be put in place. School systems derive the major portion of their revenues from tax funds. These taxes may be in the form of direct receipts from local property taxes or state appropriations and collections having various forms of taxation as the money sources.

Taxing authority for school districts is a special power that must be specifically conferred by the legislature. Not all districts have the same power. This was clearly stated in the decision in *Pirrone v. City of Boston,* 305 N.E. 2d 96 (MA, 1973), when the court held that school districts are not agencies with broad powers but are limited to powers that are expressly or by necessary implication conferred upon them by the legislature. The court held, furthermore, that the legislature could classify districts and delegate varied financial powers to them dependent upon their classification. However, such a legislative enactment does not preclude constitutional tax limitations. In *Hurd v. City of Buffalo,* 311 N.E. 2d 504 (NY, 1974), a constitutional tax limitation applicable to certain school districts in the state of New York was at issue and was allowed to stand.

Basically, there are two types of boards of education when consideration of their power to tax and raise funds is at issue. The first is the fiscally independent board of education. These boards are granted legal authority by the state legislature to set the ad valorem tax rate on real property (not personal and intangible property)—within constitutional and legislative limits—to levy and collect (or cause to be collected) taxes for the support and maintenance of the local schools, and to approve the expenditure of the funds collected. All must be in accord with the district's budget. The vast majority of the nearly sixteen thousand public school boards of education in the United States fall into the fiscally independent category. The second is the fiscally dependent board of education. In this arrangement the board of education commonly prepares and adopts a budget showing the anticipated expenditures and projecting the revenue needs. Then a different political subdivision has the responsibility for apportioning the school taxes. One example is the Virginia Code, Section 22-126.1, which provides that the local municipal governmental agency shall be the tax-levying authority. The code provides, furthermore, that local boards of education must go to their local governmental body for appropriations and budget approval. Another example is the board of education of the city of New York, which must receive approval of its budget and appropriation of funds from the board of estimate. The actual funds necessary to support the school's operating budget may come through different legal and organizational arrangements, varying from state to state.

In a number of states, statutes require that tax levies be approved by the electorate annually. This is true in the Central, Union Free, and Common School Districts in New York State but does not apply to city school districts, fifty-seven of which are limited by constitutional restrictions in the amount of money that can be raised by taxation, and the five largest city school districts (Buffalo, New York, Rochester, Syracuse, and Yonkers), which are dependent upon other municipal bodies for their funding.

In the state of Georgia county school boards of education approve their budgets and then rely, generally, upon the county tax commissioner for collection. Twenty-eight "independent" school districts (cities that are separate from the county school system) must rely upon the cities in which they are located for the funds to operate the schools. The county school districts—with a few exceptions—have a twenty-mill limitation on tax rates of real property for school operating funds.

Voter resistance to increases in property taxes for school purposes has been experienced in California—with the passage of "Proposition 13" and in Massachusetts—with the passage of "Proposition 2½." Other states, for example, Michigan and Ohio, have experienced financial setbacks when voters have rejected increased millage referendums with the result that some school districts have had to close their doors until funds become available. Others have continued, but with programs that were drastically reduced.

There have been exceptions to the taxpayer approval of spending plans. In a 1978 decision of the New Jersey commissioner of education relating to the Upper Freehold Regional board of education, the commissioner certified a local board of education's raising of additional funds by taxation when the local board found it necessary to do so because of voter reluctance to approve the funds deemed necessary for school-operating expenditures.

Frequently, procedural defects emerge in the levying of taxes. When these irregularities occur and become the focal point of a suit, the courts are faced with alternatives that may declare the irregularly levied tax invalid and, thereby, cripple the schools; or they may find the tax to be valid and thus work a hardship on the taxpayer. Usually, the court will weigh carefully the harm to the taxpayer, and where the taxpayer has not been deprived of a substantial right, the levy will be considered to be valid.

This generalization does not hold when the taxpayer has been deprived of his voice in determining whether the tax should be levied. As a rule, when there is a special referendum being held at a time and date that varies from the general election date and that has been set by the governing body (the board of education), it is the obligation of the board of education to give proper notice of the date, time, place, and purpose of the special referendum. A defect in this procedure will, in most cases, render the referendum invalid. That is, boards may not use obscurity as a technique to "sneak by" a tax increase.

Determining the amount of tax to be levied raises some interesting questions. One deals with surplus funds. Generally, a board of education cannot use its taxing power to establish a surplus fund. There are, however, exceptions to this. Section 2021.21 of the New York State Education Law provides that the anticipated balance (surplus) of the budget of a school district is limited to the amount necessary to meet expenses during the first 120 days of the fiscal year following the fiscal year in which such tax is collected. Any balance in excess of this amount must be used to reduce the new tax levy. Most states apply even more rigorous and demanding regulations upon local boards.

In *C.R.T. Corp. v. Board of Equalization,* 110 N.W. 2d 194 (NE, 1961), the Nebraska Supreme Court specifically recognized the authority to levy a tax rate that would produce a relatively small surplus should the total tax levy be collected. In this instance the court upheld a levy that was designed to produce for all purposes an amount of approximately $800,000 in a total budget of $13 million. The court allowed that there were uncertainties in fluctuations in operating expenses as well as in anticipated revenues, thus the necessity for making adequate estimates of the sums required to balance the budget. In some years actual tax collections may be only 85-90 percent of the levied amount. Some flexibility is needed.

The Georgia Supreme Court, in *Watkins v. Jackson,* 179 S.E. 2d 747 (GA, 1971), upheld a county board of education that increased its tax rate to almost twice that of the previous year. The board argued that there was considerable uncertainty over the continued availability of P.L. 874 (Impact Aid) funds. The board submitted, in evidence, a letter from a United States senator that raised the question of uncertainty. The court observed that the funds to be raised by the increase in taxation were approximately the equivalent of the money that was ordinarily expected from the federal sources.

As with other legal aspects of public school operation, the student of educational law is cautioned to review the constitutional provisions, statutes, and court decisions of each particular state in which there is some interest. Finance laws and provisions are among the most complex of those laws governing public school operation, demanding very careful scrutiny in each state, for each state has some characteristics that are unique.

Remedies for the Taxpayer Against Illegal Taxation

What rights does a taxpayer have to recover taxes that were illegally collected? Under the presumption that every man knows the law and then pays the tax knowing of its invalidity, the finding in *Cornell v. Board for Dist. No. 99,* N.E. 2d 717 (IL, 1936), was that he may not, at some future date, use his ignorance as the ground upon which to recover the payments he made. One should note that this determination is applicable when the payment is made voluntarily.

On the other hand, when payment is made under duress or compulsion, the general rule on recovery of taxes illegally collected is not applicable. In the majority of cases, it is not sufficient to establish payment under duress when paying taxes under protest. The courts must determine if, in fact, payment has been made under duress or compulsion, and if they apply a liberal construction to these terms, very often they will permit recovery of the money paid.

When a taxpayer has reason to believe that an illegal tax is being levied, the time to act is before the tax is collected. The decision in *Shaffer v. Carter,* 64 *L.Ed.* 445 (1920), seems to have settled the principle that the collection of an illegal tax may be enjoined. Thus a party who may feel aggrieved by the levying of an illegal tax may seek to have its collection enjoined. Should that take place, there is no need for such an effort as would be necessary to recover paid taxes illegally levied.

One other method used by taxpayers to protest illegal taxes is through the nonpayment of the tax that has been levied against them. The case of *City of Houston v. McCarthy,* 371 S.W. 2d 587 (TX, 1963), demonstrated that the fact that the tax is illegal is not necessarily a defense. This was an action against a taxpayer for nonpayment of taxes, and the Texas Court of Civil Appeals considered a situation in which the city of Houston and the Houston Independent School District were found to have used an illegal scheme of taxation. When the plan was put into place, the taxpayers in question did nothing. However, when the tax was levied and collections were being made, these parties refused to pay the tax and relied upon a defense based upon the illegality of the system. The court would not accept their argument and claimed that they failed to show any substantial financial loss due to the illegal system of determining and levying the taxes. The court dismissed the taxpayer suit.

Although there are remedies against illegal taxation, citizens who would successfully employ these remedies should be meticulous in following prescribed procedures. The substance of the law is important, but more cases fail for procedural defects than for substantive issues. For school administrators, the point is to stay scrupulously within the statutory boundaries for public school taxation. School district residents who feel they have been unfairly or illegally taxed are not likely to continue as pleased supporters of public education—even if they do recover their money or even if there is no real dollar loss through the illegal taxation.

Indebtedness and Fiscal Responsibility

Absent statutory authorization to the contrary, school districts are expected to operate with balanced budgets. Thus "pay as you go" is the basic premise under which these political subdivisions function. There are times when a short-fall in funds limits a district's cash flow, and the district is forced to resort to borrowings. For example, unexpectedly low tax collections may leave a school district's treasury depleted just at the time of the monthly payroll. Finance laws of the several states prescribe the types and terms of borrowings that may be undertaken by the political subdivision—school districts included. Loans are subject to many varied legal controls, depending upon the term, purpose, and form. When the power to borrow money is granted for a specific purpose, the funds borrowed must be applied to that purpose and to no other.

There are several types of borrowing. The first of them is the short-term loan. As a general rule, such loans are to provide the cash flow necessary to meet current obligations, for example, payroll and bills payable on a monthly basis. The statutes commonly require that such loans must mature and be redeemed in the same fiscal year out of revenues that are due or collectible in that year. An example of this requirement can be seen in the Pennsylvania Statutes Annotated, Title 53, Section 6780-201. Where there is more than one lending institution within the school district, a wise policy is to seek quotations (bids) from all interested lenders and then accept the one that provides the best arrangement for the school district. Other procedural conditions (advertising the nature, purpose, and amount of the loan; clearance of bond forms and terms; and prior voter approval) are not usually required for short-term loans.

The second form of borrowing is concerned with long-term debt. Such borrowing becomes necessary when there are insufficient funds to finance long-term school construction and other capital improvements. State constitutions and statutes set forth the provisions that regulate both the substance of the loans and the form and procedure of the contracts covering them. One of the primary controls is found in the establishing of debt ceilings through the enactment of debt-limitation laws. An old case, *McBean v. Fresno,* 44 P. 358 (CA, 1896), early provided the rationale for such laws by stating:

The framers had in mind the great and evergrowing evil to which the municipalities of the state were subjected by the creation of a debt in one year, which debt was not, and was not expected to be paid out of the revenue of that year, but was carried on into the next year increasing like a rolling snowball as it went until the weight of it became almost unbearable upon the taxpayers. It was to prevent this abuse that the constitutional provision was enacted.

At issue in borrowing is the calculation of "net" debt. A common definition of *net debt* is that debt which remains after deducting from the total of all outstanding debts the assets of the district that are available for the payment of existing debts. Generally, the holding is that the assets need not actually be applied to the payment of the indebtedness, but only that they be available.

One should note that borrowed money which is funded through revenue bonds rather than through general-obligation bonds is not considered a debt. This arises from the fact that holders of revenue bonds depend for their payment on income produced by the enterprise that has been financed by the bonds. Although this form of financing is not, generally, available to school districts, it is available to states and often through this means may be the source of funds the state uses to finance certain types of educational ventures. One example of revenue bonds being used directly by school districts is in those states where this is permissible and the district has embarked upon a self-liquidating project such as an athletic stadium. In this instance, the holders of the loan instruments are paid solely from revenues generated as a result of the construction of the stadium and the admission tickets sold. Such debt is not considered for funding-limitation purposes.

Another means of avoiding a debt ceiling is through using another government entity (for example, a school building authority) to finance and construct a building for long-term lease to a school district. This overlying debt is used by fiscally hard-pressed school districts in those states where the constitution and statutes permit such a procedure.

Exemption from debt-ceiling limits may be achieved through a public referendum whereby the public authorizes the board of education to contract a debt exceeding the debt limit for the construction of a new building or reconstruction of an existing building or for such other capital expenditure as is statutorily permitted. When the voters approve such a financing scheme, the courts are reluctant to overturn their decision.

Fiscal stability is the responsibility of the central administration and the board of education. The annual budget is the board's fiscal statement of the school district's educational program. The budget includes a statement of the anticipated expenditures and the revenues that are to support these expenditures. Detailed budget provisions and procedures vary from state to state. They may include but are not necessarily limited to requirements such as the format of the budget, itemization within the budget, publication of the budget, public hearings on the budget, adoption of the budget, and issuance of a tax-warrant or tax-levy order to provide the tax-revenue portion of the budget.

Courts tend to respect the right of a board of education to use its discretion about those public purposes for which school funds may be expended, but they will not permit expenditures for improper purposes. At times, arguments arise over the transfer of funds from one category to another within the budget. Particular attention should be paid to the individual state's constitution and statutes. In general, courts hold to the rule that a fund that has been raised by taxation for a specific purpose cannot be diverted to another. An illustration of this would be monies raised to pay the principal and interest on bonded indebtedness. Funds in that category, raised specifically by taxation for that purpose, may not be transferred to another section of the budget. In another instance, the state's highest court, in *Stene v. School Bd. of Beresford Independent School,* 206 N.W. 2d 69 (SD, 1973), upheld the transfer of funds from the general fund to the capital outlay fund. The court reasoned that there was no evidence that the funds that were transferred had been raised by local tax levies, and the amount of the transfer was actually less than the amount derived from sources other than local taxes.

An outgrowth of fiscal constraints on school districts has been the consideration of student fees with which to fund certain services and activities. These fees have been the subject of numerous legal tests. Just what fees may be charged and under what circumstances is dependent upon the specific wording of the statutes.

There are diverse opinions in the courts about just what activities are to be included in free public education. For purposes of convenience, we shall deal with three major classifications: instruction (including tuition, matriculation, and registration fees), materials (textbooks, other books, and instructional supplies), and special activity fees.

Under the classification of instruction, a Wisconsin court in 1974 held that pupils residing within a school district may not be subjected to general charges for admission to the public school during the normal school year. The court held, furthermore, that it made little difference whether the charge was labeled as a tuition, matriculation, or registration fee. A West Virginia court, also in 1974, held that residency, unlike domicile, depends upon bona fide physical habitation within a district with intention to remain there for an indefinite period, even though the residence is not the child's ultimate and home place. In 1973, a third court, this one in Illinois, held that residency would not be deemed to be bona fide if the sole purpose of locating within a school district is to gain tuition-free admission to its schools. Residency is a necessary qualification to escape tuition fees charged by public schools to nonresidents. By 1980 some Nebraska school districts charged nonresidency fees in excess of $3,500 a year.

There is some question about eligibility for nonrequired, or elective, courses and the charging of fees to register for them. A Missouri court used a strict reading of "free" education and held that this reading appeared to bar any course fee, but a New Mexico court held just the opposite position—that course fees were allowed for elective subjects. In general, states have seemed to follow a middle ground where the term *free public education* was interpreted to forbid fees for any courses (elective or required) if these courses qualified for credit toward graduation, were reasonably related to the school's educational goal, or were approved by the state governing body for the public elementary and secondary schools.

There is a division of opinion about furnishing free instructional materials. Here, it is important to consult the statutes of the particular state of interest. As an example, the states of Idaho, Michigan, and Montana require that a legal test be applied to textbooks and school supplies to determine if these items fall under the provision of a free public education.

272 School Law for the Practitioner

The test is to determine if these materials are essential to the public school activity or are reasonably related to the general educational goals of the school. If they are found to be essential or related, no charge may be made for them. Conversely, if they are in areas that are considered to be nonessential, a charge may be made for them.

The issue then becomes a definition of what is essential and what is nonessential—or what falls in the area of the extracurricular. Here, courts in two of the three states, above, differ. The Idaho court ruled that fees could be charged; the Montana court ruled in opposition to the charging of fees for extracurricular materials. Recently, state courts have predominantly held that reasonable fees, which are tied to actual costs, may be charged for textbooks and supplies. Michigan is one state, as an example, in which the courts have been very critical of such charges, however.

The charging of special-activity fees falls into the same relationship as charging for instructional materials. The question that must be considered is: are they consistent with the state constitutional requirement of a free public education? If that is so, have they been authorized, statutorily? In general, the courts have held that the charging of activity fees is impermissible where the activity is required of the student; the courts have been less stringent in applying this to voluntarily selected activities, but it is a variable condition from state to state.

Finally, there is a need to address fiscal responsibility dealing with expenditure controls, particularly in the area of contracts. A *contract* is an agreement or promise that is legally enforceable. In addition, these requirements pertain to contracts: the parties are sufficiently competent to enter into a contract; the parties have the legal capacity to enter into a contract; there are proper offers that are properly accepted with a sufficient consideration (an agreed-upon exchange between the parties) to be enforceable; and there is nothing illegal about the contract. All of those requirements must be present in the personnel-services contract between an employing board and all employees if it is a valid contract.

It should be noted that boards of education must take their action to enter into a contract in an open, public meeting of the board, which is properly constituted and prepared to act on the business before it. In that way, every contract becomes a matter of public record. Where boards of education never formally approved the contract, or attempted to do so in a manner unauthorized by statute, or attempted to authorize an agreement beyond its powers, or failed in some other manner (for example, reducing an oral agreement to writing) to carry out its statutorily required duties, the resulting agreements have been declared null and void and are unenforceable. Such restrictions create a protection of the public funds administered by each local board of education.

An area of great concern in contracts is that of bid laws. Most states have enacted statutes that govern public competitive bidding by outside independent contractors who want to do business with school districts. Although the need for such statutes may seem to be obvious, such legislation seeks to prevent fraud, collusion, favoritism, and improvidence in contract administration in the public sector. Furthermore, it is the intent of these statutes that there be assurance that public schools and agencies receive the best products and services at the lowest available price from a responsible bidder. Bid specifications usually place in the hands of the board of education the responsibility for using its discretion in determining what bid is actually lowest in net cost, who is a qualified or responsible bidder, the equivalency of items submitted as alternates to those that were specified, and when it is prudent to "standardize" their selection of goods and services because of special needs, services, or materials that are unique and justify a negotiated, nonbid procurement regardless of the contract amount.

From time to time, there are attempts to use unlawful devices to eliminate bidding and, thereby, circumvent the bidding statutes. The courts have tended to accept broad board discretion about how much and when work may be ordered by contract. However, an obvious attempt to avoid the bid statutes by splitting a continuous service into small successive contracts is an unlawful practice. This broad discretion is permitted, also, when dealing with alternatives. In this instance, the board of education must determine which alternative best meets its need and then must award the contract to the lowest responsible bidder within the same alternative package.

In developing bid proposals, and to ensure fair and open competition, boards of education should pay particular attention to the development of advertisement for bids. They should provide sufficient facts to enable bidders to submit intelligent bids. All facts should be disclosed fully to avoid giving any bidder an unfair advantage from undisclosed facts. The board of education's requirements should be stated in full and complete terms to avoid disqualifying bidders for not complying with intended, but unstated, requirements. The specifications for goods and services from which vendors and/or contractors prepare their bids must furnish the same information to all prospective bidders as the basic minimum fairness. Normally, the development of specifications and advertisements is a task that is assigned to central-office administrators.

Once a board of education formally accepts a low bid and awards a contract for the work or material, it cannot seek other bids for the same work or material. However, before the award of a contract, the board of education has the right to reject any and all bids—provided that such right exists by statute, charter law, or terms of the invitation to bid. Courts have upheld low-bid rejections for a bidder's failure to attach bid security in the form of a bid bond or certified check, failure to comply with the requirements of the invitation to bid, and failure to sign the bid form. The courts are not in agreement about whether a bidder has a right to a hearing before being disqualified. In at least one instance, a court has found that denial of a hearing on bidder responsibility could amount to arbitrary abuse of administrative discretion. The point of the bidding process is to assure, through open competition, that public school funds are spent in a prudent fashion but not to discriminate unjustly against some bidders.

Uses of School Buildings and Grounds

A difficult concept for most citizens to comprehend is the legal nature of school buildings. Most persons feel that since primarily local funds were used to construct and equip school buildings, the buildings belong to the local community. As one manifestation of the concept, requests come from various local groups seeking to use the school buildings for purposes that are often unrelated to education. The fact remains that, generally, school property is state property, and its use rests completely with the legislature except where there may be constitutional restrictions.

Although the use of school buildings rests with the legislature, restrictive legislation is lacking and the local board of education is given the discretion for the management and control of school buildings. In some instances, there are occasional requirements (for example, the use of schools as polling places for official elections) that must be met. Likewise, it is generally held that school buildings may not be used for some purposes—secret society activities or religious services. It is a legally justifiable action to permit the use of school buildings for school-connected activities to which parents, friends, and the general public are invited even where admission fees are charged. However, the general rule is that school buildings may not be used for commercial enterprises where there is a monetary gain for private individuals or entities.

One of the most far-reaching concepts of school building use for nonschool purposes can be found in the California Civic Center Act. This act requires boards of education to permit community use of school property free of charge for meetings to discuss subjects that in the judgment of the group "appertains to the educational, political, economic, artistic and moral interests of the citizens."

Boards of education do have the authority, unless specifically prohibited by state statute or constitution, to deny access to the school buildings to outside persons or groups. However, if it chooses to do this, all persons or groups similarly situated must be denied access. Fairness must prevail. In denying the use of the building, it is impermissible for a board of education to use constitutionally protected rights as the basis for its denial. A case in point will be found in *East Meadow Community Concerts Ass'n. v. Board of Educ.*, 219 N.E. 2d 172 (NY, 1966), where the New York Court of Appeals applied the rule that, although school authorities could close the door to all outside organizations, if they opened the door to any, they had to treat alike all organizations in the same category. Furthermore, although a board could deny use of the building if proof were presented that a clear and present danger existed that public disorder and possible damage to the building would result from a proposed use, the board could not bar an organization simply because it, or even a part of the public, might be hostile to the opinions or the program of the organization, provided the same were not unlawful per se. In this instance, the board of education sought to bar one of a series of concerts because it was to feature as a performing artist one who was a "highly controversial figure." The performer had sung a concert in Moscow and some of the songs he sang were critical of American policy in Vietnam. The court held that the board of education's reason for cancelling the concert was unconstitutional, because it rested on the unpopularity of the singer's views rather than on the unlawfulness of the concert. The court, in its opinion, stated, "The expression of controversial and unpopular views, it is hardly necessary to observe, is precisely what is protected by both the Federal and State constitutions."

There may be some question about the use of school property on a temporary basis for religious services. This use is an exception accepted by many courts to the majority view that buildings cannot be used for sectarian purposes. Frequently, this use occurs when a house of worship has been destroyed by flood, fire, tornado, or some other disaster and a meeting space is needed for the congregation. Certainly, such a use could not occur when the school itself was in regular session.

When faced with a surplus of classrooms due to declining enrollments, boards must decide the best use of the property that is no longer needed for school purposes. Disposition of this property, either by lease or sale, falls within the powers delegated to boards of education by statute. When leasing property, the board of education is required to limit the lessee to lawful uses. Furthermore, the board is required to receive, in return for the lease, a fair return on the property. Leasing at a nominal fee (for example, $1), even to a nonprofit organization, is an unlawful gift of public funds unless such an arrangement is authorized by statute.

Good fiscal management requires prudent action on the part of the board of education. A fair return in the form of rental fees is an example of good management where it pertains to buildings no longer needed for school purposes. Before property is sold, a long-range study must be made to determine if, in the foreseeable future, such property will be needed once again for school purposes. If so, the cost of replacement must be weighed against the immediate monetary gain from selling—rather than renting or leasing—the property.

Public Funds for Private Schools

Three basic principles under the establishment clause are involved when reviewing legislative enactments with respect to public funds for private schools in order to determine the Constitutionality of the statutes: Does the enactment have a secular purpose? Does the principal or primary effect of the enactment neither inhibit or advance religion? Does the enactment foster an excessive entanglement with religion? The use of these three principles can be illustrated by using two cases—Levitt I and Levitt II—from New York State. In the first, *Levitt v. Committee for Pub. Educ. and Religious Liberty,* 413 U.S. 472 (NY, 1973), the United States Supreme Court struck down a 1970 New York State statute that provided public funds to reimburse both church-sponsored and secular nonpublic schools for performing various services mandated by the state. The Court reasoned that the statute violated the establishment clause of the First Amendment. In 1974 the New York State legislature attempted to remedy the defect of the 1970 legislation by enacting a new statute that directed the commissioner of education to apportion and pay to nonpublic schools the actual cost they incurred in complying with certain state-mandated requirements. The difference in the two statutes was that in the 1974 version the state did not plan to reimburse nonpublic schools for preparation, administration, or grading of teacher-prepared tests, and this statute provided a means whereby payment of state funds could be audited to ensure that only the costs incurred were reimbursed from state funds. A federal district court, in *Committee for Pub. Educ. and Religious Liberty v. Levitt,* 414 F. Supp. 1174 (NY, 1976), invalidated this statute. Upon appeal to the United States Supreme Court, the Court vacated the district court's judgment and remanded the case for reconsideration. The district court, under the precedent of *Wolman,* ruled that the statute did not violate the establishment clause and the district court decision was again appealed to the U.S. Supreme Court. In *Committee for Pub. Educ. and Religious Liberty v. Regan,* 100 S. Ct. 840 (NY, 1980), the Supreme Court (in a five to four decision) held that the New York State statute did not violate the provisions of the First and Fourteenth Amendments. In arriving at its decision, the majority noted:

This is not to say that this case, any more than past cases, will furnish a litmus-paper test to distinguish permissible from impermissible aid to religiously oriented schools. But Establishment Clause cases are not easy; they stir deep feelings; and we are divided among ourselves, perhaps reflecting the different views on this subject of the people of this country. What is certain is that our decisions have tended to avoid categorical imperatives and absolutist approaches at either end of the range of possible outcomes. This course sacrifices clarity and predictability for flexibility, but this promises to be the case until the continuing interaction between the courts and the States—the former charged with interpreting and upholding the Constitution and the latter seeking to provide education for their youth—produces single, more encompassing construction of the Establishment Clause.

The provision of transportation to pupils who attend nonpublic schools continues to be a matter of litigation. Some states have provided the service under the child-benefit theory; others have considered the service to be unconstitutional on the theory that it actually benefits the schools where sectarian doctrines are taught.

In *Everson v. Board of Education,* 330 U.S. 1 (1947), the Supreme Court held that a New Jersey statute that permitted boards of education to arrange at public expense for the transportation of children to school was Constitutional. The Court considered the furnishing of transportation of all pupils to be in the category of a public service for all and, as such, was a general program to help parents get their children, regardless of their religion, safely and expeditiously to and from their schools. Relying upon this decision, a recent case in Pennsylvania was decided in favor of the state statute authorizing free transportation of pupils to nonpublic schools up to ten miles beyond the boundaries of the public school district. The three school districts who challenged the statute were told by the Pennsylvania Supreme Court that the statute met the three tests developed by the United States Supreme Court, and, thereby, the statute was constitutional under the Pennsylvania constitution. The districts were ordered to comply with the statute. Other states have disallowed publicly supported transportation costs for children enrolled in nonpublic schools beyond the boundaries of the public school district where the child resided.

Apportionment of State School Funds and Challenges

Beginning in the late 1960s and intensifying during the 1970s, litigation appeared attacking state public school finance systems. The attacks centered upon the systems that were based, primarily, upon property-tax revenues and took a position that children are discriminated against when their education is dependent upon the wealth or poverty of their neighbors in the school district in which they "by accident of birth" and residence were to be educated.

Two series of cases have been brought to the courts. The first series began with what is known as the *McInnis*-type cases in 1968. *McInnis v. Shapiro,* 293 F. Supp. 327 (IL, 1968), was a class-action suit brought in behalf of parents and public school students in four Cook County school districts in Illinois. The plaintiffs claimed that the Illinois system of public school finance violated the equal-protection guarantees under the Fourteenth Amendment. In addition, they claimed that there was an inequitable variation of expenditures on a per pupil basis throughout the Illinois public school systems. The plaintiffs sought relief through a permanent injunction forbidding further distribution of tax funds in accordance with the existing state statutes.

After hearing the case, the United States District court ruled against the plaintiffs. In its declaration, the court cited the following points: the Fourteenth Amendment did not require that public school expenditures be made solely on the basis of "educational need"; "educational expenses" were not the "exclusive yardstick" for measuring the quality of a child's educational opportunity; and there were no "judicially manageable standards" by which a federal court could determine if and when the equal-protection clause is satisfied or violated.

The court further expanded its opinion in stating: "the General Assembly's delegation of authority to school districts appears designed to allow individual localities to determine their own tax burden according to the importance which they place upon public schools."

In yet another case, *Burruss v. Wilkerson,* 310 F. Supp. 572 (VA, 1969), the district court dismissed the plaintiff's action brought by parents who claimed that because of the Virginia system of public school finance, their children were being denied equal educational opportunities. In dismissing the complaint, the court held that the deficiencies and disparities existing between public school districts in Virginia were not the results of purposeful discrimination by the state. Rather, the blame "is ascribable solely to the absence of taxable values sufficient to produce required moneys."

Thus in both of these cases the courts believed the legislatures of the states should remedy the existing inequities. That is, no recognition of a federal question was made, and all modifications of the public school finance structure were left in the hands of state legislatures. In one sense the *McInnis*-type cases were unsuccessful, but in another sense they provided a validation of the state's obligation for education.

In 1971 there was a complete turn of events in California, and a second series of cases began to appear. In *Serrano v. Priest* (Serrano I), 561 Cal. 3d 584 (1971), the California Supreme Court held that the California school-aid formula violated the equal-protection clauses of the Constitutions of the United States and California. In its finding the court agreed with parents living in Los Angeles County that there were inequities of educational opportunity in some districts occasioned by the state's funding plan, inequities to taxpayers in less-favored districts as a result of the heavy reliance on the property tax for schools, and discrimination between and among districts, because the system unfairly made the quality of a child's education a function of the wealth of his district.

In its holding, the court said:

By our holding today, we further the cherished idea of American education that in a democratic society free public schools shall make available to all children equally the abundant gifts of learning. This was the credo of Horace Mann, which has been the heritage and the inspiration of this country. "I believe," he wrote, "in the existence of a great, immortal, immutable principle natural law, or natural ethics—a principle antecedent to all human institutions, and incapable of being abrogated by any ordinance of man—which proves the *absolute right* to an education of every human being that comes into the world, and which, of course, proves the correlative duty of every government to see that the means of an education are provided for all. . . .

The California Supreme Court remanded the case back for trial, saying:

The richer district is favored when it can provide the same educational quality for its children with less tax effort. Furthermore, as a statistical matter, the poorer districts are financially unable to raise their taxes high enough to match the education offering of wealthier districts.

The California Supreme Court in *Serrano v. Priest* (Serrano II), 18 Cal. 3d 725 (1977), reaffirmed its stand in *Serrano I* and proceeded to list the remedies that were available to the legislature in order for the legislature to cure the malaise of the public school-finance program in California. Included in the list were the following proposals: full state funding, to be supported by a statewide property tax; consolidation of districts with boundary realignments to equalize assessed valuations of real property among school districts; retention of present school district boundaries but removal of commercial and industrial property from local tax-warrant rolls for school purposes and placement on state tax-warrant rolls for school purposes; school district power equalization; and implementation of a voucher system.

Shortly after *Serrano* was handed down, a United States District Court in Minnesota held in *Van Dusartz v. Hatfield,* 334 F. Supp. 870 (MN, 1971), that the Minnesota system of public school finance was in violation of the equal-protection clause of the Fourteenth Amendment. The finding was similar to that in *Serrano* and in other *Serrano*-type cases that have been heard more recently; namely, that students in public schools do, in fact, enjoy a right to have the level of spending for their education unaffected by variations in the taxable wealth of the school district in which they live as compared to the taxable wealth in other school districts in the state. Here, again, the court identified the legislature as the agency to provide the remedy for the inequity.

Serrano spawned a case that was heard by the United States Supreme Court. It is presented here in detail because of its importance in establishing public education as a basic responsibility of the state.

San Antonio Independent School District v. Rodriguez, 411 U.S. 1 (1973)

GENERALIZATION

Public education is not a "fundamental interest" under the equal-protection clause of the United States Constitution. If one school district is wealthier than another and a state-aid formula takes that into account, the state is not structuring a Constitutionally suspect classification.

DESCRIPTION

This suit attacking the Texas system of financing public education was initiated by Mexican-American parents whose children attended the elementary and secondary schools in the Edgewood Independent School

District, an urban school district in San Antonio, Texas. They brought a class action on behalf of schoolchildren throughout the state who were members of minority groups or who were poor and resided in school districts having a low property-tax base. Named as defendants were the state board of education, the commissioner of education, the state attorney general, and the Bexar County (San Antonio) board of trustees. The complaint was filed in the summer of 1968. In December 1971 the panel rendered its judgment in a per curiam opinion holding the Texas school-finance system unconstitutional under the equal-protection clause of the Fourteenth Amendment. The state appealed the decision to the United States Supreme Court. The Court agreed to hear the case because of the far-reaching Constitutional questions that were involved.

Justice Powell delivered the opinion of the Court.

The first Texas State Constitution, promulgated upon Texas' entry into the Union in 1845, provided for the establishment of a system of free schools. Early in its history, Texas adopted a dual approach to the financing of its schools, relying on mutual participation by the local school districts and the State. . . .

Until recent times Texas was a predominantly rural State and its population and property wealth were spread relatively evenly across the State. Sizable differences in the value of assessable property between local school districts became increasingly evident as the State became more industrialized and as rural-to-urban population shifts became more pronounced. The location of commercial and industrial property began to play a significant role in determining the amount of tax resources available to each school district. These growing disparities in population and taxable property between districts were responsible in part for increasingly notable differences in levels of local expenditure for education. . . .

We must decide, first, whether the Texas system of financing public education operates to the disadvantage of some suspect class or impinges upon a fundamental right explicitly or implicitly protected by the Constitution, thereby requiring strict judicial scrutiny. If so, the judgment of the District Court should be affirmed. If not, the Texas scheme must still be examined to determine whether it rationally furthers some legitimate, articulated state purpose and therefore does not constitute an invidious discrimination in violation of the Equal Protection Clause of the Fourteenth Amendment. . . .

In support of their charge that the system discriminates against the "poor," appellees have made no effort to demonstrate that it operates to the peculiar disadvantage of any class fairly definable or indigent, or as composed of persons whose incomes are beneath any designated poverty level. Indeed, there is reason to believe that the poorest families are not necessarily clustered in the poorest property districts. . . .

Neither appellees nor the District Court addressed the fact that . . . lack of personal resources has not occasioned an absolute deprivation of the desired benefit. The argument here is not that the children in districts having relatively low assessable property values are receiving no public education; rather, it is that they are receiving a poorer education. . . . Apart from the unsettled and disputed question whether the quality of education may be determined by the amount of money expended for it, a sufficient answer. . . . [is] that, at least where wealth is involved, the Equal Protection Clause does not require absolute equality or precisely equal advantages. Nor, indeed, in view of the infinite variables affecting the educational process, can any system assure equal quality of education except in the most relative sense.

For these two reasons—the absence of any evidence that the financing system discriminates against any definable category of "poor" people or that it results in the absolute deprivation of education—the disadvantaged class is not susceptible of identification in traditional terms. . . .

It is clear that the appellees' suit asks this Court to extend its most exacting scrutiny to review a system that allegedly discriminates against a large, diverse, and amorphous class, unified only by the common factor of residence in districts that happen to have less taxable wealth than other districts. The system of alleged discrimination and the class it defines have none of the traditional indicia of suspectness . . . .

We thus conclude that the Texas system does not operate to the peculiar disadvantage of any suspect class.

But appellees have not relied solely in this contention. They also assert that the State's system impermissibly interferes with the exercise of a "fundamental" right and that accordingly the prior decisions of this Court require the application of the strict standard of judicial review. It is this question—whether education is a fundamental right, in the sense that it is among the rights and liberties protected by the Constitution—which has so consumed the attention of courts and commentators in recent years.

. . . the key to discovering whether education is "fundamental" is not to be found in comparisons of the relative societal significance of education as opposed to subsistence or housing. . . . Rather, the answer lies in assessing whether there is a right to education explicitly or implicitly guaranteed by the Constitution. . . .

Education, of course, is not among the rights afforded explicit protection under our Federal Constitution. Nor do we find any basis for saying it is implicitly so protected . . . it is appellees' contention, however, that education is distinguishable from other services and benefits provided by the State because it bears a peculiarly close relationship to other rights and liberties accorded protection under the Constitution. Specifically, they insist that education is itself a fundamental personal right because it is essential to the effective exercise of First Amendment freedoms and to intelligent utilization of the right to vote.

. . . this is not a case in which the challenged state action must be subjected to the searching judicial scrutiny reserved for laws that create suspect classifications or impinge upon constitutionally protected rights. . . .

A century of Supreme Court adjudication under the Equal Protection Clause affirmatively supports the application of the traditional standard of review, which requires only that the State's system be shown to bear some rational relationship to legitimate state purposes. . . . We have here nothing less than a direct attack on the way in which Texas has chosen to raise and disburse state and local tax revenues. We are asked to condemn the State's judgment in conferring on political subdivisions the power to tax local property to supply revenues for local interests. In so doing, appellees would have the Court intrude in an area in which it has traditionally deferred to state legislatures.

. . . the judiciary is well advised to refrain from imposing on the States inflexible constitutional restraints that could circumscribe or handicap the continued research and experimentation so vital to finding even partial solutions to educational problems and to keeping abreast of ever-changing solutions.

Appellees do not question the propriety of Texas' dedication to local control of education. To the contrary, they attack the school-financing system precisely because, in their view, it does not provide the same level of local control and fiscal flexibility in all districts. Appellees suggest that local control could be preserved and promoted under other financing systems that resulted in more equality in educational expenditures. While it is no doubt true that reliance on local property taxation for school revenues provides less freedom of choice with respect to expenditures for some districts than for others, the existence of "some inequality" in the manner in which the State's rationale is achieved is not alone a sufficient basis for striking down the entire system. . . . It may not be condemned simply because it imperfectly effectuates the State's goals. . . .Nor must the financing system fail because, as appellees suggest, other methods of satisfying the State's interest, which occasion "less drastic" disparities in expenditures, might be conceived. Only where state action impinges on the exercise of fundamental constitutional rights or liberties must it be found to have chosen the least restrictive alternative.

The complexity of these problems is demonstrated by the lack of consensus with respect to whether it may be said with any assurance that the poor, the racial minorities, or the children in overburdened core-city school districts would be benefited by abrogation of traditional modes of financing education. . . .

We hardly need add that this Court's action today is not to be viewed as placing its judicial imprimatur on the status quo. The need is apparent for reform in tax systems which may well have relied too long and too heavily on the local property tax. And certainly innovative thinking as to public education, its methods, and its funding is necessary to assure both a higher level of quality and greater uniformity of opportunity. These matters merit the continued attention of the scholars who already have contributed much by their challenges. But the ultimate solutions must come from the lawmakers and from the democratic pressures of those who elect them.

Reversed.

Having brought to an end the attitude that education was a fundamental interest that was protected by the United States Constitution, the United States Supreme Court returned arguments regarding state financing of public school education to the state courts for determination. Since then, decisions reflecting both the *McInnis*-type and the *Serrano*-type cases have been made. Two *Serrano*-type cases worthy of mention are *Robinson v. Cahill* 303 A. 2d 273 (NJ, 1973), and *Brinkman v. Gilligan,* No. C-3-75-304 (OH, 1977).

In *Robinson* the New Jersey Supreme Court upheld a superior court ruling that New Jersey's system of financing its public elementary and secondary schools was unconstitutional. The system, in the words of the high court, relied heavily on local taxation and led to great discrepancies in dollar input per pupil and, thereby, had no relation to the state's constitutional mandate to furnish "a thorough and efficient system of public schools." In its decision, the Court ordered the state legislature immediately to devise a new financial scheme for public education in New Jersey. The aftermath of the judiciary branch ordering the legislative branch to do a prescribed act created a political struggle with more than a peripheral interest to students of school law, although, finally, new legislation was passed.

In *Brinkman* the Court of Common Pleas of Hamilton County, Ohio, declared that the state's system of school finance violated the Ohio constitution. The holding indicated that the financing system established invidious classifications among schoolchildren in violation of the equal-protection clause of the state constitution. The domain of a county court is sharply limited, but the case does represent continuation of one line of judicial thought.

One further *Serrano*-type case, *Board of Educ. Levittown v. Nyquist,* 408 N.Y.S. 2d 606 (NY, 1978), merits more detailed discussion. This case is of considerable interest, because two sets of plaintiffs each claimed the state's school-finance system to be unconstitutional but on different grounds.

GENERALIZATION

This is another case in which complaints, arguing that schoolchildren were denied equal protection of the law with respect to educational finance, had been filed. It should be noted that once a determination has been reached in a lower court, the losing side can, and frequently does, appeal to a higher court. Only when all appeals have been exhausted is the issue finally determined.

DESCRIPTION

The original plaintiffs, twenty-seven school districts and twelve schoolchildren, argued that excessive reliance by the state on revenue from property taxes levied by local school districts resulted in grossly unequal expenditures per pupil, because districts that were relatively low in real property wealth were unable to match the expenditures of districts that were relatively high in real property wealth, even when they levied taxes at rates that were substantially higher than their more fortunate neighbors.

With respect to this contention, the court concluded that New York's current system for providing state aid to public elementary and secondary schools fell short of the equal-protection requirements contained in Article 1, Section 11, of the New York constitution.

These plaintiffs contended, furthermore, that the state's school-support program did not meet the obligations established by Article XI, Section 1, of the New York State constitution, which provides, in part, that "The legislature shall provide for the maintenance and support of a system of free common schools, wherein all the children of the state may be educated." In agreeing with the plaintiffs, the court said:

. . . it is not the fact that, in attempting to fulfill the constitutional obligation, the State has delegated taxing responsibility to school districts which offends the Education Article. Rather, it is the fact that such delegation has been made without adequate recognition of the varying capabilities of districts to raise educational funds through taxes levied on disparate real property tax bases and the failure of the state to correct disparities in the availability of locally-raised educational funds by providing state aid sufficient to discharge its primary obligation.

The court held, furthermore, that the irrational nature of the state school-support program failed to pass constitutional muster.

The second group of plaintiffs—including the boards of education of the state's four largest cities, the city of New York, certain public officials of these cities, the United Parents Association of New York, Inc., and twelve schoolchildren—argued that New York's school-finance program violated the equal-protection and education clauses of the United States Constitution. It is important to note that these plaintiffs argued successfully that educational need, or "educational overburden," was demonstrably greater in the large urban school districts than in other districts. The plaintiffs claimed, furthermore, that the New York state-aid formula operated in a manner that bore no reasonable relation to the purpose of the statute. The court agreed with the contention and further concluded that

. . . the state aid statute's failure to give effect to the overburdening factors affecting large city school districts has resulted in overstating the capacity of such districts to finance public education and thereby classifying them as less deserving of state aid. Such a classification bears no reasonable relation to the statute's purpose of providing state aid to districts in proportion to their need. Because the state aid statute has been shown to operate in that way, it has in its operational effect created a classification which as to the plaintiff-intervenors lacks a rational basis and is discriminatory. It must be found therefore to constitute a denial of equal protection of the law and a violation of Article I, Section 11 of the New York Constitution.

Furthermore, the court found that the school-finance program did violate the equal-protection guarantees of the Fourteenth Amendment of the United States Constitution.

On appeal, the Supreme Court, Appellate Division, Second Department, on October 26, 1981, held that various boards of education and schoolchildren represented by parents had standing to make the current challenge; the cause was justiciable; the state method of financing did not violate the equal-protection guarantees of the Fourteenth Amendment of the federal Constitution; and the state method of financing violated the equal-protection clause and the education article of the New York State constitution.

A *McInnis*-type case was decided November 24, 1981, by the Supreme Court of Georgia, indicating that the views of the judiciary on equitable school finance are not unified.

McDaniel v. Thomas, 285 S.E. 2d 156 (GA, 1981)

GENERALIZATION

Complaints, arguing the schoolchildren are denied equal protection of the law with respect to educational finance, have been filed in over fifty instances. Since *Serrano,* decisions in more than twenty states have made fundamental changes in their educational funding policies.

DESCRIPTION

The complaint in this 1974 case was filed by parents, taxpayers, and board of education members of the Whitfield County school system in Georgia. Later, these parties were joined by the Lowndes County Property Owners Association and the County Boards of Education of Carroll and Polk Counties, all in the state of Georgia. The complaint alleged that the state of Georgia financing system and the laws that imposed it were unconstitutional and were repugnant to the equal-protection provisions of the constitution of the state of Georgia in that it did not provide funds to equalize educational opportunity or resources that were substantially equal with those enjoyed by children attending other school districts in the state.

On January 7, 1981, Judge Dan Winn, presiding over the Superior Court in Polk County, handed down a decision in which he found for the plaintiffs, declared the system to be unconstitutional, and ordered the Georgia General Assembly to provide a more equitable public education financing system.

The decision was appealed to the Supreme Court of Georgia and on November 24, 1981, Justice Smith presented the opinion of the court:

The issue presented in the main appeal is whether the trial court erred in holding that the current system of financing public education in Georgia violates the equal protection provisions of the state constitution. It is conceded that any challenge to the Georgia system under the equal protection clause of the United States Constitution is foreclosed by San Antonio v. Rodriguez. . . .

The court has construed the "adequate education" provisions of the Georgia Constitution as requiring the state to provide basic educational opportunities to its citizens, and we have found that the existing public school finance system meets constitutional requirements in this regard. The question now presented is whether the state equal protection provisions impose an *additional* obligation on the state to *equalize* educational opportunities. . . .

What is disturbing about finding such an obligation under state equal protection is the fact that an entire article of the Georgia Constitution (Article VIII) is specifically devoted to education. The article mandates that the "provision of an adequate education shall be a primary obligation of the State of Georgia."

In view of the extensive treatment afforded the subject of public education in our state constitution, we believe the absence of any provision imposing an affirmative duty on the General Assembly to equalize educational opportunities is of constitutional significance. . . .

However, even assuming that a ruling in appellees' favor is not foreclosed by the conspicuous absence of any provision relating to equalization of educational funding, we nonetheless conclude that the equal protection provisions of the Georgia Constitution do not render the existing public school finance system invalid. . . .

Appellees have argued that education is a "fundamental right" for purposes of state equal protection and that the Georgia public school finance system is therefore subject to "strict scrutiny". . . .

The "equal protection" clause of the Georgia Constitution itself provides: *"Protection to person and property is the paramount duty of government* and shall be impartial and complete."* [Emphasis supplied]

The trial court held that, even under a "rational relationship" test, the Georgia system of financing public education must fall. With this conclusion, we cannot agree. The primary purpose of the APEG (Adequate Program of Education for Georgia) system is to provide basic educational funding to children throughout the state, and with the exception of RLE (Required Local Effort) which "discriminates" in favor of property poor school districts, it does so on an essentially equal basis. Beyond APEG, the Georgia public school finance system preserves the idea of local contribution. . . . The fact that the state had not *funded* a large-scale equalization plan does not render the current public school finance system invidiously discriminatory. In terms of equalization the system is a poor one. However, the system does bear some rational relationship to legitimate state purposes and is therefore not violative of state equal protection. Accordingly, the judgment of the trial court on the main appeal must be reversed.

Our holding that the current system of financing public education in Georgia is not unconstitutional should not be construed as an endorsement by the court of the status quo. Constitutions are designed to afford *minimum* protections to society. Plaintiffs have shown that serious disparities in educational opportunities exist in Georgia and that legislation currently in effect will not eliminate them. It is clear that a great deal more can be done and needs to be done to equalize educational opportunities in this state. For the present, however, the solutions must come from our lawmakers.

Judgment reversed on main appeal. All the parties concur.

The past decade is surely an indicator of continued challenges to state public school financing systems. Whereas courts have scrutinized the systems carefully, they have never demanded that equal dollars must be spent on every child. Nonetheless, it should be expected that states will be called upon to make changes in their existing systems of public school finance, and some of those changes will be by way of court decisions.

* * *

Public schools are creatures of state and local governments. Even though the federal government is not charged with the direct financing of education, federal funds in comparatively small amounts are made available through various Congressional enactments.

School districts, as instrumentalities of the state, must develop financial plans for carrying out state constitutional mandates for educating the citizens of the state. These districts derive the major portions of their revenues from tax funds. Taxing authority to provide these funds is a special power that must be conferred by the legislature to the LEA. Such authority is possessed in different degrees, dependent upon the classification of the school district. Fiscally independent boards of education have the authority to set the ad valorem tax rate on real property, to levy and collect—or cause to be collected—taxes for the support and maintenance of the schools, and to approve the expenditure of the funds collected. Fiscally dependent boards of education depend upon another political subdivision for the funds with which to operate the school system.

Taxpayers who complain about illegal taxation would do well to act before the tax is collected. The usual process is to seek to have the collection of the tax enjoined.

School districts are expected to operate within balanced budgets. There are times when funds are needed for capital projects or for situations due to a short-fall in cash flow. Under these conditions, in accordance with state statutes and constitutional limitations, districts are permitted to borrow funds. Short-term debt is that which will be liquidated during the current tax period, and long-term debt is, usually, in the form of bonds. These bonds are in the form of general obligation bonds and differ from revenue bonds in that revenue bonds are redeemed from revenues derived from the source of revenue for which the bonds were issued, whereas general obligation bonds are a debt obligation to be paid from tax and other revenue sources.

Although boards of education have discretion to use their school funds for public purposes, they must be sure that the use is proper. The same must be said for sources of funds. One source area that raises questions is that of student fees. In general, if the course is required for graduation, if the course is related to the school's educational goal or if the course has been approved by the state board of education, fees for entry into the course are inappropriate. It should be pointed out, however, that the courts have been definitive with respect to fees that may be charged to students.

Boards of education are permitted to enter into contracts. A contract is an agreement that is legally enforceable. In addition, these requirements pertain to contracts: the parties are sufficiently competent to enter into a contract; the parties have the legal capacity to enter into a contract; there are proper offers that are properly accepted with a sufficient consideration; and there is nothing illegal about the contract.

Bidding laws permit boards of education some latitude in acquiring services and materials that they seek. However, they must be meticulous in their application of the laws.

School buildings are, generally, state property, and their use rests completely with the legislature. Broad powers have been conferred upon local boards of education in permitting the use of school buildings. It is commonly accepted that school buildings may be used for educational purposes. It is when a request for use comes from an individual or a group wanting to use the building for other than educational purposes that questions arise. If a board of education chooses to deny the use of the building to an individual or group, it must treat all other individuals and groups similarly situated in like manner.

The courts have been asked to rule on the use of public funds for private schools. In reviewing such use under the establishment clause, three basic principles must be addressed: Does the enactment have a secular purpose? Does the principal or primary effect of the enactment neither inhibit nor advance religion? Does the enactment foster an excessive entanglement with religion? Usually, moneys provided to private school pupils flow under the child-benefit theory.

Beginning in the late 1960s, intensifying in the 1970s, and sure to continue though the 1980s, litigation has appeared attacking public school-financing systems. Basically, two types of cases have appeared: the *McInnis* type, which have been largely unsuccessful in attacking the constitutionality of the state-financing systems; and the *Serrano* type, which have been successful in attacking the constitutionality of the systems. These cases have been based upon state constitutions. In *Rodriguez,* heard by the United States Supreme Court, the Court held that public education was not a "fundamental interest" under the equal-protection clause of the United States Constitution, and the financing system did not discriminate against a suspect class of citizens.

Public school systems in our nation will continue to face financial crises. To meet them, changes in state-financing systems, tax policies, taxing structures, and school-system organization, budgeting, and administration are inevitable in the decade ahead.

GLOSSARY

Abrogate: The repeal of an existing law by passing a new law, which may be either explicit or implicit.

Accident: An unforeseen event or situation that is not the result of inappropriate behavior by other persons.

Accrue: To grow or to develop; to be added onto.

Action: A proceeding that occurs in a court.

Actionable: Things done by one individual or group that may cause another to seek relief in a court action.

Adjudication: A judgment or decision rendered by a court.

Ad valorem: A duty or tax levied according to value.

Advocate: A person who pleads or presents the cause of another.

Affirm: To act positively; accepting and endorsing the judgment of a lower court; or accepting a contract and making it binding.

Agency shop: An agreed upon condition of employment in which all nonunion employees pay a fee to the union as their share of negotiation costs; a service fee.

Agreement: The statement of mutually accepted items developed through negotiations between an employer and an employee organization.

Allegation: The formal statement of what a party expects to prove.

Amicus curiae: An indirectly interested party who is allowed to present information to a court, enhancing the background from which a judgment may be made.

Appeal: An application to a higher court, seeking a rehearing of a contest from a lower court.

Appellant: The party who makes an appeal from one court to another.

Appellee: The party against whom an appeal is made to another court.

Arbitration: A method of settling labor disputes through recourse to an impartial third party, whose decision may or may not be final and binding, according to state laws.

Arbitrator: An impartial third person who enters disputes, hears arguments, and makes a decision—a settlement, often called an "award."

Assault: A threat to strike or harm another.
Attractive nuisance: A condition that is dangerous to young children because it is so enticing; it is dangerous because inexperienced (young) children cannot distinguish that latter characteristic from the attraction.

Bail bond: A pledge of value taken when a defendant is released from custody, conditioned for the timely appearance of that defendant.
Bona fide: Honestly; without deceit.
Breach of contract: Failure by either party to perform a part or the whole of a contract, without any legal basis for such failure.

Capacity: The ability to function as a majority citizen; to make contracts and possess property.
Case law: The body of law created from judicial decisions.
Caucus: A meeting of the leaders of a group to decide about the acceptability of conditions or persons.
Certificate: An official document intended as an indicator of performance, or of an event; an indication of authority or qualification.
Certiorari: An action to remove a case from a lower to a higher court, commonly a request directed to the United States Supreme Court.
Citation: A system of source identification in law books incorporating technical abbreviations; a reference to authority to support an argument.
Civil action: An action brought to redress a wrong or to recover some civil right.
Closed shop: In labor relations, a condition dictating union membership as preceding employment.
Codification: The systematic arrangement of the laws of a state or of the United States, with appropriate headings, index, and so on.
Collective bargaining: A process in which employees meet as a group and make demands and proposals about working conditions to their employer; negotiations.
Common law: That part of law that has come down through the culture, deriving its force from social consensus of what constitutes fair play.
Compensatory damages: A measure of actual loss when damages have been suffered by a party; not punitive damages.
Concurring opinion: A statement by a judge, indicating general agreement with the opinion of the court, but including the (different) reasons leading to that shared opinion.
Constitution: The supreme law of the land; the documents that include the basic legal principles of each state and of the United States.
Contempt: An intentional disobedience of public authority; commonly, disregard for the orders of a court.
Contract: An agreement based upon value, mutually acceptable to the parties to the agreement; the proof of that agreement; a document revealing commitment and considerations.
Contract action: A court action brought as a necessity to enforce the terms of a contract.
Contributory negligence: The proximate cause of an injury, in which both litigants share.

Court of record: A court that keeps a permanent record of its proceedings, and that commonly has its findings cited as precedent for subsequent actions.

Criminal action: The legal proceeding by which parties charged with crimes are brought to trial.

Damage: An injury that occurs to a person, reputation, or property that may have been caused by a wrongful act, negligence, or accident.

De facto: In fact.

De jure: In law.

Decision: The conclusion of a court, arrived at by its own reasoning, the court's judgment.

Declaratory relief: A judgment that declares certain rights of parties but does not order anything to be done.

Decree: A court order made to settle questions of equity.

Defamation: Words that are written or spoken about another that may be harmful and for which an action for damages would lie.

Defendant: The person against whom a suit is brought or against whom an indictment has been brought.

Demurrer: A plea by one party that the existence of a body of facts is not a basis to continue the action.

Dictum: A statement by a judge of a legal principle, not essential to the case at point and not forming a part of controlling precedents.

Discrimination: In school law, the inappropriate conferral of privileges upon one class of citizens, when there is lacking a reasonable basis for that distinction.

Dissenting opinion: An opinion by one (some) judge, disagreeing with the majority of the justices of the court, as an eight to one decision or a five to four decision.

Due process: The rules and systematic protection of individual rights when questions of access and property arise.

Eminent domain: The power of some governmental units, such as public school districts, to take private property for private use, with just compensation.

Enjoin: To require a person, by virtue of court order, to perform or to cease and desist from some act; to command positively.

Equity: A system of law providing a remedy where there is no complete and adequate remedy already at hand.

Estoppel: Prevention at law of a person from affirming or denying certain facts because of previous behavior or statements by that person.

Ex officio: By virtue of office.

Ex parte: An action that is not an adverse proceeding against another.

Ex post facto: After the fact; coming after an occurrence.

Ex relatione: In behalf of or upon the relation of information.

Fait accompli: An accomplished fact; already done.

Felony: An offense that is more significant than a misdemeanor.

Finding: The conclusion of a court after consideration of the facts of a case.

Forfeiture: A penalty imposed, calling for the loss of rights or property as punishment for an illegal act or negligence.

Fraud: The use of deceitful or unfair means to gain personal advantage to another's loss.

Fringe benefits: Supplements to wages or salary received by employees at some cost to employers.

Governmental immunity: Sovereign immunity; in common law, the circumstance in which the consequences of governmental functions are not actionable, even in the face of damages.

Grievance: A complaint or expressed dissatisfaction by an employee in connection with his job, pay, or other aspects of his employment.

Gross negligence: A low standard of care; less thought than even inattentive persons give to the management of their own property.

Habeas corpus: A court command to one person who is holding another to bring that person before the court.

Hearsay evidence: Testimony by a witness relating what has been told him by another, not what is personally known of firsthand.

In loco parentis: In place of the parent; carrying out conventional duties of parents in the society.

In re: Concerning; in the matter of; commonly used to identify proceedings where there are no adversarial parties.

Indictment: A written accusation against one or more persons of a crime.

Information: An accusation against a person, alleging violation of some law.

Infringement: An invasion of an individual's rights.

Injunction: A prohibitive command from a court forbidding a person or group to do, or to continue doing, some act that is injurious to the plaintiff; a restraint.

Ipse dixit: An assertion deriving to authority from an individual.

Ipso facto: By the fact itself; the consequences of an act.

Judgment: The decision of a court; also the reasons set forward by a judge to reveal the rationale of that decision.

Jurisdiction: The power of a court to decide on a matter; the geographical area over which a court has power, as the area of one of the circuit courts of appeal.

Laches: The lapse of time that is sufficient to cause a person to lose the rights to a legal remedy for redress.

Laws: Rules of human conduct to which persons are obliged to conform; statutes enacted by a legislature comprise the statutory law.

Liability: Responsibility under law.

Libel: Defamation in a written communication.

Liquidated damages: Damages in an exact amount, as the amount due from one party to another for breach of contract.

Litigation: A dispute carried into court for settlement.

Majority opinion: The statement or reasons accepted by the majority of the judges sitting to hear an argument, when a decision is less than unanimous.

Mala prohibita: Acts prohibited by law that may not run counter to generally understood standards of the culture.

Malfeasance: The commission of an act that is unlawful.

Malice: Ill will; intentionally and by design doing an unlawful act.

Mandamus: An order from a court compelling a public officer or a public body to do the thing specified in that writ.

Mediation: An attempt by an unbiased third party to assist labor negotiations toward settlement; to advise and stimulate action toward agreement.

Ministerial: The obligation of a subordinate who is bound to follow instruction; the opposite of discretionary.

Misdemeanor: Any indictable offense that is less than a felony.

Misfeasance: A wrongful act that may include the inappropriate performance of a lawful act.

Moral turpitude: An action that is base or depraved; out of harmony with the customary rules of behavior in the culture.

Municipal corporation: A voluntary political body organized for the purpose of administering local affairs; a city or village. Less precisely, any political subdivision less than a county.

Negligence: Lack of reasonable care.

Nolens volens: When done with or without consent.

Nonfeasance: Nonperformance or omission of a required duty.

Nuisance: An offensive or noxious use of property; a condition that may injure or inconvenience others; obstructing the proper use of the property.

Oath: A promise; a solemn affirmation undertaken with a sense of responsibility.

Ordinance: A rule or regulation, generally applied to the laws passed by a municipality.

Pecuniary: Having to do with money.

Per se: By itself, alone.

Perjury: A false statement made while under oath, as in a court proceeding.

Petition: An application or a prayer to the court, asking redress for some wrong.

Petitioner: The person presenting a petition; similar to the plaintiff in other kinds of cases.

Picketing: Patrol duty, typically near the place of employment, by members of the employee organization to publicize a labor relations dispute.

Plaintiff: The person who initiates a complaint by filing a complaint.

Plenary: Complete power, as the grant of power from the federal government to the states under the Tenth Amendment.

Police power: The power of the states to enact statutes for the comfort, health, and general welfare of the citizens.

Precedents: Previous court decisions that are followed by courts that, later, receive cases of parallel disputes; a system of coordinating judicial authority.

Prima facie: A first examination; evidence so strong that it will prevail unless disproved.

Quantum meruit: A contract dispute involving an amount of compensation or quality level of performance.

Quasi: Almost as if it were.

Quasi-municipal corporation: A political subdivision that functions to assist in the accomplishment of the state's obligation, for example, a public school district.

Quorum: In an organization, the minimum number necessary to constitute a lawful meeting when business can be transacted.

Ratification: The act of confirming an obligation; closing an option, as in ratification of a tendered contract.

Reasonable doubt: The circumstance of qualified conviction after comparing and considering all that can be presented in a given case.

Referee: Generally, a disinterested party to whom disagreements are referred for settlement.

Referendum: A proposition extended to voters for their acceptance or rejection; that voting procedure itself.

Remand: To send a case back to an inferior court where it was first heard, with orders to take some specific, further proceedings.

Respondent: In certain kind of cases, the defendant; the one who makes an answer.

Restrain: A court order prohibiting some action or occurrence; an injunction.

Right: A claim; a power that one party possesses against another.

Seniority: A designation of employment status useful in determining promotion, layoff, vacation, and so on.

Slander: A communication delivered by speaking that is maliciously defaming of another party's reputation or business.

Stare decisis: The adherence to precedents as a means to develop the legal principles necessary for the settlement of litigation; to cite cases already decided.

Status quo: The existing circumstance; to leave unchanged.

Statute: The law enacted by a legislature, which may be the U.S. Congress or the legislature of any state; statutes may be substantive, that is, dealing with material problems; or procedural, that is, enabling government agencies or parties to do certain things.

Strike: A temporary work stoppage by employees to express a grievance, enforce a demand, or resolve a dispute with management.

Subpoena: A legal procedure whereby a party can be commanded to appear in court and testify.

Sue: To bring a civil action in a court.

Suit: The civil action, pitting plaintiff against defendant.

Supra: A word used as an indicator in scholarly books, referring the reader to a previous part of the book.

Tacit: Understood; implied by a lack of denial or disapproval.

Tenure: Generally, a description of an employment condition indicating the expectation of continuation in position; in public employment, a demand that dismissal must be for just cause and with due process.

Tort: In civil law, a wrong committed against the person, reputation, or property of another.

Trespass: An unauthorized entry into or upon the property of another; interference with property use.

Trial: The examination of a cause before a court. The court may consist of a judge or judges, may be with or without a jury.

Ultra vires: An action, especially in contract, that exceeds the legal power of an organization.

Umpire: In labor relations, the person who decides a question in dispute.

Unfair labor practice: Action by an employer or employee group that violates labor legislation, such as a refusal to bargain in good faith.

Union shop: A provision in a contract requiring all employees to become members of the union within a short period after initial hiring. Opposite of "right-to-work" shops.

Unlawful: Contrary to the law.

Valid: Effective; with binding force.

Venue: The neighborhood; the place where an act occurred, where a trial may be held, and from where a jury is drawn.

Vested right: A right that is so obviously and specifically the possession of a party that it cannot be revoked, removed, or impaired.

Violation: An act that is contrary to another's right, which may be carried out with violence.

Void: Null; ineffective and lacking legal force, as in a contract that is defective.

Waive: To renounce or voluntarily set aside a right.

Warrant: A writ or summons; an authority.

Wilful (or Willful): To act intentionally and deliberately.

Witness: A person who sees some act performed, committed, or perpetrated.

Writ: The judicial instrument that enforces obedience to the orders of a court and its sentences.

Writ of error: In the appeals procedure, the order of a superior to an inferior court, calling for its records, which will be examined for alleged errors.

Wrong: An act infringing upon a right.

ANNOTATED BIBLIOGRAPHY

The selections for the annotated bibliography have been primarily from journals. Many selections have been included to expand the informational base of this book beyond its confines of school law, for they are concentrated on the ethical and sociological aspects of the chapter titles.

1. The Legal System and Location of Cases

Frank R. Kemerer and Kenneth L. Deutsch. *Constitutional Rights and Student Life* (St. Paul, Minn.: West, 1979), Appendixes A, B, C, and D provide information on finding and briefing cases and on legal terminology.

Arval A. Morris. *The Constitution and American Education,* 2nd ed. (St. Paul, Minn.: West, 1980). Following the United States Constitution, Chapter 1 provides a description of the judicial system and includes directions on how to use the reporter system and find cases.

William Valenti. *Law in the Schools* (Columbus, Ohio: Merrill, 1980). Chapter 1 provides a short overview of the legal system as it relates to schools, with an emphasis on the judiciary.

Martha L. Ware and Madeline Kenter Remmlein. *School Law,* 4th ed. (Danville, Ill.: Interstate, 1979). The Introduction, with Appendixes A and B, provide a strong and understandable basis for finding and reading cases.

2. The Origin of Public School Districts

Elwood P. Cubberley. *Public Education in the United States* (Boston: Houghton Mifflin, 1919). From the beginning settlements in the colonies, this history traces the character and development of American schools. Included are details such as political and philosophic debates and the developments of specific programs in both elementary and secondary schools, traced to the point of World War I.

Elwood P. Cubberley and Walter C. Eells. *An Introduction to the Study of Education* (Boston: Houghton Mifflin, 1933). Chapters 1-5 are devoted to aspects of the creation of locally controlled schools for public patronage.

H. G. Good. *A History of American Education* (New York: Macmillan, 1962). A comprehensive history of American schools, this book not only covers the events of development but provides substantial information about the personalities who became advocates for public education.

3. The Board of Education

Roald F. Campbell. *The Organization and Control of American Schools,* 4th ed. (Columbus, Ohio: Merrill, 1981). This text examines the influences and pressures that determine the character of the modern public school in the United States.

Jack L. Davidson. *Effective School Board Meetings* (West Nyack, N.Y.: Parker, 1970). This work serves as an aid to superintendents and board members as they work to effect sound decisions for education, through carefully planned, productive meetings.

William J. Hageny. *School Law* (Albany: New York State School Boards Association, 1980). This handbook for school board members is illustrative of the question-and-answer type of information that provides references to board members, administrators, teachers, and all other persons interested in school law.

Robert C. O'Reilly. "Some Expectations for New School Board Members," National School Boards Association, Dallas, 1981; and *Resources in Education,* Educational Management Clearinghouse ED 202 160, August 1981. Task categories and reasonable time allocations for them are identified, along with suggestions for assessment of personal performance.

Philip K. Piele, ed. *The Yearbook of School Law* (Topeka, Kans.: National Organization on Legal Problems in Education, 1981). This yearbook, as with predecessor editions, provides a section on governance that is an annual update of decisions relating to the board of education and the governance of the school system.

Research Report (Washington, D.C.: National School Boards Association, 1975-76). Reference is made to three titles—"What Do We Know About School Boards?" "The People Look at Their School Boards," and "School Board Meetings"—that provide valuable information about the public's perceptions about school boards.

Rennard Strickland. *Avoiding Teacher Malpractice* (New York: Hawthorn, 1976). This is a practical treatise dealing with the legal consequences of decisions made in the course of daily school operation.

Kenneth E. Underwood, James C. Fortune, and Harold W. Dodge. "Your Portrait: New Look, Concerns, Budget," *American School Board Journal,* Vol. 169, #1, 1982, pp. 17-21. From a comprehensive survey of school board members in 1981, by geographical areas, a new description of those public servants emerged.

Edward Wynne. *The Politics of School Accountability* (Berkeley, Calif.: McCutchan, 1972). The author's intent is to help members of various groups better understand where they are and where they are going so that better day-to-day decisions can be made.

4. Parents' Rights and Responsibilities

"The Changing Family," *Educational Horizons,* Vol. 59, #1, 1980. Ten essays discussing many aspects of parenting, some predictions for the family, and explanations of parental rights.

Donald T. Cundy. "Parents and Peers: Dimensions of Political Influence," *Social Science Journal,* Vol. 19, #1, 1982, pp. 13-24. (Davies pub.) Although parental influence may fall below that of peers in several areas, this research indicated its clear dominance in political matters—a communications opening for parents to offspring.

"Education for Parenthood," *Journal of Education,* Vol. 163, #3, 1981. Six essays devoted to different aspects of the child-parent-school relationships.

William R. Hazard. *Education and the Law,* 2nd ed. (New York: The Free Press, 1979). Chapter 4 focuses upon interrelationships among pupils, parents, and educators and includes one section on parental rights.

Donald R. Moore and Sharon Weitzman. "Advocacy: A Proven Method for Helping Children," *Citizen Action in Education,* Vol. 8, #2, 1981, pp. 1ff. Techniques used by groups advocating changes on six issues in public school programs are charted as they were developed in six locations over the nation.

David Schimmel. *The Rights of Parents in the Education of Their Children* (Columbia, Md: The National Committee for Citizens in Education, 1977). This work is directed primarily at parents and other interested citizens. It provides a description of court-tested common law and statutory rights that parents and schoolchildren now possess.

M. Donald Thomas. *Parents Have Rights, Too!* (Bloomington, Ind.: The Phi Delta Kappa Educational Foundation, 1978). This fastback addresses seven important parent rights: the right to have teachers employed on merit rather than by discriminatory practices; the right to attend a school of one's choice; the right to a "free, appropriate, and equal education"; the right to equal educational opportunities for both boys and girls; the right to "due process" and an informal hearing before student suspension from school; the right to receive compensatory services for handicapped children; and the right to know what schools are doing.

5. Certification, Contracts, and Retirement

Robert C. O'Reilly. "Changing Certification and Endorsement Programs," National Conference of Professors of Educational Administration, 1981; and *Resources in Education,* Educational Management Clearinghouse ED 207 193, April 1982. A survey of statutory and regulatory change in regard to teacher certification provides a background for an in-depth study of one state in a condition of change—Oklahoma.

Martha L. Ware and Madeline Kinter Remmlein. *School Law,* 4th ed. (Danville, Ill.: Interstate, 1979). Chapters 1 and 2 are devoted to certification and contract; Chapter 9 treats retirement benefits, including social security.

6. Administering Staff Personnel

Barry J. Baroni. "The Legal Ramifications of Appraisal Systems," *Supervisory Management,* Vol. 27, #1, 1981, pp. 40-44. A thoughtful analysis of the whole appraisal condition, with specific tasks examined.

Ralph H. Baxter, Jr., and John M. Farrell. "Constructive Discharge—When Quitting Means Getting Fired," *Employee Relations Law Journal,* Vol. 7, #3, 1981-82, pp. 346-68. Administrative techniques designed to reduce employer liability in terminations are identified and discussed.

William Halal and Bob S. Brown. "Participation Management: Myth or Reality," *California Management Review,* Vol. 23, #4, 1981, pp. 20-32. Extensive research on this question, carried on among organizational administrators, and in various kinds of participation, indicates that the United States is comparatively low in the use of industrial democracy.

Harry W. O'Neill. "Changing Employee Values in America," *Employee Relations Journal,* Vol. 7, #1, 1981, pp. 21-35. Based upon research in 188 companies, a condition of diminished trust between organizations, administrators, and "line" employees emerged over a twenty-five-year span. Suggestions for administrator action are set forward.

Nancy J. Pitner and Rodney T. Ogarva. "Organizational Leadership: The Case of the School Superintendent," *Educational Administration Quarterly,* Vol. 17, #2, 1981, pp. 45-65. In this study superintendents were shadowed in many work settings to provide a picture of on-the-job behavior. Much of superintending is communicating, inquiring, or informing.

7. Administering Student Personnel

Lewis Aptekar. "Sociological and Psychological Factors of Mexican American High School Students' Perception of Schools," *Education,* Vol. 102, #1, 1981, pp. 16-26. This study was done in two school systems, both of which were majority Mexican-Americans. Size of the student body, more than race, influenced students' perceptions of their schools.

Joseph E. Bryson. *Ability Grouping of Public School Students* (Charlottesville, Va.: The Michie Company, 1980). This study reviews judicial decisions dealing with the grouping and tracking of students and reviews the major court cases that have been decided in the area of classification and placement of students in special classes.

Richard Clelland. *Section 504: Civil Rights for the Handicapped* (Arlington, Va.: American Association of School Administrators, 1978). This is a good basic reference on Section 504 and the critical issues and possible problem areas related to it.

Eugene T. Connors. *Educational Tort Liability and Malpractice* (Bloomington, Ind.: Phi Delta Kappa, 1981). The author's expressed intent is to enlighten teachers, principals, superintendents, and school board members about the complexities of educational tort law. Much of the material deals with pupils.

Louis Fischer. *The Rights of Students and Teachers* (New York: Harper and Row, 1982). This book is designed to help readers become more aware of student and teacher rights and how these rights can be asserted legally. The goal of the book is to help resolve educational conflicts without going to court.

Donald Graul. *Student Rights and Responsibilities Revisited* (Arlington, Va.: National School Public Relations Association, 1976). This report takes another look at these rights and responsibilities four years after the first such report was issued. It reports, in general, that student rights appear to be duly recognized as official policy in the majority of public schools and school districts across the country.

Arthur H. Green and others. "Factors Associated with Successful and Unsuccessful Intervention with Child Abusive Factors," *Child Abuse and Neglect,* Vol. 5, #1, 1981, pp. 45-52. From research projects that treated 1,724 abusing adults, a report of positive results and procedures used provides a basis from which to reduce abuse.

A. Regula Herzog. "High School Seniors' Occupational Plans and Values: Trends in Sex Differences 1976 Through 1980," *Sociology of Education,* Vol. 55, #1, 1982, pp. 1-13. Data collected from three thousand high school students over four years revealed marked differences between the sexes in regard to occupational choices and only a slight change in preference within each sex group over the four years.

Ellen Jane Hollingsworth. "The Impact of Student Rights and Discipline Cases on Schools," *Schools and the Courts, Volume II* (Eugene, Ore.: ERIC Clearing House on Educational Management, 1979). This study deals with the law-related knowledge that teachers have about discipline and how this knowledge relates to their experience and behavior.

Eve H. Malakoff, ed. *Schools and the Law of the Handicapped* (Washington, D.C.: Council of School Attorneys, National School Boards Association, 1981). This is an update of a previous publication of the same title that provides new perspectives on P.L. 94-142 and Section 504.

Philip K. Piele, ed. *The Yearbook of School Law* (Topeka, Kans.: National Organization on Legal Problems in Education, 1981). This yearbook, as with predecessor editions, provides a section on pupils that is an annual update of decisions relating to that segment of the school population.

Stanley Smedley and Donald J. Willower. "Principals' Pupil Control Behavior and School Robustness," *Educational Administration Quarterly,* Vol. 17, #4, 1981, pp. 40-56. In this study to determine optimum techniques to control student behavior, it was found that humanistic principals tended to encourage the development of robust schools.

Linda Tigges and Leona M. Zastrow. "Alternative Model for Program Evaluation in Cultural Based Communities," *Journal of American Indian Education,* Vol. 20, #2, 1981, pp. 4-12. When Indian children come from several tribes into a single Headstart program, this research into effectiveness suggests special programmatic modifications.

8. Discrimination and Equality of Opportunity

"Black English and Equal Educational Opportunity," *Michigan Law Review,* Vol. 79, #2, 1980, p. 279. An analysis of one case, in which the court acknowledged a learning barrier within a dialect difference and ordered a remedy.

Brown v. Topeka, 1955-56 to 1979-80 (a special issue of *The Negro Educational Review*, Vol. 32, #1, 1981). From the May 1954 decision, several authors trace its effect in schools and in society generally.

Robert Lewis Gill. "The Effects of the Burger Court Decisions upon the Lives of Black Families," *Negro Educational Review*, Vol. 32, #3-4, 1981, pp. 230-51. A well-researched inquiry into the legal demands for school desegregation that is coupled to intuitive and insightful comments about current attitudes of black citizens.

David E. Hicks. "Employment Discrimination—Title VII and the Equal Pay Act," *Creighton Law Review*, Vol. 15, #2, 1981-82, p. 579. A thoroughly researched inquiry into the ambiguities of the two legislative actions aimed at pay and sex and their ambiguities.

R. A. Maidment. "The U.S. Supreme Court and Affirmative Action: The Cases of Bakke, Weber and Fullilove," *Journal of American Studies*, Vol. 15, #3, 1981, pp. 341-56. In this review of the three cases, extensive attention is devoted to the positions of the individual justices along with a commentary of censure to the Court for attempting too much.

Francis R. McKenna. "The Myth of Multiculturism," *Journal of American Indian Education*, Vol. 21, #1, 1981, pp. 1-10. By examining official government publications and other evidence, the conclusion is reached that contemporary America has very little respect for cultural differences.

Robert C. O'Reilly. "Pregnancy Cases and Legislation Affecting Equality and Costs in Schools," National Conference of Professors of Educational Administration ED 179 013, 1979. The case-law history leading to the passage of the Anti-Pregnancy Discrimination Act provides the basis for exemplary cost projections for this particular fringe benefit.

_____. "Racial Desegregation in Schools and Evolving Law: The 1980s" (a revised Educational Television [ETV] script) ED 188 288, 1980. Court cases and population data for all racial minority groups are included in this analysis and projection.

Howard Risher and Marsha Cameron. "Pay Decisions: Testing for Discrimination," *Employee Relations Law Journal*, Vol. 7, #3, 1981-82, pp. 432-53. A system for the discovery of unequal pay is detailed, along with a statistical model for achieving equalization.

Rodney A. Smolla. "Integration Maintenance: The Unconstitutionality of Benign Programs That Discourage Black Entry to Prevent White Flight," *Duke Law Journal*, Vol. 6, 1981, p. 893. The social desirability of actions to maintain racially desegregated conditions are examined and rejected as unconstitutional.

"Views of Women in Education: Past, Present, and Future," *Educational Horizons*, Vol. 60, #1, 1981. A series of eleven essays considering the place of women in education with emphasis upon new status for women by way of sex equity.

9. Injury and Negligence

Lydia Parnes and Paul Trause. "Exposure of Supervisors and Managers: Personal Liability for Managers," *The Bureaucrat*, Vol. 10, #1, 1981, pp. 23-26. Analyzing several cases that called for damages, the authors point out the expenses of suits, even when the managers are vindicated. The Civil Service Reform Act is explained.

E. Edmund Reutter, Jr., and Robert S. Hamilton. *The Law of Public Education,* 2nd ed. (Mineola, N.Y.: Foundation Press, 1976). Chapter 7 is a discussion of the liability of board members, administrators, and teachers.

Martha L. Ware and Madeline Kinter Remmlein. *School Law,* 4th ed. (Danville, Ill.: Interstate, 1979). Chapter 13 is devoted to analyzing negligence and subsequent liability for teachers and school officials.

10. Religious Influences and Public Schools

William R. Hazard. *Education and the Law,* 2nd ed. (New York: The Free Press, 1979). Chapter 2 is devoted to the church-state issues. The opening essays are insightful examinations of constitutional and common law conflicts.

M. A. McGhehey, ed. *Contemporary Legal Issues in Education* (Topeka, Kans.: National Organization on Legal Problems in Education, 1979). Three essays of this collection address some problems in the church-state conflict arena: finance, curriculum, and personnel administration.

"Religion," *Law and Contemporary Problems,* Vol. 44, #2, 1981. A series of eight articles considering the Constitutional and ethical conflicts as people try to assert religious independence and still conform to statutory demands commonly put upon all citizens, including the education of children.

11. Collective Bargaining

Arbitration and School Administration. This monthly publication provides timely, pertinent histories of teacher-arbitration cases: how and why they arose; the issues involved; the wording of the applicable contract provisions; the arbitrator's ruling and stated reasoning; and penetrating comment by practicing employee-relations advisors.

Frank H. Cassell. *Collective Bargaining in the Public Sector: Cases in Public Policy* (Columbus, Ohio: Grid, 1975). The cases in this book examine the area of labor-management relations in various dimensions. They deal with many of the critical issues and confrontations of our time.

Collective Bargaining Law Bulletin (Boston: Quinlan). This is a monthly bulletin that reports decisions on collective-bargaining cases. The cases are taken from both the public and private sectors.

Anthony M. Cresswell. *Education and Collective Bargaining* (Berkeley, Calif.: McCutchan, 1976). A prime objective of this work is to bring together some of the best analytical perspectives on a complex topic—collective bargaining in the educational world. A series of readings deals with four pertinent aspects of the process: The Environment of Collective Bargaining; The Collective Bargaining Process; Impasse Resolution and Strikes; and Economic, Political, and Organizational Outcomes.

_____. *Teachers, Unions, and Collective Bargaining* (Berkeley, Calif.: McCutchan, 1980). This book represents a comprehensive attempt to treat the most important aspects of the entire collective-bargaining system. It is arranged so each chapter is an entity unto itself.

Max W. Evans. *Trends in Collective Bargaining in Public Education* (Seven Hills, Ohio: American Association of School Personnel Administrators, 1978). This is a report of a study that sought to examine some important trends in the collective-bargaining movement as revealed in recent literature and as perceived by American Association of School Personnel Administrators members, leaders of teachers' organizations, and members of the National Association of Educational Negotiators.

Peggy Odell Gonder. *Collective Bargaining Problems and Solutions* (Arlington, Va.: American Association of School Administrators, 1981). This publication reviews the positive and negative effects of bargaining on school districts as perceived by the administrators who responded to a survey questionnaire. Special emphasis is placed on "how to" suggestions from experts and successful programs.

Government Union Review (Vienna, Va.: Public Service Research Foundation). This quarterly journal on public sector labor relations provides a forum for scholarly debate in the field of public employer-employee relations with an eye toward the role and impact of unionism and collective bargaining on that relationship and on the public.

Labor Relations in Education (Arlington, Va.: Capitol Publications). This bi-weekly newsletter deals with judicial, legislative, and administrative developments in school and college employee relations.

Myron Lieberman. *Public-Sector Bargaining* (Lexington, Mass.: D. C. Heath, 1980). In this work the author examines the feasibility of public sector bargaining.

David Lipsky. "The Effect of Collective Bargaining on Teacher Pay: A Review of the Evidence," *Educational Administration Quarterly,* Vol. 18, #1, 1982, pp. 14-42. A longitudinal examination of teacher salaries, with attention given to trends. Indications are that bargaining has, generally, helped to boost salaries.

Charles J. Namit. *Labor Relations for Principals and Other School Managers* (Washington, D.C.: National School Labor Relations Service, 1980). The purpose of this manual is to acquaint school board members and management teams with the different roles the parties play in the collective-bargaining process; the negotiating process—from the initial bargaining session through impasse resolution; and contract administration including implementation of the contract provisions through grievance handling and arbitration.

Robert C. O'Reilly. *Understanding Collective Bargaining in Education* (Metuchen, N.J.: Scarecrow, 1978). A comprehensive treatment of labor relations in schools, with interoccupation comparisons in the public employment arena.

Phillip Pagano. "Managers of the Classroom, Private University at Yeshiva University Are Not Professional Employers Under the NLRB," *Creighton Law Review,* Vol. 14, #2, 1980-81, p. 657. The facts that led to a five to four holding are set forward along with observations on the position of faculties in some private institutions.

Philip K. Piele, ed. *The Yearbook of School Law* (Topeka, Kans.: National Organization on Legal Problems in Education, 1981). This yearbook is one of a series that includes a chapter on bargaining. These chapters provide an annual update of the legal developments in the area of collective bargaining.

School Law Seminar Proceedings (Washington, D.C.: National School Boards Association, 1979). This particular issue contains a section on mandatory collective bargaining that deals with items of negotiation.

W. J. Usery, Jr., and Douglas Henne. "The American Labor Movement in the 1980s," *Employee Relations Law Journal,* Vol. 7, #2, 1981, pp. 251-60.

Current conditions are forcing labor to change, to assume a less adversarial position. Analysis leads to the position that labor-management cooperation may be the hallmark of the 1980s.

12. Finance

Charles S. Benson. *The Economics of Public Education* (Boston: Houghton Mifflin, 1978). The work deals with the economic setting and the allocation of educational finances. Two main topics are addressed: the acquisition of funds for our system of public elementary and secondary education and the use of those funds by local school administrators.

Joel S. Berke. *Answers to Inequity: An Analysis of the New School Finance* (Berkeley, Calif.: McCutchan, 1974). This book describes the role of the courts in bringing progressive change in educational finance laws and evaluates the degree to which the legal tests effectively meet the problems besetting the support of public education.

Percy E. Burrup. *Financing Education in a Climate of Change,* 3rd ed. (Boston: Allyn and Bacon, 1982). This book explores decision making in the 1980s in light of tax-limiting measures, shifts in local control, and financing a variety of educational programs equitable to all students.

Education Laws 1978: A Guide to New Directions in Federal Aid (Arlington, Va.: National School Public Relations Association, 1978). This is one of a series of Education U.S.A. Special Reports and represents an analysis of the Education Amendments of 1978 and how these changes will affect practically every school district in the nation.

Walter I. Garms. *School Finance: The Economics and Politics of Public Education* (Englewood Cliffs, N.J.: Prentice-Hall, 1978). This work provides an intense examination of the economics of education, the politics of funding and allocation, and the decision-making processes of appropriate governmental institutions.

James W. Guthrie, ed. *School Finance Policies and Practices: The 1980s: A Decade of Conflict* (Cambridge: Ballinger, 1980). This is the first annual yearbook of the American Education Finance Association. The focus of the book is on school finance policies.

Roe L. Johns. *The Economics and Financing of Education: A Systems Approach,* 3rd ed. (Englewood Cliffs, N.J.: Prentice-Hall, 1975). This edition presents insights of the authors that were gained through directing important researches financed by the United States Office of Education.

Journal of Education Finance. This quarterly journal reports studies in educational finance and comments on developments in finance and provides book reviews of current publications in the field.

John Lindelow. *Educational Vouchers* (Reston, Va.: National Association of Secondary School Principals, 1979). This monograph provides a clear and objective discussion of educational vouchers.

Allan Odden. *School Finance Reform in the States: 1981* (Denver: Educational Commission of the States, 1981). This is an excellent summary of the changes that have taken place, some trends, and reviews of major finance-policy issues.

John Vaizey. *The Political Economy of Education* (New York: John Wiley and Sons, 1972). This book is a study of the economics of education and of educational systems in the broadest sense.

Edward Wynne. *The Politics of School Accountability* (Berkeley, Calif.: McCutchan, 1972). The author examines accountability in a historic and interdisciplinary light. The book is an analysis and forecast of interactions between groups and systems. Its intention is to help members of various groups understand where they are and where they are going.

CASES

INDEX

About the Authors

Robert C. O'Reilly is Professor and Chairman of the Department of Educational Administration, Supervision, and Foundations at the University of Nebraska in Omaha. He has written *Understanding Collective Bargaining in Education, Librarians under Union Contracts,* and *Librarians and Labor Relations* (with Marjorie I. O'Reilly, Greenwood Press, 1981).

Edward T. Green's career has included positions ranging from classroom teacher and director of guidance to superintendent of schools. He is currently Associate Professor of School Administration and Supervision at Georgia Southern College in Statesboro. He served as a weekly educational columnist for the *Oneida Daily Dispatch* and the *Rondout Valley Times*.